CHARGING AND TRADING IN LOCAL GOVERNMENT

AUSTRALIA
Law Book Co.
Sydney

CANADA and USA
Carswell
Toronto

HONG KONG
Sweet & Maxwell Asia

NEW ZEALAND
Brookers
Wellington

SINGAPORE and MALAYSIA
Sweet & Maxwell Asia
Singapore and Kuala Lumpur

CHARGING AND TRADING IN LOCAL GOVERNMENT

By

John Bennett MA, LLB
Consultant Solicitor with Eversheds LLP, Solicitors and Visiting Professor, Nottingham Law School

Stephen Cirell, LLB, Solicitor
Head of Local Government, Eversheds LLP, Solicitors

In association with

LONDON
SWEET & MAXWELL
2005

First Edition 2005
Published in 2005 by Sweet & Maxwell Limited of
100 Avenue Road,
London NW3 3PF
www.sweetandmaxwell.co.uk
Typeset by LBJ Typesetting Ltd of Kingsclere
Printed in England by
Athenaeum Press

No natural forests were destroyed to make this product; only farmed
timber was used and replanted

A CIP catalogue record for this book is available from the British Library

ISBN 0 421 902 809

Dedication

John Bennett dedicates this book to Jonjo and Amanda.
Stephen Cirell dedicates this work to his daughters Daisy and Flora.

ACKNOWLEDGEMENTS

A book of this nature involves more than the efforts of the two authors. We therefore wish to thank all those who have been involved in one way or another with the production of this book.

These include all the officers and members who have attended our charging and trading courses, and whose questions and contributions have given us much food for thought. During 2004 we teamed up with the Association for Public Service Excellence to run a Charging and Trading Masterclass which was highly successful and attended by a large number of people from across local government. These were organised by Paul O'Brien, with Andy Mudd helping us to deliver them; we thank them and the APSE team for the effort that went into these events. Des Murray is also thanked for his assistance with the material on Scotland.

Once the work of the authors was done in dictating the material, the manuscript was typed by Glenda Dixon, PA to Stephen Cirell at Eversheds. Glenda's dedication to the cause was exceptional and without her hard work we could not have produced the manuscript in accordance with the agreed schedule. We are very grateful to her for her help and assistance.

The authors are members of a large team of lawyers at Eversheds LLP that undertake legal and consultancy work for local authority clients. We acknowledge the help and support of this wider team in all that we do in local government law. Particular thanks are extended to Mike Mousdale and Judith Barnes, who are partners in the Local Government Group, and who are themselves very experienced in this area. The opportunity to discuss and debate issues is always helpful and this has been the case in relation to the subject area covered by this book. We would also like to thank Anna Sweeney, who is an associate in the Commercial Department in the Leeds office of Eversheds, who assisted with the chapter on commercial issues.

We would also like to thank the team from Sweet and Maxwell, headed by Daniel Fox, for the support and encouragement that they have shown during both the planning and writing phases.

Finally, without the support and encouragement of our families we would never have climbed this particular mountain and for that we are eternally grateful.

John Bennett
Stephen Cirell
Leeds
December 31, 2004

PREFACE

The ability of local authorities to charge for and trade services with other organisations is something that the Association for Public Service Excellence (APSE) has lobbied extensively for, on behalf of its local authority membership, over the past two decades. During this period two names have become synonymous with being at the cutting edge on local authority charging and trading, Stephen Cirell and John Bennett. For that reason it is with great pleasure that APSE supports and contributes to this book. The Association shares with the authors a positive view of the role of local government in developing and leading local communities and therefore welcomes the new opportunities that arise for both charging and trading.

Over the years there have been many false dawns with regard to this issue, however, with the enactment of the Local Government Act 2003 in England and Wales, and the Local Government in Scotland Act 2003 in Scotland, we have seen powers bestowed from central government that deliver a successful conclusion to a long drawn out campaign.

It is interesting to note the impact of devolution across the United Kingdom, with Scottish legislation simply amending the Goods and Services Act 1970 to facilitate charging and trading; and Northern Ireland remaining fairly constant, with charging and trading only being allowed with other public bodies at present. Charging and Trading in England and Wales will be facilitated mainly via the powers contained in the 2003 Act, although the powers in Wales will not be restricted by the Comprehensive Performance Assessment, as in England.

In England and Wales, the difference between large scale commercial based trading for profit and charging will be significant. APSE believes that 95 per cent of activity will be covered under the discretionary charging powers, with only 5 per cent being of a nature likely to necessitate the forming of a trading company. The Association also believes that, for reasons well explained within this book, authorities would be well advised to consider carefully whether any benefits can be derived from establishing a trading company for dealing with existing contracts. It is likely to lead to a negative conclusion and may, in most cases, result in a realisation that the trading company approach is best suited to new initiatives of a commercial basis.

The main benefits of undertaking charging and trading activity for local authorities can be best summarised as:

- To meet some of the challenges thrown up by Gershon;
- To engage with a range of organisations active within their communities;
- To be involved in developing new solutions to service delivery;
- To achieve Best Value by adopting new and innovative methods;
- To make maximum use of their existing skills and capacity;
- To engage in regeneration activities;
- To promote the economic, social and environmental wellbeing for the community;
- To attract and retain a skilled workforce and provide training opportunities;
- To create, foster and promote healthy markets in the region;
- To achieve meaningful outcomes set out in their community strategies/plans.

Authorities may also wish to consider the following points when planning to charge or trade:

- What legal powers they intend using for the activity undertaken;
- How the activity fits with the community plan or strategy;
- Has a need been identified for the service;
- The development of a business plan for the activity;
- The undertaking of a thorough market analysis;
- Has a risk assessment been undertaken;
- Does the activity show clear linkages to wellbeing powers.

Although charging and trading activity has been predominately identified with local authority direct works services in the past, the new powers represent an opportunity to expand charging and trading to more Council services and to innovative projects. This book contains numerous examples of potential schemes or activity undertaken.

The opportunity to charge for and trade services has opened up significantly for local authorities as a result of the new legislative framework. This book identifies the powers, which permit activity, the process of providing the service and examples of what some authorities have done to date. One of the greatest benefits of Cirell and Bennett's works is their ability to describe the law in a fashion that lay people can understand easily, whilst maintaining the legal certainty required by their professional peers.

Paul O'Brien
Chief Executive
Association for Public Service Excellence

AUTHOR'S PREFACE

The concept of municipal trading has existed in local government for many years. However, at different points in the history of local government, the concept has become of heightened importance. In 1990 the authors wrote *Municipal Trading—A Guide To The Use Of Local Authority Powers*, which was published by Longman. This was a short work of less than 200 pages that had a dramatic impact amongst local authorities, becoming symbolic of the struggle, then ongoing, for local authorities to act innovatively and to engage in municipal enterprise at a local level.

The authors remarked that the term "municipal trading" had become pejorative and was misleading in its implication in any event. The first book was called *Municipal Trading*, simply because that was the tag by which the activity was known and this, therefore, made it the appropriate title for the work. It is commented below that, in the intervening period, a new title has emerged that can only be a good thing. The reason the term 'municipal trading' is misleading is because the real issue is nothing to do with trading but concerns the existence of powers and duties and their proper and lawful exercise by a local authority. In other words, the whole concept is founded on the legal principles of the use and abuse of local authority powers. The authors always insisted that if the debate was kept to this founding principle, then a far more clear and dispassionate discussion would take place about the activities themselves, than by starting from the standpoint that a local authority was engaging in potentially risky trading activities.

Municipal Trading always made clear that in 1990, if a simple answer to the question "can local authorities engage in municipal trading?" was required, the answer must surely be no. However, as mentioned above, it is necessary to go back to the basic legal principles and, like so many other issues in life, it cannot be oversimplified in such a way. The purpose of the first book was therefore to outline the legal framework of powers and duties in English law as they relate to local authorities and to identify recurring themes and principles. The authors commented that it would be futile to suggest that a simple list of statutory and Common Law powers would be of value to local government officers in the absence of the knowledge of how to apply the relevant principles; it was therefore an attempt to provide local authorities with the tools needed to identify powers which might have been of use and work with them. It was particularly significant that, prior to this, no other book had ever tried to bring together the disparate areas of law that deal exclusively with powers and duties from the angle of municipal trading.

The context that existed in local government at the time of *Municipal Trading* was particularly difficult. Local government law had developed over time in a somewhat haphazard way and had been described as a 'patchwork quilt' with powers and duties developing through the Parliamentary process to meet the specific needs of local authorities as and when those needs arose. Unfortunately, there was often no correlation or inter relationship between the powers which had been developed and this had the consequence that identifying powers and their proper uses was much more difficult than it needed to be. The reasons for that consequence were deeply enshrined in the English legal system itself, though not mirrored in the legal systems of our European local authority counterparts.

The intention of the authors was to generate debate and discussion amongst local authorities on this important subject; it is a sad reflection on the local government climate at the time that it became patently clear that others did not want any such debate and intended to stifle local municipal enterprise. As a result, controversy followed some of the statements made in *Municipal Trading*; needlessly so in the view of the authors. The reason that controversy arose was because the central government of the time was hostile to local authorities in general and certainly to suggestions that authorities should engage in municipal trading. The mood in government at that time was that local authorities' powers should be constrained, rather than expanded, and that civic enterprise should be replaced with private enterprise. This is clearly demonstrated through the CCT and privatisation policies operated from 1988 onwards.

Perhaps more significant was the fact that the Audit Commission at the time was also hostile to the concept of municipal trading. Taking its lead from central government, the Commission published and circulated increasingly restrictive legal advice on the use of local authority powers and seemed both intolerant of such activity and insensitive to what local authorities were trying to achieve. Every time a suggestion was made as to schemes that local authorities might engage in, a further Technical Release would appear from the Commission, based on restrictive legal advice provided by its in-house solicitor at the time, and often supported by Counsel's opinions. Classic examples are provided by Technical Release 23/90 from the Audit Commission on cross boundary tendering or on Technical Releases concerning sales of UPVC windows, charging for services and the like.

All in all this contributed to a macro scenario between central and local government, characterised by poor relations and a lack of trust. It was some time after the late 1980s and early 1990s that even in central government the realisation dawned that such poor central/local relations were damaging both sides. In relation to trading, relations were also poor with the Audit

Commission with substantial criticism being levied by each side of the other. Few arguments are black and white and to a degree both sides had a point to make and made it effectively. Unfortunately, this led to deadlock in many local authorities, the freezing of municipal enterprise and the development of a climate of fear around any activities linked to trading.

Interestingly enough, the authors commented in 1990 on the fundamental issue of centralism v localism. The system prevalent in continental Europe was considered, in the context of powers of general competence, and comparisons made. It was considered that the fundamental reason why municipal trading activity should be discussed was that local authorities, by their very nature, are elected by local people to serve their needs. It is therefore unwise to assume that central government knows best and that local government needs strict control of this type. Local authorities had had explicit powers for many trading activities (such as gas and electricity generation and distribution, water production and transport systems), for decades without any problems. So the comment was made that for central government to raise concerns over and to blame local authorities for risking tax payers money should be exposed as nothing more than a crude weapon being used by central government to restrain the locally elected authority from implementing locally supported policies. In this way, municipal trading could be seen as the tip of the iceberg in a much wider political debate, namely whether central or local government should control people's lives. As Ruth Rendall and Colin Ward explained in their book *Undermining The Central Line* (Chatto and Windus), they see the 'worm turning' end in due course:

"Just as the whole tendency in the twentieth century has been an unthinking assumption that central government knows best, so the inevitable reaction in the twenty-first century is going to be a rediscovery of the aspirations towards local democracy. There is going to be a devolution of control of essentially community concerns from district and county councils to local communities. There is going to be a devolution of control of essentially regional concerns from central government to regional bodies as federations of counties."

This was written in the late 1980s but is as true today as it was then. As mentioned below, the 'tide' is definitely on the turn.

It is of significant interest that most of the problems mentioned above that provided a particularly hostile context for municipal trading in the late 1980s and early 1990s have now substantially receded in the intervening decade and a half. As an example, whilst local government law could still be described as a 'patchwork quilt,' we now have specific powers for charging and trading as provided by the Local Government Act 2003 and examined in detail in this work. The decade that started in the year 2000 finds a central government that encourages a debate with local government about all aspects of public service, including charging and trading. Central government is now supportive of local authorities trying to improve the lot of their citizens, attempting to be innovative and generally promoting civic enterprise. This is perhaps the biggest single key factor in the transformation of the context in which charging and trading now takes place.

The other element of the regulatory control of trading mentioned above was the Audit Commission. It is interesting to note here too that there have been substantial changes. The powers under which the Audit Commission operates were consolidated in the Audit Commission Act 1998 and in the early part of this decade the new leadership under James Strachan developed a concept of 'strategic regulation' for the Audit Commission's work. This involves the work of the Commission being proportionate to local government and the principal tool of the Comprehensive Performance Assessment being used to cover a number of other disparate areas previously existing. Accordingly, the position of the new Commission on charging and trading is that it is a matter for the government and local authorities. There is no reason to believe that the Commission will not be supportive of local authorities engaging in charging and trading, using both the new statutory powers and existing powers in the context now appertaining. A wide scale conflict between the Commission and local authorities is unlikely.

Central government/local government relations are greatly improved from those earlier days. When the Labour party was elected into government in 1997 it made clear that it specifically wanted to improve central/local relations as they had degenerated to a very low ebb. The government created the Central Local Partnership signed up by both central government and the Local Government Association on behalf of local authorities. This forum has been used to build up relationships over subsequent years. In 2004 the government introduced its Vision document for the next decade as part of a consultation process and this recognises that the two sides will not always agree.

In the document that accompanied the announcement of the consultation process (*The Future of Local Government: Developing a Ten Year Vision* ODPM July 2004) it is stated that one of the challenges facing the government moving forward is to establish a more coherent and stable relationship between local and central government. At p.9 the government admits, "this relationship has sometimes been characterised by over-burdensome controls, conflicting priorities and unjoined up initiatives." The Local Government Minister, Nick Raynsford, was perhaps even more candid in an article in the *Municipal Journal* on July 27, 2004 when he said:

> "What we are working towards is not some tension-free utopia but a workable, stable relationship—a clear framework where we all understand our different roles, and where issues can be raised and resolved in a mature way. . ."

Perhaps the key factor in the ten year vision is the positive 'vibes' it contains about what local government can achieve working in partnership with central government. It is commented that:

"The investment in and reform of local government since 1997 have contributed to substantial improvement and demonstrated the enormous energy and potential within local government if it is properly funded and imaginatively led. . . But these examples of excellence, and the reforms which have underpinned them can only increase the sense that much more would be achieved across all local authorities, if the right environment is created." (At p.8).

In the years following the year 2000 the tide has also continued to move away from centralism and towards a decentralised approach. This has become known as the "new localism" agenda following the tireless work of the New Local Government Network to promote a new approach. This is illustrated in the booklet *New Localism—Re-fashioning the Centre-Local Relationship* which was written by Dan Corry and Professor Gerry Stoker and published by the New Local Government Network in December 2002. They state:

"We argue for a new localism that explicitly recognises the inherent weakness of authority-based systems of control. We are convinced that effective local and regional institutions and dynamic communities hold the key to unlocking a series of intractable problems confronting our society that no amount of sophisticated action by Whitehall will be able to tackle." (Executive Summary).

Even now the debate rumbles on. Simon Jenkins in a booklet *Big Bang Localism* in 2004 argued that the NHS should be abolished and health services decentralised, policing, planning, prisons and probation should revert to top tier councils and care homes, nurseries, parks and leisure to municipalities and parishes. This was described by *Public Finance* magazine as "naïve" and will probably never be achieved; but one thing is certain and that is that local government is an infinitely better position in 2005 than it was in 1990.

With the changing context in which charging and trading takes place, its fortunes have also ebbed and flowed. As the authors pointed out in *Municipal Trading*, in the period before the CCT regime was extended to blue collar services, there had been a period of relative stability in the interpretation of local authority powers and local government had retained a level of confidence in the innovative use of those powers. Good examples are provided by both s.111 of the Local Government Act 1972 permitting activities which facilitate or are conducive or incidental to the performance of other functions, or in relation to other key powers such as s.101 of the

Local Government Act 1972 for joint arrangements. In short, the powers had been given by Parliament, were being used and there seemed little concern at the regulatory level.

However, municipal trading went through some dark years from the introduction of CCT to blue collar services via the Local Government Act 1988, which lasted until the middle of the following decade. During these dark years, central local relations were at their lowest and against a background of the growing tide of centralism in British politics, it was predictable that the government wished to adopt a restrictive view of the use of powers by local authorities. The work of the Audit Commission in preventing local authorities from acting innovatively was significant and extensive, and this represented a distinct change from previous years. In the past, the role of the external auditor in relation to local government had been one of assisting the authority in identifying powers and contributing to schemes coming to fruition. That all changed during this period, as described in Ch.13. It did not go unnoticed in local government circles that in parallel to the restrictive views of the government and the over-enthusiasm of the Audit Commission to enforce a restrictive line, the courts also delivered some damning judgments on local authority powers. Three particular judgments stand out as indicative of the judicial swing towards a more restrictive line and these are the Hammersmith and Fulham interest rate swaps case, the North Tyneside severance case and the McCarthy and Stone case. All of these had a profound effect on local government and are fully considered in Ch.13.

The triple effect of pressure from central government, the Audit Commission and the courts created a climate of fear amongst local authorities in terms of their use of, often fairly established, legal powers. The legacy of this period was the stifling of municipal enterprise at a time when most local authorities in the country had experience of not pursuing one scheme or another due to doubts about whether it was *ultra vires* or not.

Fortunately a renaissance did arrive in the mid-1990s, by way of a legal opinion surrounding the reorganisation in Wales and a new case giving Court of Appeal authority for a more liberal view of statutory powers. This time in relation to another key power, namely the Local Authorities (Goods and Services) Act 1970. If the metaphor of the 'tide turning' is to be used, this was surely it.

Of course the Labour Party entered government in 1997 for the first time in eighteen years and introduced its 'Modernisation Agenda.' There were many facets to Labour's new Agenda, including the improvement of central/local relations, the greater empowering of local authorities and the abolition of the despised CCT regime. Over the course of the next two Parliamentary terms, the government introduced the Best Value regime under the Local Government Act 1998, new powers of community initiative under the Local Government Act 2000 and followed this in 2003 with the passing of the Local Government Act giving specific powers for charging and trading. Slowly but surely following the election in 1997, the new government dismantled the legacy of the late 1980s and early 1990s and dealt with the baggage that local authorities had been left with in terms of their confidence to take decisions on the use of powers.

So, in 2005, the new context for municipal trading emerged, involving full governmental support, a new brace of statutory powers and a clear way forward. As part of this reinvigoration of such activity, a new term also emerged to replace the pejorative tag of municipal trading, namely "charging and trading." This is, therefore, the term used in this book.

Consequently, the authors have re-written the original text of *Municipal Trading* that was so popular with local government and have placed it firmly in the modern context existing in the mid 2000s. The character of the original text has been preserved, in terms of a fiercely positive approach to the issue of powers, and providing ways of interpreting available powers purposively in order to achieve legitimate goals for civic enterprise. It is a source of some irony that the views characterised in *Municipal Trading* that were so heavily criticised by the government of the time (and the Audit Commission) remain and now find more solid support from all quarters, including the judiciary and leading Counsel.

We hope that this work will be as useful to officers and members in local government as the predecessor was for explaining the operation of charging and trading powers and encouraging local authorities to use them.

CONTENTS

	Page
Acknowledgments	vii
Preface—Paul O'Brien, Chief Executive, Association for Public Service Excellence	ix
Author's Preface	xiii
Table of Cases	xxv
Table of Statutes	xxix
Table of Statutory Instruments	xxxvii

Part One—Introduction and Context

	Paras
Chapter 1—Introduction and Context	1.1
Chapter 2—The Legal Basis for Charging and Trading	2.1
Introduction	2.1
The *Ultra Vires* Doctrine-Capacity	2.2
The *Ultra Vires* Doctrine-Exercise of Powers	2.17
Dealing with the impact of the *Ultra Vires* Doctrine?	2.24
Case Law on Charging and Trading	2.28
Conclusion	2.32
Chapter 3—Strategic Planning	3.1
Introduction	3.1
Which of the Three Routes to Follow?	3.2
Factors in the Choice between Charging and Trading Powers	3.3
Developing a strategy for Charging and Trading	3.15
An Incremental Three Year Plan for Trading	3.16
A Strategy for Discretionary Charging	3.23
A Commercial Trading Strategy	3.25

Part Two—Charging and Trading Powers

Chapter 4—Charging and Trading under Existing Powers	4.1
Introduction	4.1
Key Powers for Charging and Trading Activity	4.2
Incidental Powers	4.24
Spare Capacity	4.25
Local Legislation and Other Special Powers	4.28

Specific Charging Powers   4.32
Conclusion   4.34
Chapter 5—Powers to Charge for Discretionary Services under
    Section 93 of the Local Government Act 2003   5.1
Introduction   5.1
Conclusion   5.12
Chapter 6—Examples of Using the Charging Powers   6.1
Introduction   6.1
Conclusion   6.8
Chapter 7—Commercial Trading   7.1
Introduction   7.1
The Legal Framework   7.2
The CPA and Better Performing Authorities   7.6
Trading Companies   7.7
The Distinction between Powers to Charge for Discretionary
    Services and Commercial Trading   7.12
The Impact on Existing Powers to Trade   7.13
Conclusion   7.14
Chapter 8—Establishment of Companies for Trading   8.1
Introduction   8.1
Issues to Consider before Forming any Company   8.2
The Legal Constraints   8.10
The General Governance Framework   8.20
Staffing, Personnel and Employment issues   8.27
Funding and Other Assistance to the company   8.28
State Aid and Competition Law   8.29
Business Planning   8.31
Exit Strategies   8.32
Taxation   8.33
Conclusion   8.34
Chapter 9—Commercial Trading in Practice   9.1
Introduction   9.1
The Example of a Wholly Owned Company   9.2
The Example of a Joint Venture Company   9.9
Conclusion   9.16

Part Three—Practical Implementation

Chapter 10—Practical Implementation Issues   10.1
Introduction   10.1
The Business Plan   10.2
The Risk Analysis   10.4
The Market Analysis   10.6
User Surveys   10.7

Performance Levels   10.8
A Cost/Benefit Analysis   10.9
Economic, Social and Environmental Wellbeing Cases   10.10
Management and Organisational Issues   10.11
Accountability   10.13
Tactical Issues   10.14
Risk of Challenge   10.15
Conclusion   10.17
Chapter 11—Commercial and Consumer Issues   11.1
Introduction   11.1
Pre-Contractual Statements   11.2
Determining the terms of the contract   11.3
Contractual terms implied by the Law   11.6
Advertising Controls   11.13
The Distance selling regulations   11.14
Codes of Practice   11.15
Competition Law   11.16
Tax and VAT   11.19
VAT   11.21
Conclusion   11.22
Chapter 12—Employee and Member Related Issues   12.1
Introduction   12.1
Managing Change   12.2
Secondment   12.11
VAT   12.15
Fixed Term Employees   12.19
Staff Transfer Issues—The Framework under the Local
   Government Act 2003   12.20
TUPE Rights   12.28
Pensions   12.29
Indemnities for Officers and Members   12.36
Conclusion   12.37

Part Four—Context and History

Chapter 13—An Introduction to Local Government and the History
             of the Trading Debate   13.1
Introduction   13.1
The Structure of Local Government   13.2
The Relationship between Central and Local Government   13.4
The Role of the Courts in Controlling Trading   13.7
Moves to Abolish the *Ultra Vires* Doctrine   13.9
A Softening of attitudes towards Trading by Local Authorities   13.10
Conclusion   13.15

CONTENTS

Part Five—Charging and Trading in Scotland, Wales and Northern Ireland

Chapter 14—Charging and Trading in Scotland, Wales and Northern
Ireland   14.1
  Introduction   14.1
  Charging and Trading in Northern Ireland   14.2
  Trading and Charging in Wales   14.7
  Charging and Trading in Scotland   14.20
  The Legal Provisions   14.21
  How will trading in Scotland operate?   14.26
  Conclusion   14.33

Part Six—Conclusion

Chapter 15—Conclusion   15.1

Appendix One: Legislation and Statutory Instruments   16.1
Appendix Two: Guidance on Charging and Trading   17.1
Appendix Three: Miscellaneous documentation in relation to
              Charging and Trading   18.1

                               Page
Index   385

TABLE OF CASES

A/S Sameiling v Grain Importers (Eire) Ltd [1952] 2 All E.R. 315;
[1952] 1 Lloyd's Rep. 313; [1952] 1 T.L.R. 847, QBD 11.7
Alexandra Palace Ski Centre v Haringey LBC [1994] E.G.C.S. 99;
[1994] N.P.C. 73; *The Times*, May 25, 1994, CA 2.29, 4.24
Allsop v North Tyneside MBC. *See* North Tyneside MBC v Allsop
Associated Provincial Picture Houses Ltd v Wednesbury Corp [1948]
1 K.B. 223; [1947] 2 All E.R. 680; 63 T.L.R. 623; 112 J.P. 55;
45 L.G.R. 635; [1948] L.J.R. 190; 177 L.T. 641; 92 S.J. 26,
CA 2.18, 2.20
Attorney General v Great Eastern Railway Co (1879–80) L.R. 5
App. Cas. 473, HL 2.9, 13.7
Attorney General v London County Council [1907] A.C. 131 .... 13.7
Attorney General v Manchester Corp [1906] 1 Ch. 643, Ch D 2.16
Attorney General v Smethwick Corp [1932] 1 Ch. 562, CA 4.24, 13.8
Attorney General v Wilts United Dairies Ltd (1922) 38 T.L.R. 781,
HL 2.14

BRS v Arthur Crutchley Limited [1968] 1 All E.R. 811 .... 11.4
Baroness Wenlock v River Dee Co (No.1) (1884–85) L.R. 10 App.
Cas. 354, HL 13.7
Beckmann v Dynamco Whicheloe Macfarlane Ltd (C-164/00); sub
nom. Beckman v Dynamco Whicheloe Macfarlane Ltd [2002] All
E.R. (EC) 865; [2002] 2 C.M.L.R. 45; [2002] C.E.C. 547; [2003]
I.C.R. 50; [2002] Emp. L.R. 970; [2002] O.P.L.R. 289; [2002]
Pens. L.R. 287; *The Times*, June 17, 2002, ECJ 12.32
Blake (Valuation Officer) v Hendon Corp (No.1) [1962] 1 Q.B. 283;
[1961] 3 W.L.R. 951; [1961] 3 All E.R. 601; 125 J.P. 620; 59
L.G.R. 515; [1961] R.V.R. 552; 105 S.J. 666, CA 2.11
Bromley LBC v Greater London Council [1983] 1 A.C. 768; [1982] 2
W.L.R. 92; [1982] 1 All E.R. 153; 126 S.J. 16, HL 2.19
Bullard v Croydon Hospital Group Management Committee [1953]
1 Q.B. 511; [1953] 2 W.L.R. 470; [1953] 1 All E.R. 596; 97 S.J.
155, QBD 12.36
Butler Machine Tool Co v Ex-cell-o Corp (England) [1979] 1
W.L.R. 401; [1979] 1 All E.R. 965; 121 S.J. 406, CA 11.4

Celtec Ltd v Astley; sub nom. Astley v Celtec Ltd [2002] EWCA Civ
1035; [2002] 3 C.M.L.R. 15; [2002] I.C.R. 1289; [2002] I.R.L.R.
629; [2002] Emp. L.R. 1064; (2002) 99(37) L.S.G. 38; *The Times*,
August 9, 2002, CA 12.13

Commission v Germany (Case 126/03) 8.11
Commission v Spain (Case 84/03) 8.11
Congreve v Home Office [1976] Q.B. 629; [1976] 2 W.L.R. 291;
   [1976] 1 All E.R. 697; 119 S.J. 847; *The Times*, December 9, 1975,
   CA 2.14
Council of Civil Service Unions v Minister for the Civil Service
   [1985] A.C. 374; [1984] 1 W.L.R. 1174; [1984] 3 All E.R. 935;
   [1985] I.C.R. 14; [1985] I.R.L.R. 28; (1985) 82 L.S.G. 437; (1984)
   128 S.J. 837, HL 2.18

D and J Nicol v The Trustees of the Harbour of Dundee [1914] A.C.
   550 .... 4.27
Department of Health and Social Security v Envoy Farmers Ltd
   [1976] 1 W.L.R. 1018; [1976] 2 All E.R. 173; [1976] I.C.R. 573;
   120 S.J. 330, QBD 2.9
Donoghue v Poplar Housing & Regeneration Community Association Ltd. *See* Poplar Housing & Regeneration Community Association Ltd v Donoghue

European Communities v Italian Republic, January 2003, ECJ 5.9,
                                                     17.64, 17.80
Forrest v Manchester, Sheffield and Lincolnshire Railway Company
   [1861] 30 BEAV 39 .... 4.27

Hazell v Hammersmith and Fulham LBC [1992] 2 A.C. 1; [1991] 2
   W.L.R. 372; [1991] 1 All E.R. 545; 89 L.G.R. 271; (1991) 3
   Admin. L.R. 549; [1991] R.V.R. 28; (1991) 155 J.P.N. 527; (1991)
   155 L.G. Rev. 527; (1991) 88(8) L.S.G. 36; (1991) 141 N.L.J. 127,
   HL 2.1, 2.9, 2.10, 2.25, 4.24, 13.8, 13.9
Henke v Gemeinde Schierke (C-298/94) [1997] All E.R. (EC) 173;
   [1996] E.C.R. I-4989; [1997] 1 C.M.L.R. 373; [1997] I.C.R. 746;
   [1996] I.R.L.R. 701, ECJ 12.21
Hertford Foods Ltd v Lidl UK GmbH. *See* Lidl UK GmbH v
   Hertford Foods Ltd

Jonescu v Royal Free Hospital Board of Governors (1965) 109 S.J.
   534, CA 11.7

Lidl UK GmbH v Hertford Foods Ltd; sub nom. Hertford Foods
   Ltd v Lidl UK GmbH [2001] EWCA Civ 938, CA 11.4

McCarthy & Stone (Developments) Ltd v Richmond upon Thames
   LBC; sub nom. R v Richmond upon Thames LBC Ex p.
   McCarthy & Stone (Developments) Ltd [1992] 2 A.C. 48; [1991]
   3 W.L.R. 941; [1991] 4 All E.R. 897; 90 L.G.R. 1; (1992) 4
   Admin. L.R. 223; (1992) 63 P. & C.R. 234; [1992] 1 P.L.R. 131;
   [1992] J.P.L. 467; [1991] E.G.C.S. 118; (1992) 89(3) L.S.G. 33;
   (1991) 141 N.L.J. 1589; (1991) 135 S.J.L.B. 206; [1991] N.P.C.
   118; *The Times*, November 15, 1991; *Independent*, November 15,
   1991, HL 2.13, 2.16, 4.24, 4.27, 5.3, 10.14, 10.16, 13.11

North Tyneside MBC v Allsop [1992] I.C.R. 639; 90 L.G.R. 462; (1992) 4 Admin. L.R. 550, CA 2.2, 2.15

Pepper (Inspector of Taxes) v Hart [1993] A.C. 593; [1992] 3 W.L.R. 1032; [1993] 1 All E.R. 42; [1992] S.T.C. 898; [1993] I.C.R. 291; [1993] I.R.L.R. 33; [1993] R.V.R. 127; (1993) 143 N.L.J. 17; [1992] N.P.C. 154, HL 2.2

Poplar Housing & Regeneration Community Association Ltd v Donoghue; sub nom. Donoghue v Poplar Housing & Regeneration Community Association Ltd; Poplar Housing & Regeneration Community Association Ltd v Donaghue [2001] EWCA Civ 595; [2002] Q.B. 48; [2001] 3 W.L.R. 183; [2001] 4 All E.R. 604; [2001] 2 F.L.R. 284; [2001] 3 F.C.R. 74; [2001] U.K.H.R.R. 693; (2001) 33 H.L.R. 73; (2001) 3 L.G.L.R. 41; [2001] B.L.G.R. 489; [2001] A.C.D. 76; [2001] Fam. Law 588; [2001] 19 E.G.C.S. 141; (2001) 98(19) L.S.G. 38; (2001) 98(23) L.S.G. 38; (2001) 145 S.J.L.B. 122; [2001] N.P.C. 84; *The Times*, June 21, 2001; *Independent*, May 2, 2001; *Daily Telegraph*, May 8, 2001, CA 17.37

R. v Ealing LBC Ex p. Times Newspapers Ltd [1987] I.R.L.R. 129; 85 L.G.R. 316; (1987) 151 L.G. Rev. 530; *The Times*, November 6, 1986, DC 2.20

R. v Greater Manchester Police Authority Ex p. Century Motors (Farnworth) Ltd; *The Times*, May 31, 1996, QBD 2.30

R. v Hackney LBC Ex p. Secretary of State for the Environment, 88 L.G.R. 96; (1990) 154 L.G. Rev. 453, DC 4.6

R. v Inner London Education Authority Ex p. Westminster City Council [1986] 1 W.L.R. 28; [1986] 1 All E.R. 19; 84 L.G.R. 120; (1986) 83 L.S.G. 359; (1986) 130 S.J. 51; *The Times*, December 31, 1984, QBD 2.21

R. v Manchester City Council Ex p. King, 89 L.G.R. 696; [1991] C.O.D. 422; *The Times*, April 3, 1991; *Daily Telegraph*, April 12, 1991, DC 2.21

R. v Richmond upon Thames LBC Ex p. McCarthy & Stone (Developments) Ltd. *See* McCarthy & Stone (Developments) Ltd v Richmond upon Thames LBC

R. v Yorkshire Purchasing Organisation Ex p. British Educational Suppliers Ltd; sub nom. R v Yorkshire Purchasing Organisation Ex p. British Educational Suppliers Association [1998] E.L.R. 195; [1997] C.O.D. 473; *The Times*, July 10, 1997, CA .. 2.26, 4.7, 4.27, 10.16, 13.12

Rhyl Urban DC v Rhyl Amusements Ltd [1959] 1 W.L.R. 465; [1959] 1 All E.R. 257; 57 L.G.R. 19; 103 S.J. 327, Ch D 2.1

Roberts v Hopwood; sub nom. R. v Roberts Ex p. Scurr; R. v Roberts Ex p. Scurr [1925] A.C. 578, HL 13.7, 13.8

St Albans DC v ICL [1996] All E.R. 481 .... 11.12

Sauter Automation Ltd v HC Goodman (Mechanical Services) Ltd (In Liquidation)(1986) 34 B.L.R. 81; *Financial Times*, May 14, 1986, Ch D 11.4

Short v Poole Corp [1926] Ch. 66, CA 2.18
Simpson v Westminster Palace Hotel Co Ltd [1860] Ch 29 .... 4.27
Stadt Halle and Others (Case 36/03) 8.11

Teckal Srl v Comune di Viano (Reggio Emilia) (C-107/98) [1999]
    E.C.R. I-8121, ECJ 8.10, 8.11, 15.1

United Dominions Trust (Commercial) v Eagle Aircraft Services;
    sub nom. United Dominions Trust (Commercial) v Eagle Avia-
    tion [1968] 1 W.L.R. 74; [1968] 1 All E.R. 104; (1967) 111 S.J.
    849, CA 11.7

Wards Construction (Medway) Ltd v Kent CC [1999] B.L.G.R. 675;
    [1999] 2 P.L.R. 61; [1999] J.P.L. 738; [1999] E.G.C.S. 18; [1999]
    N.P.C. 16; *The Times*, March 3, 1999; *Independent*, February 22,
    1999, CA 2.31
Westminster Corp v London & North Western Railway Co; sub
    nom. London & North Western Railway Co v Westminster Corp
    [1905] A.C. 426, HL 2.21

TABLE OF STATUTES

1835 Municipal Corpora-
tions Act (5 & 6
Will. 4 c.76) 13.7

1855 Metropolis Manage-
ment Act (18 &
19 Vict. c.120)
s.62 .... 13.7

1875 Public Health Act (38
& 39 Vict. c.55) .. 2.11
s.265 .... 12.36

1900 Alexandra Park and
Palace (Public
Purposes) Act (63
& 64 Vict.
c.cclix) 2.29

1908 Smallholdings and
Allotments Act (8
Edw.7 c.36)
s.49 .... App.3

1933 Local Government Act
(23 & 24 Geo.5
c.51) 2.11, 4.10

1944 Education Act (7 & 8
Geo.6 c.31) App.3
s.100(1)(b) App.3

1945 Water Act (8 & 9
Geo.6 c.42) 13.2

1946 Education Act (9 & 10
Geo.6 c.50) App.3
National Health
Service Act (9 &
10 Geo.6 c.81) .. App.3

1947 Civic Restaurants Act
(10 & 11 Geo.6
c.22) ... 3.18, 4.1, 4.15,
7.2, 14.11, 17.9
s.1 .... 4.11

1947 Civic Restaurants Act
—cont.
s.3(2) 4.15

1948 Children Act (11 & 12
Geo.6 c.43) App.3
Criminal Justice Act
(11 & 12 Geo.6
c.58)
s.45 .... App.3
s.46(1) App.3
Sch.5 .... App.3

1959 Education Act (7 & 8
Eliz.2 c.60) App.3

1962 Education Act (10 &
11 Eliz.2 c.12) .. App.3

1963 Local Authorities
(Land) Act
(c.29) .. 2.11, 4.10, 4.14
s.2 .... 2.11
s.3 .... 4.14
s.4 .... 4.14

1964 Police Act (c.48)
s.2 .... App.3
s.3 .... App.3
s.4 .... 2.30
Public Libraries and
Museums Act
(c.75) 2.20, 5.5, 5.9
Education Act
(c.82) App.3

1965 Industrial and Provident Societies Act
(c.12) 7.7, 8.4, 8.8,
9.1, 17.20

1967 Education Act
(c.3) App.3

1967 Criminal Justice Act
(c.80)
s.96(1) App.3
1968 Education Act
(c.17) App.3
Trade Descriptions Act
(c.29) 11.13
Social Work (Scotland)
Act (c.49)
s.2(4) App.3
s.3(9) App.3
s.7(8) App.3
s.21(3) App.3
s.95(2) App.3
Sch.9 .... App.3
1969 Children and Young
Persons Act
(c.54) App.3
1970 Local Authorities
(Goods and
Services) Act
(c.39) ... 1.1, 2.11, 3.1,
3.13, 3.16, 4.3, 4.5,
4.7, 4.8, 4.14, 5.10,
6.4, 7.5, 11.20,
12.12, 13.12, 14.3,
14.4, 14.8, 14.11,
14.20, 14.21, 14.22,
14.23, 14.27, 14.28,
16.3, 16.4, 17.6,
17.9, 17.16, App.3
s.1 ... 2.26, 3.17, 4.2, 4.4,
4.6, 4.8, 4.10, 4.23,
4.30, 4.31, 7.13, 9.9
(2) 2.11, 4.14
(a) 4.6
(b) 4.6
(3) 4.3
(4) 4.4, 4.5, 4.6
(5) 4.4, 17.9
(6) 4.4
s.2(1) 4.4
(2) App.3
s.65 .... App.3
s.120 .... App.3
Sch.8, para.5 ..... App.3
Sch.22, para.13 ... App.3

1970 Equal Pay Act
(c.41) 12.24
1971 Education Act App.3
1972 Kensington and
Chelsea Act 4.28
Local Government
(Northern Ireland)
Act (c.9) 14.2
Superannuation Act
(c.11)
s.7 .... 12.30
Local Government Act
(c.70) 3.23, 14.2
s.100A(4) 17.33
s.101 .. 4.2, 4.8, 4.9, 4.10,
4.11, 4.24
(12) 4.11
(14) 4.10
s.111 ...... 2.8, 2.9, 2.13,
2.14, 2.15, 2.16,
2.25, 3.17, 3.19,
3.22, 4.2, 4.4, 4.8,
4.11, 4.13, 4.14,
4.24, 4.27, 5.2, 5.5,
5.9, 5.12, 6.2, 7.11,
7.13, 8.28, 12.12,
12.36, 13.8, 17.14
(1) 2.13, 2.30,
17.53, 17.69
(3) 2.14, 17.14
s.112 .... 3.17, 12.12
s.113 .... 12.11
s.137 .... 2.11
s.137(1) 2.11
s.144 .... 4.1
s.145 .... 4.11, 4.17, 4.18,
4.31, 5.5, 17.9
(2) 4.17
(c) 5.5
Sch.12A 17.33
Sch.13 .... 7.13
1973 Supply of Goods
(Implied Terms)
Act (c.13) 11.8
Water Act (c.37) 13.2
Powers of Criminal
Courts Act (c.62)
s.56(2) App.3

1973　Powers of Criminal
　　　　Courts Act—*cont.*
　　　　Sch.6 . . . . App.3
1976　Local Government
　　　　(Miscellaneous
　　　　Provisions) Act
　　　　(c.57) 3.18, 12.36,
　　　　　　　　　　　　　14.11
　　　　s.19 . . 2.3, 2.7, 4.11, 4.19,
　　　　　　　　4.31, 10.7, 17.9
　　　　(1) 4.20
　　　　(2) 4.19
　　　　s.32 . . . . 4.23
　　　　s.38 . . . 2.27, 4.1, 4.2, 4.8,
　　　　　　　　4.11, 4.21, 4.31, 7.2,
　　　　　　　　　　　　　17.9
　　　　(1) 4.22
　　　　(2) 2.27, 4.22
　　　　(3) 4.22
1977　National Health
　　　　Service Act (c.49)
　　　　s.28 . . . . App.3
　　　　s.129 . . . . App.3
　　　　Sch.14, paras 1–3　App.3
　　　　Sch.16 . . . . App.3
　　　　Unfair Contract Terms
　　　　Act ("UCTA")
　　　　(c.50) 11.6, 11.8,
　　　　　　　　　　11.10, 11.12
　　　　Pt I 11.12
　　　　Sch.2 . . . . 11.12
1978　Interpretation Act
　　　　(c.30) 5.3
1979　Sale of Goods Act
　　　　(c.54) 11.8, 11.9,
　　　　　　　　　　11.10, 11.12
　　　　s.8 . . . . 11.10
　　　　s.10(1) 11.10
　　　　s.13 . . . . 11.10
　　　　s.14 . . . . 11.10
　　　　(2B) 11.10
　　　　(3) 11.10
　　　　s.15 . . . . 11.10
　　　　s.20 . . . . 11.10
1980　Child Care Act (c.5)
　　　　s.89(1) App.3
　　　　(3) App.3

1980　Child Care Act—*cont.*
　　　　Sch.4, para.9 . . . . . App.3
　　　　Sch.6 . . . . App.3
　　　　Education Act (c.20)
　　　　s.22(5) App.3
　　　　s.38(6) App.3
　　　　Sch.7 . . . . App.3
　　　　Local Government
　　　　Planning and
　　　　Land Act (c.65)　14.23
　　　　Pt X 6.4
　　　　s.163(1) App.3
　　　　Highways Act (c.66)
　　　　s.278 . . . . 2.31
1981　Animal Health Act
　　　　(c.22) 4.11
　　　　Acquisition of Land
　　　　Act (c.67)
　　　　s.25 . . . . 2.31
1982　Supply of Goods and
　　　　Services Act
　　　　(c.29) 11.8, 11.9,
　　　　　　　　　　11.11, 11.12
　　　　ss.3–5 . . . . 11.11
　　　　s.12(4) 11.11
　　　　s.13 . . . . 11.11
　　　　s.14(1) 11.11
　　　　(2) 11.11
　　　　s.15(1) 11.11
　　　　(2) 11.11
　　　　s.16 . . . . 11.11
　　　　Local Government
　　　　(Miscellaneous
　　　　Provisions) Act
　　　　(c.30) 2.21
1985　Companies Act (c.6) . . . 7.8,
　　　　　　　　8.1, 8.6, 8.23, 9.7,
　　　　　　　　　　　　　17.20
　　　　s.1(2) 8.5
　　　　s.159(A) 17.11
　　　　s.736 . . . . 8.12
　　　　s.832 . . . . 11.20
　　　　Sch.10A, para.4 . . . . . 8.12
　　　　Local Government Act
　　　　(c.51) 13.2
　　　　Housing Act (c.68)
　　　　s.27 . . . . App.3

1985 Housing Associations
        Act (c.69) 6.4
     Birmingham City
        Council Act 4.28
1986 Local Government Act
        (c.10)
        s.1 . . . . 4.13
        s.2 . . . . 2.4, 8.17
     Insolvency Act (c.45) . . . 8.6
1987 Consumer Protection
        Act (c.43) 11.13
1988 Income and Corpora-
        tion Taxes Act
        (c.1) 11.20
        s.6(1) 11.20
        (4)(a) 11.20
     Education Reform Act
        (c.40)
        Sch.12, para.11 . . . App.3
        Sch.12, para.68 . . . App.3
     Housing Act (c.50)
        Pt III App.3
1989 Water Act (c.15) 13.2
     Companies Act (c.40) . . 8.6
     Local Government and
        Housing Act (c.42)
        Pt IV 7.9
        Pt V . . . 7.3, 7.7, 7.9, 7.10,
            8.1, 8.4, 8.5, 8.12,
            8.21, 8.28, 9.14,
            14.16, 17.14, 17.15,
            17.20, 17.28, 17.50,
            17.66
        s.33 . . . . 14.3
        s.67 . . . . 7.7
        (1) 7.7, 8.8
        (b) 8.5
        (c) 8.5
        (4) 7.7
        (5) 7.7
        ss.67–70 . . . . 7.9
        s.70(1) 7.3, 8.12
        s.71 . . . . 7.9
        s.72 . . . . 7.9
        s.73 . . . . 7.9
        s.150 . . . . 2.12, 4.24, 4.31,
            4.32, 4.33, 13.11,
            17.9

1989 Local Government and
        Housing Act—
        cont.
        s.150(1) 4.33
        (c) 4.32
        s.190(1) 4.33
1989 Greater Manchester
        Act 4.28
1990 Enterprise and New
        Towns (Scotland)
        Act (c.35)
        s.19 . . . . App.3
     Environmental Protec-
        tion Act (c.43)
        s.46 . . . . 2.3, 2.8
1991 New Roads and Street
        Works Act (c.22)
        s.23 . . . . 2.31
     Water Industry Act
        (c.56)
        Pt V App.3
     Water Resources Act
        (c.57)
        s.4(4) App.3
        s.158 . . . . App.3
     Water Consolidation
        (Consequential
        Provisions) Act
        (c.60) App.3
1992 Further and Higher
        Education Act
        (c.13)
        Sch.8, Pt II,
        para.71(1) App.3
1994 Local Government
        (Wales) Act
        (c.19) 13.12
        Sch.13, para.26 . . . App.3
     Value Added Tax Act
        (c.23)
        s.33 . . . . 17.36
     Deregulation and
        Contracting Out
        Act (c.40) 17.14
1995 Environment Act
        (c.25) App.3
        Sch.8, para.5 . . . . . App.3
        Sch.22, para.13 . . . App.3

1996 Police Act (c.16)
    s.3 .... 7.2, App.3
    s.6 .... 4.29
    s.25 .... 4.29
    s.25(1) 4.29
    s.103(3) App.3
    Sch.9 .... App.3
  Housing Act (c.52) 6.4
  Education Act (c.56)
    s.13 .... 4.30
    s.16 .... 4.30
    s.32(6) App.3
    s.482 .... App.3
    s.497A(4) App.3
    s.582(2) App.3
    (3) App.3
    Sch.5, para.1 ..... App.3
    Sch.38 .... App.3
    Sch.39, para.39(1) App.3
  Government of Wales
    Act 14.7
1997 Education Act (c.44)
    Sch.7, para.2 ..... App.3
  Local Government
    (Contracts) Act
    (c.65) 17.16
1998 Audit Commission Act
    (c.18) 10.16
  Data Protection Act
    ('DPA') (c.29) .. 11.13,
      17.33
  Teaching and Higher
    Education Act
    (c.30)
    s.44(2) App.3
    Sch.4 .... App.3
  School Standards and
    Framework Act
    (c.31)
    Sch.30, para.2(1) .. App.3
  Competition Act
    (c.41) 8.30, 11.16,
      11.18, 17.39
  Pt 1 .... 13.6
  Human Rights Act
    (c.42) 17.37

1998 Regional Development
    Agencies Act
    (c.45)
    Sch.7, para.3 ..... App.3
1999 Health Act (c.8) App.3
  Local Government Act
    (c.27) .. 5.2, 7.3, 12.23,
      13.5, 14.1, 14.3,
      14.5, 14.10, 17.68
    s.1 ..... 7.2, 17.49, 17.65
    (1)(a) 7.2
    (2) .. 7.2, 7.3, 7.4, 17.5
    s.3 .... 13.5
    s.15 .... 13.5
    s.16 ...... 7.1, 7.11, 13.6,
      13.13, 13.14, 14.5,
      14.8, 17.6
  Greater London
    Authority Act
    (c.29) 13.2
    s.2 .... 4.31
    s.30 .... 4.31
    (1) 4.31
    (2) 4.31
    (4) 4.31
    (5) 4.31
    (7) 4.31
    (9) 4.31
    s.31 .... 4.31
    s.34(2) 5.9, 17.54
    s.41(1) 4.31
    s.388 .... 4.5, App.3
2000 Local Government Act
    (c.22) .. 2.23, 3.16, 4.2,
      4.10, 5.1, 5.6, 5.12,
      6.1, 7.3, 7.5, 13.9,
      13.13, 14.1, 14.3,
      17.9, 17.51, 17.53,
      17.67, 17.69, 17.79
    Pt 1 .... 2.6, 12.12
    s.2 ... 2.3, 2.6, 2.27, 3.19,
      4.2, 4.11, 4.12, 4.13,
      4.14, 4.24, 4.25,
      4.26, 4.28, 5.2, 5.3,
      5.9, 6.2, 6.4, 6.6,
      7.11, 10.10, 17.16,
      17.54, 17.70, App.3

2000 Local Government Act
—*cont.*
s.2(1) 2.6, 4.12, 4.13,
7.11, 9.13, 17.9
(2) 2.6
(4) 4.13
(c) 4.13
(f) 4.13, 12.12
s.3 ...... 2.6, 4.13, 10.10
(1) 2.6, 4.13
(2) .. 4.12, 4.13, 12.12,
17.9, 17.54, 17.70
(3) 4.13
s.4 .... 2.6, 3.4, 7.3
s.101 .... 17.25
Freedom of Informa-
tion Act ('the
FOIA')(c.36) 17.33
s.5(1)(b) 17.33
Criminal Justice and
Court Services Act
(c.43)
s.4 .... App.3
Sch.7, Pt 2,
para.44 .... App.3
National Parks
(Scotland) Act
(asp 10)
Sch.2, para.11 .... App.3
2001 Housing (Scotland)
Act (asp.10)
s.107(1) App.3
2002 Local Government
(Best Value)
(Northern Ireland)
Act (c.4) 14.3, 14.5
s.1(1) 14.5
(2) 14.5
s.3 .... 14.5
National Health
Service Reform
and Health Care
Professions Act
(c.17)
s.6(2) App.3
Sch.5, para.4 ..... App.3
para.12(a) .. App.3
Enterprise Act (c.40) .. 8.30

2002 Water Industry (Scotland) Act (asp.3)
s.61 .... App.3
2003 Local Government Act
(c.26) 1.1, 1.2, 2.2,
3.23, 4.1, 4.2, 4.25,
4.34, 5.1, 5.6, 7.1,
7.2, 7.5, 7.6, 7.7,
7.9, 8.3, 9.1, 9.14,
9.16, 10.16, 12.20,
12.21, 13.3, 13.14,
13.15, 14.1, 14.3,
14.4, 14.10, 14.11,
14.32, 15.1, 16.2,
16.3, 17.9, 17.49,
17.51, 17.52, 17.53,
17.55, 17.61, 17.65,
17.67, 17.68, 17.77
Pt 1 .... 17.15
s.2 .... 4.8, 17.15
s.3 .... 17.15
s.4 .... 17.15
s.18 .... 14.16, 17.15
s.93 .... 1.1, 1.2, 2.3, 2.6,
2.8, 2.12, 2.15, 2.32,
3.1, 3.2, 3.4, 3.10,
3.12, 3.13, 3.15,
3.16, 3.19, 3.20,
3.21, 3.23, 3.24,
3.26, 4.1, 4.3, 4.11,
4.12, 4.13, 4.14,
4.15, 4.17, 4.19,
4.22, 4.23, 4.24,
4.26, 4.27, 4.32, 5.1,
5.2, 5.3, 5.5, 5.6,
5.7, 5.9, 5.10, 5.11,
5.12, 6.1, 6.2, 6.3,
6.4, 6.5, 6.6, 6.7,
6.8, 7.2, 7.5, 9.1,
10.1, 10.2, 10.3,
10.6, 10.8, 10.10,
10.11, 10.12, 10.14,
10.15, 12.12, 14.10,
14.12, 15.1, 15.2,
17.8, 17.16, 17.49,
17.65, 17.69, 17.78
(1) .. 5.3, 5.10, 17.49,
17.53, 17.65, 17.69

2003 Local Government Act
      —cont.
    s.93(1)(b) 5.4
      (2) . . 5.5, 17.49, 17.65
      (a) 5.5
      (3) . . . 3.21, 3.23, 5.7,
        5.8, 5.9, 5.11, 6.1,
        6.3, 6.5, 6.6, 10.3,
        10.7, 17.56, 17.57,
        17.72, 17.73
      (4) . . 5.8, 17.57, 17.73
      (5) 5.8
      (6) 5.1, 14.12, 17.49,
        17.65
      (7) . . . 2.6, 5.9, 17.54,
        17.70
      (a) . . . 17.53, 17.69
      (8) 5.3
    ss.93–94 . . . . 17.51, 17.67
    ss.93–97 . . . . 16.2
    s.94 . . . . . 5.1, 5.10, 14.10,
      14.12, 17.8, 17.51,
      17.62, 17.67, 17.78
    s.95 . . . . 1.1, 1.2, 1.3, 2.8,
      2.9, 2.21, 2.25, 2.27,
      2.32, 3.1, 3.2, 3.4,
      3.5, 3.10, 3.12, 3.13,
      3.14, 3.15, 3.16,
      3.21, 3.25, 3.26,
      3.28, 4.1, 4.8, 4.12,
      4.22, 4.26, 5.1, 5.2,
      5.3, 5.10, 6.1, 7.1,
      7.2, 7.3, 7.7, 7.11,
      7.13, 8.1, 8.28, 9.2,
      9.13, 9.16, 10.1,
      10.2, 10.3, 10.6,
      10.11, 10.15, 13.5,
      13.8, 14.3, 14.8,
      14.10, 14.13, 14.17,
      14.32, 15.1, 15.2,
      17.3, 17.4, 17.5,
      17.7, 17.9, 17.12,
      17.14, 17.16, 17.20,
      17.24, 17.38, 17.49,
      17.50, 17.65, 17.66,
      17.78
      (1) 17.2, 17.16,
      17.50, 17.66

2003 Local Government Act
      —cont.
    s.95(1)(a) 7.2, 17.9
      (b) 7.2
      (2) 7.2
      (b) 17.9
      (3) 7.3
      (4) 7.3, 7.7, 14.22
      (5) 7.3
      (6) 7.3
      (7) 7.2, 7.3, 7.4,
      17.4
    s.96 . . . . . 7.1, 14.10, 17.3,
      17.4, 17.5, 17.9,
      17.14, 17.31, 17.50,
      17.66
      (1) 7.3
      (1) 17.3
      (2) 7.3, 17.3
    s.97 . . 5.1, 7.1, 7.3, 14.10,
      14.18, 17.63, 17.79
      (1) 7.3, 14.18
      (2) 5.10, 14.18
      (6) 7.3
      (7) 14.18
      (11) 7.2
    ss.97–98 . . . . 17.51, 17.67
    s.98 . . . . . . 7.1, 7.3, 17.63,
      17.79
    s.99 . . . . 7.6
      (4) 17.4, 17.5
    s.100 . . . . 14.8, 14.9
    s.101 . . 12.1, 12.21, 12.36,
      12.37, 17.29, 17.31
    s.102 . . 12.1, 12.21, 12.31,
      12.37, 17.31
    s.117 . . . . 17.15
    s.122 . . . . 14.8
    s.123 . . . . 17.62, 17.78
    s.124 . . . . 14.10
  Local Government in
    Scotland Act (asp
    1) 1.2, 4.12, 14.1,
      14.3, 14.29, 14.33
    s.1 . . . . 14.25
      (1) 14.25, 14.27,
      14.28

2003 Local Government in
          Scotland Act—
          cont.
          s.10 . . . . 14.20
          ss.10–12 . . . . 14.20
          s.11 . . 14.20, 14.21, 14.25

2003 Local Government in
          Scotland Act—
          cont.
          s.11A 14.20, 14.23
          s.12 . . 14.22, 14.24, 14.30,
                                              14.32
          s.14 . . . . 14.24

TABLE OF STATUTORY INSTRUMENTS

1972 Local Authorities
(Goods and
Services) (Public
Bodies) Order (SI
1972/853) 16.4,
App.3

1975 Local Authorities
(Goods and
Services) (Public
Bodies) Order (SI
1975/193) 6.4, 16.4,
App.3

1981 Local Authorities
(Goods and
Services) (Public
Bodies) Order (SI
1981/1049) 16.4,
App.3

1981 Transfer of
Undertakings
(Protection of
Employment)
Regulations (SI
1981/1794) 17.29,
17.31

1990 Local Authorities
(Goods and
Services) (Public
Bodies) Order (SI
1990/433)   16.4, App.3

1991 Houses in Multiple
Occupation
(Charges for
Registration
Schemes)
Regulations (SI
1991/982) . . 2.12, 13.11

1992 Local Government
(Miscellaneous
Provisions)
(Northern Ireland)
Order (SI
1992/810) 14.4

1992 Local Authorities
(Goods and
Services) (Public
Bodies) Order (SI
1992/2830) 16.4,
App.3

1993 Local Authorities
(Goods and
Services) (Public
Bodies) Order (SI
1993/2097) 16.4,
App.3

Public Services
Contracts
Regulations (SI
1993/3228)
reg.3 . . . . 8.4
reg.6(k) . . . 4.8, 4.10, 4.11

1994 Local Authorities
(Goods and
Services) (Public
Bodies) Order (SI
1994/37) . . 16.4, App.3

Local Authorities
(Goods and
Services) (Public
Bodies) (No.2)
Order (SI
1994/1389) 16.4,
App.3

1995 Local Authorities (Com-
         panies) Order (SI
         1995/849) 7.9, 8.1,
                 8.12, 8.13, 8.14,
                 8.22, 9.14, 17.14
      regs 12-18 . . . . 7.9
      Local Authorities
         (Goods and
         Services) (Public
         Bodies) (Meat
         Hygiene) Order
         (SI 1995/2626) . . . 16.4,
                              App.3
1996 Local Authorities
         (Goods and
         Services) (Public
         Bodies) (Trunk
         Roads) Order (SI
         1996/342) 4.5, 16.4,
                              App.3
      Local Authorities
         (Goods and
         Services) (Public
         Bodies) (Trunk
         Roads) (No.2)
         Order (SI
         1996/1814) 16.4,
                              App.3
      Local Authorities
         (Goods and
         Services) (Public
         Bodies) (The Julie
         Rose Stadium)
         Order (SI
         1996/2534) 16.4,
                              App.3
      Local Authorities
         (Goods and
         Services) (Public
         Bodies) (Sports
         Councils) Order
         (SI 1996/3092) . . . 16.4,
                              App.3
1997 Local Authorities
         (Goods and
         Services) (Public
         Bodies) Order (SI
         1997/101)   16.4, App.3

1997 Local Authorities
         (Goods and Ser-
         vices) (Public
         Bodies) (Trunk
         Roads) (No.1)
         Order (SI 1997/
         204) 16.4,App.3
      Local Authorities
         (Goods and Ser-
         vices) (Public
         Bodies) (Greater
         London Enterprise
         Limited) Order
         (SI 1997/809) 16.4,
                              App.3
      Local Authorities
         (Goods and Ser-
         vices) (Public
         Bodies) (Trunk
         Roads) (Amend-
         ment) Order (SI
         1997/849) 4.5, 16.4,
                              App.3
      Local Authorities
         (Goods and Ser-
         vices) (Public
         Bodies) (Trunk
         Roads) (No.2)
         Order (SI
         1997/850) 16.4,
                              App.3
      Local Government
         Pension Scheme
         Regulations (SI
         1997/1612) 12.30
      Local Authorities
         (Goods and Ser-
         vices) (Public
         Bodies) (English
         Heritage) Order
         (SI 1997/1835) . . . 16.4,
                              App.3
      Local Authorities
         (Goods and Ser-
         vices) (Public
         Bodies) Order (SI
         1997/2095) 16.4,
                              App.3

1997 Secretary of State for the Environment, Transport and the Regions Order (SI 1997/2971)

Art.6 . . . . App.3

1998 Local Authorities (Goods and Services) (Public Bodies) Order (SI 1998/308) 16.4, App.3

Local Authorities (Goods and Services) (Public Bodies) (No.2) Order (SI 1998/868) App.3

Local Authorities (Goods and Services) (Public Bodies) (No.3) Order (SI 1998/1123) 16.4, App.3

Local Authorities (Goods and Services) (Public Bodies) (No.4) Order (SI 1998/1574) 16.4, App.3

Local Authorities (Goods and Services) (Public Bodies) (No.5) Order (SI 1998/2956) 16.4, App.3

Local Authorities (Goods and Services) (Public Bodies) (No.6) Order (SI 1998/3095) 16.4, App.3

1999 Local Authorities (Goods and Services) (Public Bodies) (No.1) Order (SI 1999/421) 16.4, App.3

Local Authorities (Goods and Services) (Public Bodies) (No.2) Order (SI 1999/1754) 16.4, App.3

Unfair Terms in Consumer Contracts Regulations (SI 1999/2083) 11.8
reg.5 . . . . 11.8
reg.7 . . . . 11.8
Sch.2 . . . . 11.8

2000 Local Authorities (Goods and Services) (Public Bodies) Order (SI 2000/63) . . 16.4, App.3

Local Authorities (Goods and Services) (Public Bodies) (Scotland) Order (SSI 2000/207) 16.4, App.3

Local Authorities (Goods and Services) (Public Bodies) (No.2) (Scotland) Order (SSI 2000/403) . . . 16.4, App.3

2000 Local Authorities (Goods and Services) (Public Bodies) (No.2) Order (SI 2000/1027) 16.4, App.3

Consumer Protection (Distance Selling) Regulations (SI 2000/2334) 11.14

2001 Local Authorities
(Goods and Ser-
vices) (Public
Bodies) (England)
Order (SI
2001/243) 16.4,
App.3

Local Authorities
(Goods and Ser-
vices) (Public
Bodies) (England)
(No.2) Order (SI
2001/691) 16.4,
App.3

Local Authorities
(Goods and Ser-
vices) (Public
Bodies) (England)
(No.3) Order (SI
2001/1823) 16.4,
App.3

Local Authorities
(Goods and Ser-
vices) (Public
Bodies) (England)
(No.4) Order (SI
2001/3347) 16.4,
App.3

2002 Local Authorities
(Goods and Ser-
vices) (Public
Bodies) (England)
Order (SI
2002/522) 16.4,
App.3

Local Authorities
(Goods and Ser-
vices) (Public
Bodies) (Wales)
Order (SI
2002/1729) 16.4,
App.3

Fixed-term Employees
(Prevention of
Less Favourable
Treatment) Regu-
lations (SI
2002/2034) 12.19

2002 Local Authorities
(Goods and Ser-
vices) (Public
Bodies) (England)
(No.2) Order (SI
2002/2244) 16.4,
App.3

Local Authorities
(Goods and Ser-
vices) (Public
Bodies) (England)
(No.3) Order (SI
2002/2624) 16.4,
App.3

Local Government
(Miscellaneous
Provisions)
(Northern Ireland)
Order (SI
2002/3149) 14.3

2003 Local Authorities
(Goods and Ser-
vices) (Public
Bodies) (England)
Order (SI
2003/354) 16.4,
App.3

Local Authorities
(Goods and Ser-
vices) (Public
Bodies) (England)
(No.2) Order (SI
2003/1018) 16.4,
App.3

Local Authorities
(Goods and Ser-
vices) (Public
Bodies) (England)
(No.3) Order (SI
2003/2069) 16.4,
App.3

Local Authorities
(Goods and Ser-
vices) (Public
Bodies) (England)
(No.4) Order (SI
2003/2558) 16.4,
App.3

2004 Local Authorities
(Goods and
Services) (Public
Bodies) (England)
Order (SI 2004/
485) 16.4, App.3
Local Authorities
(Capital Finance)
(Consequential
Transitional and
Savings
Provisions) Order
(SI 2004/533) 7.9,
8.12, 17.14
Local Authorities
(Categorisation)
(England) Order
(SI 2004/1704) 7.6,
17.3
Local Government
(Best Value Auth-
orities) (Power to
Trade) (England)
Order (SI
2004/1705) ... 2.17, 7.2,
7.4, 8.1, 16.3, 17.3,
17.5
reg.1 .... 7.4
(3) 7.4
reg.2 .... 7.4
(2) 7.4, 8.3
(3) 7.4, 8.28
(4) 7.4
reg.3 .... 7.4, 8.32
reg.4 .... 8.15
reg.5 .... 8.16
reg.6 .... 8.18
reg.7 .... 8.19
reg.9 .... 8.18

2004 Local Government
(Best Value Auth-
orities) (Power to
Trade) (England)
(Amendment
No.1) Order (SI
2004/2307) 16.3
Local Authorities
(Goods and
Services) (Public
Bodies) (England)
(No.2) Order (SI
2004/2475) 16.4,
App.3
Local Government
(Best Value Auth-
orities) (Power to
Trade) (England)
(Amendment
No.2) Order (SI
2004/2573) 16.3
Local Authorities
(Goods and
Services) (Public
Bodies) (Wales)
Order (SI
2004/2878) 14.11,
16.4, App.3
Local Authorities
(Indemnities for
Members and
Officers) Order
(SI 2004/3082) .. 12.36

Part One

Introduction and Context

CHAPTER 1

INTRODUCTION AND CONTEXT

The author's preface explains the reasons for writing this book. In **1.1** particular, there has been a change in approach by central government with greater "freedoms and flexibilities" offered to local authorities by the Local Government Act 2003. That Act provided for new powers to charge for discretionary services (which came into effect in November 2003) and new powers of commercial trading (which came into effect in July 2004).

At the end of 2004, when this book was completed, the use of these powers presented a mixed picture across the country as a whole. The attitude of authorities ranged from those who were actively looking at setting up commercial trading companies, through to those who were taking a more cautious approach by experimenting with the charging power, to those who had no plans to use any of the new powers. The powers do need careful consideration, in the light of the need to meet the Gershon efficiency savings. In simple terms, commercial trading may deliver profit for cashable savings whilst charging for discretionary services may deliver enhanced civic benefit or value, for non-cashable efficiency gains. Obviously a local authority's performance in delivering the Gershon efficiencies will now feed back into its overall CPA classification. Against this background, it is likely that considerable attention will be paid to these powers.

Part 1 of this book, contains three Chapters. This introduction is the first and is followed by Ch.2 on the legal basis for charging and trading and then Ch.3 on strategic planning.

Chapter 2 explains the fundamental principle of local government administrative law: the so called *ultra vires* doctrine. Local authorities are statutory corporations and are only able to act in the manner which Parliament permits them to act; otherwise they are acting unlawfully and in an *ultra vires* manner (roughly translated as: outside of their powers). The powers of any council to undertake any action are contained in a patchwork quilt of statutes and statutory instruments (a form of delegated legislation). Trading activity is like any other activity and may only be undertaken by finding the necessary power contained in a statutory provision. This work is intended to provide a comprehensive overview of the subject matter and that requires some knowledge of the *ultra vires* doctrine. Those who are lawyers and understand the doctrine will probably only use Ch.2 as a reminder; those who wish to consider the relevant powers which permit trading, without understanding the doctrine itself, will find those powers within Pt 3.

Chapter 3, reminds authorities of the need to act strategically in all that they do, and trading is again no different to other activities. The Comprehensive Performance Assessment, has emphasised the need for strategic planning and a strategic approach to all major decision making. Questions such as: "is trading the right approach for us?"; "what type of trading activity should we embark upon?" and "how should we implement a trading strategy?" will all be easier to answer by those who have taken the trouble to read Ch.3.

Part 2 contains the main part of this work, which is a detailed consideration of the charging and trading powers introduced in the Local Government Act 2003, as well as the existing trading powers which remain and have not been repealed. This contains six Chapters all relating to charging and trading powers. This analyses in detail the three limbs that make up the new law. The first of these is the existing powers, principally the Local Authorities (Goods and Services) Act 1970 (but supported by other important powers examined in Ch.4); the second part is the new powers to charge for discretionary services under s.93 of the Local Government Act 2003 considered in Ch.5; and the final part provided by Ch.7, which looks at s.95 of the Local Government Act 2003, authorising local authorities in certain circumstances to engage in commercial trading operations. Ch.8 considers the establishment of companies for commercial trading as this is a legal requirement of the new power. Also featured in Part Two are Chs 6 and 9 giving practical examples of both charging and trading activity respectively.

1.2 The power in s.93 of the Local Government Act 2003 is a completely new specific power to levy a charge for the provision of discretionary services. This means that all of those activities that were previously authorised by wellbeing powers (but where there was some doubt as to where the charges could be levied) are now able to be provided and their costs born by the user. User charging was placed in centre stage on the political agenda with congestion charging in London and more and more authorities are now realising that the only way to meet increased demand for public services, in a climate of reluctance to pay increased council tax, is through a form of user charging for certain services. Discretionary services may deliver enhanced civic benefit and wider value to the local authority and are much more flexible than at first thought. Local authorities appear to have been put off by the suggestion that cost recovery is rather mundane and unexciting and provides little flexibility. On the contrary, the effect of these powers will be profound over the next five years and could transform local authorities that seek to use them extensively.

The new commercial trading powers in s.95 of the Local Government Act 2003 allows local authorities for the first time to trade commercially to make profits; but requires those services to be provided by a company. For the sake of clarity, it should be said that the way that local authorities have acted over the past decade (acting *commercially*) is really talking about *efficiency*. It means performing services properly, being well organised, having good financial management and leadership. However, it is the delivery of public services for the general public good that we are talking about here. In the parlance of s.95, the term *commercial* has a different meaning. It means operating with the primary motive of generating a profit; rather than for civic purposes. In simple terms it means acting like the private sector, rather than the public sector. Whilst this sounds fairly reasonable, local authorities may not have appreciated that by setting up trading companies, they need to act in an inherently private sector way and temper the public sector ethos to which they are normally so committed. Many legal issues are raised by trading companies, though they will perform an important role depending on the circumstances.

Part 3 considers practical implementation issues. It commences with Ch.10 which looks at a variety of those issues and making the case for charging and trading. Local authorities have, of course, become much more experienced on the commercial front in the last ten to fifteen years and this experience will now be instrumental in ensuring that charging and trading activity is undertaken properly. In particular, some of the planning documentation required to support the activity (such as business cases, risk analyses, market impact analyses and so on) is examined and practical guidance given on preparation of such documentation.

Chapter 11, considers some of the commercial issues faced by local authorities when undertaking charging and trading activity. This Chapter explains the need for proper contract documentation and outlines some of the new legal issues which will have to be faced by those operating in this new legal environment. Whilst only a brief overview, it does give local authorities an idea of the sort of commercial issues that will arise. Chapter 12 considers some of the employment and related issues which will need to be faced. These range from potential changes to the contract of employment, the potential impact on pensions and such matters as indemnities for both officers and members.

Part 4, contains a single chapter: Ch.13. This provides a background Chapter of the history of trading and charging. Those who have come only recently into this area of work may wish to review the twists and turns which this subject has taken over the past few decades and are outlined in this Chapter.

Part 5 considers charging and trading elsewhere in the United Kingdom as the basic text focuses on England, where central government is based in

Whitehall and the Local Government Act 2003 operates. In Wales, the Local Government Act 2003 does have force, though the Welsh Assembly Government also has a role to play. Northern Ireland is not only without the Local Government Act 2003 but also other key powers such as wellbeing, and so charging and trading relies extensively on existing powers there. Scotland is also different, with its own legislation (the Local Government in Scotland Act 2003) which permits charging and trading activity, though using an entirely different route to England. All of these areas are considered in Ch.14.

1.3   Part 6 is the conclusion where the authors look forward in Ch.15 to how these new powers in England will develop and how they will link to the government's ten year vision mentioned above. Comparisons with other jurisdictions (principally Scotland) are also likely to see how the different powers to permit charging and trading have developed.

This book is written for local government officers and members alike. It is intended to be a readable and practical guide to existing powers and duties, and to the new provisions in the Local Government Act 2003. Inevitably, some elements of the work are legalistic by nature but the authors have a reputation for producing material in an easily understandable format, particularly relating to the explanation of legal subjects for non-lawyers. It should always be borne in mind, however, that general advice on this area can never be a complete guide and the application of powers will usually relate heavily to local circumstances and, almost always, require specific detailed legal advice. This is particularly so in relation to the use of the new s.95 powers to establish trading companies.

If the book does no more than create a platform upon which officers and members question the ability of their local authority to enter into innovative new schemes and to derive greater public benefit from them, it will have succeeded. It goes without saying that the views expressed in this book are those of the authors personally and it is also predictable that, in the words of the age old phrase "other views are available!" However, the views of the authors have withstood the test of time and did not waver during the dark years of the late 1980s and early 1990s, when considerable doubt was cast by many on whether the powers could be used innovatively to authorise a variety of activities. The fact that particular storm was weathered augers well for the next phase in the development of charging and trading and the authors look forward to commenting on this over the next decade.

CHAPTER 2

THE LEGAL BASIS FOR CHARGING AND TRADING

INTRODUCTION

This Chapter provides background information on the legal framework **2.1** which underpins all local government activity; including that of charging and trading. Chapter 13, which describes the history of the subject, describes the legal framework as a "patchwork quilt" of different statutory provisions built up over the years. Whilst the political and social context has changed, the framework of administrative law has remained remarkably constant. There are literally hundreds of different Acts of Parliament, each of which provides a power or duty on local authorities and regulates the work undertaken by that authority. At the heart of the judicial controls over local authorities is the *ultra vires* doctrine. That doctrine means that local authorities, which are statutory corporations, must have the power to undertake an activity and must undertake that activity "reasonably", if they do not—they will have acted outside of their powers (hence *ultra vires*).

The impact of an *ultra vires* decision by a court is that the transaction is deemed never to have happened (see, for example, *Rhyl UDC v Rhyl Amusements Ltd* [1959] 1 WLR 465; where a lease was declared void following an *ultra vires* action of the council). In general, the parties are restored to the position they were in before the transaction ever happened. In a trading context this would mean that the authority concerned would have to repay the money it had earned from that *ultra vires* activity. This impact was summarised in advice given in a Technical Release issued in 1991 by the Audit Commission, following the House of Lords' decision in the case of *Hazell v Hammersmith and Fulham LBC* [1992] 2 AC 1. That advice states at para.2:

"The effect of the decision of the House of Lords is that interest rate swaps and similar contracts entered into by local authorities are *ultra vires* and void. Obligations purportedly created are unenforceable. There is no default in non-performance. Default and cross default clauses are ineffective. Damages for breach of contract cannot be recovered. No further payments may be made or received by local authorities."

The situation about the recovery of sums already made is complex, although on general principles the courts should unpick the transaction and restore the parties to their original positions. This Chapter only provides selective coverage of this interesting legal area and the *ultra vires* doctrine is covered in detail in legal textbooks on administrative law, for example: *Local Government Constitutional and Administrative Law—Arden, Manning and Collins* (Sweet and Maxwell—1999).

In outline, there is a "system" which applies to the use and abuse of statutory powers and it is this system that will come into play in relation to any charging and trading activity. This Chapter explains that "system" so that readers can understand the foundations upon which the three types of charging and trading powers are built. Existing powers are considered in Ch.4; the new power to charge for discretionary services is considered in Ch.5; and the new power of commercial trading is considered in Ch.7. Additional relevant material on older cases will be found in Ch.13.

This Chapter commences with an examination of the two "limbs" of the *ultra vires* doctrine; firstly an examination of whether there is a power or duty permitting the activity (has the authority the *capacity*?) and secondly, whether it has exercised that power or duty "reasonably", which is known as *exercise*. Within the first area of *capacity*, there is an examination of the difference between powers and duties, and an outline of the different groupings of powers (general, specific, express and implied) which may be encountered.

THE *ULTRA VIRES* DOCTRINE—CAPACITY

Introduction to Capacity

2.2   In terms of the first hurdle, this requires an interpretation of the wording and scope of relevant statutory provision under consideration. This examination is necessary to determine whether the type of trading or charging activity which is being contemplated is permitted by that particular Act of Parliament or whether recourse is necessary to a different statutory power. This process has become considerably simpler with the new provisions in the Local Government Act 2003. As Parker L.J. said in the Court of Appeal when considering whether North Tyneside MBC had power to make enhanced severance payments:

"I should add that in the course of some very complex and refined arguments on both sides we were referred to a number of authorities. I have referred to none of them because in my judgment the question for determination is simply one of construction of the relevant statutory provisions in accordance with well established principles." (Transcript of the case of *Allsop v North Tyneside Borough Council* (1992) at pp.19 and 20).

If there is true ambiguity on the face of a statute, the case of *Pepper v Hart* [1993] 1 All ER 42 has indicated that the debate in Parliament, as recorded in Hansard, may be used in interpretation; although this must be done cautiously.

Those contemplating charging or trading will find the most relevant powers explained in Pt 2 of this work.

The Distinction between Powers and Duties

The logical place to begin in any consideration of the generalities of powers and duties is the distinction between the two terms. A power usually contains permissive language, for example, "a local authority *may* provide . . . recreational facilities." By contrast, a duty normally involves mandatory language, for example, "it *shall* be the duty of each waste collection authority . . . to arrange for the collection of household waste in its area". The examples given, which come from the Local Government (Miscellaneous Provisions) Act 1976, s.19, and the Environmental Protection Act 1990, s.46, respectively, are clear in their scope; there may, however, be cases where a power given by way of permissive language is in fact coupled with a duty to exercise it in certain circumstances. Accordingly, it is necessary to carefully consider the Act of Parliament which confers the powers. **2.3**

Generally speaking the primary functions of a local authority will be duties, for example, those governing the areas of eduction, social services, highways, libraries and the like. The funding for these duties comes from local and national taxation rather than any payment at the point of use. In practice the scope for trading activity in these areas is normally in offering an "enhanced" service which builds onto the duties undertaken; for example the cleaning of refuse bins. That enhanced service will have to be offered under a power, for example, the wellbeing power under s.2 of the Local Government Act 2000, which is considered *below* and also in context in Ch.4. Other areas of activity are undertaken by local authorities as a discretionary activity, for example, the provision of leisure. These discretionary areas are sometimes part funded by service users (for example the users of the leisure facility); and now any discretionary service can, potentially, be charged for by using the charging power within s.93 of the Local Government Act 2003, as desribed in Ch.5.

Express Prohibitions

2.4   There are few express prohibitions; because the whole nature of the legal framework of administrative law is based on the need to find the power to act. Nevertheless, as an example, the Local Government Act 1986, s.2, introduced a prohibition on political publicity. The section provides that a local authority, "shall not publish any material which . . . appears to be designed to affect public support for a political party".

This is only likely to impact indirectly on trading activity; for example of the authority sought to promote its actions as being permitted by "legis-laton introduced by the Labour party" or it it sought to say that its activities were motivated by "Envronmental concerns supported by the Conservative Party." In those circumstances, whilst the existence of the statutory power may exist, the manner in which the local authority has exercised the power would offended this express prohibition.

Different Types of Powers

2.5   Whilst duties are relatively straightforward; powers are more complex. There are four broad types of power:

- General powers; these are powers of "first resort," offering a wide source of legal authority;

- Specific powers; relating to a particular area of activity;

- Incidental powers; where the activity is supportive of another activity; and

- Implied powers; where the requisite authority is derived from a necessary implication of the language used in the specific power.

In simple terms, the solidity of the legal foundation offered by each of these powers gets progressively weaker as the list is moved down. In other words, general powers are particularly wide and therefore effective in providing legal capacity to undertake an activity while the use of implied and incidental powers offer much more scope for debate and disagreement and their legal foundation is markedly less secure. All of these different types of powers are considered further below.

General Powers

2.6   A general power is a wide source of legal authority that can be used by local authorities as a power of "first resort". As Ch.13 explains, the key wellbeing power was introduced in 2000, to permit local authorities to deliver their new role of community leadership and to undertake innovative schemes which may have been challenged before on the absence of suitable powers.

The power in Pt 1 of the Local Government Act 2000 is sometimes known as the power of "community initiative." More specifically, the power in s.2 of that Act authorise local authorities to do anything which is likely to promote or improve the economic, social or environmental wellbeing of their area. The power was framed to link into the modernisation agenda, for example Best Value, the community leadership role and to other key areas of government policy such as sustainable development. Each local authority has to develop a community strategy under s.4 of the Local Government Act 2000 and the operation of the wellbeing powers is linked to each community strategy.

The government issued guidance in relation to the powers of community initiative, to which local authorities must have regard. The guidance *Power To Promote Or Improve Economic, Social Or Environmental Wellbeing* (March 2001 DETR), specifically confirmed that local authorities needed new powers to achieve their various goals. Paragraph 5 comments:

"For many years, innovative actions by local authorities have been stifled by concerns over the scope of their powers. Whilst some legislation contains deliberate and specific constraints over local authority activities, there has been considerable uncertainty over the extent of the enabling powers that have been conferred on councils. The result has been a necessarily cautious approach to innovation and joint action, and a concomitant limitation of council's contribution to the improvement of their communities' quality of life. . . . The government's purpose in introducing the wellbeing power is to reverse that traditionally cautious approach, and to encourage innovation and closer joint working betwen local authorities and their partners to improve communities' quality of life."

Accordingly, the power granted by the Local Government Act 2000 was described by the government as "a power of first resort." This means that rather than searching for a specific power elsewhere in statute in order to take a particular action, councils can instead look to the wellbeing power in the first instance and provided it passes a number of tests (such as whether it does constitute promotion of wellbeing and is not prohibited elsewhere), the power will be available.

There is an important limitation within s.3 of the Local Government Act 2000. Subsection (1) of this section states that: "the power under s.2(1) does not enable a local authority to do anything which they are unable to do by virtue of any prohibition, restriction or limitation on their powers, which is contained in any enactment. . ." This is supplemented by subs. (2) which confirms, "the power under s.2(1) does not enable a local authority to raise money (whether by precepts, borrowing or otherwise)."

This means that s.2(1) of the Local Government Act 2000, of itself, does not permit authorities to raise money; but this does not prevent the power being used as the basis for undertaking the activity and then using another power (principally s.93 of the Local Government Act 2003) to charge for that activity. If there were any doubt in the matter, that doubt has been removed by the provision within s.93(7) of the 2003 Act as discussed in Ch.5.

The combination of the wide discretionary power in s.2 LGA 2000 and the charging power in s.93 LGA 2003 is likely to meet the needs of many authorites to achieve efficiency targets and derive income by charing users for the services they need. Examples of this combination of powers is given in Ch.6.

Specific Powers

2.7   An example of a specific power is that for local authorities to provide recreational facilities. Section 19 of the Local Government (Miscellaneous Provisions) Act 1976 states: "A local authority may provide, inside or outside its area, such recreational facilities as it thinks fit. . . ."

The power in s.19 is widely drawn, with local authorities free to provide any of the recreational facilities specifically included within the six subss. but the power is even wider than that because those subss. are not exhaustive. The phrase, "without prejudice to the generality of the powers conferred . . ." makes it clear that if a local authority can identify a recreational facility which is not specifically covered, then it may still provide that facility using this power. The fact that Parliament intended this power to be entirely self-contained is illustrated by the final sentence of subs. (1) whereby the general power to provide facilities includes powers to "provide buildings, equipment, supplies and assistance of any kind". In these circumstances, it is difficult to imagine a situation legitimately falling within the provision of recreational facilities which cannot be achieved by use of this power.

Incidental Powers

2.8   It has long been accepted by the courts that when considering the drafting of a statutory power, activity incidental to that power may also be permissible. In the words of one old case:

> "the limitations on their activities "ought to be reasonably, and not unreasonably, undertood and applied, and that whatever may fairly be regarded as incidental to, or consequential upon, those things which the legislature has authoriesd ought not (unless expressly prohibited) to be held, by judicial construction, to be *ultra vires*." Lord Selborne in *Attorney-General v Great Eastern Railway* (1880) 5 HL 473.

This doctrine of incidental or consequential powers was given statutory effect by s.111 of the Local Government Act 1972; although the argument remains that there is still a common law doctrine of similar effect.

Section 111, is discussed in Chapter 4 and provides:

"Without prejudice to any powers exercisable apart from this section but subject to the provisions of this Act and any other enactment passed before or after this Act, a local authority shall have power to do any thing (whether or not involving expenditure, borrowing or lending of money or the acquisition or disposal of any property or rights) which is calculated to facilitate or is conducive or incidental to, the discharge of any of their functions."

The key words are "incidental" and "functions." The former word was considered in a case outside of the trading arena. *DHSS v Envoy Farmers Ltd* [1976] 2 All ER 173 considered the meaning of the word "incidental." It adopted the Oxford English Dictionary definition, namely that something is incidental if it "occurs in subordinate conjunction with something else." This confirms that incidental powers may not stand alone. It must always be added to another power or duty. Hence the argument that the power to set up a company to trade under s.95 of the Local Government Act 2003 relies both on s.95 itself and an incidental power.

The word "functions" has been given a wide meaning to include all of a local authority's normal activities. This relies upon the *dicta* of the Divisional Court, (later approved by higher courts) in the case of *Hazell v Hammersmith and Fulham LBC* [1992] 2 AC 1 (see below).

Local Authority Functions

Hazell v Hammersmith and Fulham LBC [1992] 2 AC 1, was the famous **2.9** case on local authority interest rate swaps and as part of the judgement had to determine the scope of implied powers to trade in those swaps. Consideration had to be given to the word *functions*. Wolf L.J. in the Divisional Court determined:

"what is a function for the purposes of the subsection is not expressly defined but in our view there can be little doubt that in this context "functions", refers to the multiplicity of specific statutory activities the Council is expressly or impliedly under a duty to perform or has power to perform under the other provisions of the Act of 1972 or other relevant legislation . . .".

This wide definition was approved by the Court of Appeal. It was held that:

"We agree with the Divisional Court that in this subsection the word "functions", which is accompanied by no statutory definition, is used in a broad sense, and is apt to embrace all the duties and powers of a local authority: the sum total of the activities Parliament has entrusted to it. Those activities are its functions."

This approach was subsequently approved by the House of Lords.

Implied Powers

2.10   In most situations it is not advisable to rely on implied powers to undertake any innovative activity of a trading or charging nature as this is likely to lead to challenge. With the ability to use the wide general power of wellbeing linked to the charging power in s.93 of the Local Government Act 2003 (see Ch.6); the use of implied powers is likely to be regarded as somewhat academic and it is only addressed for the sake of completeness.

The concept of an incidental power is difficult to explain. It is inherent in the nature of drafting that sometimes, those interpreting that drafting will be able to say that an activity not expressly covered was nevertheless implied by the wording. An example is the power to set up a company to engage in commercial trading under s.95 of the Local Government Act 2003. The section states that the power, "shall only be exercisable through a company." However, there is no express power for a local authority to establish a company. As Ch.7 explains, most authorities will use their "incidental power" within s.111 of the Local Government Act 1972 (see below) but other lawyers have argued that it must be implicit within s.95 that there is power to form a company; and the power therefore derives from the obligation in s.95.

A similar issue arises with matters such as vehicle purchase and vehicle maintenance. Whilst the duty to collect refuse is contained within a statute (see Environmental Protection Act 1990, s.46 above); there is no express power to buy refuse freighters. Therefore the purchase of vehicles must either be implied or the incidental power of s.111 of the Local Government Act 1972 must be used. If the incidental power is used under s.111; what power is there then to maintain those vehicles? As the case law shows, the courts have been reluctant to allow the incidental power within s.111 to be used twice in relation to the same activity (the so called "incidental to the incidental" argument which is considered above).

Does More Than One Power Cover the Activity?

2.11   Sometimes powers and duties may overlap and a particular purpose may be achieved by more than one route. Also one power or duty may conflict with another under some circumstances. Examples of direct conflict are difficult to find as Parliament normally considers the effect of new legislation on existing powers and duties prior to its enactment. This will often lead to saving provisions being included in legislation to prevent conflict arising. Where conflicting powers arise in relation to land, the Court of Appeal has indicated that the object for which the land is held must be ascertained. In the case of *Blake v Hendon Corporation* [1961] 1 QB 283, this rule was confirmed. In this case the land was held under a power for public walks and pleasure grounds, pursuant to the Public Health Act 1875. The court held that exercise of any other power, such as that to grant leases under the Local Government Act 1933, could only be sanctioned if the exercise of that power was consistent with the full use of the land by the public as public walks and pleasure grounds. Accordingly, the dominant power prevailed over inconsistent alternative powers.

Whilst it is difficult to generalise in this area, it is not normally the case that one power will restrict the use of another in any absolute way, unless this is specifically provided. The point is illustrated by use of the Local Authorities (Land) Act 1963 for the purposes of construction works for other local authorities or public bodies. A specific restriction appears in the Local Authorities (Goods and Services) Act 1970 under s.1(2) regarding new building works. This prevents the use of the 1970 Act as the source of legal power to construct buildings for another public body. However, the 1970 Act is enabling in nature and, therefore, if an alternative power can be identified, the 1970 Act will have no relevance to the use of that alternative power. Section 2 of the 1963 Act provides that, "a local authority may, for the benefit or improvement of their area, erect any building and construct or carry out works on land . . ." Manchester City Council relied upon this power to construct flats for a local housing association in the early 1990's. The District Auditor claimed that the 1970 Act prevented such use; this was clearly a fundamental misunderstanding of the legal nature of the powers concerned.

One rare exception to this rule is s.137 of the Local Government Act 1972. This power may not be used to overcome deficiencies in any other power by virtue of the wording of s.137(1). Thankfully, such generally restricting powers are not prevalent within local government law and the s.137 provision will be seen to be an unusual provision itself.

Charging Powers

Express Powers to Charge

The Local Government and Housing Act 1989, s.150, introduced a **2.12** regulation making power for the Secretary of State to permit charges to be levied by local authorities for a number of purposes.

The power is widely drawn and covers activities where there is no current power or duty to impose a charge. As with many other modern legislative provisions, the law may be changed by regulation, although a positive resolution by each House of Parliament is required. Regulations may impose minimum or maximum charges; specify types of activities which may be covered and a multiplicity of other matters. The power has, to date, only been used infrequently, for example to produce the Houses in Multiple Occupation (Charges for Registration Schemes) Regulations 1991 (SI 1991/982). These enable local housing authorities to levy charges for dealing with notifications in respect of houses in multiple occupation and applications for registration as part of an overall scheme of management.

Chapter 5 discusses in considerable detail the power in s.93 of the Local Government Act 2003 to charge for discretionary services. With the advent of this new charging power it seems unlikely that the regulation making power within s.150 of the Local Government and Housing Act 1989 will be used to the same extent in the future.

The Use of the Incidental Power in s.111 of the Local Government Act 1972 to Charge?

2.13   In the light of a widely drafted power to charge for discretionary services, any discussion of an alternative power may be thought to be only of academic interest. The authors summarise this discussion because during the early days of the 2003 Act some lawyers have given a restrictive view of its scope (See Ch.5). While that view is not shared by the authors, it may become necessary at some time in the future to revitalise the old arguments relating to the use of s.111 of the Local Government Act 1972 as a charging power.

This debate came to the fore in the case of *R. v Richmond-upon-Thames LBC ex parte McCarthy and Stone (Developments)* [1992] AC 48. The case considered the duty to consider planning applications and the choice of the authority to offer "pre-planning inquiries" for a fee. The House of Lords held that whilst the pre-planning inquiries were incidental to the planning function (and therefore permitted by s.111 of the 1972 Act); charging for those services was "incidental to the incidental" and therefore required use of another power.

The case went all the way to the House of Lords. It is worthy of note, however, that the treatment accorded to the case in the Court of Appeal and the House of Lords differed widely and summarises the respective positions of the wide and narrow interpretations of statutory and Common Law powers to charge. The local authority succeeded in the Divisional Court and the Court of Appeal, but the developer's appeal was upheld before the House of Lords.

The determination of the case by the Court of Appeal is worthy of comment. Slade L.J. delivered the principal judgment. He differentiated the position in respect of a *duty*, a *power* and an *incidental power*. He said that where there is a duty on a local authority to provide a service, then there is a correlative right on the part of members of the public to receive the service. In these circumstances, where no power to charge was expressly conferred, it is not possible to levy a charge. To do so, would of course be asking members of the public to pay for a right, which cannot be achieved by using s.111 of the 1972 Act. However, where there was a power rather than a duty, the door was left open as to whether a charge could be levied. In some cases, express power had been conferred for the sake of clarity; in other cases it might be implicit from the statutory formulation of the power that a charge could not be levied. In these circumstances, it would depend on the facts of each case. The Court of Appeal stated:

"in our judgment, it is clearly open to the council to regard the making of such an arrangement of this kind as falling within the subsidiary powers conferred by s 111(1) of the Act of 1972, provided only that such an arrangement is not objectionable on *Wednesbuy* grounds."

The House of Lords was clearly influenced by the fact that local **2.14** authorities are given taxation powers and that only the clearest wording of a statute may permit taxation to be levied. Support for this contention was to be gained from the case of *Attorney General v Wilts United Dairies Ltd* (1921) (*The Times*, July 22), where an attempt by governmental authorities to impose charges was held to be *ultra vires*. The taxation argument was also considered in *Congreve v Home Office* [1976] 1 All ER 697. In the former the government charged a fee as the condition of issuing a licence to purchase milk, and the latter a charge was made as the price for refraining from revoking a valid and subsisting TV licence. In both cases the charges were held to be *ultra vires*; but the cases did not relate to trading but rather requiring payments for "the exercise of a privilege," that is a form of taxation.

The House of Lords concluded ultimately that the view of s.111 forwarded by Richmond-upon-Thames LBC would, "allow it to charge for the performance of every function, both obligatory and discretionary which provided a service". For this reason it was held that it was not justified and a restrictive view would be taken. However, Lord Lowry went on to state:

"I would not be prepared to say . . . that in the absence of express statutory power, there can never be a case in which the power to charge arises by necessary implication, but I have heard no convincing argument to show how the present facts could support such an implication."

Lord Lowry also considered the restrictions on raising money within s.111(3) of the 1972 Act which prevents the section to raise money: "whether by means of rates, precepts or borrowing." He made a fairly ambiguous statement on the statutory interpretation of the words of the 1972 Act. This was: "The developers argument (that charging was pro-hibited by s.111(3)) would require the addition of the words "or otherwise" after borrowing to get off the ground, and even then, in the context of "rates, precepts or borrowing," indicated in the House of Lords that, "to equate charging for a service with the raising of money appears to me to demand a very forced interpretation of language. I therefore agree with the conclusion of the Court of Appeal that s.111(3) imposes no restrictions on the council's powers. . . .".

This suggests that there may be circumstances where using the powers of s.111 of the Local Government Act 1972 to charge will be lawful; thus leaving the door ajar, rather than firmly closed in the face of local authorities.

Do the Statutory Powers to Charge Provide a Code?

2.15   The case of *Allsop v North Tyneside Borough Council* (1992) 90 LGR 462 related to the exercise of powers by a local authority in the context of making enhanced severance payments to staff over and above those permitted in the Superannuation Act 1972. The authority sought to rely on s.111 of the Local Government Act 1972, allied to its function of staff recruitment and good labour relations, but was prevented. The court held, in that case, that the powers of the authority were purely within that detailed "Code"; and therefore the s.111 could not be used because of the wording within that statutory provision (see above) which states that the s.111 power is "subject to the provisions of this Act and any other enactment passed before or after this Act." In effect the detailed provisions governing superannuation amounted to a prohibition to use other powers to get round that restriction.

This gives rise to the argument as to whether the power in s.93 of the Local Government Act 2003 provides a "statutory code", thereby preventing the incidental powers within s.111 of the Local Government Act 1972 also being used as a charging power. Whilst this argument may be superficially attractive, it is not persuasive when consideration is given to the manner in which the new powers were introduced. The Government made it clear in the document *General Power for Best Value Authorities to Charge for Discretionary Services—Guidance on the Power in the Local Government Act 2003* (ODPM November 2003) at para.4 that the guidance: " does not apply to charges levied under other legislation through which an authority has a power to charge. Where an authority has the benefit of a separate power to charge for a discretionary service (either now or in the future) that power will remain in force and the new general power to charge for discretionary services as s.93 will not be available. . ."

Incidental Powers—The "Incidental to the Incidental" Argument

2.16   *R. v Richmond-upon-Thames LBC ex parte McCarthy and Stone (Developments)* [1992] AC 48 was really decided on the argument that, whilst the holding of pre-planning enquiries was properly calculated to facilitate, conducive or incidental to the function of determining planning applications; this had exhausted the use of s.111 of the 1972 Act. Therefore no further use could be made of that incidental power for example to levy a charge. The House of Lords held that the making of the charge was incidental to an activity which was *itself* incidental to the function. Authority for this point was cited as the case of *Attorney General v Manchester Corporation* [1906] 1 Ch. 643; although that case was decided on another point and may be distinguished. In the *Manchester* case the court was dealing with the issue of running *another* service off the back of a service which was itself incidental. This is fundamentally different in nature from charging for the provision of the service *itself*. The authors consider that the better view is that levying a charge *also* facilitates the performance of the function of determining planning applications as by making such a charge, the authority is smoothing the way by resolving difficulties before any formal application is forthcoming. This argument suggests that different incidental matters may be viewed as satellites of the function as opposed to the linear concept adopted by the House of Lords. These issues are illustrated in diagrammatic form in Figure 2.1.

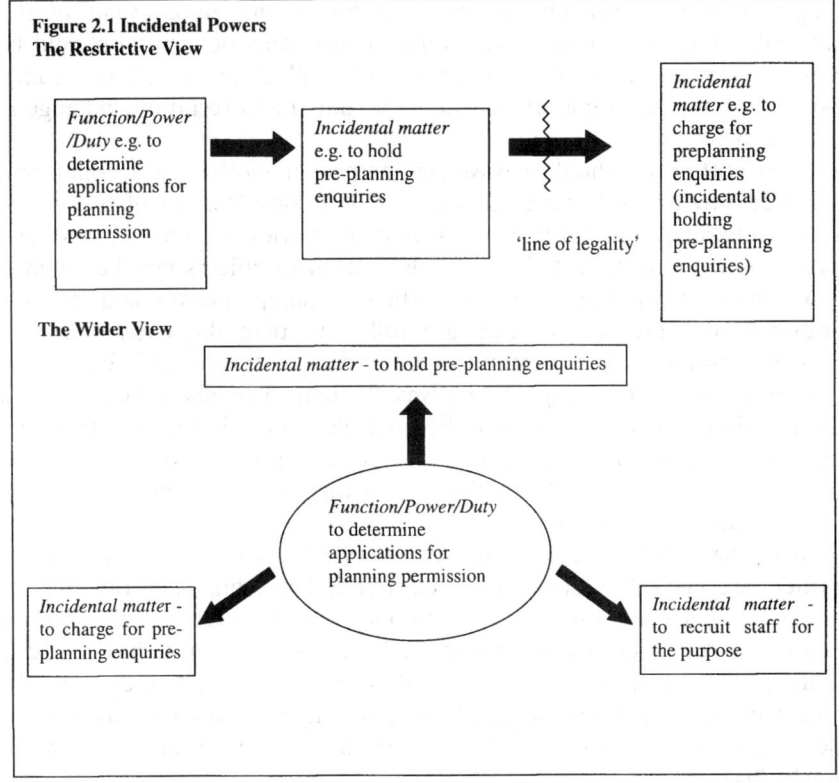

Figure 2.1 Incidental Powers
The Restrictive View

Function/Power /Duty e.g. to determine applications for planning permission

Incidental matter e.g. to hold pre-planning enquiries

'line of legality'

Incidental matter e.g. to charge for preplanning enquiries (incidental to holding pre-planning enquiries)

The Wider View

Incidental matter - to hold pre-planning enquiries

Function/Power/Duty to determine applications for planning permission

Incidental matter - to charge for pre-planning enquiries

Incidental matter - to recruit staff for the purpose

THE *ULTRA VIRES* DOCTRINE—EXERCISE OF POWERS

Introduction to "Exercise"

2.17   This Chapter explains that there are two "limbs" of the *ultra vires* doctrine; firstly an examination of whether there is a power or duty permitting the activity (known as *capacity*) and secondly, whether it has exercised that power or duty "reasonably", which is known as *exercise*.

The principles governing the proper exercise of powers have been widely commented upon elsewhere. The authors do not consider it appropriate to embark on any lengthy review of the relevant principles in this work. Instead, an attempt will be made to outline the core of the legal rules and illustrate by way of examples some of the practices which are highly likely to render the exercise of powers improper, followed by factors to be borne in mind when striving to stay within the balance of lawfulness.

Proper exercise of powers is largely a matter of common sense. Local authorities should always act within their own standing orders and terms of reference which they have previously determined. Advice should always be sought from appropriately qualified officers in the employment of the authority and, where necessary, external consultants or counsel should be used to provide opinions. This golden rule will often be self rewarding, particularly where an important scheme is ruined as a result of challenge in the courts.

Local authorities should always act for proper motives in an open and unbiased way and following full and detailed consideration of the issues. Where charging and trading is concerned, in view of the controversial nature of some of the activities, full delegation to officers may be deemed unwise and committee reports need to be both comprehensive and carefully prepared. If these simple rules are followed, then the likelihood of a challenge on the exercise of statutory powers is greatly reduced. Even in the difficult days when trading activity was challenged regularly by the Audit Commission (see Ch.13), it soon became clear that district auditors very rarely challenged a local authority on exercise of powers alone; the normal scenario was a claim that the authority is acting *ultra vires* under both of its limbs: *capacity* and *exercise*.

Any judgement as to exercise of powers relates to an examination of earlier case law where abuse has been found. These highlight a number of principles which the courts will take into account, for example, whether the motive of the authority is proper, and whether or not it has properly followed the required procedures laid down in the statute (for example the requirement for a business case before setting up a trading company as explained in Ch.6 which is a requirement of the Trading Order—SI 2004/1705).

The Importance of "Reasonableness"

This is perhaps the most important of all the grounds upon which the **2.18** decision of a local authority may be challenged. Many officers and members of local authorities will have heard the phrase, *Wednesbury reasonableness*. This is because the standard laid down in the famous case of *Associated Provincial Picture Houses Ltd v The Wednesbury Corporation* [1948] 1 KB 223, by Lord Greene MR has long been held as one of the clearest expositions of the law. He said:

"It is true that discretion must be exercised reasonably. Now what does that mean? Lawyers familiar with the phraseology used in relation to exercise of statutory discretions often use the word "unreasonable" in a rather comprehensive sense. It has frequently been used and is frequently used as a general description of the things that must not be done. For instance, a person entrusted with the discretion must, so to speak, direct himself properly in law. He must call his own attention to the matters which he is bound to consider. He must exclude from his consideration matters which are irrelevant to what he has to consider. If he does not obey those rules, it may truly be said, and often is said, to be acting "unreasonably." Similarly, there may be something so absurd that no sensible person could ever dream that it lay within the powers of the authority. Warrington L.J. in *Short v Poole Corporation* gave the example of the red haired teacher, dismissed because she had red hair. This is unreasonable in one sense. In another it is taking into consideration extraneous matters. It is so unreasonable that it might almost be described as being done in bad faith; and, in fact, all these things run into one another."

Another exposition unreasonableness was given by Lord Diplock in the case of *Council of Civil Service Unions v Minister for the Civil Service* [1985] AC 410. He described an unreasonable decision as one which is "so outrageous in its defiance of logic or of accepted moral standards that no sensible person who had applied his mind to the question to be decided could have arrived at it".

It should be clear from the extracts above how the law will determine reasonableness or unreasonableness. It is certainly true that in administrative law unreasonableness has a meaning aside from its generally understood meaning.

It is also clear from the *dicta* of Lord Greene that a number of the different elements of exercising statutory powers considered above will overlap. For example, to take into account an irrelevant consideration may itself be unreasonable as may be the reliance on an improper motive or policy. In this sense, the courts will often bundle a number of grounds together to found a declaration of *ultra vires*, without really explaining how the facts fit into each category. According to Lord Greene it was not important to categorise such matters in any event, so long as such a decision was overturned as unlawful.

Improper exercise of powers

2.19   The following are examples of limitations which the courts will read into statutory powers and the contravention of which will lead to challenge as being *ultra vires* the authority.

Blind reliance on policy

Where a local authority has discretion vested in it by a statutory power, it is imperative that it exercises that discretion validly. The inevitable result of a local authority not considering each case on its merits but simply imposing a decision in blind reliance on a policy is therefore *ultra vires* action. There are many examples of where a local authority has fettered its discretion in advance leading to the exercise of its statutory powers being struck down in the courts. A useful illustration is provided by the case of *Bromley London Borough Council v Greater London Council* [1983] 1 AC 768. In this case, the GLC had promised in its election campaign to subsidise the public transport services in London. Upon assuming power, the subsidies were implemented without proper consideration having been given to the decision. Accordingly, the court held that the local authority had fettered its discretion in advance and declared the decision *ultra vires*.

Relevant and Irrelevant Considerations

2.20   It has long been a principle that a local authority in exercising its powers must have regard to all relevant matters and be seen to disregard all irrelevant matters in the formulation of its decisions. This is discussed above in the context of *Associated Provincial Picture Houses v The Wednesbury Corporation* [1948] 1 KB 223. The courts will therefore strike down local authority action where it is clear that it is based on matters which Parliament had not intended to be taken into account or are wholly irrelevant to the activities under consideration.

An example outside of the sphere of trading is provided by the case of *R. v Ealing London Borough Council, ex p. The Times* [1986] 85 LGR 316. In this case a number of local authorities banned Times Newspapers from their libraries because of the actions of Rupert Murdoch in dealing with his striking workers. The court had no difficulty in holding that this political object was irrelevant to the statutory duty to provide a comprehensive and efficient library service under the Public Libraries and Museums Act 1964.

A similar result would be likely if a local authority ignored a relevant consideration in framing its decision, for example if a local authority in entering into charging activity did not act prudently by taking account of the fact that it could, potentially, make a loss.

Improper Motives

An example of the improper motive of income generation was seen in **2.21** the case of *R. v Manchester CC, ex p. King* (1991) (unreported). In that case the Council had sought to use its licensing powers to require street traders to pay a commercial fee for use of highways in the ownership of the council for these purposes.

The court confirmed that the Local Government (Miscellaneous Provisions) Act 1982, in allowing the local authority to "charge such fees as they consider reasonable for the grant or renewal of a street trading licence", did not authorise the council to use its licensing powers as an income producing asset. In fact the powers had to be exercised within the policy and objects of the Act. This meant that the level of fees must be related to the cost to the council of operating the street trading scheme. The court also found that the local authority had not paid sufficient regard to the ability of the street traders to absorb the additional cost, which was an increase of over one thousand per cent. In failing to take into account this material consideration, the council had also acted unlawfully.

Another example of improper motive would be trading activity designed to undermine the commercial success of legitimate businesses which the authority could not control through planning powers.

For the sake of completeness, it should also be noted that a motive of pure commercial profit in many such arrangements may also taint the agreements with improper purposes and render them *ultra vires* (unless they are under the s.95 powers in the Local Government Act 2003).

Sometimes the authority may have a mixed motive; in these circumstances, the law will seek to identify which was the dominant purpose and determine whether or not that purpose is legitimate. If it is, then the fact that a wholly ancillary purpose has also been achieved will not invalidate the decision, even if the ancillary purpose alone could still be challenged as *ultra vires*.

The principle is usefully illustrated by the case of *Westminster Corporation v London and North Western Railway* [1905] AC 426. In that case the corporation constructed public conveniences beneath Whitehall with an entrance from either side of the street. Accordingly, a subway was also created, although the corporation had no statutory power to provide subways. The House of Lords considered the purposes of the corporation's actions. It concluded that, "the primary object of the council was the construction of the conveniences with the requisite and proper means of approach thereto and exit therefrom." The corporation's actions were held to be lawful.

However, where the ancillary aim is held to be really the dominant purpose, or was sufficiently important to the decision to have been of significant influence in its making, the courts will strike down the actions as *ultra vires*. This is illustrated in the case of *R. v Inner London Education Authority, ex p Westminster Ciy Council* [1986] 1 WLR 28, where the court did not really distinguish in which of the two categories the decision lay. In that case the ILEA, although having power to publish information in the public interest, was held to have done so for the dominant purpose of political persuasion. The action was declared *ultra vires*.

Acting In Bad Faith

2.22   In this sense bad faith does not mean dishonesty but rather acting without authorisation, unreasonably, mistakenly or on improper grounds. It can readily be seen, therefore that bad faith may be imputed together with a number of other grounds for overturning a particular decision.

Procedural Impropriety

2.23   It will be seen when considering possible challenge in the next section that procedural impropriety may found an action for judicial review. Local authorities disregard procedural fairness at their peril, many decisions having been struck down on this ground, which often merges into natural justice. It is therefore essential that local authorities follow their own published standing orders, financial regulations, terms of reference and constitution. Failure to do so may lead to an allegation that the local authority has not complied with its own procedures. As an example, if an executive decision is taken outside of the cabinet in a 'leader and cabinet' model, it will not have been conducted in accordance with the authority's proper procedures or under the law as laid down in the Local Government Act 2000.

DEALING WITH THE IMPACT OF THE *ULTRA VIRES* DOCTRINE?

2.24   The authority will need to consider both limbs of the *ultra vires* doctrine; that is whether they have the necessary powers and whether or not they are exercising those powers lawfully and in a reasonable manner. Different types of powers give rise to different risks, with the use of express powers being the safest route. The overall approach may be expressed in a diagrammatic form, as in Figure 2.2.

Figure 2.2
The Approach to Powers

Proposed scheme

▼

Identify duty/power/implied power to be relied upon

▼

Is it incidental?
Will incidental powers be necessary?

▼

Exercise of powers in a reasonable manner, for proper motives and
within their statutory context

▼

Legitimate consequences which follow from use of powers. Examples
include efficiency savings (more staff; increased plant and machinery,
increased output) or cashable savings.

Issues Which May Need To Be Managed

Scale and Planning of the Activity

The importance of proper planning and documentation is highlighted in **2.25**
the case of *Hazell v Hammersmith and Fulham LBC* [1992] 2 AC 1. That
case is mentioned above, under the discussion on the incidental power
within s.111 of the Local Government Act 1972, and related to the activities
of the council in undertaking interest rate swaps.

Although the case was ultimately decided on absence of powers (*i.e.* a
capacity issue), the discussion of the facts in the Court of Appeal is worthy
of examination. In general terms, the authority entered into 562 swaps with
a total value of over £6 billion, when its own annual budget was in the
region of £45.5 million. Clearly the scale of the activity was a major factor
in suggesting that the motive was not prudent debt management, but so was
the lack of planning and evaluation of the risks by the council. The Court of
Appeal commented:

"... having carefully considered all the submissions of counsel and all
the material drawn to our attention, we are satisfied that all the
transactions to which the challenged items of account relate during the
first two periods are shown by the auditor to have been tainted with the
improper purpose of trading.

We base this conclusion primarily on one clinching fact fatal to the inference that any of the transactions was entered into for a purpose which could have been proper: neither before the transactions began, nor at any time before July 1988, did the council or its officers make any careful and detailed analysis of the interest which was due to be paid or received at any time in the future, or of the losses which the council might suffer, or of the risk that those losses might eventuate, or of the steps which it was desirable to take to mitigate or secure protection against those losses . . . As time went on and the pattern of the council's activity became established, the inference that it was engaged in trade (or speculation) becomes even clearer." ([1990] 2 WLR 1038 at p.1073).

This case also illustrates the important principle that essentially the same activity can be ruled lawful, or indeed unlawful, depending on the motive for which it was undertaken. If the motive is purely one of speculation to make a profit, it is likely to be ruled unlawful as an abuse of power, unless the power in s.95 of the Local Government Act 2003 is relied upon (see Ch.7). It also illustrates that where a local authority does not properly consider the implications of its actions, then it may be challenged.

Taking on Additional Resources?

2.26   Taking on extra resources to undertake trading activity is really a matter of proper strategic and business planning (see Chs 3 and 10); and is part of the issue of whether the authority is acting "reasonably" or not. One issue which caused difficulties in the past, particularly with external auditors, was the taking on of extra resources. This gave rise to arguments over whether or not authorities could only trade within the limits of their own "spare capacity." Trading under s.1 of the Local Authorities (Goods and Services) Act 1970 was said in the 1980s to be reliant upon "spare capacity." This view emanated from a Counsel's opinion obtained by the in house solicitor to the Audit Commission in 1988. In that opinion, Counsel expressed the following view:

"It would be a strong indication in my view that a local authority was doing that which it was not authorised to do by the 1970 Act if the undertaking it is conducting is not reasonably related in capacity in terms of staff, vehicles, plant and apparatus to what it may reasonably require in order to discharge its own functions and obligations arising other than under the 1970 Act."

So far as the 1970 Act is concerned, this opinion was *not* accepted in the case of *R. v Yorkshire Purchasing Organisation Ex p. British Educational Suppliers Ltd* (1997) *The Times*, July 10, 1997. As explained in Ch.4, the Court of Appeal has now confirmed that local authorities can purchase goods speculatively in the hope of selling them on and also take on the necessary extra staff and other resources to comply with their obligations under the 1970 Act. This means that they are not limited to using "spare capacity"; providing they are acting reasonably under the second limb of the *ultra vires* doctrine.

The Motive of Profit

This is another difficult area that had been the source of much **2.27** controversy in relation to pre-existing powers, prior to the enactment of the Local Government Act 2003. Obviously, s.95 of the 2003 Act commits a local authority to engage in risk based commercial trading for profit (see Ch.7). Outside of s.95, however, having the single motive of profit is a much more difficult issue.

The starting point should be to say that local authorities are empowered by Parliament to provide community leadership, deliver services, be the stakeholders of public money and generally operate within the public law framework; their powers to act relate to those functions. Accordingly, profit should never be the *primary* motive of a local authority unless it is trading commercially under s.95 of the 2003 Act. Nevertheless, authorities will not wish to make a loss and profit may be the lawful consequence of the exercise of a lawful motive.

In undertaking any activity, the local authority would need to show that its primary motive was an appropriate public law outcome, related to the particular statutory provision relied upon. Therefore if the power in s.2 Local Government Act 2000 is relied upon; the primary motive must be community leadership, or the achievement of wellbeing. That said, it does not mean that profit will not be a relevant consideration.

As another example, the power within s.38 of the Local Government (Miscellaneous Provisions) Act 1976, (see Ch.4) expressly permits a local authority to provide computer based services from its own computers to third parties on a commercial basis. The drafting of s.38(2) expressly requires the authority to include provisions in the contractual arrangments which the authority consider are those on which others would reasonably be expected to provide the facility; *i.e.* it must charge a commercial rate. The motive here would merely be to dispose of spare capacity to achieve efficiency savings, and a commercial rate (or profit) would have to be realised as that is required by the relevant statutory power.

Chapter 4 mentions a range of other powers, and provided the relevance of the profit element is properly characterised, either expressly within the statutory provision or impliedly as a relevant consideration, then the consequence of obtaining a profit will be perfectly lawful.

CASE LAW ON CHARGING AND TRADING

2.28   There have been many cases on powers and duties that have been relevant to charging and trading, many of which are mentioned in this chapter; there have been fewer cases on trading itself, but these do come before the courts now and again. The following are three cases that were determined during the last part of the 1990's specifically on this subject.

Alexandra Palace Ski Centre v Haringey LBC, (*The Times*, May 25, 1994, [1994] E.G.C.S. 99)

2.29   The case turned on an interpretation of the Alexandra Park and Palace (Public Purposes) Act 1900 as amended. The Council had given the Ski centre a lease under which it was allowed to charge admission to the ski centre. The Council were challenged as the 1900 Act did not permit charging. The court determined that, although the Act did not expressly authorise an admission charge to be made for the public to enter any part of the land; and implied power could be found because the trustees were given power to enter lease agreements. This would impliedly give power to permit lessees to charge the public for admission.

R. v Greater Manchester Police Authority Ex p. Century Motors (Farnworth) Ltd, (*The Times*, May 3, 1996)

2.30   The police authority externalised vehicle recovery to the Automobile Association and this was challenged by a third party (Century Motors) on the basis that there was no statutory power to do this. The case considered the statutory powers within the Police Act 1964 s.4, and the Local Government Act 1972 s.111(1). It was held that the combination of these powers gave power to the authority, in discharging its function of maintaining an efficient force, to appoint contactors for those purposes. Although there was no express provision to levy charges for the scheme, it was a necessary implication that the police authority was entitled to charge for this service.

Wards Construction (Medway) Ltd v Kent CC, [1999], (JPL, 738, *The Times*, March 3, 1999)

2.31   The construction company entered into an agreement with the council to pay 65 per cent of the costs of acquiring land and building a roundabout close to its housing development. The power used by the council was s.278 of the Highways Act 1980 (now replaced by s.23 New Roads and Street Works Act 1991). The land owner wanted £9,000 for the land which the construction company valued at only £7,000. The council therefore CPO'd the land. Subsequently, a Lands Tribunal assessed the compensation to be paid by the council to the owner at over £2 million; due to the "ransom" value of the land. The construction company did not want to pay 65 per cent of that vastly higher figure and argued that the it was not bound by the agreement.

Although the court accepted, as a preliminary issue, that the s.278 agreement was unenforceable it separated out the council's actions in relation to the CPO from that agreement. The CPO was justified on both a traffic case and a planning case at the local inquiry level; the need for it was therefore independent of the s.278 agreement and was not tainted with any illegality under s.278. In any event, another statutory provision (the Acquisition of Land Act 1981 s.25) could have provided a defence to the challenge of the compulsory purchase order.

CONCLUSION

It can be seen that the legal basis for charging and trading can be complex, but if properly explained is a relatively straightforward legal analysis of capacity to act and the proper exercise of the power or duty concerned. **2.32**

The government introduced powers under the Local Government Act 2003 to simplify charging and trading law. Where those powers in s.93 and s.95 apply, it will not be necessary to give consideration to any other legal powers, simply to the justification for the new specific statutory powers to apply and the proper exercise of the relevant powers. However, as mentioned above, the powers will not apply on every occasion and if this is the case, then a range of pre-existing powers may come into play. Some of these relate to public to public activity, others in relation to public to private trading and some govern the ability of local authorities to provide services to members of the public. Where these powers apply, greater scrutiny is likely to be forthcoming on the activities of the authority and so it is important to ensure that the legal system has been properly followed. Further advice on the relevant powers is provided in Pt 2 of this work.

CHAPTER 3
STRATEGIC PLANNING

INTRODUCTION

The current climate of local authority activity means that authorities **3.1** need to act strategically in all that they do; and trading is again no different to other activities. The Comprehensive Performance Assessment, has emphasised the need for strategic planning and a strategic approach to all major decision making. Questions such as: "is trading the right approach for us?"; "what type of trading activity should we embark upon?" and "how should we implement a trading strategy?" should all be easier to answer by those who have taken the trouble to read this Chapter.

In Pt 3 of this work, the authors have detailed the three areas of powers available to local authorities for charging and trading activity, namely: use of existing powers (such as the Local Authorities (Goods and Services) Act 1970); powers to charge for discretionary services using s.93 of the Local Government Act 2003; and powers of commercial trading using s.95 of the local Government Act 2003. This chapter looks at one of the most important parts of the whole process *i.e.* how to decide which route is the best for the local authority in question.

This decision will depend upon a number of factors and will need careful consideration. Few local authorities considered the detailed implications of using a trading company during 2004. This was hardly surprising because the commercial trading powers were, at that time, only newly introduced. During this period, however, many authorities had already determined that extensive use of the s.93 powers would fit them best; even though they had no record of using the existing charging and trading powers widely at all. Those authorities, therefore, had no current charging and trading "culture" developed. Still, more local authorities have yet to decide anything about the use of trading powers. As an example, the *Local Government Chronicle* on December 3, 2004 reported that in a survey of 244 local authorities by the Local Government Association, only 2 per cent had used the trading powers in s.95 of the 2003 Act and only 3 per cent had used the discretionary power to charge. At this stage, of course, the charging powers had been in for over twelve months and the trading powers for nearly six months. This surprising result demonstrates that local authorities across the country do need to apply themselves to the strategic planning exercises outlined in this chapter in relation to their charging and trading activity.

The chapter considers the choice that every local authority has between, essentially, the obtaining of civic benefit or general wellbeing and the generation of profit. It looks at the factors that will impact on any local authority making this decision.

In view of the fact that commercial, risk based trading will be more high risk, more difficult and more complex, the authors would urge caution in going down the s.95 route, without a full analysis of the implications; whilst the use of the s.93 power or existing powers may be operated on a smaller scale. Either way, once the local authority has decided exactly what route is appropriate for it, it needs to develop a detailed strategy for that particular area. Once the legal framework is clear, some of the more practical issues highlighted Pt 3 of this work (Chs 10–12) are likely to be of interest in relation to the implementation of the chosen strategy.

WHICH OF THE THREE ROUTES TO FOLLOW?

3.2 Most local authorities have the choice of the full range of charging and trading activity. Any local authority can use the existing powers described in Ch.4 and the s.93 powers described in Ch.5. Those local authorities in *excellent, good* or *fair* categories of the Comprehensive Performance Assessment can also use the s.95 powers for commercial trading too. The Audit Commission had made announcements by December 2004 for all unitary, county and district councils. This data illustrates that there were 16 principal authorities that fell in the *weak* or *poor* groups and a further 35 District councils. This is, of course, a relatively small percentage of the total. Obviously, these authorities only have the first two of the available areas of powers and not the company option. The comments in the remainder of this chapter assume that a local authority does qualify to use s.95 powers to establish trading companies and does therefore have the full choice available.

Perhaps the key deciding issue of which route is to be followed depends on the motive of the authority. Essentially the choice of motive can be distilled down to only two factors: civic benefit/wellbeing or financial benefit/profit. This is illustrated in Figure 3.1 below. Use of existing powers and the undertaking of discretionary services with a charge attached normally deliver civic benefit or wellbeing; whilst the use of a trading company via the powers in s.95 of the Local Government Act 2003 are normally aimed at delivery of profit for investment into the authority via the subsidisation of council tax, defraying expenditure elsewhere or providing investment. Another way of looking at it is that s.93 and the use of existing powers are about acting as the *public sector* does (though acting in a more commercial manner); whilst the use of a trading company under s.95 of the 2003 Act is about acting like the *private sector*.

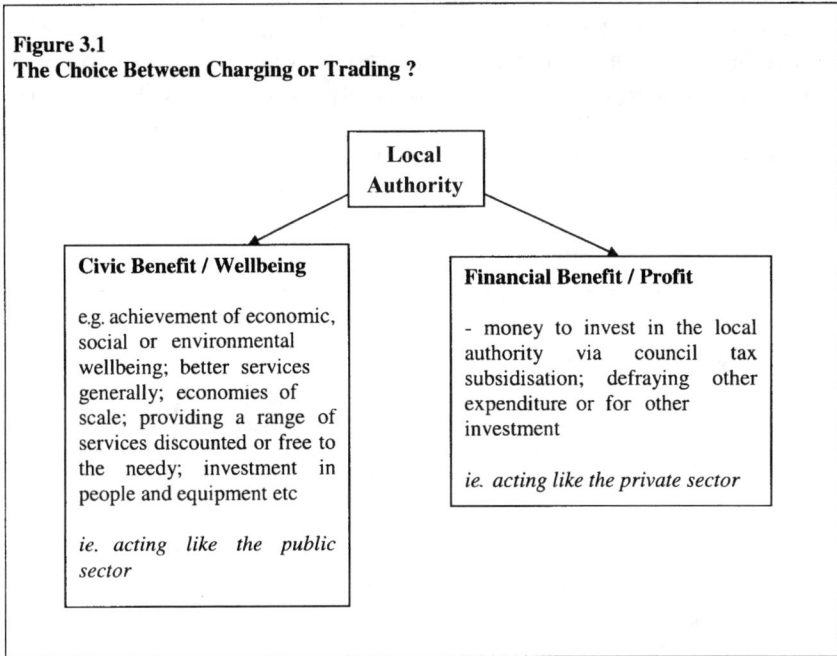

Figure 3.1
The Choice Between Charging or Trading ?

The Association for Public Service Excellence has illustrated this distinction in a slightly different way in Figure 3.2. This demonstrates that charging activity under s.93 has less risk and commercial, risk based trading under s.95 has more risk. Either way though, in theory, the benefits get back to the local authority via one route or another.

Whilst the primary motive may well be either financial profit or civic benefits; each authority will also need to consider a number of key factors that will be relevant to this decision. These are considered below.

FACTORS IN THE CHOICE BETWEEN CHARGING AND TRADING POWERS

Any local authority faced with this choice needs to decide very carefully. **3.3** The following are the key areas that will need to be considered:

Who Are We?

The starting point is with the local authority in question. It was **3.4** mentioned above that the CPA classification each local authority is given by the Audit Commission will be important to its overall standing. In relation to trading activity, the CPA classification has to be *fair* or above this status for this avenue to be open. However, on a more general point early questions include: "Are we 'excellent'?" *i.e.* recognised as a very well run local authority across the board. If so, this type of authority may wish to consider all types of charging and trading activity. In an excellent authority, the members might have confidence to move forward with a s.95 company or to authorise a wide variety of s.93 activity, knowing that it is built on strong foundations. If the local authority is not yet "excellent", how is it going to get to be "excellent?" Again, this will be relevant as the authority will have determined areas of importance to improve its performance. If charging and trading activity can assist with these areas, then a double benefit will have been gained.

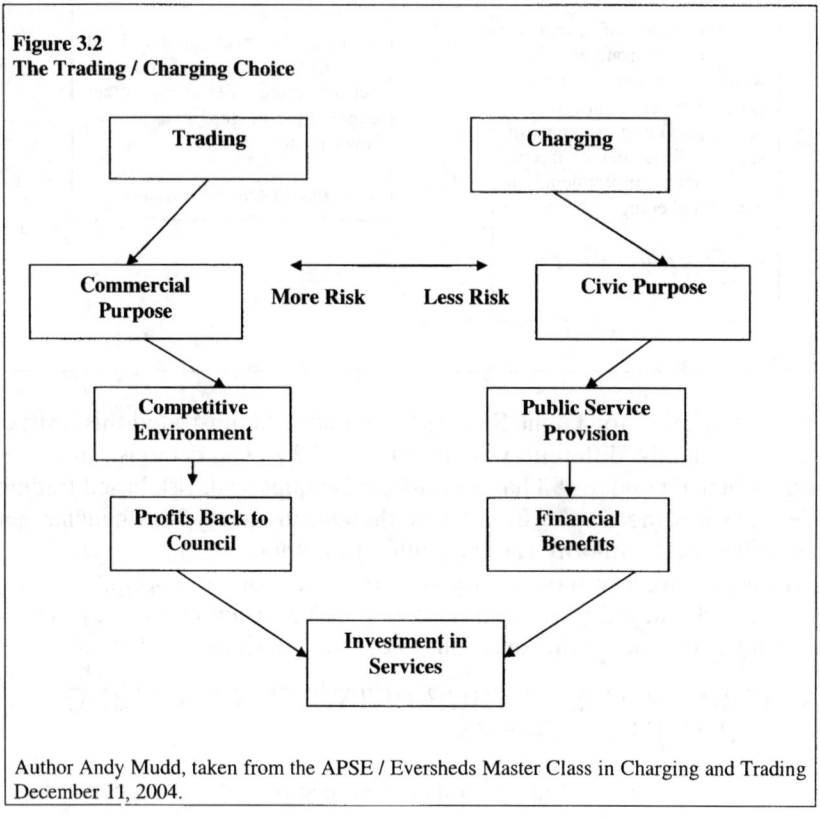

Figure 3.2
The Trading / Charging Choice

Author Andy Mudd, taken from the APSE / Eversheds Master Class in Charging and Trading December 11, 2004.

It is vital that local authorities do not look at charging and trading in isolation but as a "means to an end." The difficult issue is to determine what that ultimate end is intended to be! This means that every local authority should start with its own community strategy, prepared under s.4 of the Local Government Act 2000. As the government's Wellbeing

Guidance explains, the community strategy is intended to be the document that sets down the vision for the local community which the local authority has produced in conjunction with its Local Strategic Partnership and/or other partners. It should include the aims for the local authority and put the position of the council in question in context.

Questions need to be asked about how these community aims can be achieved or assisted by charging and trading activity. An example might be that the community strategy has, as one of its main strands, the improvement of community safety (usually termed "making Barchester a safer place"). It might be that the perceived fears of the elderly community are important to that particular strand. Introducing some form of service for the elderly, such as that discussed in Ch.6, would therefore help directly with the achievement of this element of the community strategy.

The next step is to look at its performance levels under Best Value. **3.5** Obviously, these will have fed into the CPA scores under the service blocks, as well as the corporate assessment. So far as Best Value is concerned, are there areas where we are outstanding? An example in relation to a district council is provided by the benefits service. During 2004, only one district council achieved an 'excellent' score for its benefits service under a Best Value review. This being the case, it could be an area that that local authority wants to provide to others. Conversely, are there areas where our service is poor, as evidenced by Best Value reports and inspections, which might best be avoided in relation to this type of activity?

The council's financial position will also be very relevant. What is its financial position? Is the council suffering from historical problems? Is there a particular squeeze on revenue? Also, whether the authority is debt free may have an impact in this area.

Mentioned in the conclusion (see Ch.15) is the issue about whether a local authority is willing to change in order to accommodate its charging and trading activity. The authors have indicated that it is not possible for a local authority to stay the same and simply earn profit from trading activity. If it wants to go down the commercial trading route, then it has to do so via a company (see Ch.7) and this will involve substantial change. This raises the question as to whether the authority is open to change. This may be answered by considering whether the authority's organisation has been the same for many years or whether it has continuously evolved and changed as time has gone on. Obviously, an authority that is more used to change is more likely to be able to undertake the practical requirements needed to implement the changes, as described in Ch.10.

Another relevant point will be the authority's current track record for charging and trading. If a local authority is taking a narrow legalistic view of its ability to engage in this activity and has therefore done little of it, it would be a big jump to dive straight into commercial, risk based trading activity. The "culture" of the authority for charging and trading is also relevant. If the authority has traditionally been focused on its own services rather than anything else, then it may not be experienced in external delivery or have a culture which easily permits this. Other authorities have offered services externally for some time and have traditionally worked for the public or private sectors. In such an authority, a trading culture will have developed over time, giving that authority a far better insight into what will be necessary to implement a new strategy. In the view of the authors, a trading "culture" cannot be developed overnight. Hence the view of the authors featured below that a three year plan towards more risk based trading might be a better idea. Obviously, in order to answer these questions, a local authority will need to be in possession of the data indicating what its current level of charging and trading activity is. While this sounds obvious, it may well be that such records have never been kept in this particular form and if so this will need to be remedied.

Political leadership and senior management are also key issues in charging and trading. Does the authority have strong political management and strong direction from its senior management? Again, this will be relevant to the CPA (this time more the corporate assessment) but may also be relevant to charging and trading activities. An example here is Westminster City Council, which has publicised the desire to become a "trading council" and reduce its level of council tax to nil. As Westminster is an *excellent* authority under the CPA, few would doubt that it has the capability to do this.

The issue of the extent to which a local authority wishes to embrace the commercial ethos of the private sector is potentially an emotive and controversial subject. Once concern with the language used in drafting the powers in the Local Government Act 2003 is the confusion over the word "commercial". Section 95 of the Local Government Act 2003 mentioned "commercial" trading, though this does not equate well to the idea of local authority in house operatives acting "commercially" which is more related to efficiency. Whilst many local authorities are happy to be efficient, a large number do not want to behave like the private sector but instead want to remain delivering core services primarily for civic benefit. In this regard, the distinguishing feature is the focus of the private sector on profits. Whilst many private sector businesses do have an enviable record in balancing priorities and acting ethically; ultimately they are profit driven. Any local authority setting up a commercial trading company to operate in this environment will have to decide how far it is willing to go to make a profit. Would this embrace reducing pay and conditions to increase profit? Alternatively, would this involve reducing investment or permitting aggressive take over activity? It is therefore fundamental whether a local authority is happy to act in a private sector way or not. It goes without saying that if an authority is not willing to operate in this truly "commercial" environment; then it will not want to go down the s.95 route.

The Marketplace

It is also necessary to look at the market, whether local, regional, **3.6** national or international. One way to start this exercise is to ask: "where is there a gap in the market?" Are there areas of activity where users are willing to pay charges for a service that could be delivered by the council?

The Council may wish to fill gaps in the market

It will also be necessary to look at who is providing services in the **3.7** community and to what standard? What knowledge does the council have of areas of skill or business shortage in their community? Are there gaps in the market, for example it may be that finding reliable basic level property maintenance is a problem, even though it may be possible to find a builder to undertake a loft extension, completely refit a kitchen or build a garage. Perhaps the former activity is harder to manage and may need a wider range of skills; both of which will be available to an authority but may be absent from a small specialist firm.

The Council may wish to regulate the market by its participation

Alternatively, there may be firms willing to operate in a particular **3.8** market; but the level of service may be poor and may have led to a significant level of complaints about quality or reliability. The complaints may be coming from just one sector which is under-served or where particular requirements are not met. Services to the elderly and other vulnerable groups may be such a market.

The Council is likely to be unwilling to disturb a properly functioning market

A former Circular on Best Value (DETR 10/99) talked about the **3.9** maturity of local markets. If there is an immature market, where existing service providers are thin on the ground or have not been providing services for very long, then there might be value in the local authority also providing services to help the market mature. Alternatively, there could be a normal healthy marketplace or even over-supply. In this latter case there would be little reason for the authority to enter that particular market.

Also relevant will be whether the local authority will create a market impact in its chosen activity? This will be relevant to EU competition law, (as discussed in Ch.8) and also in relation to the risk of legal challenge, as discussed in Ch.2.

The Non-Financial Resources

The third area that the authority needs to focus on is the resource levels **3.10** available to it which will be relevant to this strategy exercise. Here, the authors are talking about non-financial resources as opposed to funding. So the first question is what resource levels does the authority have?

In relation to many manual services, a sub-question will arise, namely is work performed in house by the authority or has it been outsourced? This will affect the strategy as s.93 discretionary charging benefits would be much slower and less effective in an authority that does not provide services itself. This is because it does not have the people, assets or equipment to receive the consequential and knock-on benefits. It is possible, of course, to get the outsourced service provider to undertake this work, though then many of the benefits will be lost. Equally, if an authority wants to go down the commercial trading route under s.95, it would have to tailor these to the outsourcing arrangement (see Ch.9).

Asset Availability

3.11   Asset availability will be fundamental to the authority's ability to engage in charging and trading activity. The authority will need to consider assets such as equipment and vehicles. Charging activity to local citizens is less likely to be available to an in-house operation where the primary assets are depots, salt barns, specialist gritting equipment and the like (although this may be useful for trading with other authorities). Conversely an in-house operation well equipped with chain saws, small mowers and hedge-trimming apparatus will have the equipment for charging to citizens (but this is less relevant to work for other authorities).

Staff Resources

3.12   On the people front, what skills do the people have? If the operation has good general skills available to it; this will hold it in good stead. Alternatively, the authority may have specialist skills, such as the excellent benefits team mentioned above or specialists in land drainage, archaeology or winter maintenance. Depending on the type of staff, different types of activity will be relevant.

The ability to attract new staff will also be relevant. In some areas recruitment is a real problem, for example in London and the south east where housing costs are high. If a local authority cannot attract new staff to perform extra services under either s.93 or s.95, the strategy will not work.

Closely allied to the issue of attracting new staff will be pay levels. Does the local authority traditionally pay higher than the norm? If it does, it probably has better chances of recruiting new staff. If its pay has traditionally been in the medium or lower quartiles, then it may be difficult. Again, recruitment and pay in London and the South East is often a problem.

Finally, does the authority have spare capacity in relation to its people, assets, equipment or vehicles? This may well not be the case, though the authority needs to know if there are areas where extra value can be squeezed out of current resource.

Specialist Areas

There are two areas that could be relevant under the issue of specialisms. **3.13** These are: asset based specialist areas or skill based specialist areas. Turning to asset based areas first, there are a number of examples that could be forwarded. An obvious one is an authority that has developed a UPVC window manufacturing factory. In the former days of local authorities owning substantial social housing stocks, it was not unusual for an authority to develop a UPVC window manufacturing capability. The idea, of course, was to manufacture the windows to fit in its own properties, thereby improving their standards and longevity. If a local authority did go down this route, then matters have usually changed quite substantially. Obviously, many authorities have now disposed of their stocks via LSVT or other arrangements; even those that have not, should have replaced all or most of the windows of the main stock, thereby meaning that the UPVC factory has an uncertain future. Whilst it would be possible for a local authority to charge for the supply and fit windows using s.93 powers, as described in Ch.6, there would certainly be issues about the geographical boundaries within which such activity could take place.

If the authority simply wanted to undertake this work freely anywhere in the country and for profit, then s.95 might be the better route. A UPVC window factory may well be a self contained, specialist operation with little interface generally with the local authority. As such, it may be ideal for this type of approach. Similar comments could be made about other asset based specialist areas such as large grounds maintenance nurseries, vehicle maintenance workshops (particularly specialist ones such as refuse collection vehicles) and so on.

The other specialist area worthy of note is skill based specialist services. Here, a local authority may have a body of people who have developed specialist skills in a particular area that might be more widely utilised. One example would be a local authority's land drainage team. If the authority in question has suffered from land drainage problems, it may well have developed expertise over many years which are encapsulated within a small team of officers. However, if the land drainage issues in relation to the geographical areas of that local authority have been brought under control, there may be insufficient work for that team of officers to undertake. Again, s.93 of the Local Government Act 2003 could be used to offer services, but geographical boundaries would again be an issue. Whilst this would not be the case with the Local Authorities (Goods and Services) Act 1970, private sector customers could not be dealt with using this power. Again, this specialist area may therefore benefit from being considered for the s.95 route. The same comments could be made for other skill based specialist service areas such as an archaeological team or in the area of engineering.

Delivering Efficiency

3.14   The Gershon review requires substantial efficiency savings to be made across government, including local authorities. Each local authority has to decide where the efficiency savings are to be made, some of them "cashable" and others providing different benefits. Collectively, local authorities have to achieve £6.4 billion of savings by 2007/2008.

This is also relevant to an authority's consideration of its charging and trading strategy. The question is how is the authority going to find the Gershon savings? Is it confident that it can improve efficiency to meet those targets? This is relevant because charging and trading activity can generally improve economies of scale and s.95 companies have potential for cash generation.

All of these matters will need to be properly taken into account in order for the local authority to determine its position, *i.e.* what it wants to achieve from its trading activity. The various headings are summarised in Figure 3.3 below.

Figure 3.3
Summary of Key Areas in Deciding on the Strategy

Who Are We?

- Community strategy
- CPA classification
- Best Value performance
- Financial position
- Openness to change
- Political leadership
- Management
- Track record for charging and trading
- Current culture of charging and trading
- Current level of charging and trading activity
- How far are we willing to go in embracing the philosophy of potential private sector rivals?

The Marketplace?

- What is there a demand for?
- Who is providing services?

- Are they doing it well?

- Are there gaps in the market?

- Are there complaints regarding private sector provision?

- Is there an immature market, a normal healthy market or over-supply?

- Would the local authority involved create a market impact?

The Non-Financial Resources

- Non-financial resources available to the authority

- What resources do we have?

- Do we perform work ourselves or have we outsourced?

- What assets, equipment and vehicles do we have?

- What skills do our people have?

- Can we attract new staff?

- What are our pay levels in comparison to others?

- Is there spare capacity in people, assets, equipment or vehicles?

Specialist Areas

- Do we have any asset based specialist areas *e.g.*

  — UPVC window factory
  — extensive vehicle maintenance workshops
  — extensive nurseries

- Do we have any specialist skill based areas *e.g.*

  — land drainage section
  — archaeology team
  — winter maintenance

Delivering Gershon

- How are we going to find the efficiency savings to deal with Gershon?

- Do we have the confidence that we can further improve efficiency?

DEVELOPING A STRATEGY FOR CHARGING AND TRADING

3.15   Once the basic strategic audit has been undertaken; a report (or business case) will need to be prepared to support the recommended course of action. This will be placed before members, via the cabinet or other governance arrangements that are in place, to confirm the local authority's position.

Having examined the factors outlined above; the report is likely to explain the three available areas (existing powers, s.93 and s.95) and reflect on the culture of the authority, its performance levels and general position before recommending the appropriate course of action.

As mentioned above, the authority has three potential routes to take (or a combination of these three routes). Once the authority has decided which route to choose, its strategy will need to be developed. It should be noted that even if a local authority does want to go down the s.95 route, it may be unrealistic for it to do so, bearing on mind its current resources, CPA performance or culture. Evidence from the first year or so of the provisions coming into force suggests that most local authorities will not move directly to the commercial trading route but will choose to delivery civic benefit through charging, at least in the first instance.

One of the reasons for choosing the civic benefit route might be uncertainty as to whether any more risk based commercial trading operation would be successful. It is for this reason that some authorities have adopted an incremental three year plan, as detailed below.

AN INCREMENTAL THREE YEAR PLAN FOR TRADING?

3.16   The authors have worked with a large number of local authorities on charging and trading work, spanning more than a decade. Experience to date, is that few local authorities have determined to commence with s.95 risk based trading, nor would it be sensible for them to do so. Instead they prefer to have a plan to ease the authority into this activity, whilst continually reviewing its position and strategy.

In legal terms there is a progression of powers which may be used for trading. These are featured in Figure 3.4 below. This demonstrates that the most familiar legal foundations are at the top of the chart (for example, the Goods and Services Act), whilst the highest risk (company based commercial trading) are at the bottom. Many would suggest that it would be unwise to start with company based commercial trading, without extensive experience of the areas above to rely upon.

42

Figure 3.4
The Progression of Powers

- The Local Authorities (Goods and Services) Act 1970
- Other specific powers
- The Local Government Act 2000 Wellbeing powers
- Incidental powers
- Discretionary charging powers under s.93 LGA 2003
- Commercial trading powers under s.95 LGA 2003

A better suggestion would therefore be to work down the various powers, ensuring that those with the most familiar legal foundations are exploited first. This would include the following:

The Goods and Services Act

All authorities will be familiar with the concept of 'public to public' **3.17** trading activity using the Goods and Services Act. Since the YPO case mentioned in Ch.4, it is clear law that a local authority may offer services to other local authorities and public bodies contained in s.1 of the 1970 Act. The Court of Appeal's judgment in the YPO case also indicated that a local authority can use this trading power speculatively, can buy goods on the basis it will sell them on later and can enter into substantial agreements. It is also possible for local authorities to take on staff via s.112 of the Local Government Act 1972, attach incidental powers to the 1970 Act via s.111 of the Local Government Act 1972 and provided the authority acts reasonably and in accordance with public law (under the second limb of the *ultra vires* doctrine) this activity will be lawful.

The Goods and Services Act are more familiar than the new powers and it therefore offers an excellent way for an authority to expand its experience of working for others.

Other specific powers

There are many examples of these, mentioned in Ch.4. Obvious examples **3.18** would be leisure powers under the Local Government (Miscellaneous Provisions) Act 1976, restaurants and food outlets under the Civic Restaurants Act 1947; and the sale of spare computer capacity under the Local Government (Miscellaneous Provisions) Act 1976. There are numerous other powers, including powers of tourism, entertainment and car parking.

Any authority that wants to move forward in its charging and trading activity should be making full use of these powers.

Wellbeing powers

3.19   Chapter 4 explains the powers in s.2 of the Local Government Act 2000 which permit a local authority to do anything that is likely to have the effect of promoting or improving the economic, social or environmental wellbeing of its area. Having fought for so long to obtain these powers (which may be equated to powers of general competence within the three designated areas), it is something of a surprise that local authorities are not using the powers to the full. The ODPM has expressed surprise at this and is puzzled as to why local authorities are not making more use of their wellbeing powers. However, this can soon be remedied and the addition of s.93 powers to charge for wellbeing powers might well prove the necessary spur to this. However, the authors have indicated in Ch.2, earlier that there is an argument that in any event a charge can be levied using wellbeing powers via s.111 of the Local Government Act 1972.

Discretionary charging powers

3.20   The new discretionary charging power under s.93 of the Local Government Act 2003 is discussed in detail in Ch.5 and full examples are given in Ch.6. This is an extremely flexible power that is likely to be used extensively by local authorities.

Commercial trading powers

3.21   The new commercial trading powers under s.95 of the Local Government Act 2003 are considered in Chs 7 to 9 in detail. A local authority needs to set up a company in order to trade commercially and a number of other legal rules and requirements will need to be observed. Legally speaking, this is the most complex of the charging and trading routes.

All these routes are considered in detail in Pt 2 of this work. For illustrative purposes, however, the point is made that in the earlier years of a trading and charging strategy extensive experience could be gained of working for others, structuring new activities and monitoring costs (particularly in relation to the duty to balance the books under s.93(3)) allowing a further review to be undertaken at the end of the three year period.

If a local authority did not want to go down the commercial trading route at the start due to insufficient experience, this may well have been remedied after a couple of years, thereby giving the opportunity of reconsidering this position. It will also be the case that other local authorities will have used the s.95 powers in the interim, thereby creating precedents. Figure 3.5 summarises a potential three year plan.

Figure 3.5
A Potential Three Year Charging and Trading Plan

Year 1

- Full initial review of position;

- Re-embrace Goods and Services Act work;

- Use existing statutory powers to the full;

- Evaluate charging and trading position;

- Influence culture of local authority;

- Brainstorm uses of s.93.

Year 2

- Increase charging activity using existing powers;

- Review organisation of the local authority and its progress;

- Greatly extend use of s.93 to provide new services.

Year 3

- Undertake market analysis (see **Ch.10**);

- Consolidate activities;

- Review areas where s.95 might be appropriate and review experience and culture.

Figure 3.5 assumes there are no specialist areas capable of benefiting from the s.95 treatment earlier, such as the UPVC window factory mentioned above. If the three year plan is appropriate and followed, any local authority will be in a position by the end of year 3 to decide is risk based trading is appropriate for it or not. It could be that the local authority has improved its charging and trading activity in the interim and is not confident enough to attempt a bolder venture; on the other hand it could be that the authority has found it harder than it thought, and accordingly is dissuaded from any more aggressive trading ventures.

Incidental powers

The original Common Law power enabling a local authority to do **3.22** anything that is incidental to or consequential upon the performance of its functions is now enshrined in s.111 of the Local Government Act 1972.

This authorises a local authority to do anything that facilitates or is conducive or incidental to the performance of its functions. However, a number of cases in the 1980s and 1990s led to restrictive interpretations being placed on s.111. These cases are discussed in Ch.2. Notwithstanding these judgments, the government is now being far more supportive of local authorities using their powers purposively in order to achieve civic benefit. This being the case, there are many more things that could be authorised using the power in s.111 and local authorities may find innovative ways of using these powers.

A STRATEGY FOR DISCRETIONARY CHARGING

3.23   Assuming the local authority wants to go down the route of offering discretionary services and levying a charge for them, the authority needs to decide what services it can provide and what civic benefit will be delivered as a result.

A report to members will be necessary for approval of the authority's approach. This is likely to include:

- an explanation of the new powers under s.93 of the Local Government Act 2003 with a view on how useful those might be if used by the authority;
- a request that decisions to engage in marginal discretionary services are delegated to officers;
- authorisation to establish an appropriate control and accountability mechanism to govern this activity.

So far as the development of a system of controls is concerned, this is considered further in Ch.10. It should include the requirement to have a business plan for each activity, combined with some form of risk analysis, market analysis and justification for the powers relied upon. The authors have suggested in Ch.10 that this could be by way of a series of precedent documents which need to be completed by the appropriate officer at the appropriate time in order to demonstrate that the matter has been approached adequately and that a legal and financial audit trail is available.

On a practical level, one of the most important elements of using s.93 of the Local Government Act 2003 is the actual identification of services the authority could provide and what might be charged for them. On this front, the authors have suggested getting groups of officers together in order to "brainstorm" the services that are currently provided for the authority itself and how spin offs might be developed. In the experience of the authors, such meetings could be highly productive in identifying new areas that can then be taken forward.

As part of the s.93 strategy the local authority also needs to establish a charging policy. This policy has to distinguish between the newer style charging for discretionary services under the powers in s.93 of the Local Government Act 2003 and the more traditional charging areas, utilising other specific powers. In Ch.6 the example of developing a service of loaning art works to the private sector is considered; this would have to be contrasted to the existing provision by a local authority of car parks using other powers and how the charges in relation to those car parks should be determined. Obviously, the duty to balance the books under s.93(3) of the Local Government Act 2003 only applies to the use of those new powers. In relation to existing charging powers, the authority may have more or less flexibility. It will have less where it is a regulatory function and Parliament has set down the exact charges; it may have more where the ability to levy a charge and determine that charge itself was included in the primary Act. Examples in this latter category might be entertainment and tourism powers contained in the Local Government Act 1972.

The Audit Commission produced a paper in September 1999 entitled *The Price Is Right? Charges For Council Services*. This highlighted the importance of charges to service provision generally and concluded that charges can underpin the continuous improvement of local authority services and deliver Best Value. Whilst the paper was written long before the Local Government Act 2003 came into effect, its comments provide helpful guidance on the effect properly considering what level of charges should be applicable can have on the service itself. Under the section on "the Power of Charging" it comments that few local authorities are getting the best out of charging, though with notable exceptions that demonstrates what can be done. Para.20 goes on:

"These examples counter the commonly held view that user charges are just about raising money. A thoughtful review of the role and level of charges can underpin the continuous improvement of services that is envisaged by Best Value. The challenges raised by the issue of charging should lie at the heart of any searching Best Value review:

- Why are we providing this service at all?
- Who benefits from the service—individuals or the wider community?
- Why do we subsidise it? What are we trying to achieve by subsidising it? and
- How much do residents and businesses value the service? How willing are they to pay for it?"

The paper goes on in the following paragraphs to illustrate how user **3.24** charges levied by councils can connect directly to the top social and service objectives contained in the authority's community strategy. Six categories are outlined:

- Targeting subsidy and top priorities;
  this is about recovering more of the costs of lower priority services through charges, in order that the income raised can be directed towards higher priorities. In relation to s.93 activities, this could also be interpreted to mean providing a wider range of services within a particular service definition, so that there is available income to provide services discounted or freely to the needy.

- Improving services;
  this refers to the idea that income generated through charges can be used to improve services through investment in improved facilities, improved accessibility or extended opening hours.

- Delivering corporate priorities;
  the Audit Commission makes the point that charges can help in delivering corporate priorities. For example discretionary charges to help tackle social exclusion as part of an anti poverty strategy or parking charges in support of environmental transport strategies.

- Generating income;
  this paragraph shows the age of the paper by indicating that surplus income can be generated by identifying where services are under-priced compared with what users would be prepared to pay. Obviously, this will only be applicable where s.93 does not apply, due to the legal duty to balance income and expenditure when using that power. However, it may still be relevant in relation to s.93 by creating income that then needs to be matched by expenditure, for example via concessionary pricing. It is also ironic that a local authority that is charging below the going rate for any particular service may well be more vulnerable to challenge than if it were charging the going rate.

- Managing demand for services;
  here the point is made that well designed charges can increase take up of services by priority users by way of creative charging techniques including concessions, discounts and eligibility criteria.

- Communicating a message;
  the final point is that there may be times when it is better to levy a charge for a service than to provide it for nothing. There is a widely held view that people do not value that which they receive for free and it may be useful to the council to indicate that charges will be levied (albeit with discretionary charging elements) for services.

The general thrust of *The Price Is Right?* paper is that local authorities are not determining, managing and recovering charges to deliver strategic objectives. In particular, it found little evidence that charging policies were driven by policy priorities or systematic planning on behalf of the authority. This must be the central message that local authorities take into new strategies, particularly using s.93 powers. The Commission concluded that the area of local authority charging needed a thorough review.

As para.32 notes:

"These consequences combine to provide a compelling argument for councils to think again about charges in terms of:

- the positive power of charges to help deliver top local priorities and needs being largely untapped;

- users and residents finding the existing pattern of charges illogical, unfair and confusing;

- money being wasted as subsidy is misdirected;

- potential income being lost;

- services being cut or starved of investment when users would be willing to pay more; and

- the failure to address the challenge questions raised by the charges means that councils may not meet their new duty of Best Value."

It is the reference to Best Value that is interesting as the authors would agree that this offers an excellent way forward. If a local authority were to apply the four Cs to its charging area, the following could be analysed:

- The *challenge* questions;
  These are featured above from the Audit Commission but would include why do we provide this service? Do we need to provide it? Could somebody else provide it better? Are the charges we levy for it the right ones? etc.

- The *compare* issues;
  This would include proper comparisons with other local authorities' charging policies but also comparisons with similar service providers in the private sector in their area, for example, for car parks and other types of services. Obviously, a local authority, wants to be charging about the right amount for a service, subject to its legal duties.

- The *consult* issues;
  Mentioned in Ch.10 is the issue of a user survey, *i.e.* the ability to ask users of the service what they think about the charging policies. There could also be internal consultation with those who provide the service and with other functional areas of the council that would be

able to comment on the targeting of the service towards the community strategy aims.

- The *competition* issues;
  It would be possible to look at how competitive the local authority services are compared with other service providers in terms of both quality and cost.

This would give a thorough grounding for the local authority in determining whether it is providing the right services, charging the right amount for them and so on.

Featured in Ch.10 are more practical implementation issues for a s.93 strategy.

A COMMERCIAL TRADING STRATEGY

3.25 Essentially, if a local authority determines to go for profit generation, it would only have a smaller number of issues to consider, outside of the many different elements that would comprise the establishment of the company itself. From the authority's side, the main issues would be: the role of the company and the extent to which it has complete commercial freedom; how to control the operations of an arm's length company (via the shareholding or the board of directors—see Ch.7), the short and long-term funding needs and what the long term exit strategy will be.

Issues of control of the company are considered in Ch.7 and will need to be the subject of careful consideration by the authority. In particular, the authority wants to ensure that the company does not become a renegade and continues to adhere to the chosen path.

So far as income or capital growth is concerned, the authority will need to decide what it wants. It might be that it expects a certain level of financial contribution towards revenue each year from the company's profits; or it could be that the plan is to reach a certain capital value by a certain date. Either way, the authority should be clear on what it is trying to achieve.

The latter issue may well be relevant to the exit strategy too. If the plan of the authority is to build up the capital value of the company to a certain amount by a certain date, it may then be intended to sell it to obtain a capital gain. On the other hand, if the company's purpose is to continually generate revenue that can be used to subsidise the council tax, then it will intend to keep the company indefinitely. Such matters should be considered as part of the business case for the company in the first place, as required by s.95 and the Trading Order.

A s.95 strategy could also involve outsourcing of the current in house provision in total, entering into a joint venture or trading via contract. Practical examples of the activities of authorities are considered in Ch.9.

Outsourcing the Whole Operation

One solution is to take part of the in house service delivery operation **3.26** (for example a DSO or DLO) and outsource it to kick start the s.95 activity. An example might be a building maintenance DLO where the authority determines to transfer its whole operation to a s.95 company on the basis that that company will then both provide services to the council and trade more widely using the people, assets and equipment transferred.

Whilst this is an option, it is not without difficulties, as discussed in Ch.8. The difficulties predominantly revolve around the ability of the company to undertake work for its parent local authority, without entering into further competitive tendering. As is pointed out in that chapter, any contract between the local authority and a commercial trading company (even where wholly owned) involves the procurement of services for which a competitive tendering exercise is likely to be required under the EU Procurement rules.

Another formidable difficulty is the effective outsourcing of the ability for the council to use the s.93 powers to charge for provision of discretionary services. In short, the local authority can only get the s.93 benefit if it has people undertaking work who will benefit from the economies of scale that can be achieved. In Ch.6 the example is given of undertaking grounds maintenance work for an RSL. Essentially, the council undertakes the work using its current capacity plus some extra resource that can be recruited using those powers. As a result, the in-house council's ground maintenance service obtains more people, better equipment and other knock-on benefits. Predictably, this will not be the case if it does not perform grounds maintenance work itself. Here, the only option is to get the company to do the s.93 type work (which will then ironically mean it is s.95 trading) but the only benefit the council gets is via the profits generated by the company rather than any consequential civic benefit.

Joint Ventures

Another option is the join venture option whereby a local authority joins **3.27** with others in order to provide services. Whilst it is possible for local authorities to join together with other authorities to form publicly owned ventures, it is more likely that authorities might join with a private sector suitor in order to give the authority the edge of commercial operation and experience. The significant advantage of a share based company is the ability for a range of share holdings and even of different types of shares.

An example emerged in 2004 of a district council that had a good DLO operation with a successful service base and turnover which sought a joint venture partner from the private sector in order to trade externally together. The idea was that the local authority's own work would continue to be performed by its own DLO; though the joint venture would look for new work from other authorities and/or the private sector in the relevant area. Obviously, if a local authority does want to pursue an option such as this, it needs to be clear on what it intends to get out of it.

Trading via an Existing Private Sector Company

3.28   The final strategy is to use the s.95 powers but without ever having formal ownership or control in the company that does the trading. In reality this is likely to be rare because an authority will normally wish to have at least a small shareholding so that it can take advantage of capital growth. If there is some share ownership, this would technically be a joint-venture company.

Section 95 is structured in such a manner that it is permissible for a local authority to engage in trading via a company owned or controlled by others. Put simply, this means that the local authority seeks a private sector company that has the capability and capacity to trade in a chosen area and enters a contract with that company whereby the company offers services on behalf of the authority. In legal terms, it is perfectly appropriate for the company to trade using the authority's name (as provided for in the contract between the parties). The sharing of profit would also be a matter covered by agreement.

An example might be provided by a police authority that offers anger management and dispute resolution courses via a trading company. It would be appropriate for the company to use the authority's crest, indicate that the courses are provided on behalf of the police authority and then to pay the authority 15 per cent of all income generated. In this way, the authority is "trading", though it has no share holding or other interest in the company undertaking the services.

Although this option may seem superficially attractive as a way of obtaining reward without risk; the authority must consider the potential reputation risk. It will be difficult for most authorities to allow a company which it cannot control to trade in its name.

CONCLUSION

3.29   Each authority has a range of powers which it may use to undertake charging and trading activity. It will need to review the availability of those options in the context of its own strategic objectives. Determining what the authority wants to achieve is probably the most important area of all in relation to charging and trading. This will set the direction or path that the local authority will go down and whilst the practical implementation steps examined in detail in Ch.10 are also important, if the local authority is on the wrong path, then no matter how well it undertakes its preparation, it will never achieve its ultimate aims. It is therefore essential that local authorities invest appropriate time in the work mentioned in this Chapter, do the necessary analyses that will underpin the decision and carefully determine the best way forward. There is plenty of advice on strategic planning generally, and with the material within this Chapter it should be possible for authorities to fit their trading and charging strategy within this wider context.

Part Two

Charging and Trading Powers

CHAPTER 4

CHARGING AND TRADING UNDER EXISTING POWERS

INTRODUCTION

Part I of this work outlines the legal framework of trading; and explains **4.1** that in order to undertake "trading activity" a local authority needs to indentify a suitable power which permits the activity. It then needs to exercise that power in a permitted manner; that is, the power must not be abused. The main emphasis of this work is on the two powers which were introduced by the Local Government Act 2003: the power to charge for discretionary services (see Ch.5) and the power to undertake commercial risk based trading through a company (see Ch.7).

Notwithstanding these new powers, local authorities have been undertaking trading type activity for decades, using other powers outside of those provided for by the 2003 Act. Those powers were not repealed in 2003 and remain available, to be used where appropriate. The Trading Guidance expressly mentions five of these powers at para.20. These five powers are examined below, along with some other powers which have been traditionally used for these purposes.

It should be noted that some of the existing powers authorise the undertaking of activities akin to municipal trading, which might be used in conjuction with the new powers to charge for discretionary services under s.93 of the 2003 Act. Others are specific and existing powers to charge. It is vital to distinguish between the two, as existing powers to act may be combined with the new powers, whereas existing powers to charge specifically preclude operation of the new powers. An example might be the Civic Restaurants Act 1947 mentioned below, which includes a specific power to charge for restaurant meals. This means that no local authority could lawfully use s.93 to charge for the discretionary service of providing meals. However, s.144 of the Local Government Act 1972 is a tourism power, which enables a local authority to take steps to attract people to its area, but without a specific charging power being inlcuded in the section. Section

93 of the 2003 Act may therefore be added to that power to charge people for tourism services. On occasion, it may be advantageous to use an older power as it may enable commercial trading with the private sector; as an example, the sale of spare computer capacity under s.38 of the 1976 Act may offer advantages over the power in s.95 of the Local Government Act 2003, as there is no linkage to the CPA nor any requirement to set up a trading company.

This Chapter outlines those powers which enable trading type activity to be undertaken, and offers examples of specific charging powers that existed pre 2003 and will still apply; it also looks at a number of special powers that are available to bodies such as the Greater London Authority and police authorities and forces; incidental powers will also be of relevance, as local authorities may have to rely upon them if the s.93 power is not available; the Chapter finishes with a summary of the law relating to the charging for use of "spare capacity" a practice which has largely been superceded by the new discretionary charging provisions in the 2003 Act.

As Ch.3 emphasises, it is important to plan strategically and then find the appropriate power to deliver those strategic aims. The most important powers which were in existence before the 2003 Act as described in this Chapter can in this context be considered alongside the newer s.93 and s.95 powers examined in subsequent Chapters. There are many other specific powers which exist; and this Chapter does not set out to be comprehensive. Instead the intention is to offer the reader sufficient information to make an informed choice between the three groupings of available powers. Once a decision is made to charge or trade, it is important to be clear which power is utilised and the advantages and disadvantages of the route followed.

KEY POWERS FOR CHARGING AND TRADING ACTIVITY

Introduction

4.2   It was mentioned in Part 1 of this work that there are three sources of charging and trading powers for a local authority to choose from, namely: existing powers, the new charging power under the 2003 Act or the new commercial trading power under the 2003 Act. It was also mentioned that the three client groups that can be the subject of such activity are the public sector, the private sector and members of the public. Whilst this chapter seeks to deal only with the existing powers to charge or trade, it covers all of the possible client groups. However, in order to avoid duplication, each relevant statute is considered below, with Figure 4.1 summarising those powers relevant to charging or trading with the public sector; Figure 4.2 summarising those that are relevant to charging or trading with the private sector; and Figure 4.3 summarising those available to authorise dealing with the public. Naturally, some key powers will be available in more than one group, for example the wellbeing powers under the Local Government Act 2000.

Figure 4.1
Charging or Trading With The Public Sector

Available powers include:

- The Local Authorities (Goods and Services) Act 1970 s.1
- Local Government Act 2000 s.2
- Local Government Act 1972 s.101
- Local Government (Miscellaneous Provisions) Act 1976 s.38
- Local Government Act 1972 s.111

Trading With Other Public Bodies—The Local Authorities (Goods and Services) Act 1970

This Act will be familiar to many within local government being a long **4.3** existing power for a local authority to enter into agreements with other local authorities and a defined group of public bodies, for the purposes permitted by the Act. The Act contains its own charging power (see s.1(3) below) which means that similar activity cannot be undertaken using the s.93 discretionary charging power.

The linkage to the defined public bodies means that it cannot be used for trading with the private sector, or with local citizens, which are the primary restrictions on its usage. Outside of those restrictions it provides an important power for public sector trading, which is not restricted to mere cost recovery (see s.1(3)); that is profit may legitimately be made from the use of the power.

It is a power which is mentioned in the ODPM Trading Guidance at para.16. This states that:

"The Local Authorities (Goods and Services) Act 1970 has served local government well. Authorities have made extensive use of these powers to provide goods and services to other authorities, both to make use of surplus capacity and to secure the benefit of economies of scale. However, the 1970 Act restricts the type of services to be provided and the bodies with whom an authority can trade. The new trading powers contain no such restrictions."

The reference in this paragraph to "surplus capacity" in this statement is an echo of an old argument relating to an implied (rather than express) limitation on this power which is discussed below in the context of the important case involving the Yorkshire Purchasing Organisation.

The Drafting of the Power

4.4 Section 1 is the key section. This states:

"1. (1) Subject to the provisions of this section, a local authority and any public body within the meaning of this section may enter into an agreement for all or any of the following purposes, that is to say:

(a) the supply by the authority to the body of any goods or materials;

(b) the provision by the authority for the body of any administrative, professional or technical services;

(c) use by the body of any vehicle, plant or apparatus belonging to the authority and, without prejudice to para.(b) above, the placing at the disposal of the body of the services of any person employed in connection with the vehicle or other property in question;

(d) the carrying out by the authority of works of maintenance in connection with land or buildings for the maintenance of which the body is responsible;

and a local authority may purchase and store any goods or materials which in their opinion they may require for the purposes of para.(a) of this subsection.

(2) Nothing in paragraphs (a) to (c) of the preceding subsection authorises a local authority:

(a) to construct any buildings or works; or

(b) to be supplied with any property or provided with any service except for the purposes of functions conferred on the authority otherwise than by this Act.

(3) Any agreement made in pursuance of subsection (1) of this section may contain such terms as to payment or otherwise as the parties consider appropriate."

Section 1(4) provides a number of important definitions, namely: "local authority", "public body" and "works of maintenance." The definition of public body expressly includes other local authorities, thus permitting one local authority to enter into contractual relationships with another local authority.

An important power is conferred on the Secretary of State by s.1(5) whereby that person may:

"by order made by statutory instrument provide that any person who is specified in the order or is of a description so specified, being a person

. . . exercising functions of a public nature, shall be a public body for the purposes of this Act."

This is the provision whereby the Secretary of State may extend the current grouping of bodies that are considered to be public bodies for the purposes of the Act's provisions. These are listed in Appendix 3. Control of the provisions is exercised through s.1(6) where the Secretary of State is given power to restrict agreements which may be entered into. Thus the power to extend the scope to new public bodies may contain express limitations. In passing it is worth noting that it is unlikely, given the new powers within the 2003 Act, that new public bodies will be added to the list of permitted contracting parties, though the 1970 Act is likely to remain an important power for the forseeable future.

Section 2(1) indicates that "nothing in s.1 of this Act shall be construed as derogating from any powers exerciseable by any public body apart from that section". This means that other statutory powers are not limited in any way and therefore this provides only one of a number of different powers that a local authority may use, including *implied* powers and s.111 of the Local Government Act 1972 (see below) as there is no "comprehensive code" which prevents the use of s.111.

The public bodies with whom a local authority may trade

It should be emphasised that the power only authorises a local authority   **4.5**
to enter into an agreement with a party which falls within the defined group of public bodies (this includes other local authorities, by virtue of s.1(4)). That definition has been updated to include local government reorganisation in London by the addition of the Greater London Authority, the London Fire and Emergency Planning Authority, Transport for London and the London Development Agency (see the Greater London Authority Act 1999, s.388). In Scotland the 1970 Act has been treated very differently, and is the main vehicle for charging and trading activity, as discussed in Ch.14.

Leaving aside the local authority market, there are hundreds of other defined "public bodies" which can provide a market for public sector trading activity by local authorities. Incidentally, this Act does not authorise individual public bodies to enter into agreements with other public bodies, a local authority must always be involved. The range of public bodies reflects the growing trend of fragmentation of the public sector since the Act was first introduced. In his book *Local Government Constitutional and Administrative Law*, Andrew Arden QC mentions the following from the list in Appendix 3:

"the Commission for the New Towns, the Arts Council, the British Film Institute, the Sports Councils, the Tourist Boards, the National Council for Social Services and the Council for Social Service for Wales, Crown Agents, H.M. Chief Inspectors of Schools, the Welsh Development Agency, English Heritage, as well as organisations related to hospitals, education, police, probation services, Citizen's Advice Bureaux, marriage guidance and family planning, community relations, community associations, old people's associations, nursery schools and play groups (pre-school and hospital), allotments, registered social landlords, social services, arts, sports, tourism, transport, small industry, industrial development, disablement, charities (*e.g.* WRVS, St John's Ambulance, British Red Cross Society, Age Concern, RSPCA, Richmond Fellowship, Samaritans, St. Dunstan's)." (at p.78).

Appendix 3 contains the full list of public bodies designated under the Local Authorities (Goods and Services) Act 1970, whether by Statutory Instrument or by other legislation. Appendix 1 sets out the relevant statutory instruments which have been made under the Act up to the close of 2004. More recent statutory instruments have tended to designate individual bodies, for example Special Purpose Companies which were set up to deliver PFI services to individual authorities (see for example, the Local Authorities (Goods and Services) (Public Bodies) (Trunk Roads) Order 1996 (SI 1996/342), as amdended by SI 1997/849). In view of the fact that no more Statutory Instruments on this area are likely to be made, this list may well be complete.

The services that may be provided

4.6 It should be noted that any trading activity must fit within the defined purposes of the Act; and must not be expressly excluded. Section 1 provides that local authorities may enter into agreements with other public bodies for four main purposes. These are the supply of goods or materials, the provision of services, the use of vehicles plant or apparatus (including the staff who operate them) and undertaking works of maintenance.

Authorities must bear in mind the restriction within s.1(2)(a), which expressly excludes from the ambit of the Act, any power to "construct any buildings or works", although new build may be permitted under entirely different statutory provisions, as indicated below. This prohibition prevents an authority for using this statutory provision to under take what might generally be termed "construction" rather than "maintenance." "Works of maintance" are partially defined in s.1(4) so as to: "include minor renewals, minor improvements and minor extensions".

The nature of maintenance may be planned or responsive and case law has determined that the value of the maintenance may be substantial, provided it is "maintenance"—see *R. v Hackney LBC, ex p. Secretary of State for the Environment* (1989) 88 L.G.R. 96. Minor renewals for example those often undertaken on housing stock would generally be regarded as falling within the scope of permitted maintenance (see the partial definition within s.1(4)).

The other restriction contained in s.1(2)(b) is that any agreement entered must be for the purposes of functions already conferred on the receiving authority. As an example, this means that the recepient authority must itself have power to undertake the activity which is being performed for it; therefore a district council in a two tier area could not use this provision to receive education services, as it is not an education authority (see Ch.2 for a fuller discussion of the meaning of "functions").

In practice it is likely that the greatest use of s.1 of the 1970 Act will be to support joint service delivery or joint procurement activity as prompted by the Gershon efficiency review. This would, for example, permit a group of councils within a single geographical area to contract with one of their number to provide ICT services across all the authorities for a profit, these being "administrative, professional or technical services" which fall within the ambit of the Act. As discussed below, there are other powers which would also permit this activity.

Implied limitations and the surplus capacity argument

The 1970 Act has suffered more than any other provision from the perjorative tag of "municipal trading". During the dark days of CCT, the Audit Commission issued a restrictive interpretation of its coverage (principally for the purpose of discouraging so called 'cross boundary tendering') and specifically stated that the Act could only be used if the authority had "surplus capacity"; by virtue of the fact that the Act was originally introduced to allow local authorities to enter agreements with public bodies in order to take advantage of economies of scale and to reduce costs by the sharing of resources.

4.7

Whilst this narrow and restrictive interpretation was accepted by the then Department of the Environment at the time, the Department subsequently changed its position in 1995, following the receipt of further advice from leading counsel. The uncertainty had been caused by an absence of case-law on the subject and therefore it was possible for different lawyers to give different views on the scope and usage of the powers; some lawyers gave a wide interpretation but others gave a very narrow view as to their scope.

However, matters came before the courts in 1997 in a case involving a purchasing organisation which had been set up as a joint committee. The YPO case (*R. v Yorkshire Purchasing Organisation ex parte British Educational Suppliers Ltd* [1998] ELR 195) expressly decided that the powers in the 1970 Act need not be interprteted restrictively and that there was no implied limitation that it only permitted trading where it utilised capacity it did not need for its own functions. The Yorkshire Purchasing Organisation was by 1994 employing over 300 full-time equivalent staff and operated in 31 local authority areas, outside those of its own members. It bought and held stock of educational and other supplies, which it later marketed and sold to local authorities and other public bodies. This practice of buying in goods and then attempting to find a market for them was clearly not an example of relying on "spare capacity"; but rather speculative trading. This practice was challenged by another supplier, BES Ltd, which argued that there was no power under the 1970 Act to acquire and store goods unless it had a pre-existing agreement under which it was obliged to sell them to a specific public body.

The court recognised that the purpose of the Act was to allow authorities to benefit from bulk buying and economies of scale; and that this could be "best be achieved if the purchasing authority is free to go into the market to buy in such quantities and at such times as sound business sense dictates, unconstrained by the limitations which would be imposed if it could buy only to statisfy already established requirements" (per Simon Brown L.J. at p.198 of the judgement). He then went on to state: . . . "that those enacting this legislation would have been surprised, perhaps even shocked, to see the limits to which YPO has taken it, I have little doubt. But I can see no basis whatsoever for construing this leglislation restrictively so as to prevent it" (at p.199).

BES Ltd did, however, succeed on a second complaint, which was that the Act did not permit the authority to provide a call-off service with third parties and take a fee from the activity under the definition of "administrative services." This was because the Act permits the entering into of contractual agreements for payment; and YPO had no agreement with the third parties to provide procurement services of that type. This illustrates that any activity must always fall within the wording of the statutue.

4.8   It should be noted that, in common with any exercise of a power, a local authority may be challenged if it "abuses" that power. Examples of "abuse" are given in Ch.2; and one example could be the geographical territory within which public sector trading was taking place. As an example, whilst in the view of the authors it would be possible for one authority to undertake grounds maintenance work for a neighbouring authority or one in the geographical vicinity, it would be much harder to justify this practice if the services were provided to a far distant local authority. This is because of the extra commercial risks which would be involved and the lack of linkage to the supplying authority.

Perhaps the greatest practical limitation (outside of the restriction to "maintenance") is that provided by the EU public procurement regime, which is discussed in the context of its impact on local authority companies in Ch.9. This provision impacts on the awarding of proposed contracts and largely requires the awarding authority to advertise any higher value contracts in OJEU to ensure satisfactory public competition. There are no specific exemptions which expressly permit one local authority to award a contract to another local authority without competition (although other exemptions may apply). The provisions of reg.6(k) of the Public Services

Contract Regulations 1993 (SI 1993/3228 as amended) which permits special arrangements between public bodies is discussed below in relation to s.101 of the 1972 Act. In the view of the authors, this provision would not exclude contracts under s.1 of the 1970 Act although the matter is untested by the courts and authorities should take their own advice on this matter.

The Local Authorities (Goods and Services) Act 1970 is therefore seen to be a key provision for local authorities seeking to charge or trade. As a full trading power (outside of s.95 and therefore not requiring a company) it is incredibly useful for authorities to work for one another and other public bodies. There are almost 500 authorities in the United Kingdom and a similar number of designated public bodies, giving extensive scope for agreements to be entered. The confirmation by the *YPO case* that it is permissible to trade speculatively and make a profit is very helpful. However, in the experience of the authors, very few authorities have made full use of their 1970 Act powers to date.

Figure 4.2
Charging or Trading with the Private Sector

Available powers include:

- Local Government Act 2003 s.2
- Local Government (Miscellaneous Powers) Act 1976 s.38
- Local Government Act 1972 s.111
- Spare capacity

Joint Arrangements—Section 101 of the Local Government Act 1972

4.9 The Local Government Act 1972 is perhaps the seminal statute for local government as it sets up the current system operating within the UK. Within its provisions is s.101 which authorises arrangements to be made for the discharge of a local authority's functions.

The Drafting of the Power

4.10 The first part of Section 101 states:

"(1) Subject to any express provision contained in this Act or any Act passed after this Act, a local authority may arrange for the discharge of any of their functions:

(a) by a committee, a sub committee or an officer of the authority; or

(b) by any other local authority".

The provision was added to by the Local Government Act 2000, to take account of the new executive arrangements permitted under that Act. In brief, the discharge of arrangements by another authority is prohibited where that function is the responsibility of the executive rather than the authority.

The purpose of s.101 is to confer flexibility on local authorities in the manner in which they discharge their statutory functions. Earlier legislation, such as the Local Government Act 1933, had used different terms such as "delegation" and "agency." As noted in the *Encyclopedia of Local Government Law* at para.2–209, the new phrase "arrange for the discharge of any of their functions" was intended to allow, "greater flexibility in organisation and enabling modern management techniques to be more easily adopted" as had been recommended by the Baines Report, *The New Local Authorities: Management and Structure* (HMSO, 1972).

This provision of the Act is expressly stated not to affect the operation of the Local Authorities (Goods and Services) Act 1970, nor the Local Authorities (Land) Act 1963 (see s.101(14)).

The power is widely used for agency arrangements; for example where the highways maintenance function which falls on the county council in two tier arrangements is actually discharged by the relevant disctrict council in its geographical area. In these circumstances an "agency agreement" is operated between the parties to determine the terms of that arrangement. This will include suitable terms for reimbursement; thus permitting trading type activity. One potential advantage of an agency arrangement over the use of s.1 of the 1970 Act (see above), is that this is a special arrangement between local authorities and is of an administrative nature rather than a contractual nature. As such it is easier to argue that the arrangement falls within the specific exclusion under reg.6(k) of the Public Services Contract Regulations 1993 (SI 1993/3228 as amended).

Regulation 6(k) provides that public tendering in OJEU need not be undertaken where the arrangement is between two different contracting authorities under an "exclusive right—(i) to provide the services, or (ii) which is necessary for the provision of the services, pursuant to any published law, regulation or administrative provision which is compatible with the EEC Treaty." Again, different lawyers have different views as to the precise meaning of this phrase but in the view of the authors it is at least arguable that the provision applies to agency arrangements under s.101 of the 1972 Act (in contrast to the position under s.1 of the 1970 Act); but again specific legal advice should be taken as necessary.

Outside of agency arranangements, s.101 authorises local authorities to act in a number of important ways. Functions may be discharged by joint committees, officers or even other local authorities. Innumerable such agreements have been made between authorities, although flexibility is preserved by subs. (4), which expressly permits the authority whose functions are being undertaken by another pursuant to an agreement, to concurrently exercise those functions itself.

As usual, Parliament did intend there to be some limitations on the **4.11** exercise of this power. Accordingly, a number of exceptions are included within the section itself and others are provided by separate and subsequent Acts of Parliament. One particular exclusion provided by the Act itself is the levying of rates, which can only be undertaken by the local authority for the area (see subs. (6)). A number of other miscellaneous exclusions exist such as under the Animal Health Act 1981. The authors consider that it can safely be inferred that such exceptions as there are exclusively comprise those which were intended by Parliament. Aside from these, it is perfectly proper that the section should be viewed as a wide and flexible power, reflecting the intentions of the legislature at the time of its making.

Finally, this section is a useful example of a situation where the legislature has fully intended the power to be all encompassing. Accordingly, by virtue of s.101(12) the power includes, "the doing of anything which is calculated to facilitate, or is conducive or incidental to, the discharge of any of those functions." This is a clear incorporation of the incidental powers parallel to those provided by s.111 of the Local Government Act 1972 within the section. As such, incidental matters are specifically authorised within the four corners of the original power and no recourse need be made to s.111 itself. This will permit the purchase of equipment and assets and so on to be undertaken by the local authority which is discharging the functions of another authority. It should also be noted that this wording is not "subject to the provisions of this Act and any other enactment passed before or after this Act" as s.111 itself is. In effect, once the agreement is lawfully made, the functions of the other authority effectively become those of the authority undertaking the function.

In practice it is likely that one of the main usages of s.101 of the 1972 Act will be to support joint service delivery or joint procurement activity as prompted by the Gershon review. It is possible, for example for a group of councils within a single geographical area to set up a joint committee and to delegate to that committe the responsibility of delivering various support services to the councils. This initial delegatation of the function to the joint committee would not, in the view of the authors, constitute a procurement activity which would trigger the public procurement regime requirements, due to reg.6(k) of the 1993 regulations as discussed above. That joint committee could then engage contractors (by following the EU regime where necessary) to supply the IT software and related services to deliver those support services.

Section 101 of the 1972 Act does not contain any charging provisions which mean the use of s.93 of the 2003 Act is not prohibitied for similar activity.

Figure 4.3
Charging or Trading with the Public

Available powers include:

- Local Government Act 2000 s.2
- Civic Restaurants Act 1947 s.1
- Local Government Act 1972 s.145
- Local Government (Miscellaneous Provisions) Act 1976 s.19
- Local Government (Miscellaneous Provisions) Act 1976 s.38
- Local Government Act 1972 s.111
- Spare capacity

Wellbeing Powers—Section 2 of the Local Government Act 2000

4.12   Section 2 of the Local Government Act 2000 is a very widely drafted provision which was introduced to permit local authorities to be able to deliver the community leadership role that the Government is keen to encourage. It is therefore considered firstly in the context of arrangements within the public sector; although its drafting is wide enough to embrace arrangements with the private sector and local citizenry. Indeed, when supported by the charging power within s.93 of the Local Government Act 2003 (see Ch.5) it is likely to permit most forms of charging activity.

Chapter 13 mentions the wellbeing powers in the context of the new environment in which local authorities operate. Local authorities had for some time requested powers of general competence, and the key power to promote economic, social and environmental wellbeing is very close to such a general power. Wellbeing powers were introduced to Scotland in the Local Government (Scotland) Act 2003 and are discussed in Ch.14.

The Trading Guidance refers to the underpinning provided by the 2000 Act at para.17 as follows:—

"Section 2(1) of the Local Government Act 2000 ('the 2000 Act') permits local authorities to engage in a range of activities including the provision of staff, goods, services and accommodation to any person, in connection with their powers to promote the economic, environmental and social wellbeing of their area. The power is constrained by s.3(2) of the 2000 Act which prevents authorities from exercising their 'wellbeing' powers simply in order to raise money".

Paragraph 18 of the Trading Guidance refers to the fact that the power to undertake commercial trading activity through a company (s.95 of the

2003 Act—see Ch.7); requires the authority to be undertaking function related activity (that is one which is legally permissible if undertaken not for commercial purposes). Section 2 of the 2000 Act therefore provides a useful underpinning power in this context also, because it widens the ordinary functions of the authority and therefore gives greater scope for the trading company's activities.

The Drafting of the Power

Section 2, provides: **4.13**

"Every local authority are to have power to do anything which they consider is likely to achieve any one or more of the following objects:

(a) the promotion or improvement of the economic wellbeing of their area,
(b) the promotion or improvement of the social wellbeing of their area,
(c) the promotion or improvement of the environmental wellbeing of their area."

There can be no doubt that these are extremely wide powers and were intended to be so by the Government. It is clear both from the terms of the Act and also from the circular guidance subsequently produced. It should also be noted that the drafting is "subjective"; in that the authority only has to "consider" that the activity is likely to achieve wellbeing; it is the aim rather than the result which is therefore important.

Section 2(4) provides some examples of how the power may be used, for example "to enter into arrangements or agreements with any person" (s.2(4)(c)), or "to provide staff, goods, services or accommodation to any person" (s.2(4)(f)). It is the very breadth of the provisions, which clearly permit a local authority to enter contracts with "any person" (including those in the private sector) which has excited interest from those wishing to pursue income generation activities. There are also powers to delegate functions to others, to give financial assistance and to engage in co-operation, co-ordination and facilitation of the activities of others.

Section 3 of the Act contains specific limits on the exercise of the power. The first is a limitation on using this power to circumvent other restrictions placed on local authorities in other pieces of legislation (s.3(1)). The second clarifies the fact that the power does not enable the raising of money ("whether by precepts, borrowing or otherwise") in s.3(2). This confirms that the wellbeing powers cannot be used as a form of indirect taxation or other money making activity. This means that any trading type activity facilitated by using the power within s.2(1) must be motivated by civic purposes rather than income generation and must be intended to deliver wellbeing.

The government argued that s.2(1) does not of itself provide a power to charge for the activities performed with wellbeing in mind, and therefore any wellbeing activity needs to be supported by another statutory power which would permit the authority to charge for those services performed in the name of wellbeing. Mention is made below of s.111 of the Local Government Act 1972 which can be added to a power to facilitate is use; but since the introduction of the specific charging power in s.93 there is generally no need to seek further for a power to receive payment. The combination of s.2(1) of the 2000 Act and s.93 of the 2003 Act provides a complete package of powers both to undertake a wide range of activity with "any person" and to charge for that activity; unless other charging provisions are available (see Ch.5).

The third limitation is that s.3(3) gives the Secretary of State power to make an order which prevents local authorities from using the wellbeing powers for certain activities. This limitation was described in Parliament as a "reserve power".

It is also necessary to consider the first limitation within s.3(1). The first point to make is that the limitation covers only *express* limitations and not *implied* limitations. Secondly, the prohibition only applies to a current, specific prohibition, as mentioned in another Act or subordinate legislation. An example is provided by s.1 of the Local Government Act 1986, which prevents local authorities from promoting political parties in official publicity. This is obviously a specific prohibition and it could not therefore be said that to promote a particular party in local authority publicity under particular circumstances somehow benefited the wellbeing of the community. That prohibition would prevent the use of the wellbeing powers in that circumstance.

4.14 However, confusion has arisen where limitations exist in an Act of Parliament that simply prevents the powers conferred by *that* Act being used for a particular purpose. A good example is provided above when looking at s.1(2) of the Local Authorities (Goods & Services) Act 1970, which authorises local authorities to enter into transactions for specified purposes but indicates that the powers are not to be used for constructing new buildings. This prevents local authorities from using the 1970 Act to undertake new build activities but, of course, does not provide a general prohibition to local authorities constructing buildings. Where another power can be identified for this purpose, for example in the Housing Acts for the construction of social housing, or the Local Authorities (Land) Act 1963 more generally, then this would be permissible. This distinction achieves enhanced importance when construing the provisions of s.3.

Local authorities also have to have regard to the guidance produced by the Government (see *Power to Promote or Improve the Economic, Social or Environmental Wellbeing—Guidance to Local Authorities from the DETR - March 2001)* though this was very positive in its content and tone. It specifically mentioned that in the past local authority enterprise had been hampered by restrictive interpretations of legal powers and that this new suite of powers was given to overcome that difficulty. It is important that the powers are seen in this light.

The exercise of the power has to be undertaken within the concept of a community strategy. This is triggered by s.4, which confers a duty on every local authority to prepare a strategy for promoting or improving the economic, social and environmental wellbeing of its area, and contributing to the achievement of sustainable development. Most community strategies are now produced in partnership with other community bodies, such as through the Local Strategic Partnership.

The breadth of the provisions included in this Act raised the spectre of local authority trading during the Parliamentary stage of the Bill. The Government Minister sought to scotch this talk immediately and said: "nothing in the Bill would change authorities' ability to trade goods and services, as defined by the Local Authorities (Goods and Services) Act 1970." This was a reaction to taunts from the opposition that the wellbeing powers are so wide that they would provide a charter for increased local authority trading. However, this debate was destructive in the context that it resulted in the government confirming its view that the wellbeing powers could not themselves be used to levy a charge. On the face of the provisions, this view seems misplaced but it created sufficient uncertainty for most authorities to seek to avoid using the wellbeing provisions for this purpose. This means that an alternative power had to be found and pre 2003 Act this was in the form of s.111 of the Local Government Act 1972, as discussed below. This will still be required if for some reason s.93 of the 2003 Act is not available.

The powers conferred by s.2 of the 2000 Act are very wide and it has always been inevitable that some local authorities would consider them to be useful in the context of trading. This is a difficult issue because many local authorities will lawfully undertake activities primarily for the economic, social and environmental wellbeing but might then indirectly generate income. In these circumstances, the primary and civic purpose of the activity needs to be examined; and it is important that the authority plan any such activity carefully with the correct motives in mind (see Ch.2). If the primary motive of the authority is to generate income, the wellbeing power should not be used and an alternative power will need to be found.

Catering for the Public—The Civic Restaurants Act 1947

This Act permits certain authorities to establish and operate restaurants **4.15** along with incidental activities. Section 3(2) requires authorities to use their best endeavours to ensure that their income under the Act is sufficient to off set the expenditure and therefore the Act contains its own implied charging provision; which would rule out parallel activity under the discretionary charging provisions of s.93 of the 2003 Act.

4.16   The Act has been much amended and the relevant provisions now provide:

"1(1) The following authorities, that is to say:

   a) in Greater London, the Council of the London borough or the Common Council of the City of London;
   b) elsewhere in England and Wales, the council of a district;

may establish and carry on restaurants and otherwise provide for the supply to the public of meals and refreshments, and may carry on such activities as are reasonably incidental or ancillary as aforesaid."

The Provision of Entertainments—Section 145 of the Local Government Act 1972

4.17   Section 145 is a widely drafted entertainment power which contains its own charging power within within subs.(2). By virtue of the charging power; this activity could not be undertaken under the discretionary charging power of s.93 of the 2003 Act. One unusual feature of the provision is that the authority may use this power outside of its own geographical area; subject always to the need not to abuse the power which itself would impose certain practical or geographical limitations. This is one of the existing "trading" powers mentioned at para.20 of the Trading Guidance.

Drafting of the Provision

4.18   The key part of Section 145 provides:

"(1) A local authority may do, or arrange for the doing of, or contribute towards the expenses of the doing of, anything (whether inside or outside their area) necessary or expedient for any of the following purposes, that is to say:

   a) the provisions of an entertainment of any nature or of facilities for dancing;
   b) the provisions of a theatre, concert hall, dance hall or other premises suitable for the giving of entertainments or the holding of dances;
   c) the maintenance of a band or orchestra;
   d) the development and improvement of the knowledge, understanding and practice of the arts and the crafts which serve the arts;

e) any purpose incidental to the matters aforesaid, including the provision of refreshments or programmes and the advertising of any entertainment given or dance or exhibition of arts or crafts held by them.

(2) Without prejudice to the generality of the provisions of subsection (1) above, a local authority:

a) may for the purposes therein specified enclose or set apart any part of a park or pleasure ground belonging to the authority or under their control;

b) may permit any theatre, concert hall, dance hall or other premises provided by them for the purposes of subsection (1) above and any part of a park or pleasure ground enclosed or set apart as aforesaid to be used by any other person, on such terms as to payment or otherwise as the authority think fit, and may authorise that other person to make charges for admission thereto;

c) may themselves make charges for admission to any entertainment given or dance or exhibition of arts or crafts held by them and for any refreshment or programmes supplied thereat".

Leisure Powers—Section 19 of the Local Government (Miscellaneous Provisions) Act 1976

Section 19 of the 1976 Act is a widely drafted power to provide **4.19** recreational facilities and crucially contains its own charging power within subs.(2). By virtue of the charging power; this activity could not be undertaken under the discretionary charging power of s.93 of the 2003 Act.

It not only permits the provision of the facilities themselves (for example a municipal swimming pool) but also attendant facilities "by way of parking spaces and places at which food, drink and tobacco may be bought from the authority or another person."

It is another of the existing "trading" powers which is mentioned at para.20 of the Trading Guidance.

Drafting of the Provision

The key part of Section 19(1) provides: **4.20**

"A Local Authority may provide, inside or outside its area, such recreational facilities as it thinks fit and, without prejudice to the generality of the powers conferred by the preceding provisions of this subsection, those powers include in particular powers to provide:

a) indoor facilities consisting of sports centres, swimming pools, skating rinks, tennis, squash and badminton courts, bowling centres, dance studios and riding schools;

    b) outdoor facilities consisting of pitches for team games, athletics grounds, swimming pools, tennis courts, cycle tracks, golf courses, bowling greens, riding schools, camp sites and facilities for gliding;

    c) facilities for boating and water ski-ing on inland and costal waters and for fishing in such waters;

    d) premises for the use of clubs or societies having athletic, social or recreational objects;

    e) staff, including instructors, in connection with any such facilities or premises as are mentioned in the preceding paragraphs and in connection with any other recreational facilities provided by the authority;

    f) such facilities in connection with any other recreational facilities as the authority considers it appropriate to provide including, without prejudice to the generality of the preceding provisions of this paragraph, facilities by way of parking spaces and places at which food, drink and tobacco may be bought from the authority or another person;

and it is hereby declared that the powers conferred by this subsection to provide facilities include powers to provide buildings, equipment, supplies and assistance of any kind.

(2) A local authority may make any facilities provided by it in pursuance of the preceding subsection available for use by such persons as the authority thinks fit either without charge or on payment of such charges as the authority thinks fit.

(3) A local authority may contribute:

    a) by way of grant or loan towards the expenses incurred or to be incurred by any voluntary organisation in providing any recreational facilities which the authority has power to provide by virtue of subsection (1) of this section; and

    b) by way of grant towards the expenses incurred or to be incurred by any other local authority in providing such facilities;

and in this subsection "voluntary organisation" means any person carrying on or proposing to carry on an undertaking otherwise than for profit."

This power has been extensively used by local authorities since its inception. It also featured in the *Allerdale* case where the provision of timeshare units was held by the court not to be within its remit.

Spare Computer Capacity—Section 38 of the Local Government (Miscellaneous Provisions) Act 1976

4.21   This statutory provision permits a local authority to provide computer based services from its own computers to third parties on a commercial basis. At the time the power was introduced the provision was intended to enable spare capacity on a local authority mainframe computer to be sold in order to encourage the authority to obtain a sufficiently large computer capacity for its future needs. Those drafting the provision can have had very little expectation of the extent to which computers have come to dominate all aspects of local government and commercial life some thirty years later. The drafting of the provision is extremely wide and would, for example, potentially permit an authority to sell computer aided design (CAD) services or CCTV based security services to the private sector at a commercial rate.

It is another of the existing "trading" powers mentioned at para.20 of the Trading Guidance.

Drafting of the Provision

Section 38(1) provides: **4.22**

"If a local authority—

   (a) has provided a computer for the purposes of enabling the authority to perform any of its functions other than functions under this section;
   and
   (b) considers that the computer can, without detriment to its use for that purpose, be used for the benefit of the authority in pursuance of the following provisions of this section,

the authority may enter into agreements with other persons for the provision by the authority of facilities for using the computer or of services provided by means of the computer.

(2) An agreement in pursuance of this section may contain such terms as to payment or otherwise as the parties consider appropriate; and it shall be the duty of a local authority, in settling the terms of such agreement, to ensure that they are terms on which the authority considers that a person other than a local authority could reasonably be expected to provide the facilities or services in question.

(3) In this section "computer" means any device for storing and processing information."

The drafting is clear and precise; it should be noted that the computer must have been bought originally for the local authority's own purposes not for trading activity and that the definition of "computer" is very wide (subs. (3)). It is permitted to provide "services by means of the computer", hence the examples of CAD or CCTV which rely on computer software but are basically services.

Section 38(2) provides a payment provision which rules out the parallel use of the discretionary charging provisions within s.93 of the 2003 Act.

Unusually, the provision also expressly states that the payment provisions should be "commercial" in nature and do not provide an indirect subsidy to the private sector. This limitation is referred to later in connection with the restriction in s.95 of the Local Government Act 2003 which do not permit those powers to be used where existing commercial trading powers exist (see Ch.7).

As with any power there must not be any abuse but leaving aside this general restriction the power is very wide and may be used accordingly.

Working Outside Your Area—Section 32 of the Local Government (Miscellaneous Provisions) Act 1976

4.23   This is a short enabling provision which is a supplementary power which adds weight to certain other provisions. Section 32 provides that: "any power to execute works which is conferred on a local authority by any enactment, may, unless the contrary intention appears in that or any other enactment, be exercised outside as well as inside the area of the authority."

This means that, for example, providing a power is found to construct housing works within the authority itself; similar power may be found to undertake similar works in a neighbouring authority. It is therefore a supporting power rather than a power of first resort as that initial power to construct works must always be found; assuming this is the case it could be used for new build which would not be permitted by s.1 of the 1970 Act which only permits "maintenance" to be undertaken in other authorities.

Section 32 does not contain any charging provisions which mean the use of s.93 of the 2003 Act is not prohibitied for similar activity.

INCIDENTAL POWERS

Section 111 of the Local Government Act 1972

4.24   Section 111 of the Local Government Act 1972 is probably one of the best known local authority powers. It provides:

"Without prejudice to any powers exercisable apart from this section, but subject to the provisions of this Act and any other enactment passed before or after this Act, a local authority shall have power to do any thing (whether or not involving expenditure, borrowing or lending of money or the acquisition or disposal of any property or rights) which is calculated to facilitate or is conducive or incidental to, the discharge of any of their functions."

The key word is "functions"; it is now generally accepted that the "functions" of a local authority include all of its normal activities. This relies upon the *dicta* of the Divisional Court, Court of Appeal and House of

Lords in the case of *Hazell v Hammersmith and Fulham LBC* [1992] 2 AC 1 where the term "functions" was given a wide definition.

The purposes of s.101 were made clear in the government circular issued at the time (DOE Circular 121/72) which indicated that the power was positively viewed by Parliament. It stated:

"The Act includes a new provision (s111) which puts beyond doubt that local authorities have power to do any thing which is calculated to facilitate, or is conducive or incidental to, the discharge of any of their functions, even if they have no specific statutory power for that action. This proposition has long represented the law (see in particular *Attorney General v Smethwick Corporation* [1932] 1 Ch 562), but the section has been included for the avoidance of any doubt which might hamper local initiative".

This provision was used for many years as the basis of any innovative local government activity and therefore has produced a huge raft of case law, much of it interpreting the provisions narrowly. In many ways it has now been overtaken by the wellbeing power of s.2 of the Local Government Act 2000; this is a widely drafted general power which was designed to enable authorities to undertake innovative activiites without fear of challenge. In a similar vein, s.150 of the Local Government Housing Act 1989 was intended as a charging power which would permit the government to control the ability of local authorities to raise revenue; this has relevance to the use of s.111 to permit charging.

Whether s.111 of the 1972 Act itself permitted charging when added to a power which permitted delivery of a particular power, itself containing no provisions relating to charging is a major issue which lawyers have debated for some time. This had often been thought to be the case and was so held by the lower courts in the case which finally came to the House of Lords as *R. v Richmond-upon-Thames LBC ex parte McCarthy and Stone (Developments)* [1992] AC 48. The case is summarised in Ch.2 and considered the duty to consider planning applications and the choice of the authority to offer "pre-planning inquiries" for a fee.

The House of Lords held that whilst the pre-planning inquiries were incidental to the planning function (and therefore permitted by s.111 of the 1972 Act); charging for those services was "incidental to the incidental" and therefore required use of another power. Outside of that restriction, which related to the lack of direct linkage between the activity provided under the statutory function (the duty to consider planning inquiries) and the charging, it is at least arguable that s.111 may be used as a charging power as discussed in Ch.2. As an example, in *Alexandra Palace Ski Centre Ltd v Haringey LBC* the authority granted a lease which permitted the tenant to charge for admission; even though the Acts under which the authority held the land as trustees did not empower charging. Nevertheless, in many ways the use of s.111 purely for charging has become somewhat of an academic argument in the face of the power within s.93 of the Local Government Act 2003.

SPARE CAPACITY

4.25   The use of "spare capacity" for trading activity will be well known to those who have followed the municipal trading debate for many years. In the absence of both the 2003 Act trading powers and the power within s.2 of the Local Government Act 2000, spare capacity used to provide one of the few grounds for interaction with the private sector.

What is Spare Capacity?

4.26   It has long been recognised that if a local authority has produced items for itself in pursuance of its statutory powers but has some left over, that these may be sold rather than dumped. An example might be a local authority nursery which legitimately produces flowers for a garden festival to be held within its area but does not need all of the flowers produced. What is the local authority to do with these flowers, is it to simply throw them away?

Another example of spare capacity arises in relation to cyclical work. A local authority's building department may have an expertise in asbestos removal which it needs to maintain but is not fully utilised on local authority work due to the planned nature of removal work. It would obviously be unreasonable to expect the local authority to discharge employees who it is known will be needed in the immediate future just because there is insufficient work in the meantime. What is the local authority supposed to do in the circumstances? Is it to allow its staff to remain idle or to undertake work for others?

Finally, the example of where some form of factory has been set up to accommodate the needs of the local authority and its production has temporarily dropped, thereby leaving spare capacity in the products made. This has arisen for certain authorities in respect of UPVC windows.

In the light of the Modernisation Agenda, it must be assumed that a Best Value review has been undertaken of all the major local authority functions and the above examples are normal incidences of local government operation. It may be that new horticultural techniques may be adopted which prevent the production of spare plants; or the window factory (having served its purpose) is sold. However, it is likely that some element of spare capacity (for example that of a cyclical nature) will exist in even the best run local authorities.

The authority therefore has a number of options. It could make use of the s.95 of the Local Government Act 2003 power and create an asbestos removal company which could trade commercially in line with those wide powers (see Ch.7). It could embark on a programme of environmental improvement throughout the geographical area of the authority using the wellbeing powes in s.2 of the Local Government Act 2000 which would be a civic benefit. It could charge for that discretionary service using the s.93 of the Local Government Act 2003 power (see Ch.5). In these circumstances it is difficult to see how the old debate regarding spare capacity needs to be reopened. However, this debate is summarised below.

The Legal Foundation of the power to trade in spare capacity

The legal basis for using spare capacity has long been uncertain. Old case law suggested that the basis may lie in prudent use of resources; something incidental to the fiduciary duty to look after other peoples' money properly. In the company arena (which led to the development of the *ultra vires* doctrine) there are examples of instances where the courts have upheld use of spare capacity as incidental to other statutory or common law functions. As long ago as the case of *Simpson v Westminster Palace Hotel Co Ltd* [1860] Ch.29 561, the House of Lords held that a company established for the purposes of running a hotel and tavern (together with incidental purposes) could let out parts of the hotel for use as offices. The facts of the case reveal that whilst the hotel was structurally complete, it had not been fully fitted out and the letting of offices would generate useful income for this purpose. A year later, the case of *Forrest v Manchester, Sheffield and Lincolnshire Railway Company* [1861] 30 BEAV 39 held that where a company was empowered to operate a ferry service between two points, it could conduct excursions when the steamboats were not required for ferrying purposes. In a later case, limitations were placed on this power which should be noted. This was the case of *D and J Nicol v The Trustees of the Harbour of Dundee* [1914] AC 550. In this case, the steamers maintained by the trustees for the purposes of the ferry across the River Tay were hired by them from time to time for excursions beyond the ferry limits. The House of Lords determined that this use of the ferry was *ultra vires* as the trustees had no specific power to operate the ferries outside of the limits where the ferries would be subjected to new risks and it could not be said to be incidental to their lawful operation. This sensible judgment revolves around a key issue which is rarely highlighted. This is simply that the activity was held to be *ultra vires* because of the differing nature of the activities to which the steamers had been put in comparison to that for which they were normally lawfully employed. In the words of Lord Dunedin, the pleasure trips subjected, "the boats to new and different risks to which they are subjected in the ordinary ferry business . . ." and accordingly were unacceptable. Had the ferry not been transgressing the ferry limits, then the decision would be in line with the earlier and rarely quoted *Forrest* case.

More recent case law also considered the matter. Particularly the case of *R. v Richmond-upon-Thames LBC ex parte McCarthy and Stone (Develop-*

4.27

ments) [1992] AC 48 where Lord Lowry gave judicial approval to the sale of surplus assets. He said:

> "The power to sell, for example, old motor cars for which the council no longer has a use necessarily implies that, in the interests of the ratepayers, the council will recover from a commercial transaction the return which any seller would expect to receive, as a normal incident of local government administration."

This statement did not form part of the main ruling (it was *obiter dicta*) and it was made in the context of the scope of the incidental power within s.111 Local Government Act 1972 (see below). This left matters on a somewhat uncertain legal foundation; as he seemed to be giving the view that the power is implicit and linked to fiduciary duty. One view is that utilisation of spare capacity relies on s.111; an alternative view is that there is an "implied power" to utilise spare capacity and that s.111 is not therefore necessary.

After decades of argument about spare capacity, modern judicial approval was finally secured in the YPO case (*R. v Yorkshire Purchasing Organisation ex parte British Educational Suppliers Limited* (1998) ELR 195). There an argument had been made by the BES that the Yorkshire Purchasing Organisation could not use spare capacity as part of its operations. Mr Justic Owen said:

> "Without more ado I accept the principle for which the respondent argues and accept that the legislature having given a local authority power to purchase eg educational goods for supply to its schools, the sale of goods generally bought for its purposes but proving surplus to its requirements, at the best price possible to other educational establishments, even private educational establishments, would be incidental to and concequental upon that power and would be *intra vires*."

This confirms, once and for all, that the concept of spare capacity does exist in law and can be lawful. However, in some ways this debate has been overtaken by the existence of the wide power of wellbeing supported by the charging power within s.93 of the Local Government Act 2003.

LOCAL LEGISLATION AND OTHER SPECIAL POWERS

4.28   Legislation which applies only to local authorities in a certain area is commonplace. Many local acts have been passed containing provisions specific to a particular area. A proliferation of such legislation has reached the statute book regarding the London area. Local legislation may be regional in nature, for example, the Greater Manchester Act 1989, or even broken down into a specific district, for example the Kensington and Chelsea Act 1972.

Local legislation performs a number of important functions, including the amendment of national legislation, the conferring of special provisions over and above those available elsewhere or the authorisation of a particular activity. As an example, the Birmingham City Council Act 1985 which authorises the city centre to be used for the purposes of motor racing on specified occasions. Such an Act was required because no general power to this effect existed at that time to permit the activity. The wide general power in s.2 of the 2000 Act is likely to mean that recouse may be had to this provision without the need for specific legislation in most cases of civic activity.

Different types of authorities may have been granted special powers which assist in trading activity. Three provisions only are mentioned, by way of example.

Section 25 of the Police Act 1996

Section 6 of the Police Act imposes the general duty on police authorities to secure the maintenance of an effective and efficient police force for their area. Policing objectives are to be developed in consultation with the chief constable; and published in an annaual report and local policing plan. **4.29**

Section 25 (1) of that same Act provides:

"The chief officer of police of a police force may provide, at the request of any person, special police services at any premises or in any locality in the police area for which the force is maintained, subject to the payment to the police authority of charges on such scales as may be determined by that authority".

Section 13 of the Education Act 1996

A local education authority is the same legal entity as the relevant local authority and therefore has similar powers, for example those explored earlier under s.1 of the 1970 Act. Nevertheless the LEA has specific powers of it own. As an example, s.16 provides: **4.30**

"(1) For the purpose of fulfilling their functions under this Act, a local education authority may—

    (a) establish primary schools and secondary schools;
    b) maintain primary and secondary schools, whether established by them or not; and
    (c) assist any primary or secondary school which is not maintained by them.

(2) A local education authority may under subsection (1) establish, maintain and assist schools outside as well as inside their area."

Section 30 of the Greater London Authority Act 1999

4.31   Section 30 is the general power of the authority and in many ways its drafting echoes s.2 of the 1999 Act. The drafting is of a framework nature and it contains limitiations within certain of the subsections (for example s.30(4) and s.30(5)); and the power may be supported by guidance given by the government (s.30(7)) through s.30(9)). Limitations are provided in s.31.
Section 30(1) and (2) provide:

"(1) The Authority shall have power to do anything which it considers will further any one or more of its principal purposes.

(2) Any reference in this Act to the principal purposes of the Authority is a reference to the purposes of—

    (a) promoting economic development and wealth creation in Greater London;

    (b) promoting social development in Greater London; and

    (c) promoting the improvement of the environment in Greater London.

The drafting also recognises the particular role of the Mayor (as executive) and the Assembly (as scruitinising body). The power of the Mayor is largely strategic and therefore this power links with the duties set out in s.41(1) relating to transport; planning, boidiversity, waste management, air quality, noise and culture.

SPECIFIC CHARGING POWERS

Figure 4.4
Specific Charging Powers for Local Authorities

Examples of specific charging powers are:

- Local Authorities (Goods and Services) Act 1970 s.1

- Local Government Act 1972 s.145

- Local Government (Miscellaneous Provisions) Act 1976 s.38 and s.19

- Local Government and Housing Act 1989 s.150

Section 150 of the Local Government and Housing Act 1989

As part of the pressure to permit trading type activity and permit cost **4.32** recovery, the government introduced s.150 of the Local Government and Housing Act 1989. This is another of the existing "trading" powers which is mentioned at para.20 of the Trading Guidance. Section 150 is a power given to the Secretary of State to provide power to local authorities to charge for various discretionary services. The power is exercised by statutory instrument. The Secretary of State has scope to control the pricing by setting a maximum, or a fixed amount or the like. The regulations are not available in respect of any current statutory provision which already contains an existing power or duty to charge (s.150(1)(c)).

The Trading Guidance, at para.20, instances the following areas where charges are permitted under this provision:

"HMSOs Charges for Registration Schemes, Recovery of Costs for Public Path Orders, Charges for Land Searches and Charges for Overseas Assistance and Public Path Orders."

In the light of the charging power within s.93 of the 2003 Act, which is a delegated power within the control of individual authorities, s.150 of the 1989 Act is unlikely to be used in the future. This will give authorities, rather than the Secretary of State, the control over charging.

Drafting of the Provision

The key part of Section 150 provides: **4.33**

"150(1)—The Secretary of State may make regulations providing that a charge may be imposed in respect of anything:

a) which is done by any relevant authority of a prescribed description;

b) which is prescribed or falls within a prescribed description;

c) in respect of which there is no power or duty to impose a charge apart from the regulations; and

d) which is not done in the course of exercising an excepted function.

(2) The regulations may include such provision as the Secretary of State sees fit as regards charges for which the regulations provide; and nothing in subsections (3) to (5) below or section 190(1) below is to prejudice this.

(3) The regulations:

a) may be made as regards services rendered, documents issued, or any other thing done by an authority (whether in pursuance of a power or a duty);

b) may provide that the amount of a charge (if imposed) is to be at the authority's discretion or to be at its discretion subject to a maximum.

(4) Where the regulations provide that a charge may not exceed a maximum amount they may:

a) provide for one amount, or a scale of amounts to cover different prescribed cases;
b) prescribe, as regards any amount, a sum or a method of calculating the amount.

(5) The regulations may include such supplementary, incidental, consequential or transitional provisions as appear to the Secretary of State to be necessary or expedient.

(6) No regulations may be made under this section unless a draft of them has been laid before and approved by a resolution of each House of Parliament."

CONCLUSION

4.34   Local authorities have been undertaking trading type activity for decades; well before the advent of the Local Government Act 2003. This actively relied upon existing powers which form part of the patchwork quilt of the statutory framework within which all authorities operate. Those powers were not repealed in 2003 and remain available, to be used where appropriate. The subsequent Chapters of this work consider the two powers which were introduced by the Local Government Act 2003. The power to charge for discretionary services (see Ch.5) and the power to undertake commercial risk based trading through a company (see Ch.7). However, it is vital that cognisance is taken of the fact that these powers may not be available if an alternative pre-existing power is available.

THE POWERS TO CHARGE FOR DISCRETIONARY SERVICES UNDER SECTION 93 OF THE LOCAL GOVERNMENT ACT 2003

INTRODUCTION

As mentioned in Chapter 4 the new statutory powers in the Local **5.1** Government Act 2003 will not always apply, hence the need for that chapter to have looked at the existing powers to engage in charging and trading activity, *i.e.* those powers outside of the new provisions in the Local Government Act 2003. This chapter looks at the first of the new powers in the 2003 Act, namely that to charge for discretionary services under s.93. Chapter 7 considers the final area, namely the new powers to engage in commercial trading activity under s.95 of the Local Government Act 2003.

Turning to the power in s.93, the distinction immediately needs to be made between powers to charge for discretionary services and commercial trading, governed s.95 of the 2003 Act. Essentially, the government is seeking to differentiate between two different types of activity. The first is the provision by local authority of a service by which it has the power to provide, but where the power to charge might be uncertain. The second is to enable local authorities to engage in full risk based commercial trading where appropriate. The simplest way to differentiate these two types of activity is to determine the essential purpose of the local authority's activity. Where the dominant purpose of the activity is "for a commercial purpose", then s.95 will apply; where the dominant purpose of the activity is a "civic purpose", then the activity will fall outside of s.95 and must be undertaken using s.93 or other existing legal powers. The authors stress the dominant purpose test because it will often be the case that there will be more than one purpose underlying each activity. As an example, essentially commercial activity under s.95 may still have some civic benefits, though these will be ancillary; by the same token, activities undertaken for civic benefit may result in income being received. However, it is the dominant or main purpose that will determine which is the appropriate power to be relied upon.

The government has made clear that charging for discretionary services under s.93 of the Local Government Act 2003 will have no relevance to the Comprehensive Performance Assessment introduced by the same Act. Whilst only those authorities in the upper three categories will be able to trade commercially, as described in Ch.7, charging for discretionary services will be available to all local authorities whatever their level of performance. However, this is subject to the disapplication provisions in s.94 (which allow the Secretary of State to take away the new power in s.93) and further provisions in s.97 of the Act (which permits the government to remove any other discretionary charging power). These are described below.

The government has supplemented the provisions in s.93 of the Local Government Act 2003 with guidance. By virtue of s.93(6) the "appropriate person" (in effect the Secretary of State) may issue guidance under the section and, "a Best Value authority shall have regard to such guidance. . ."

In November 2003 the ODPM issued the government's guidance. Entitled *General Power For Best Value Authorities To Charge For Discretionary Services—Guidance On The Power Of The Local Government Act 2003"* (the "Charging Guidance"), the Office of the Deputy Prime Minister explains why the power has been given and how it will work. The guidance is succinct, covering just over 10 pages and is written very positively, in a similar vein to the guidance supporting the wellbeing powers under the Local Government Act 2000. It should be noted that separate guidance applies in Wales, as indicated by Ch.14.

Substantive elements of the Charging Guidance are featured below when looking at the various provisions relating to charging for discretionary services. It should be noted, however, that notwithstanding the fact that a local authority has to have regard to the guidance, that does not mean that it actually has to follow it. It means that the local authority has to take into account what the guidance says and if it chooses another path, would have to have proper justification for that. In many ways, the guidance is so purposively written that this is only a minor issue.

The Section 93 Power

5.2   Section 93 of the Local Government Act 2003 gives a new, free standing, power to charge for discretionary services. Section 93 states:

"Subject to the following provisions, a Best Value authority may charge a person for providing a service to him if—

(a) the authority is authorised, but not required, by an enactment to provide the service to him, and

(b) he has agreed to its provision."

The first point to note about s.93 is that the power is given to the local authority direct. This is to be contrasted with s.95, where the power is given to the Secretary of State to authorise local authorities to act. Secondly, notwithstanding the fact this is a free standing power, the power is only to *charge*, it does not provide legal authority to *do anything*. Accordingly, the local authority must be able to identify its capacity to act elsewhere. As Ch.2 notes, capacity may be provided by general, specific, implied or incidental powers. Due to the extent of the new wellbeing powers provided by s.2 of the Local Government Act 2000, it may well be that local authorities most often rely on this as that legal authority. Alternatively, other specific powers might be available in appropriate circumstances. It is important to note, however, that local authorities may also rely upon implied or incidental powers (the latter being under s.111 of the Local Government Act 1972) to authorise activity and s.93 may be attached as a charging power to both implied and incidental powers. This is clear from the guidance which indicates at para.12 that matters reasonably incidental to an authority's express powers may also be used to attach s.93 to.

It is also worthy of note that the power contained in s.93 is entirely discretionary itself, *i.e.* it is not a *requirement* that any local authority has to charge for the provision of a discretionary service: such services may be provided free of charge, funded by the council tax, or be the subject of differential pricing, as discussed below.

The power in s.93 will be available to any "Best Value authority." Those authorities are defined in the Local Government Act 1999, which is the legislation that introduced the Best Value regime. As the government's guidance confirms, there are 552 Best Value authorities in total, including County councils, London Borough councils, Metropolitan authorities, Unitary councils and Districts; together with a range of other bodies undertaking fire, police, transport and waste functions. Included within the Best Value authority definition are also the Greater London Authority and its family bodies.

The Section 93 Activities

The s.93 power applies to what are generally referred to as "discretionary services." In the formal language of the Local Government Act 2003 this is expressed as a service that the authority is "authorised, but not required, by an enactment to provide. . . ." (s.93(1)). It should be noted that the definition of "enactment" by virtue of s.93(8) includes subordinate legislation within the meaning of the Interpretation Act 1978; in other words, legal authority provided by regulations, orders and statutory instruments will also comply. **5.3**

Essentially, the nature of a discretionary service is that it is not a duty, *i.e.* the authority does not have to perform the service and does so voluntarily. Such is the nature of discretionary services that often the legislation that creates them is silent about the prospect of charging, thereby meaning that uncertainty has grown up over time about whether charges could be levied, exacerbated by cases such as *R. v Richmond-upon-Thames LBC ex parte McCarthy and Stone (Developments)* [1992] AC 48. There was also a particular issue over different interpretations of ambiguous statutory wording. Accordingly, the government has granted this specific charging power. It is fortunate that most functions are discretionary in nature, with the modern legislative trend being away from direct imposition of duties by Parliament but rather giving local authorities more choice. This means that the s.93 provision is particularly wide as there will be literally hundreds of discretionary services to which it might be attached.

It is also important to comment on the fact that it is discretionary *services* that are covered by s.93. This has led some to claim that only services will be included, as opposed to contracts for *works* or *supplies*. However, it is perfectly clear from the Government's statements on this area that it intends this power to refer to *activities*, not only something that would qualify as a service, for example under the EU procurement regime. To adopt a more restrictive interpretation would be to frustrate the purposes of the Act, namely to allow authorities to achieve civic benefit by undertaking activities that have to be funded via a charge.

This is perhaps best illustrated by reference to the wellbeing power in s.2 of the Local Government Act 2000. This authorises *anything* that is likely to have the effect of promoting or improving the wellbeing of an area, not only any service that would do so. It would be a curious result if it was determined that a council could provide a traditional service, levy a charge and therefore realise wellbeing; but could not undertake minor works for a wellbeing effect or supply goods to someone due to the fact that if a charge cannot be recovered, they cannot be funded any other way.

Another early issue that arose in respect of the s.93 power is whether limitations are provided by the nature of the activity (whether it would in ordinary parlance be described as commercial in nature) or scale. The authors consider these to be little more than distractions as the legal position here is quite clear. The new power of commercial trading provided by s.95 of the 2003 Act covers commercial activity, *i.e.* where there is a "commercial purpose." If there is not a commercial purpose behind what the authority is doing, then the fact it is involved in a commercial transaction (such as providing discretionary services to a PFI special purpose vehicle under a school's PFI scheme) would be irrelevant. On the scale front, there is no rule of law that s.93 only permits marginal activity; provided a local authority does not offend the second limb of the *ultra vires* doctrine, its actions would be unreasonable due to their scale, then there will not be a problem.

The government has added the extra element into the new statutory **5.4** provisions of agreement by the party who is to be the recipient of the service in question. This is featured in s.93(1)(b) and is to a large extent stating the obvious. In the words of the statutory guidance, "authorities will not be able to require a person to pay for discretionary services that they do not wish to receive or use. The power will operate on the basis that the discretionary service is offered at a charge and that anyone who requires the service agrees to take it up on those terms" (see para.27).

In terms of examples of discretionary services, these are illustrated at para.10 of the government's guidance. This is reproduced as Figure 5.1 below.

Figure 5.1
Discretionary Services Offered By Authorities

Local authorities are currently involved in a wide range of discretionary services that include discrete areas of activity and examples of extensions to statutory services.

Some of the discretionary services most frequently offered are large scale, well established and are often regarded as part of the mainstream activities of the local authorities. For example, many authorities are major suppliers of leisure services, including sports, recreation and parks and countryside facilities, museums, galleries, theatres and concert halls. One metropolitan authority is now extending its galleries service by offering works of art on loan to local businesses and residents.

Extensions to statutory services include a range of advisory services linked to planning and development control. These are not a statutory requirement, but can make an important contribution to the operation of the statutory services. Local authorities have chosen to enhance their Social Services support by offering assistance to vulnerable young people and their families in the home, and supporting elderly residents leaving hospital. A district council in the South East of England is committing significant resource to providing key worker housing, going beyond its specific responsibilities as a housing authority.

General Power for Best Value Authorities to Charge for Discretionary Services—Guidance on the Power in the Local Government Act 2003 (ODPM November 2003).

Restrictions on the Section 93 Power

In determining whether s.93 will be available to a local authority, **5.5** consideration has to be given to a brace of restrictions, to be found in s.93(2). This states that the power in s.93 will not apply if the authority:

"(a) has power apart from this section to charge for the provision of the service, or

(b) is expressly prohibited from charging for the provision of the service."

So a local authority may not use s.93 to levy a charge where another charging power already exists or where Parliament has made its intention clear that the authority should not charge for the service in question. These merit further scrutiny.

In relation to the first proposition, this may not be as simple as it first seems. Obviously, the wording in s.93(2)(a) will cover specific charging powers included in other legislation. A good example would be powers to provide entertainments under s.145 of the Local Government Act 1972. By virtue of s.145(2)(c), local authorities "may themselves make charges for admission to any entertainment given or dance or exhibition of arts or crafts held by them and for any refreshment or programme supplied thereat." However, "has power apart from this section to charge . . .." may be interpreted to be broader than just *specific* powers. As noted in Ch.2, a number of different types of powers exist. Leaving aside *express* powers, (whether general or specific) *implied* or *incidental* might also be relevant. The authors have discussed elsewhere the argument that s.111 of the Local Government Act 1972 might confer legal authority to levy a charge but that this remains open to doubt. The s.93 power removes the need to rely on this argument and in the authors' view; the purposive construction of the Act would be thwarted if any other construction were applied to the limitation that this wording is intended to relate to *express* charging provisions, rather than anything else.

The second restriction referred to above is that a local authority will not be able to rely upon the s.93 power where there is a statute expressly prohibiting the levying of a charge. This is often the case where a duty is involved, *i.e.* the local authority has to provide a service such as under the Public Libraries and Museums Act 1964. Here, basic library services have to be provided free of charge and it would not be possible for a local authority to determine that the power under the Public Libraries and Museums Act 1964 should be added to s.93 in order to levy a charge. That said, it is possible for a local authority to provide alternative or additional services over and above those where levying a charge is specifically prohibited, as described below. A good example in relation to libraries might be the provision of a CD or DVD loan service, which does not form part of the basic service and where charges could be and are lawfully levied.

Policy Issues

5.6 The government made clear in framing the new powers under the Local Government Act 2003 that charging for discretionary services was intended to involve the recovery of costs only. It was mentioned in Pt 1 of this work that local authorities had eagerly anticipated the new powers of community initiative, granted by the Local Government Act 2000. The powers to undertake activities that promote or improve economic, social or environmental wellbeing of an area were particularly welcomed. However, the government subsequently confirmed that the wellbeing powers could be used to authorise various activities, but could not authorise the levying of charges. This came as a big disappointment to local authorities who immediately indicated that many activities would, in effect, be withdrawn as a result of this as they could not be funded from the council tax due to other priorities and if legal uncertainty existed as to whether charges could be levied, they would simply not be undertaken.

The government listened to these concerns and brought s.93 forward as the answer to them. The government's guidance at para.15 explained its aim:

"By providing a power to charge for discretionary services the government's aim is to encourage authorities to provide these sorts of services they would otherwise decide not to provide (or improve) at all because they cannot justify or afford to provide them for free or improve them. The aim is not to provide a new source of income for authorities, but to allow them to recover their costs."

It is therefore clear why the powers have been given and attention therefore turns to how tightly the provisions are drawn to limit income received exactly to expended costs. This issue is examined in detail below.

Calculating The Charges

In the experience of the authors, many local authorities have given a **5.7** lukewarm welcome to the new powers in s.93 due to the fact that they only permit cost recovery. However, it should be emphasised that the way the provisions are drawn provides a significant degree of flexibility on the part of local authorities as to how charges are constructed. The beneficial effects of this analysis are best explained by looking at examples, which are contained in Ch.6.

The government was clearly worried about this in advance of finalising the legislation as in the draft Bill that subsequently became the Local Government Act 2003, there was included provision for the Secretary of State to make regulations and for the amount of any charge levied by a local authority to be controlled. Naturally, this was the subject of significant criticism by the local government community generally and ultimately the government decided to drop the clause seeking to set out in detail how such charges should be calculated, in favour of more general provisions.

Section 93(3) now provides that a local authority is under a duty:

"to secure that, taking one financial year with another, the income from charges under that sub-section does not exceed the cost of provision."

The first thing to note is that this avoids any necessity for over-regulation by statutory instrument and leaves matters largely in the hands of local authorities themselves. Secondly, as described below, it recognises that income and expenditure may be monitored over more than one financial year. The government's guidance coins the phrase, "balancing the books" as a simple way of explaining the legal duty. Whilst this is a helpful simplification in general terms, there are in fact a number of important elements to be taken into account in this balance, as described below. The government recognises that this gives flexibility, "without having to have detailed prescription either on the face of the Act or in secondary legislation." It also recognises that there might be under-recovery, surpluses or deficits as time moves on, though indicated that these "should be addressed by an authority when setting its charges for future periods so that over time income equated to costs" (see para.17).

5.8   Having explained the basic proposition, it is necessary to look at a number of key elements that will be taken into account in the calculation of charges:

- *The definition of the service;*

    Section 93(4) indicates that the duty to balance the books shall apply "separately in relation to each kind of service." On the face of the Act, therefore, each "service" that the local authority provides requires a separate exercise of determining income and expenditure. However, that belies the fact that the definition of "a service" is left entirely to the local authority. This theme is taken up by the government's guidance at para.24 which indicates that the provisions "offer some flexibility to group services together when assessing compliance with the duty imposed by s.93(3) of the 2003 Act." In other words, either a narrow or a wider definition could be relied upon. An example of a narrow definition would be "the removal of wasps' nests" in which case all of the income and expenditure in relation to that activity would need to be separately determined. On the other hand, a local authority could decide that the service in question is "environmental services", with forty or more sub-areas coming under that service heading, including the removal of wasps' nests. If this wider definition is adopted, then hugely more flexibility is available to the local authority in terms of how to meet the duty to balance the books.

- *The time period;*

    The second area that needs to be examined in respect of meeting the charging duty is the time period over which the books have to be balanced. The only wording in the Act in relation to this is included in the duty itself, namely "taking one financial year with another. . . ." The exact meaning of this phrase is not entirely clear but it is implicit that more than one year must be involved. The reason why the provision was framed in this way was laudable, in that the government did not want to create practical problems for local authorities engaged in charging activity by constraining the income and expenditure determination into too small a time frame. Accordingly, the statutory wording indicates that more than one year can be involved and this theme is further developed by the government's guidance at para.22, where it is stated that, "the 2003 Act does not specify a period over which charges should be calculated: this is left to authorities' discretion." It goes on to say that authorities may find it useful to try a period of not less than one year and no more than three years, though in certain circumstances (such as where the costs of establishing a service would normally be amortised over a longer period) a longer time period than this may be chosen.

- *Methodology of calculation;*

The way in which the local authority calculates income and expenditure is also left to authorities' discretion. There are no provisions in the Act about this at all and the only official indication of how this should be done is to be found in the government's guidance. This indicates that "each local authority will need to establish a robust methodology for assessing the cost to the authority of providing each discretionary service." However, it indicates that authorities are free to decide what methodology they wish to adopt, though this would normally be based on the CIPFA Best Value Accounting Code of Practice. Whilst professional financial advice on this will be necessary, suffice to say the sort of costs that can be included under the Best Value Code are: employee costs, asset costs including premises and transport, supplies and services, third party payments and administrative costs. The government also indicates in the guidance that authorities may wish to take into account, "an appropriate contribution for corporate and democratic core and non-distributed costs, as those terms are identified in the CIPFA code, as part of the costs of provision." In other words, the government is happy for an element of central establishment charges to be included in the authorities' calculation of expenditure on any particular service.

- *Discretion in charging policy;*

It is also important to note that not only does a local authority not have to levy a charge for discretionary services, it can legitimately adopt a differential charging policy. This might entail ordinary members of the public being charged the full cost for provision of a particular service; students being able to enjoy a reduced cost with old age pensioners receiving the service free. Provided that the overall income and expenditure balance at the end of the day under the methodology chosen and over the correct time period, then this will be perfectly legitimate. This illustrates a further element of flexibility in that local authorities can fund the subsidisation of services to more vulnerable parts of the community using these powers. This is confirmed in Section 93(5) of the Act which indicates that, "a best value authority may set charges as it thinks fit."

It can therefore be seen that essential building blocks of the charge for a discretionary service are very flexible indeed. A combination of defining a wide service, in conjunction with a flexible time period such as three years, a discretionary charging policy and a methodology that includes all relevant costs, will put local authorities in good position. However, there are further areas that need to be examined in order to appreciate the full extent of the powers. These are considered below.

Key areas in relation to charging

5.9   There are still areas where uncertainty exists on the part of some local authorities about how the charging provisions work. The following are the main areas that need to be taken into consideration:

- *Total or Marginal Costs?*

    This one is relatively easy, as explained above. The Act simply provides in s.93(3) that it is "the cost of provision" that must be taken into account. The government's guidance makes clear that this refers to *total* cost rather than *marginal* cost. This is clear by reference to the Best Value Code of Practice by CIPFA.

    In effect, this means that if a person (or a share of an FTE), assets or equipment are required to provide a service then the full costs of all of those things can be taken into account in the calculation. This is particularly important where a local authority has to have an asset in order to provide a service, as that will permit the full cost to be allocated to the service. This is illustrated in the example in relation to loaning paintings from the Art Gallery included in Ch.6.

- *How do we Deal with Contingencies, Surpluses and Adjustments?*

    The issue in relation to contingencies, surpluses and adjustments also needs brief examination. As the basic rule of balancing the books is set down as a legal duty in s.93(3), it is important that each local authority complies with it. However, in practical terms, it may not be as easy as it sounds to balance income and expenditure. This will be particularly so if the local authority chooses a wide service area over which to make the calculation.

Fortunately, the government's guidance recognises this point and at para.26 notes that "there may circumstances where an authority inadvertently recovers more than its costs and thus generates a surplus. Where surpluses or deficits of income in relation to costs result from the use of estimated income and expenditure information or from unexpectedly high or low uptake for a service, such services or deficits should be taken into account when setting charges in the following period . . . . ." This means that where a local authority has chosen a reasonable time period over which to make its calculation, it has substantial flexibility in managing its operations. It may well be that a local authority is well ahead in terms of income in early years and needs to reduce charges; alternatively, it might be making a loss and the converse would be true in that it would need to raise charges. Either way, provided the books balance by the end of the time period across the service that has been determined, the duty will be complied with.

The issue of contingencies might also be controversial, but this should not be the case. Any organisation running services will wish to give itself a cushion in terms of its calculation of charges, in case its calculations prove to be inaccurate. In the view of the authors it could be lawfully be said that the costs mentioned above under the Best Value Code of Practice could include a modest contingency of 5–10 per cent. This would then come within the calculation of "cost" and the local authority would be complying with its duty under the Act.

- *The Prohibition on Raising Money;*

The issue of raising money has been at the centre of the problems in relation to levying charges for discretionary services for some time. In effect, a number of key statutory provisions in the past have given powers authorising local authorities to do things but have specifically limited the ability of the local authorities to use these powers to raise money. The obvious example is s.111 of the Local Government Act 1972 which, whilst permitting local authorities to do anything which facilitates or is conducive or incidental to the performance of a function, specifically states this power cannot be used to levy a tax; similarly, the provision introducing powers of community initiative in s.2 of the Local Government Act 2000, whilst allowing activities which promote or improve the economic, social or environmental wellbeing of the authority's area, specifically denied the use of these powers for raising money. In the past, those commentators who take a restrictive view of local authority powers have concluded that any prohibition on raising money would also prohibit the levying of a charge. The authors have always disagreed with this, believing that payment for a service to be a very different incident to raising money, which is more akin to levying of a tax. This point is examined in detail in Ch.2.

However, it was predictable that some might raise the argument that levying the charge under s.93 of the Local Government Act 2003 might be described as "raising money" and therefore prohibited. Accordingly, s.93(7) of the Local Government Act 2003 specifically indicates that the powers referred to above (namely s.111 of the 1972 Act and s.2 of the 2000 Act, together with s.34(2) of the Greater London Authority Act 1999 applicable only to the GLA) be disregarded when construing these provisions.

This is provided for in s.93(7) but it is a difficult provision to understand. Put simply, it provides that when looking at applying the s.93 charging power, a local authority can ignore the prohibitions in that other legislation on raising money. In other words, a local authority can levy a charge in relation to the use of well being powers, or the use of incidental powers under s.111, without offending the prohibitions in those various Acts against raising money.

This was clarified in a letter by Nick Raynsford, the Local Government Minister, to the Association for Public Service Excellence as follows:

"As you know, certain specific powers in other legislation preventing authorities raising money, including in relation to the well being provisions in the 2000 Act, are specifically disapplied in relation to Orders made under this provision. Thus, if a local authority wished to use powers set out in any order made under the new provisions and undertake trading under its well being function, there will be no potential conflict with the 2000 Act provision on raising money . . . . indeed by disapplying the restriction on raising money, the Act would actually pave the way to extending the power's scope."

- *Enhancing Services Performed Under A Duty;*

It was mentioned above that local authorities cannot use the s.93 power to charge for services that are granted to the public by Parliament as a right. Normally, when Parliament grants a duty *i.e.*, provides for a service to which everyone has a natural right, it will say specifically whether local authorities are able to charge for that service or not. In the absence of an expressed charging power the law would determine that no charge may be made.

However, an interesting twist on this scenario arises in relation to local authorities providing enhanced services over and above their legal duties. An example is mentioned above in relation to the Public Libraries and Museums Act 1964, where there is a legal duty on every local authority to provide a free public library service: though local authorities are able to offer enhanced services over and above the basic service from their library premises, such as loan services for CDs or DVDs. In relation to those enhanced services, charges may be levied.

This is recognised by the government in its guidance at para.11. This states that:

"Services that an authority has mandated or has a duty to provide are not discretionary services and will not benefit from the new power at s.93 of the 2003 Act. However, additions or enhancements to such mandatory services above the level or standard that an authority has a duty to provide may be discretionary services."

Another example is in relation to refuse collection, where the basic duty is to collect domestic refuse. However, there are various ways in which this duty may be enhanced, such as more frequent collections (the basic duty has never been clarified as to exactly how often the bins need collecting), or additional services in relation to recycling or bin washing.

Whilst the principle in relation to this matter is relatively straight-forward, and the two examples above are easy ones to envisage, the authors do foresee uncertainties in some areas in relation to this issue. A particularly difficult example is presented by educational services, where local authorities are under a duty to provide basic schooling free of charge. To what extent, therefore, could a local authority determine that having provided its free education via state schools, it will provide an enhanced service in the guise of a private school for which charges may be levied. This is an interesting scenario, because it is clear that the nature and scale of the enhanced service may actually have a direct effect on the performance of the legal duty itself. In these circumstances, it is by no means clear that this would be legally permissible.

- *Discrimination Against Other EU Countries;*

A small point, but one which is important to mention, is provided by the case of *European Communities v Italian Republic* (ECJ, January 2003). Here, the Italian government was subject to a case under EU law relating to concessionary rates for access to local museums, monuments, galleries and so on. The European Court of Justice held that any member state of the EU is not permitted to grant concessionary rates for access to cultural sites for its own nationals only. To do so would be discriminatory under EU law and prohibited. All this means if local authorities are to provide for subsidies etc they have to be non discriminatory in EU terms. In other words, if there is to be a reduced rate for students, this would need to apply equally to students from other EU states; similarly, if services are to be provided free to old age pensioners, this could not only mean UK pensioners.

Powers To Modify Charging Powers

5.10   As mentioned above, the government introduced the charging and trading powers as part of its new "carrot and stick" approach to local government following the General Election in 2001. On the one hand there is the Comprehensive Performance Assessment, with each local authority being graded into one of five categories; on the other there are the "freedoms and flexibilities" that are allocated in accordance with those classifications. This means that the better performing authorities obtain benefits such as inspection holidays and also access to new powers, in particular the commercial trading power under s.95 of the Local Government Act 2003 described in Ch.7.

The government made clear at the time that the new power to charge for discretionary services under s.93 was granted that it would not be dependent on CPA classifications. Put simply, any local authority, whatever its level of performance, could rely upon this particular power.

However, mention should be made here of s.94 and s.97(2) of the Local Government Act 2003. Section 94 is a short, but important, provision. It provides that the Secretary of State may "by order disapply s.93(1). . ." What this means in practice is that where the Secretary of State has exercised this power, s.93 would not be available for local authority to rely upon in order to levy a charge for the performance of a discretionary service. It should be noted that this does not mean that the authority could not rely on other powers that might permit charges for discretionary services; but it could not rely on s.93.

The power in s.94 enables the Secretary of State to remove s.93 by reference to particular descriptions of authority, particular authorities or particular kinds of service. This means that the provisions are very flexible and could be used to target a single authority that the secretary of state wanted to remove the powers from; types of authority which would enable a link to the CPA in future if the government so desired; or types of service, for example if the government became aware that local authorities were using this power to provide a certain type of service of which it did not approve.

The government's guidance takes up the matter at para.33, seeking to play down the existence of this power by claiming that the government would expect to use it "only exceptionally." The examples given in the subsequent paragraphs are: in the event of unfair competition; where an authority was found to be making a commercial return on charges levied; or where the particular service is not in the public interest. Local authorities will no doubt follow with interest the application of the s.94 power.

Section 97(2) is an even more extensive power whereby the secretary of state may "amend, repeal, revoke or disapply an enactment (whether passed or made), other than s.93, which makes in relation to a Best Value authority provision for, or in connection with, powers to charge for the provision of a discretionary service." On a normal construction of this provision, this would mean that the Secretary of State has, in effect, power to take away any other charging power that might exist in other legislation, including the Local Authorities (Goods and Services) Act 1970, and so on. Whilst this would leave a local authority completely powerless, with no way that could be arguably lawful to levy a charge for a discretionary service, the government has stressed that these are only reserve powers.

Administrative Matters

A number of administrative matters arise by virtue of s.93 powers. **5.11** Obviously, if a local authority is to balance the books in accordance with the duty in s.93(3), then it will need to keep records of its income and expenditure for this purpose. Where services are being provided to members of the public, the authority must be sure what the legal terms on which those services are based.

These matters are considered in Ch.10, practical implementation issues, and are not further examined here. The government's guidance does mention this matter at para.28, where it advises that authorities should make "appropriate administrative arrangements", which might include determining terms and conditions for the provision of services; information about charges (for example discounts, annual increases etc); and billing/payment arrangements. Also mentioned is professional liability insurance and regulatory compliance. All of these matters are considered in Ch.10.

CONCLUSION

The power to levy charges in relation to the provision of discretionary **5.12** services under s.93 of the Local Government Act 2003 is an extremely useful power that has been welcomed by local authorities across the country. There was clearly legal uncertainty in relation to the levying of charges under other provisions, particularly using s.111 of the Local Government Act 1972 or the new wellbeing provisions in the Local Government Act 2000. Accordingly, it has been helpful that the government has provided a new free standing power to impose such charges. The fact that the framing of the power is such that it is very flexible has also been particularly useful and the authors believe that this power will be widely used over coming years to engage in a whole variety of activities to achieve Best Value, community leadership and to promote wellbeing in an authority's area.

Chapter 6 considers some examples of how these powers may be applied in practice, illustrating their full extent.

CHAPTER 6

EXAMPLES OF USING THE CHARGING POWERS

INTRODUCTION

In Ch.5 the authors looked at the provisions in s.93 of the Local **6.1** Government Act 2003 in detail. It was seen that the Government introduced this new provision as an important free standing power offering the authorities the ability to charge for a range of discretionary services provided under other powers. The Government's framing of the legislation makes clear that it is intended to be interpreted in a purposive and positive manner, to allow local authorities to achieve key civic benefits.

The purpose of this chapter is to give some examples that demonstrate how these important powers work in practice.

It was seen in Ch.5 that some preliminary legal tests need to be applied in order to determine whether it will be possible to use the s.93 power. The preliminary steps can be summarised as follows:

- What is the Council's power to undertake the proposed activity?
- Is another charging power available?
- Is there a prohibition on a charge being levied?

These three preliminary legal tests are very important. Obviously, the local authority has to have the legal authority to undertake the activity in order to attach s.93 to that power to legally authorise the charge. Even once the primary power (which may well be the well-being power in the Local Government Act 2000) has been identified, it is necessary to authoritatively determine that another charging power does not exist. If this is the case, then the alternative charging power must be used and not s.93. Furthermore, it is equally important to authoritatively conclude that there is no prohibition on a charge being levied. These aspects of the preliminary work will need to be the subject of specific legal advice.

Once those matters have been determined, the local authority can then decide that s.93 will be available and attention turns to what services the local authority can provide and the charges that can be levied for them. Here, the duty in s.93(3) of the 2003 Act needs to be complied with, namely that income and expenditure over the given period, for the service in question, are properly balanced.

Included in this chapter are three examples. These relate to the three primary areas that will be involved in charging and trading activity, namely:

- *Charging the Public*: this involves the local authority providing services directly to the public and levying charges;

- *Public to Public* activity: this involves a local authority engaging with another public body or local authority; and

- *Public to Private* activity: this involves the local authority engaging with private sector commercial entities.

An example is provided below in relation to each category. It should be assumed for the purposes of the examples that the local authority has done the necessary strategic work outlined in Ch.3 and the practical implementation work mentioned in Ch.10. This would include elements such as preparing a business plan, ascertaining the relevant market (*i.e.* whether anyone else is providing the services and so on) and some form of risk analysis. The authors have pointed out that where charging activity using s.93 of the Local Government Act of 2003 is concerned, this preliminary work may be lower key than when a local authority engages in commercial trading under s.95, when it becomes essential. However, these are important matters that need to be properly capped off. It is also assumed that the local authority has chosen the service definition, the period of calculation and the methodology to be employed in meeting the duty in s.93 (3) of the 2003 Act.

Charging Members of the Public

6.2   The first example is in relation to services for the public and is a support service to the elderly. In this example the local authority has a population including a significant elderly element, but as this is a seaside area, many of the retired people enjoy a well off lifestyle, and poverty is not, in the main, an issue.

This elderly population requires support services and has both a willingness and an ability to pay for the right services. However, there is a reticence to deal with many private sector providers based on the fear of crime, poor services with extortionate prices and generally being "ripped off."

Services required by this group might include:

- Garden maintenance;
- Minor building repairs and maintenance;
- Painting and decorating;
- Security, including alarms, locks, fences and grilles;
- Emergency help call out;
- Shopping;
- Transport;
- Advice whether including consumer matters, legal or financial.

These services are simply not available in any comprehensive way in this particular area and the local authority has determined this by appropriate enquiries as discussed in Ch.10. The local authority therefore devises a discretionary support service to the elderly. The council could seek to be involved in many of the areas mentioned above but the example featured below is simply on the issue of building maintenance.

As usual, the three preliminary legal tests need to be applied:

- What is the council's power to act? Here it would be s.2 of the Local Government Act 2000, *i.e.*, the wellbeing powers. The primary element here would be *social* wellbeing, evidenced by the community safety elements, fear of crime etc in this elderly population. There would also be other social benefits consequential upon the operation of the services available from differential pricing and described below.

  It is unlikely that there would be any issue in relation to the powers of the local authority to provide this service but should this be the case other avenues of legal authority would be available. An example would be s.111 of the Local Government Act 1972 which permits a local authority to do anything that facilitates or is conducive or incidental to the performance of any of its functions. In order to provide functions local authorities need buildings and it would be incidental to the ownership of any building to provide building maintenance. If a local authority is able to provide building services for its own buildings then under s.93, it can provide them to others.

- Is there another charging power available?—the answer to this is no.
- Is there a prohibition to charging?—the answer to this is no.

6.3 Having gone through the preliminary tests, the council concludes that it can use the s.93 charging power, plus wellbeing, to provide this service.

In this particular example the client is a member of the public and there may therefore be policy reasons why the local authority wishes to limit the charges. However, if its market research indicates that the vast majority of the clients can meet the charges, then this may not be the case. Obviously, if the council wants to benefit other parts of the community with the income (*i.e.* by differential pricing) it needs to ensure that appropriate charges are made.

The duty in s.93(3) of the Local Government Act 2003 requires that income must equate to expenditure, over the given time period, for the service in question. Here, the expenditure to be taken into account could include the following:

- People undertaking the work, including plumbers, plasterers and electricians; it may well be the case that the authority has to recruit new staff for this purpose;

- The cost of assets, *e.g.*, depot space;

- The cost of vehicles used by the people in question; it may be that new vehicles will be needed;

- The cost of equipment including electrical circuit checkers and other tools;

- The cost of disposables including fuse wire, plaster, bricks and cement; and

- Plus a share of central establishment charges as described in Ch.5.

It is obviously the case that to provide such a service would be beneficial to the recipients of that minor building maintenance. Those people would be pleased that they are able to obtain services offering value for money from a body that has an excellent covenant, is trustworthy, employs appropriately trained staff and which operates proper systems of security.

However, other consequential advantages might be achieved via this service also. These may include the following:

- Differential pricing benefits are possible; this means that the ones who can pay for such services do pay the full cost and the services are also provided by the Council to others who cannot pay, either on a reduced rate or in some circumstances free of charge;

- The local authority could develop a whole team of people doing this work that would expand the services and achieve a greater well being effect;

- The benefits achieved could assist in supporting the council's social services and housing functions. One example would be that by keeping people out of social housing or care homes by supporting them in their own homes in this way, the council is improving its social services and housing functions, as space in social housing and care homes is under severe pressure. Those providing the services may also develop close liaison links with social services and other professionals working within the authority for the benefit of clients of those departments;

- This work could be linked to other important work such as disabled access and home modifications, where the council is involved in giving grants; and

- The costs may support the giving of extra training to staff and the purchase of new equipment.

Again, this is an excellent example of the s.93 provisions in practice. Whilst the council would have no requirement to provide services that are freely and properly available elsewhere, it may well wish to develop services where there is a gap in the market. Depending on the take up of these services, there is no reason that the council could not add significant additional services (such as shopping, advice etc) into this package. Indeed, the council could also transfer the funding arrangements of such services onto a subscription service provided that the duty in s.93(3) is properly observed. If this were to be the case then the Council would know in advance the funds that it would have available and could then gauge the discretionary pricing elements accordingly.

There may be issues of risk, for example, if the local authority was required to get into areas where it did not have the appropriate expertise or capacity. The example is predicated on the basis that the authority would only be undertaking those services that it currently provides elsewhere. Whilst it would not be legally prohibited in developing new services, this would raise new risks that would need to be properly considered.

Public to Public Charging

The second area to look at is public to public activity. Working for the public sector will always be attractive, as it goes without saying that any work or services rendered to another public body will usually involve some civic benefit to the area in question. However, the vast majority of public to public charging and trading will be undertaken via the Local Authorities (Goods and Services) Act (1970) (see Ch.4), rather than under the provisions of s.93 of the Local Government Act 2003. As Chapter 4 points out, the Goods and Services Act permits a local authority to enter an agreement for four specified purposes with another designated public body, the definition of which includes local authorities. **6.4**

Not all public bodies are designated as such under the provisions of the 1970 Act though. The various Orders that have been made under the 1970

Act (see Appendix 3) are predominantly old (for example the Local Authorities (Goods and Services) (Public Bodies) Order 1975—SI 1975/193, which designated bodies such as the Association of Metropolitan Authorities, the Association of District Councils and the Association of County Councils) and there have been many changes in the nature of public bodies since (for example these three bodies have now been superseded by the Local Government Association). The first instance where a problem may arise, therefore, is where a designated body has ceased to exist and the new body has not been designated under the 1970 Act.

The second scenario is where a body has never been designated. It is unclear, in some circumstances, whether other public bodies should have been included but were not or were deliberately omitted for some policy reason. Nonetheless, bodies such as the BBC, the Post Office and British Coal are examples of bodies that the Government itself considered to be public bodies but are not covered by any designation under the 1970 Act. Part X of the Local Government Planning and Land Act 1980 was enacted to permit action by the Secretary of State against local authorities and other public bodies in relation to superfluous land holdings. Under these old provisions, the three organisations mentioned are public bodies—thereby enabling the Secretary of State to act against them—but they are not so for 1970 Act purposes *i.e.* a local authority cannot enter a specified agreement with them.If a local authority wanted to contract with any public body in this category, then it would not be able to avail itself of the 1970 Act and would need to use the 2003 Act provisions.

It is worth making the point that the government sees no need to further extend the list of public bodies under the 1970 Act, now that the new provisions are available. Accordingly, it would be very difficult—if not impossible—to get a new designation approved by the ODPM.

The example featured below applies to a residential social landlord that is providing housing services for the public sector but is not a housing association under the Housing Act 1996. Whilst the Housing Associations Act 1985 created housing associations that were subsequently designated under the 1970 Act (see the 1975 Order mentioned above), the Housing Act 1996 permitted bodies other than housing associations to be residential social landlords. This means that a housing association will be a designated body but an RSL that is not a housing association will not. As such, the Local Authorities (Goods and Services) Act 1970 will not be available in that latter instance.

The example is in relation to grounds maintenance on the garden areas provided as part of the housing of that residential social landlord, carried out within the area of the local authority. This would utilise the wellbeing power, plus s.93 of the 2003 Act, although it should be noted that the local authority may have to tender for this work under the EU Public Procurement Regime, depending on the value of work concerned.

So in order to determine whether the local authority can undertake grounds maintenance work the following preliminary stages would need to be applied:

- What power does the local authority have to act? Here the power would be provided the provisions of s.2 of the Local Government Act 2000, *i.e.*, the wellbeing powers. The local authority would need to make the case that the wellbeing powers would apply but it would seem that grounds maintenance work would be relevant to the environmental wellbeing of the area: it may also be the case that the social wellbeing of the tenants in the housing accommodation would be benefited by such services. The local authority would need to prepare its case accordingly.

- Is there another charging power available?—the answer to this would be no;

- Is there a prohibition on charging for such services? —the answer to this would also be no.

Having undertaken these preliminary stages, and having come to the conclusion that the s.93 power will be available, the issue then turns to what can the local authority charge for these services? **6.5**

The duty in s.93(3) of the Local Government Act 2003 requires income to equate to expenditure, over the given period, in relation to the services in question. As this service is being provided to another independent public body, the local authority will wish to recover its full costs in the provision of the services. In calculating the charges to be levied, the following expenditure can be included:

- The cost of people undertaking the work, *e.g.* the gardeners; this may well include the recruitment of new staff to undertake this work;

- The cost of assets employed, *e.g.* depot space; in this regard, changes may need to be made to the current arrangements that the council operates;

- The cost of vehicles required for the services, *e.g.* open backed wagons; again, new vehicles may need to be procured for the purposes of the new services;

- The cost of equipment, *e.g.* rollers, mowers and rakes;

- The cost of disposables, *e.g.* plants, weed killer and fertiliser; and

- A share of central establishment charges as described in Ch.5.

It should be noted that the *total* cost of these services, not the *marginal* cost, can be taken into account. Any equipment that might be specifically required for these services can therefore be purchased and the full costs applied to the calculation under s.93(3).

A number of advantages might arise from this type of arrangement, over and above the obvious civic or wellbeing effect that the new service is designed to create. This may include:

- More staff to undertake the services; this might have a knock on capacity impact on the local authority's own work, as more people will be employed and more flexibility available in staff rotas;

- Purchase of new equipment; it might be that better or more modern equipment is needed and this will then be available to use on the authority's own work as well;

- Training; it may be that further or better training for staff engaged on these services is needed, which would then have a knock on effect on the workforce generally, as staff may rotate and therefore everyone needs to be included in such training;

- Efficiency gains; reviewing the current operation of the system, including the staffing, application of equipment etc. This may lead the council to derive greater efficiencies in the operation of the overall services;

- Procurement; the council may derive procurement benefits from the purchase of goods and supplies due to greater quantities;

All of these aspects should generally result in a better organised and supported service to the local authority itself for grounds maintenance.

Public to Private Charging

6.6   The final area is in relation to charging the private sector. Here there may well be greater risk than in the other two areas. Where one public body is assisting another in relation to some public service, it is unlikely that difficulties would arise in the relationship and even if there was contractual default, the nature of the bodies and service would suggest that practical solutions would be sought out. However, when a local authority is providing a service to the private sector, it should expect to be treated exactly the same as any other provider; this may well mean enforcement and damages if there is a breach of contract. For this reason, local authorities may regard this area as the least attractive of the three examined under charging powers. Nonetheless, there are some good opportunities to be had here, as the example below demonstrates.

Here the example is the loan of art works to private sector corporate bodies. The facts are based on a city council that has an art gallery, housing a substantial (though ageing) art collection. The collection includes ethnic art from local artists linked to the region. The art gallery is on a city centre site but only displays 50 per cent of the total works with the rest being in storage at the back of the gallery premises. The council supports the arts and the members genuinely believe that the art gallery performs an important public function, though it has difficulty in being financially supported in competition with funding more pressing educational and social services needs. The art gallery has a backlog of problems of repair, restoration and other cleaning to the art work. The collection is not catalogued and has no IT support.

The local authority therefore decides to use the s.93 route to develop a new service to loan art works to corporate bodies in the city, as a number of major companies have their headquarters in this area. It is assumed that there is a market for this service and that local businesses would wish to avail themselves of it.

In order to determine whether s.93 will be available, the preliminary legal tests need to be addressed as follows:—

- What is our power to undertake this activity? This would be s.2 of the Local Government Act, *i.e.* the wellbeing powers. It could be argued that social wellbeing of the area would be improved by having art works that would otherwise be in storage and not be displayed to anyone displayed in these corporate headquarters. There would also be economic benefits to the local authority in its ability to buy more art.
- Is there another power to charge?—The answer here is no.
- Is there a prohibition to charging?—The answer to this is no.

The council concludes that it can use the s.93 charging provision together with the wellbeing power.

The attention then turns to what the local authority may charge for this service? Here there is a corporate client and therefore the "going rate" may be higher than in relation to a service provided to members of the public. In other words, there would be no policy issues requiring the subsidisation of charges.

The duty in s.93(3) of the Local Government Act 2003 requires income to equate to expenditure, over the given period, for the service in question. Here the expenditure could include the following:

- Cataloguing the whole art collection; this would be necessary in order to keep a proper record of the art works being loaned out.
- Cleaning, restoration and repair of the whole collection; this would be necessary as the art will be rotated and all art works in the collection may be the subject of loan at some stage.

- Reviewing the security arrangements in the art gallery for the transportation of items and in the general operation of the scheme; it is important to ensure that proper security arrangements are maintained and that this may well necessitate a preliminary review.

- Modifications to the art gallery to ensure the swift turnaround of the art and to better facilitate the new services; at the start, having the art works that are not being displayed in cupboards at the back of the art gallery does not facilitate their easy circulation under the new services. It is therefore perfectly reasonable to undertake some modifications to the fabric of the art gallery to facilitate this.

- Modifications to the art gallery for security under the new arrangements; this may include the security relating to the rotation of artworks.

- Purchase of assets, *e.g.* a vehicle to transport the art to the new corporate clients; any such vehicle would have to be properly secure and be an appropriate vehicle for this purpose, with a GPS system and other key facets.

- Establishing an appropriate staffing of the services, including share of the curator time to choose the most appropriate art to supply, security time to load the transport and ensure delivery, plus administrative support.

- Establishing the administrative functions in support; this would include office, IT, finance and legal input, billing and customer care systems.

6.7   Chapter 4 makes clear that it is the *total* cost of the steps mentioned above, not the *marginal* cost that can be taken into account. The rule of thumb should be that if something is *required* to provide the service then its full cost should be counted in the calculation of expenditure.

In relation to the art gallery, this means that the full costs of establishing and running the scheme could well be in excess of £200,000, thereby allowing the local authority to charge 20 corporate enterprises £10,000 per annum for the benefit of the service.

Some costs included in the list above may be one off costs, *e.g.* purchase of the vehicle and the building works to the art gallery; however, other new costs may be incurred as the services take off. An obvious cost associated with this particular service is the purchase of new art to include in the scheme. It is therefore unlikely that the local authority would be in a position whereby it had to reduce the charges.

The purpose of this scheme is civic benefit in terms of improving the wellbeing of the community in social and economic terms. This is a lawful purpose and will authorise the commissioning of the scheme. However, there are a number of consequential effects that will be beneficial to the local authority as follows:

- An improved art gallery for the people of the city in general; in particular this may include the better running of the establishment, more staff being available, cleaner, better quality art presented in a more professional manner;

- The costs of the new service will be charged to the private sector but there will be a consequential benefit to the council taxpayers of the area, partly because they are getting services that would not otherwise have been achieved, such as the cataloguing of the arts and the repair and restoration work; and they are not subsequently paying for elements of the art gallery's operation that would have fallen on the council tax.

This example illustrates really well the flexibility of s.93 provisions and how they can be used imaginatively. Provided the purposes is properly civic benefit rather than any commercial gain the resultant benefits will be lawful.

CONCLUSION

The new power to charge for discretionary services under s.93 of the **6.8** Local Government Act 2003 is a very flexible power. It is likely to be extremely useful to local authorities in the provision of services more generally and, as the examples show, can have significant civic benefits. These will be in kind rather than in cash but may nonetheless be important and be attractive to members. An example is the consequential improvement to the general service delivery on the back of the new equipment and assets, better training and the like funded through the discretionary services.

There are numerous other examples that the authors could give using s.93. Figure 6.1 gives some suggestions that have already been made by local authorities across the country. It is unnecessary to go through each and every example as the same "system" applies to each proposal. This system is explained in relation to each of the examples above and requires the preliminary legal tests to be applied, followed by a proper determination of what expenditure can lawfully be taken into account.

Figure 6.1
Possible Discretionary Services for Use with S93 of the Local Government Act 2003

- Loaning works of art to local businesses from art galleries, museum exhibits from museums etc;

- Earlier access to premises at an extra charge;

- Additional cleaning services, lighting or other benefits to city centre premises;

- Accounting and other professional services for small business/ charities;

- Recruitment services for social enterprise ventures;

- Catering services to promote nutritional standards, provision of specialist ethnic meals etc;

- Landscaping and grounds maintenance to areas adjacent to council property;

- Archives—whether selling copies of important documents, arranging viewings etc, including rare books;

- exploitation of a local authority's own intellectual property;

- Use of locations for filming, *e.g.* city hall for the Greater London Authority, hiring out buildings and guided tours;

- Civic ceremonies, weddings and other meetings including catering and other services;

- Provision of design services for relevant functions, *e.g.* educational design;

- Training on relevant areas, *e.g.* community safety;

- Undertaking work to allow for disabled access;

- Advisory services including how to apply for government grants, permissions and consents;

- Specialist cleaning, such as deep cleaning in restaurants to meet stringent food hygiene regulations;

- Translation services;

- Graffiti removal for private businesses;

- Creation of ID cards, security passes and the like;

- Services for the elderly including shopping, gardening, cleaning and security;

- Building maintenance including Disability Discrimination Act, gas equipment servicing, health and safety checks, asbestos surveys and remedial work, maintenance and installation of stair lifts, passenger lists and goods lifts, equipment testing generally;

- Secondment of specialist staff to other organisations.

Once these principles are understood then local government officers will be able to apply the rules to any area of service. However, the authors should stress that legal advice should be sought on each opportunity, as difficulties will arise if the tests are not applied properly.

Examples of the sort of costs that can be taken into account in relation to such activities are illustrated in Figure 6.2. Many of these elements have already been seen in the examples cited above.

Figure 6.2
Examples of "Costs" That Can Be Taken Into Account In Relation To The s.93 Charging Power

- Recruitment of staff;

- Rearrangement of assets, to facilitate new services;

- Purchase of vehicles and equipment;

- Purchase of supplies, goods and disposables;

- Physical works to buildings to adapt accommodation, create public reception areas etc;

- Review of security and necessary improvements and changes;

- Establishment of administrative functions in support of new services;

- Establishment of IT systems to support new services;

- Printing of business cards, adverts, flyers and brochures;

- Cost of advertising and publicity;

- Establishment of customer relationship management systems, appointment systems and other necessary business requirements using IT;

- Introduction of new systems such as bar coding as necessary;
- Installation of GPS systems in council vehicles

It seems to be the case that the real issue here is not about the application of the law but a cultural issue for local authorities. In order to make the most of these powers, the officers and members of local authorities have to start thinking "out of the box", *i.e.*, imaginatively and purposively about what they want to achieve in civic benefits and develop a strategy to deliver that. If the powers are approached in a narrow and restricted way then marginal benefits are all that will ever be achieved.

CHAPTER 7

COMMERCIAL TRADING

INTRODUCTION

The possibility that local authorities would be given new powers to **7.1** provide goods and services to the private sector was first raised in 2001 in the consultation paper: *Working with Others to Achieve Best Value: Section 16 of the Local Government Act 1999—A Consultation Paper on Changes to the Legal Framework to Facilitate Partnership Working* (DETR 2001). This was in the context of promoting partnership working through PPPs, rather than as a revenue raising power. The White Paper, *Strong Local Leadership—Quality Public Services* (DTLR 2001); went further by indicating that the government would certainly give authorities power to trade commercially, where this helped Best Value and the delivery of public services. This was part of the new "freedom and flexibilities" to be given to those better performing authorities under the government's Comprehensive Performance Framework.

The Local Government Act 2003 was enacted on September 18, 2003 and the provisions relating to both commercial trading and discretionary charging (see Ch.5) came into force two months later. Section 95 provides a power to trade in function related activities. This is a power given to the "appropriate person" to authorise the activity; not a power given directly to local authorities. The "appropriate person" in England is the Secretary of State and in Wales is the Welsh Assembly. The generic term "relevant Minister" is used in this Chapter, except where differences apply between England and Wales. It is an enabling provision and local authorities will have discretion as to whether or not they embark on trading activity. Nevertheless, s.95 heralds a sea change in attitude. As Ch.1 recounts, trading has been important to local authorities for several decades but has been severely hampered by legal uncertainty and the unwillingness of the government of any political hue to support the activity. Section 95 represents a new era of permissive, although regulated, commercial trading.

The legal framework for commercial trading is more complex than that for charging for discretionary services. The use of statutory instruments means that s.95 is supported by the regulation and guidance making power in s.96 which actually permits the activity. There is also the power in s.97 to amend legislation which impedes these provisions, using the procedure outlined in s.98. The Act permits guidance to be issued by the relevant government office (for example when the Act was passed, the ODPM in England and the Welsh Office in Wales).

There are two key limitations on the government's willingness to permit commercial trading under s.95. The first is that, in England at least, this will be a privilege given only to those better performing authorities under the CPA (see below). The second is that the power may only be exercised through a company, not directly by the local authority itself. Both of these limitations are considered below. In Wales, all authorities are to be given the power, but again only through a company. Those English authorities which do not achieve a grading of *fair* or higher in the CPA must look to other powers within this book, as must those who refuse to countenance the setting up of a company to undertake the activity.

This Chapter concentrates on the law relating to commercial trading under s.95 Local Government Act 2003. Chapter 8 discusses the key practical issues; particularly those involving the use of a company structure, and Chapter 9 gives examples of the use of the power.

THE LEGAL FRAMEWORK

The Act

7.2   Relevant extracts from the Local Government Act 2003 are contained in Appendix 1. A full copy of the Act is available from the Stationery Office website: http://*www.hmso.gov.uk/acts/acts2003/20030026.pdf*. Section 95 of the Act enables the relevant Minister to do two things. The first is "to authorise Best Value authorities to do for a commercial purpose anything which they are authorised to do for the purpose of carrying on any of their ordinary functions. . . ." (s.95(1)(a)). The second is to "make provision about the persons in relation to whom authority under para.(a) is exercisable" (s.95(1)(b)). This is both an enabling power and power to impose limits to that power. The first "Trading Order" was made in 2004 (see the Local Government (Best Value Authorities) (Power to Trade) (England) Order 2004, SI 2004/1705 also reproduced in Appendix 1), and is discussed below.

The potential class of authorities who may be granted these powers is very wide. "Best Value authorities" are defined in s.1 of the Local Government Act 1999 and number over 500. This wide grouping includes all local authorities (s.1(1)(a) of the 1999 Act); as well as many single purpose authorities, for example, a National Park authority and a police or fire authority; although s.95(7) limits the class for the purposes of s.95. This means that the relevant Minister could not give the power to trade to police authorities established under s.3 of the Police Act 1996 or the London Development Agency. Section 1(2) of the 1999 Act defines "local authority" in England as: a county council, a district council, a London borough council, a parish council or a parish meeting of a parish which does not have a separate parish council; the Council of the Isles of Scilly: the Common Council of the City of London in its capacity as a local authority; or the GLA in so far as it exercises it functions through the Mayor.

There is no definition of "doing for a commercial purpose," though the only sensible interpretation of this is for the purpose of profit, largely distinguishing it from the charging provisions in s.93 of the Act. So far as "ordinary functions" is concerned, this is defined in s.97(11) as the general functions of the authority which are not contained in s.95 (*i.e.* all those outside of the specific trading function). In other words, a local authority must have the statutory power to undertake an activity before it can consider whether or not to trade commercially in it (see, generally, Ch.2, on *ultra vires*). This is subject to the further limitations outlined below.

The power given to the relevant Minister in s.95 of the Act is constrained by two factors, within s.95(2). The first is that the trading power will not be available where a local authority is "required" to do something under its ordinary functions. This means that where a local authority is under a *duty* to do something under its functions, for example, the provision of education services, it cannot then trade in that function. This is because it was clearly Parliament's intention that these services be provided free of charge; not as a commercial activity. The second limitation is that the trading power should not replace any existing commercial activity which is already authorised. One of the very rare examples of this is s.38 of the Local Government (Miscellaneous Provisions) Act 1976, which authorises the sale of spare computer capacity commercially (see Ch.4). Whilst statutory duties of local authorities are many, those which authorise commercial activity are very rare and the s.38 example above is one of the few that are likely to be identified. It remains a moot point whether a local authority can establish a company to trade in areas authorised elsewhere, for example, the Civic Restaurants Act 1947; or indeed whether a general trading company established by a local authority has the power to undertake such activities.

The second part of the authorisation permits the relevant Minister to **7.3** limit the categories of Best Value authority which are permitted to exercise the power. Section 95(3) clarifies this, so that the limitation may be applied not only to categories of best value authorities but also (under s.95(3)(b)) to particular functional areas. In 2004, the Trading Order limited the power to trade in England to local authorities as defined in s.1(2) of the 1999 Act; and only those authorities who achieved a categorisation of *excellent, good* or *fair* under the CPA.

Section 95(4) contains the other key control on trading. This is that the activity can only be done via a company regulated by Pt V of the Local

Government and Housing Act 1989 (this, for example, excludes the use of limited liability partnerships). The use of the company mechanism gives rise to a range of legal complications and these are outlined in Ch.8. Section 95(5) confirms that if a Best Value authority is not ordinarily a local authority, it will be so treated for the purposes of Pt V of the 1989 Act in so far as it is acting through a company. Section 95(6) constrains the order making power within s.70(1) of the 1989 Act to those issues which are related to commercial trading.

Section 95(7) clarifies the provisions as discussed above. It therefore limits the range of Best Value authorities who may be given the power by excluding police authorities from that scope. In contrast, temporary trading powers were given to fire authorities under two subsequent trading orders (SI 2004/2307 and SI 2004/2573).

Section 96(1) of the Act gives the relevant Minister power to issue regulations which "impose conditions" in relation to the exercise by local authorities of their power to trade commercially and their power to do anything via a company; the relevant statutory instruments are discussed below. Section 96 (2) of the Act gives the power to issue regulations guidance which authorities "shall have regarded to." Relevant guidance was first issued in England in July 2004, and subsequently updated as discussed below. Together these are wide provisions, which give the relevant Minister considerable control and influence over commercial trading activity.

Sections 97 and 98 are wide enabling powers to modify enactments and to permit these statutory provisions to work properly. Section 97 (1) gives the Secretary of State the power to sweep aside any prior enactment which seems to prevent or obstruct trading for a commercial purpose, as covered by s.95. It also extends the power to do the same in relation to charging for discretionary services (discussed in Ch.5). The drafting permits the Secretary of State to "amend, repeal, revoke or disapply the enactment." This provision is becoming increasingly common in local government legislation and enables Parliament to deal with limitations which emerge in existing legislation, without the need for new primary legislation. Section 97(6) is a safeguard to reassure those who might see these provisions as turning local authorities into purely commercial entities; which is such a major step that it could only be done by primary legislation. Similarly, the power to remove an obstruction to trading cannot be used to allow a local authority to trade in an area where it has a legal obligation under its ordinary functions to perform a service. Section 97 preserves the autonomy of the National Assembly for Wales, in the regulation of local authorities and best value within that country.

Section 98 sets down the procedure for orders under s.97. Basically, the Secretary of State is under a duty to consult appropriate persons (including the Welsh Assembly) before making his proposals and the procedure is very similar to that contained in the Local Government Act 1999 in relation to Best Value orders. In effect, the Secretary of State has to lay before each

House of Parliament a paper, which explains his proposals, encloses a draft Order and gives details of the consultation he has adopted. The provisions must be formally approved in a positive resolution and no order can be laid until 60 days after the explanatory document has been put before Parliament.

Interestingly, there is no express linkage of the power to the best value regime; or to the community strategy which must be developed under s.4 of the Local Government Act 2000. The government perhaps considers these limitations to be implicit; or perhaps it has faith that as the power is given only to better performing authorities, they would not seek to use the power other than for the better performance of their overall functions. In any event, if there were perceived to be abuse, the regulation making powers are sufficient to ensure proper control.

The Trading Orders

The power to permit commercial trading needed to be triggered by **7.4** statutory instrument. The first statutory Order, is the Local Government (Best Value Authorities) (Power to Trade) (England) Order 2004, (SI 2004/1705). This is reproduced in the Appendix 1. Where necessary to distinguish between statutory instruments, this is referred to as the "Trading Order" within this book. The Order came into force in July 2004 and has two main provisions. Regulation 1 limits trading activity to those "best value authorities" which are also "local authorities" as defined in s.1(2) of the Local Government Act 1999. It also limits that grouping to those better performing authorities under the CPA, that is those who achieve the top three categorisations "excellent," "good" or "fair." Regulation 1(3), limits the category of local authorities by excluding certain fire authorities: any non-metropolitan county council; a non-metropolitan district council in areas where there is no county council or the Council of the Isles of Scilly.

Regulation 2 lays down the key limitations. The Order confirms that the power only relates to "ordinary functions" as defined in s.95(7) of the 2003 Act. Regulation 2(2) covers the key procedural step which must be complied with, which is that "the authority shall—(a) prepare a business case in support of the proposed exercise of that power; and (b) approve the business case." "Business case" is clarified in reg.2(4). The purpose and contents of a business case are considered further in Ch.8. Regulation 2(3) is the key financial step, which is that the authority must recover the costs of "any accommodation, goods, services, staff or other thing that it supplies" to its trading company. This is important to avoid State Aid restrictions as described below.

Regulation 3 lays down certain transitional arrangements which are relevant to the fact that an authority's CPA categorisation may change annually; if it reduces, this could mean that an authority is no longer permitted to operate the company. Where a local authority is re-categorised as below *fair*; it will only be able to complete that trading work which it has already started and any agreements or arrangements which it has entered into as the authority will cease by operation of law after two years. This would mean, for example, that a secondment agreement to supply staff to the company would end. It would not however end the life of the company or impact legally on the contracts entered into by the company (although it may impact practically on the ability of the company to deliver under those contracts).

As of November 2004, no statutory instrument had been published in Wales to bring the trading powers into operation for Welsh authorities. The Welsh Assembly has indicated that, in relation to Wales, the "power will be available to those Welsh authorities that have been assessed as eligible to trade via their performance under the Welsh Programme for Improvement". (At para.6 of *General Power for Best Value Authorities in Wales to Charge for Discretionary Services—Guidance on the Power in the Local Government Act 2003* Welsh Assembly—2004 also reproduced in Appendix 1). Trading in Wales is discussed in detail in Ch.14.

The Guidance

7.5   When draft regulations on commercial trading were issued for consultation in May 2004, draft guidance was issued at the same time. That guidance was comprehensive, comprising 35 pages of guidance entitled: *General power for local authorities to trade in function related activities through a company—guidance on the power in the Local Government Act 2003*. Following consultation, the guidance was reissued in slightly expanded from both to local authority lawyers and others by way of a letter to ACSeS on July 28, 2004; and by publication on the ODPM web-site. The guidance was re-issued in slightly amended form in October 2004; and is referred to in this book as the "Trading Guidance" to distinguish it from that issued by the Welsh Assembly. It is reproduced in Appendix 1. However, to obtain the latest copy of the guidance it is available from: *http://www.odpm.gov.uk.*

The Welsh Assembly published guidance on the discretionary power to charge *General Power for Best Value Authorities in Wales to Charge for Discretionary Services—Guidance on the Power in the Local Government Act 2003* soon after the commencement date of the Act. This is reproduced in Appendix 1 but is also available from the Assembly web-site: *www.wales.gov.uk.* As its name suggests this largely deals with the s.93 power discussed in Ch.5; but does also mention the trading powers in the 2003 Act (at paras 6 and 7). It is anticipated that further guidance will be published once the necessary statutory instrument to permit trading has been made. Two trading orders covering English fire authorities were published in 2004: the Local Government (Best Value Authorities) (Power to Trade) (England) (Amendment) Order 2004 (SI 2004/2307) and the

Local Government (Best Value Authorities) (Power to Trade) (England) (Amendment No.2) Order 2004 (SI 2004/2573).

As well as general sections relating to charging and trading and the context of trading; the ODPM's Trading Guidance also provides specific advice on preparing a business case and business planning. This production and approval of a business case is a necessary precondition to commercial trading by virtue of the Trading Order discussed above. The guidance then includes a major section on "trading through a company" and this embraces governance issues, the problems of potential conflicts of interest, staff and personnel issues and matters relating to assistance and state aid.

The Trading Guidance contains 12 key sections and is supported by four annexes. The sections are summarised in Figure 7.1. The aim of the drafting is to promote awareness of the issues to be faced and is very helpful for those who are contemplating commercial trading. It largely avoids giving advice, being clear that this is a matter for the authority and its advisors. The guidance is considered in context, largely in Ch.8.

Figure 7.1
Sections within the ODPM's Trading Guidance (2004)

- The following sections are included:
- — Introduction
- — Background
- — Context for Trading
- — Charging and Trading
- — Relationship with Local Authorities (Goods and Services) Act 1970 and Local Government Acts 2000 and 2003
- — Comprehensive Performance Assessment
- — Trading through a Company
- — Preparing to Trade
- — Making a Business Case and Business Planning
- — Trading through a Company
- — Anti-competition Legalisation and Competition with Local Businesses
- — Exit Strategy

- The four Annexes are:
- — A: Preparing to Trade

— B: Business Case and Business Plans

— C: State Aid

— D: Acknowledgements

THE CPA AND BETTER PERFORMING AUTHORITIES

7.6 The Comprehensive Performance Assessment or CPA was placed on a statutory footing by the Local Government Act 2003. Under s.99 of that Act the Audit Commission is obliged to produce a report on its findings in relation to the performance of English local authorities. That report categorises English local authorities into five different categories based on a balanced score card assessment of their overall performance.

The first formal categorisation under that statutory duty was published in 2004. The Local Authorities (Categorisation) (England) Order (SI 2004/1704) listed all authorities and their position on July 1, 2004. The Order is supported by a series of Schedules from 1 through 5 according to each of the five categories. It is anticipated that a number of similar orders will be made on a regular basis and for this reason the CPA Orders are not reproduced. A copy of this Order and other statutory instruments may be obtained from *http://www.hmso.gov.uk*; by following the links for the relevant year of the statutory instrument sought.

The permissive power in the Trading Order relates only to local authorities that are in the top three categories (*excellent*, *good* and *fair*). Only they can trade commercially, whereas those in the bottom two (*weak* and *poor*) cannot. Transitional provisions apply, as discussed under the Trading Order above. If an authority finds itself in the difficult position of having dropped from *fair* to *weak* after having set up its trading company it will have two years to rectify the position; after that time it will no longer have the power to trade. This does not however impact on the status of the company itself. Therefore a local authority which found itself in this position could, as an example, sell its shares in the company to a commercial operator or to another local authority with a higher categorisation and the company itself could carry on as normal. If there is a group of local authorities, provision would need to be made to deal with this eventuality and one arrangement may be to have a shareholder's agreement which prevented the poorly performing authority from taking dividends or voting or even forced it to sell its shares to another shareholder.

TRADING COMPANIES

The Legal Requirement for a Company

7.7 Section 95, which enables the relevant Minster to permit categories of local authority to trade, makes it a statutory requirement that the commercial trading must be undertaken through a company. There are no *de minimis* provisions so any level of trading activity "for a commercial purpose" must be by the company route. Section 95(4) indicates that this must be a company regulated by Pt V of the Local Government and Housing Act 1989.

There are a number of reasons why the Government has included the requirement to trade via a company. One is to make it "a level playing field" (see ODPM's Trading Guidance, at para.10), as most competitors will usually be companies. Another is for tax reasons, as local authorities would otherwise have a tax advantage over the competition; a third reason might be to ensure the necessary transparency for competition law and state aid purposes. These matters are discussed in Ch.8. However, the main reason must surely be to protect the council tax payers; by insulating the authority through the mechanism of a limited liability company; in the same way as other shareholders are protected if a company fails. In the view of the authors this is nothing more than a legal technicality as the authority cannot escape reputational risk from the actions of its trading company.

Section 67(1) of the 1989 Act defines companies to which Pt V applies, and this wide ranging definition covers four broad groupings: companies limited by shares, companies limited by guarantee with or without a share capital, unlimited companies and societies registered under the Industrial and Provident Societies Act 1965. Section 67(4) enables an order to be made under this provision regulating those companies, and a new provision (added by the Local Government Act 2003) in s.67(5) means that different provisions may be made for different local authorities (for example linking the provisions to CPA categorisation). The drafting of s.67(1) means that the only type of corporate vehicle which may be used is one of those four groups. Notably, s.67 does not mention charitable trusts, non-charitable trusts, joint committees and limited liability partnerships (LLPs) or unlimited partnerships. These latter vehicles cannot therefore be used for commercial trading.

Features of corporations

The common thread which links all incorporated bodies is that they are **7.8** legal entities which exist in their own right. The act of incorporation creates a separate, incorporeal entity. All corporations are legal person with rights and obligations which are different from those of its members (or shareholders). They hold property in their own right and name and can sue and are sued in their own names. Corporations are formed by incorporation in the manner laid down in the relevant legislation. Most corporations are companies are formed under the Companies Act 1985.

Figure 7.2 illustrates the key features of companies.

Figure 7.2
Key Features of Companies

- A company is a new legal entity, separate from the authority(ies) which have formed it and is able to undertake transactions (*e.g.* enter contracts) in its own name;

- Most companies offer the protection of limited liability;

- A company will have its own staff (although these may be seconded from the authority);

- A company has its own assets (although these may be leased from the authority);

- A company offers a range of different managerial and administrative structures;

- The directors of a company owe duties to the company rather than simply representing the narrow interests of their own organisation;

- A company vehicle facilitates speed in decision making;

- A company offers a "single face" to third parties.

The regulatory regime for local authority companies

7.9   Part V of the 1989 Act was a framework and was itself only brought into force some six years after enactment. The Local Government and Housing Act (Commencement No.16) Order (1993) brought into force ss.67–70, 72 and 73 of the 1989 Act; and the (Commencement No.17) Order brought into force s.71 (relating to control of minority interest in companies). Part V needed supplementing by statutory instrument and this came in 1995 with the Local Authorities (Companies) Order 1995 (SI 1995/849). Overall, Pt V determines which categories a company falls into (controlled, influenced) and then links into the 1995 Order which applies two further tests to determine whether the company is then "regulated" or "unregulated". Regulated companies were subject to two sets of controls, "financial" and "proprietary."

The financial controls on regulated companies were designed to prevent local authorities seeking to use companies to avoid the limits on borrowing under the regime in Pt IV of the 1989 Act. This had legal effect in the 1995 Companies Order, where Regulations 12–18 applied the provisions of Pt IV of the 1989 Act to regulated companies so that these were deemed to be the actions of the controlling local authority themselves. These borrowing controls have now been replaced by the prudential finance regime, itself introduced in the Local Government Act 2003. A subsequent statutory instrument (the Local Authorities (Capital Finance) (Consequential, Transitional and Savings Provisions) Order 2004—SI 2004/533) repealed the relevant regulations in the 1995 Companies Order so that all companies are brought within the prudential controls. The proprietary controls remain, and therefore the Pt V framework and the Local Authorities (Companies) Order 1995 is still relevant, in part at least. The recent prudential financial controls and the longstanding proprietary controls are discussed in Ch.8.

Which type of company vehicle should be used?

The legal requirement is to adopt one of four structures, by virtue of the **7.10** linkage to Pt V of the Local Government and Housing Act 1989. The ODPM's Trading Guidance states at para.42: "an unlimited company is unlikely to offer the level of protection the authority would want"; therefore, this will really be a choice of three models: companies limited by shares, companies limited by guarantee and Industrial and Provident Societies Act Companies.

These models are summarised in Ch.8; but before choosing between them, the authority needs to be clear as to the aims and for the company and in particular why it is undertaking trading activity. It is important therefore not to focus too much on the vehicle until the necessary business case has been considered and a clear business plan adopted.

Power to set up a company?

Legal arguments continue to arise in relation to powers for part of local **7.11** authorities to establish companies. There are some lawyers who believe that a local authority has no power to establish a company for a trading purpose; despite the wide ranging power in s.2 of the Local Government Act 2000 (wellbeing) and the requirement for a company imposed by s.95 of the Local Government Act 2003. The government's view is that the incidental power within s.111 of the Local Government Act 1972, when used in conjunction with s.95 of the 2003 Act provides the requisite power. This point was made in the Frequently Asked Questions sheet published by the ODPM in July 2003 and referred to above. Its answer is reproduced in Figure 7.3 below.

> **Figure 7.3**
> **FAQs—ODPM July 2003**
>
> Q: What powers can local authorities rely on to form or participate in such companies?
>
> A: Based upon ordinary principles, an authority has the power to do anything reasonably incidental to its express powers. The power to trade in functions and related activities under s.95 is an expressed power. Accordingly, if for example it appeared to an authority that the arrangements for carrying out of function related trading would be most appropriately handled by an "in house company", the authority would be able to form a company for that purpose under its subsidiary powers.
>
> *Local Government Bill—Power To Trade In Function Related Activities Through A Company—Frequently Asked Questions* ODPM July 3, 2003

Earlier advice from the government was that the wide general power of s.2(1) of the Local Government Act 2000 (the wellbeing power) enables local authorities to participate in companies (see *Working with Others to Achieve Best Value*, DETR Consultation Paper of 2001). Paragraph 3.12 of that paper reminds authorities of the important limitation on the exercise of this power: "provided they are satisfied that the primary purpose behind the formation of, or participation in, a particular company is likely to achieve the promotion or improvement of the economic, social or environmental wellbeing of the authority's area." For a number of years it has been said that the government will issue an order, under s.16 of the Local Government Act 1999 to give an express power to establish companies and this will remove any lingering doubts on this issue.

As well as this limitation, the *ultra vires* rule also requires authorities to be satisfied that they are not using the power for an improper purpose nor are acting imprudently. This requirement not to act imprudently, means for example that the authority has considered all the relevant issues, has taken advice where necessary and that it will not act imprudently, for example in providing excessive initial start up capital etc for the company.

THE DISTINCTION BETWEEN POWERS TO CHARGE FOR DISCRETIONARY SERVICES AND COMMERCIAL TRADING

7.12   Essentially the Government is seeking to differentiate between two different types of activity. The first is the provision by a local authority of a service, which it has the power to provide, but where the power to charge might be uncertain, thereby creating uncertainty as to whether it can recover its costs. The second is to enable local authorities to engage in full risk based trading where appropriate. In view of the fact that the Government has drawn a distinct line between these two different types of activity, different provisions apply to each.

According to the ODPM's Trading Guidance (at para.15), there are four main differences in the powers. These are examined in Figure 7.4 below.

Figure 7.4
The Four Main Differences Between Charging and Trading

1. Charging relates only to discretionary services, whereas the power to trade is for all services;

2. All best value authorities can use the power to charge whereas the power to trade is only available to councils rated *fair*, *good* or *excellent* under the CPA;

3. Charging is limited to the recovery of the cost of providing the service whereas trading can be at profit;

4. The power to trade is only exercisable through a company.

THE IMPACT ON EXISTING POWERS TO TRADE

In Ch.4, mention is made of the ability to use s.111 Local Government **7.13** Act 1972 in support of another specific power to permit municipal trading type activity. That Chapter also mentions the case law relating to the effect of a provision amounting to a "code." Cases such as *Hazell v Hammersmith & Fulham LBC* [1992] AC 1 have established that s.111 cannot be used to authorise activity which is already comprehensively regulated by another statutory provision. Therefore in *Hazell*, it was not possible to justify the use of interest rate swaps as a tool of debt management because the Sch.13 of the Local Government Act 1972 contained what was (at that time) considered to be a comprehensive code of statutory provisions regulating borrowing.

This raises the issue as to whether, s.95 of the Local Government Act 2003 and the Trading Order provide a statutory code for commercial trading and therefore prohibit any other trading activity using different statutory powers. The government does not think so. In the 2004 guidance it expressly considers the link with s.1 of the Local Authorities (Goods and Services) Act 1970 which permits trading with public bodies and which has not been repealed by the s.95 power.

What has happened is that the government has created a new power to permit commercial trading; but has not sought to remove the existing framework. This may make matters more complicated (in so far as it is necessary to determine the best power to use), but it has not provided a single route which amounts to a comprehensive code.

CONCLUSION

7.14   The power to permit commercial trading for local authorities represents a sea change in attitude. Previously, the government had sought to prevent local authorities undertaking any aspect of risk based trading; now it has been expressly recognised that this is a legitimate part of a local authority's functions—although within controls. Whether this power, with the added complication of the company route, is used as extensively as discretionary charging seems unlikely. However, the position may change. Those who wish to take this step need to be aware of the implications of the company route and these are described in Chapter 8.

CHAPTER 8

ESTABLISHMENT OF COMPANIES FOR TRADING

INTRODUCTION

Chapter 7 explained the provisions introduced by s.95 of the Local **8.1** Government Act 2003, and the two key limitations on commercial trading. The first is that, in England at least, this will be a privilege given only to those better performing authorities under the CPA (*i.e.* those categorised as *excellent*, *good* or *fair*). The second is that the power may only be exercised through a company; not directly by the local authority itself. In Wales, all authorities are to be given the power, but again only when acting through a company.

This Chapter explains some of the key issues, which need to be considered by an authority using a company for trading. It commences by considering the steps which a local authority should undertake before forming a company: for example the legal requirement for the authority to consider a business case which was introduced in the Trading Order (SI 2004/1705) and discussed in Ch.7. As part of these pre-incorporation issues it also considers the fundamental issue of whether the authority wishes the company to act as an arm's length commercial entity or one set up as a not-for-profit community enterprise. Different types of company vehicle are suitable for each usage, and other issues flow from that categorisation, for example the extent to which the EU public procurement regime will impact on the company's procurement. Governance issues will also need to be examined.

The second broad area which needs to be considered is the manner in which companies operate. Companies are regulated by a body of law arising generally under the Companies Act 1985. There are also specific legal controls for local authority companies (under the Local Authorities (Companies) Order 1995, being part of the regime put in place by Pt V of the Local Government and Housing Act 1989). Since the introduction of the prudential accounting framework, it is the proprietary controls (rather than borrowing controls) which have the most relevance and these are discussed below. Within the operational area is the important issue of the opportunities for the company to obtain work from the parent authority and whether this must be done in competition because of the impact of the EC public procurement regime. This section also considers the restrictions on the authority subsidising the company (for example by providing cheap loans or guarantees); here too the Trading Order impacts, but so do State Aid and other competition rules.

ISSUES TO CONSIDER BEFORE FORMING ANY COMPANY

Governance Issues

8.2   An authority needs to be clear about some basic issues before it proceeds with a proposal to form a company for trading purposes. It is likely that it will need to take advice on these matters before seeking to set up the company. Those matters upon which early advice is typically sought include:

- The preparation of a "business case";

- Advice on the type of company required, depending on the aims and objectives of the authority;

- The legal constraints which will impact on the manner in which any trading vehicle may be used, for example whether or not it will have to tender in open competition for work from its parent local authority and the impact of local authority financial and propriety controls.

Guidance on these key issues will be provided from within the authority or through external advisors. The material below is designed to outline why these matters are important. Chapter 3 considers strategic issues and Chapter 10, practical implementation issues. The considerations raised below may well be relevant to either assessment. Further reference material specifically on companies and which may be of assistance is the Partnerships UK paper—*A Guidance Note for Public Sector Bodies forming Joint Venture Companies with the Private Sector*—(PUK 2001). This is available on the web-site: *www.partnershipsuk.org.uk/guidance*.

The Need for a Business Case

8.3   Regulation 2(2) of the Trading Order covers the key procedural step which must be complied with before commercial trading commences. This is that "the authority shall—(a) prepare a business case in support of the proposed exercise of that power; and (b) approve the business case." The order uses the phrase "prepare a business case in support of the proposed exercise of that power" which suggests that the business case may be generic (for example to set up the trading company) rather than specific (for example to enter into a particular contract). This interpretation is supported by the definition of "business case" in art.2(4) which indicates that this is a statement covering matters such as the objectives of the business, the investment requirements, the risks and the financial and other outcomes to be expected.

The ODPM's Trading Guidance (*General power for local authorities to trade in function related activities through a company—guidance on the power in the Local Government Act 2003*) provides further explanation of this requirement. The guidance reminds authorities of the overall controls provided by the *ultra vires* doctrine and their fiduciary duty (at para.36), which has led the government to require formal consideration of a business case. Paragraph 36 indicates that there are a number of steps which need to be considered by authorities when preparing to trade, and draws attention to Annex A of the guidance. Annex A is summarised below in Figure 8.1, whilst the complete guidance is reproduced in Appendix 2.

Figure 8.1—Summary of Steps before Preparing to Trade

- Market analysis;
- Customer research;
- Service/Product research;
- Competition research;
- Risk Analysis;
- Sources of analysis and research
    - market data;
    - competitive data;
    - internal data;
    - projected future for the product or service
- Different research methodologies

Based on Annex A of the ODPM's Trading Guidance 2004

Paragraph 37, distinguishes between the business case (which is a formal risk assessment which determines whether to proceed at all) and a business plan, which is much more about the manner in which the business will operate. In practical terms, both will be necessary although it is the "business case" which is the legal requirement.

131

Annex B of the Trading Guidance provides an outline of the matters which a business case should consider and several pages of guidance on developing a business plan. The suggested steps which those preparing the business case should undertake are summarised below in Figure 8.2. It is only where the risks are acceptable that the authority should consider undertaking the trading activity and forming the company.

Figure 8.2—Summary Of Steps Needed To Prepare A Business Case

- Analysis of current activities;

- Identify business risks;

- SWOT analysis;

- Option analysis in light of SWOT;

- Analysis of long term trends, *e.g.* political, economic, social and technical (PEST);

- Prepare Customer/service matrix;

- Revisit SWOT;

- Assess likelihood of risks occurring;

- If risks are too high, then do not proceed.

Based on Annex B of the ODPM's Trading Guidance 2004

What Type of Company?

Commercial or Community Aims

8.4   Chapter 7 and the text below explain the linkage to Pt V Local Government and Housing Act 1989. Part V was set up for a different purpose, namely to regulate companies in which local authorities had interests and divided companies into five different types. In practice, because of the risks of operating through unlimited companies and changes in the law in 1985, this will really be a choice of three models: companies limited by shares, companies limited by guarantee (without any share capital) and Industrial and Provident Societies Act (IPS) companies. These three models are summarised below, but before choosing between them, the authority needs to consider the aims and objectives for the company and in particular why it is undertaking trading activity.

Most companies are formed in the commercial world with a key view to profit; that is to make money. Financial value is generated both by the payment of surplus profit to members of the company and by the increase in the value of the shares, which may then be traded. If a company is set up for these purposes it will have a defined commercial character and the local authority involvement will be very much as an investor. If, however, the authority wishes to set up a company, where the generation of income is secondary to a community purpose (for example, a sheltered workshop set up to provide employment for a disadvantaged group), the aims and objectives will be different. The authority may be willing to subsidise the enterprise, but in any event will be looking for it to deliver needs in the general public interest rather than as a commercial entity in its own right. Whilst in practice many authorities will want aspects of both, the legal distinction is significant and therefore a determination of which of those two broad aims: commercial or community purposes needs to be made.

One example of the legal importance of the distinction is the treatment of the company under the EC public procurement regime. If the company is set up as a commercial trading entity; that company will not be itself subject to the EC public procurement regime (even though the parent authority is). However, if the company is set up to meet needs in the general interest, both it and the parent company are likely to be subject to tendering requirements introduced by that regime. This is because of the definition of contracting authorities under the regime (see, for example, reg.3 of SI 1993/3228 governing services). The definition of contracting authority embraces any corporation which is largely financed by a local authority or subject to management supervision by the authority or where more than half or the board or more than half of the members are appointed by the local authority; provided always it set up to meet needs in the general interest and does not have a commercial character.

Another important need to make the distinction is to choose the right corporate vehicle. Whilst a company limited by shares is an appropriate vehicle for commercial trading, a company limited by guarantee or an IPS company would be better suited if the aim were community purposes.

Company vehicles which could be used for trading

As Ch.7 explains, the legal requirement is to adopt one of five corporate **8.5** structures, by virtue of the linkage to Part V of the Local Government and Housing Act 1989. Part V divides guarantee companies into two different types: s.67(1)(b) of the 1989 Act mentions "a company limited by guarantee and not having a share capital"; whilst s.67(1)(c) mentions "companies limited by guarantee and having a share capital." That latter form of entity has not been available since the mid 1980s, in that s.1(2) of the Companies Act 1985 makes it clear that it is no longer possible to set up "companies limited by guarantee and having a share capital." This reduces the five possible types to four. The fourth model, that of unlimited company, is "unlikely to offer the level of protection the authority would want" according to the ODPM's Trading Guidance (at para.42). It is only mentioned below, therefore, for the sake of completeness.

The types of company which can now be formed for trading purposes are therefore: companies limited by shares, companies limited by guarantee (without any share capital) and IPS companies.

Companies limited by shares

8.6   A company limited by shares has long been the favoured vehicle for commercial trading activities within the United Kingdom. Its usage within local authority circles has therefore been rare, in the absence of specific powers permitting commercial trading. The ODPM's Trading Guidance states: "A trading company is likely to be limited by shares" (at para.42).

Companies limited by shares must be registered at the Companies House in Cardiff and must comply with the requirements of the Companies Acts 1985 and 1989 and the Insolvency Act 1986.

Perhaps the key advantage of this vehicle is that the liability of the members (the local authority shareholder(s)) is defined to a fixed financial limit. In the event of a liquidation, liability is limited to the amount (if any) which remains unpaid on any shares owned. The amount already paid will form the working capital, which is of course also vulnerable on liquidation. Nevertheless the liability is fixed, irrespective of the actual debts of the company on liquidation.

The working capital of the company is made up of equity (which is provided in exchange for shares), and debt, which is the corporate borrowing of the company. If all shares are issued fully paid, there is no further liability of shareholders. Shareholders control the company and, for example, decisions made by shareholders will include the payment of dividends and the appointment of directors. Normally shares will each have one vote, therefore the party with the largest shareholding (the majority shareholder) will control the company. The trading income earned by the company (after deduction of operating expenses, taxes, wages and directors fees) is available to shareholders who can choose to plough these profits back into the company or pay them out to themselves in the form of a dividend. On winding up any surplus capital of a company limited by such is refunded to its members.

The fact that different classes of shares may be created with different voting rights and different dividend rights means that a share company is a very flexible entity. As an example; this would allow an investment stake in the company to be sold to private sector trading partners—whilst still retaining overall control over the company in the hands of the local authority. This flexibility is reflected in the controls over local authority companies; because share based companies may be regulated or unregulated depending on the exact balance of control between the public and private sectors (see Financial and Proprietary Controls—below).

It is not a particularly favoured model for community purposes as the assets of the company are effectively owned by the shareholders. Such a company would not usually be able to obtain charitable status and therefore would not be able to take advantage of the fiscal exemptions enjoyed by charities.

The key features of this type of company are summarised in Figure 8.3 below.

Figure 8.3—Key Features of Companies Limited by Shares

- A company's share capital (equity) provides its initial working capital;

- A company may borrow money (debt funding);

- The flexibility to allow both equity and debt funding which may be particularly attractive depending on the needs of the company;

- Participation by way of equity will allow shareholders to share in the longer term growth in the value of the company;

- Profits are paid as a dividend on shares or retained within the company to fund future growth;

- Voting rights depend on the number and type of shares held;

- A majority of shares (51 per cent) is normally enough to control the Board of Directors;

- The shareholders may agree to protect minority shareholders by providing them with veto rights over key decisions (*e.g.* winding up the company) and company law provides certain protection for minority shareholders;

- A key consideration is the extent to which shares may be sold to third parties (thus transferring control and ownership);

- Joint Venture Companies (*e.g.* those with some shares allocated to the private sector) are normally supported by a shareholder's agreement, which determines how the shareholders will work together;

- Different shareholding may give different rights, this provides flexibility in structuring particular projects with a range of different partners;

- Sale of shares offers an alternative to obtaining profit by dividend.

- Attention needs to be given to the "Exit stage" and how and at what cost shares would be transferred.

Companies limited by guarantee

8.7   It is possible to set up companies which are limited by guarantee rather than shares. This is a vehicle often used for 'not for profit' organisations who wish to take advantage of limited liability and a separate legal entity. It is the model used for community organisations, because there is generally no wish to trade, or to raise capital by the issue of shares, or to pay dividends to shareholders. Guarantee companies are often used to manage community facilities and may also obtain charitable status. The liability of members is limited by the memorandum to the amount which the members undertake to contribute in the event of the company being wound up, which is usually a nominal figure of £10 or so. The ODPM's Trading Guidance indicates that: " . . . vehicles such as companies limited by guarantee (with or without share capital) are unlikely to be appropriate vehicles for a trading company as these are more appropriate for a 'not for profit' company which may also be registered as a charity." (At para.42). The mention again of guarantee companies with shares may seem unusual, but it could be that a local authority has a company limited by guarantee with share capital which was formed before 1985. However, this would be a rare occurrence.

Industrial and Provident Societies Act Companies

8.8   An IPS company is a society which is set up to conduct business either as a co-operative (that is for the benefit of its members) or, alternatively, for the benefit of the community. It must be registered in conformity with the Industrial and Provident Societies Act 1965. Once the registration is approved it has the form of a legal entity and may be used for certain types of trading activity. It is used for businesses without share capital such as various forms of workers' co-operatives, some social enterprises, and for housing associations. In the local authority arena, they have been used for leisure trusts, primarily because of the fact that it is generally possible to obtain charitable status as exempt charities which do not have to register with the the appropriate authority (in England and Wales the Charity Commission). Charitable status would clearly not be possible for a trading company.

The distinguishing feature is that they are run, co-operatively, for the mutual benefit of their members, with any surplus usually being ploughed back into the organisation to provide better services and facilities. If they are run for the wider benefit of the community they will need to satisfy the regulator (the Financial Services Authority) of special reasons why the society should not be registered as a company.

The FSA has the responsibility to ensure, through the examination and registration of rules and other documents, that these societies always comply with the registration requirements of Industrial and Provident

Societies legislation. There are a number of sponsoring bodies which represent a wide spectrum of societies which have "model rules" approved by the FSA. The adoption of one of these models provides a recognised framework that is known to meet the requirements of the relevant legislation, enabling registration to be undertaken more speedily and cheaply. Once formed, any IPS company must submit its annual returns and accounts within seven months of their year end. Societies must submit a set of accounts with their annual return form, and (as an absolute minimum) these must contain an income and expenditure account, a balance sheet and an auditor's report.

Under s.67(1) of the Local Government and Housing Act 1989, an IPS company will be a regulated company and subject to financial and proprietary controls provided its main customer is the local authority (see below).

Unlimited companies

Unlimited companies are, as the name suggests, corporate entities which **8.9** do not enjoy limited liability and are therefore only theoretically suitable for commercial trading. Their main advantage is in the limited disclosure requirements under the Companies Act. If an unlimited company goes into liquidation the members must contribute the amounts required to meet the debts of the company. The risk is not that the creditors can sue the members, it is that the liquidator can call for the necessary contribution from members to meet the debts. It is the lack of limited liability which has caused the ODPM to consider that this model does not offer suitable protection.

THE LEGAL CONSTRAINTS

Tendering for own authority work

The EU public procurement regime requires all public sector contracts **8.10** over particular threshold levels to be publicly advertised in the Official Journal of the European Union (OJEU). This is to ensure adequate access Europe wide. All contracts below the threshold are subject to rules prohibiting non-discriminatory behaviour (for example favouring local contractors over European contractors). In 2005, those values were £153,376 for service and supplies contracts let by local authorities and £3,834,411 for works contracts. There are aggregation rules to prevent authorities splitting up contracts to avoid triggering those thresholds.

The mere setting up of a trading company does not trigger any EU procurement requirements. The difficulty arises with the award of contracts to that company or any wish to novate contracts into that entity. An attempt to do this would be the award of a contract to a new legal entity.

Advice on the impact of the EU regime is likely to be necessary, as the advice within the ODPM's Trading Guidance is of a very general nature. Paragraph 76 states that: "The EU procurement rules may apply where the authority provides services, supplies or staff to the trading company, where the authority buys services, supplies or staff from the company or where the company itself buys services." In reality, much depends on the nature and value of the contracts let by the authority.

As an example, the EU regime means that if the local authority wished to award an engineering and design contract to a local authority owned engineering company and the total value of that contract was likely to exceed £153,376 that contract would have to be advertised EU wide and won in open competition, unless, of course, an exemption could be found. If the company is heavily reliant on local authority work for its income stream this will be a major consideration and may even persuade the authority against setting up a trading company for these purposes.

Authorities may wish to consider the potential case law exception offered by Case C–107/98, *Teckal Srl v Comune di Viano and AGAC*. In that case it was recognised that: "where the local authority exercises over the person concerned a control which is similar to that which it exercises over its own departments and, at the same time, that person carries out the essential part of its activities with the controlling local authority or authorities"— awards of contracts would not trigger the regime. However, there are three notes of caution to be sounded in relation to this. The first is the limitation to the need only to be providing the "essential part of its activities" to the parent local authority. Most commercial vehicles will be set up with the intention of widescale trading, not merely working for the parent authority, and therefore this requirement will not be met. The second note of caution is that the exemption only applies to "services," not to supplies or works. The third note of caution is that towards the end of 2004 there were three cases pending on the precise scope of this exemption and all seemed likely to limit rather than expand the exemption.

Specific advice is likely to be necessary, as it may be that other exemptions apply but if the company is envisaging a major source of its income stream coming from contractual work from the parent authority it will need to know whether this may be awarded as of right or will have to be tendered for. At the time of writing (2004) it seems as though the *Teckal* exemption will be limited and is likely only to apply where the company is an "in-house" company rather than one set up to trade more widely.

If the company does tender, it must be treated on an equal basis to other competing entities. In many ways this puts any newly formed company at a disadvantage; because a new company will not have the financial standing and track record of a well established rival.

In addition, if the company has been set up to meet community purposes rather than being a purely commercial trading entity and the authority controls the company, that company itself will be deemed to be a contracting entity for the purposes of the public procurement regime. The company's own contracts (*i.e.* the supplies and services to it) may need to be tendered and only be awarded following OJEU advertising. In the early days of trading at least the value of the contracts should be below threshold levels. The legal power of local authorities to provide services to trading companies is covered at para.34 of the ODPM's Trading Guidance.

Perhaps the only silver lining in this particular cloud is that any other local authority or public body is likely to have to tender above threshold work and this could provide a ready market for the new company.

Arguments for placing contracts with in-house companies without the need for competition

It is no surprise that the ingenuity of lawyers has been put to use to try **8.11** and find a lawful way in which contacts may be placed by a local authority with its in-house trading company without the need for competition. As at January 2005, their efforts have largely been focussed on a liberal interpretation of the *Teckal* (Case C–107/98), as discussed above.

Local authority lawyers have raised a number of possible courses of action. One which has been widely canvassed is to award the work in-house when the trading company is first formed and then later tender for other, third party, work. The suggestion is that it is open to an authority, firstly to set up an in-house, non-trading company to perform its own work and then at a later date to make a second decision to "convert" that company to a trading vehicle after it had won the in-house work. If the two decisions are taken entirely independently and with a period of time between these two events, this would seem to fall within the letter of the law.

Any such actions should however carefully consider the emerging case law on the subject as outlined *below*. To put the matter in context, it should not be forgotten that a court needs to interpret this European based law teleologically that is according to the aim or sprit of the law rather than its exact wording. The very setting up of a company to trade outside the authority would itself seem to rule out the *Teckal* exemption. Of course the purpose of the company will be obvious to any observer because of the need to provide a business case to the authority to set up such a vehicle (a requirement of the Trading Order, as discussed in Ch.7).

The authors draw attention in particular to the following cases:

- *Stadt Halle and Others* (Case C–36/03)—where the court determined that any arrangement with a company in which the private sector held shares would fall outside of the *Teckal* exemption; because that type of company was liable to follow "considerations proper to private interests and pursue(s) objectives of a different kind" an arrangement with an in-house department (at para.50). Although the matter has yet to be determined; these are exactly the type of

139

considerations which a local authority trading company are likely to follow.

- *Commission v Spain* (Case C–84/03)—where Spain was found not to have properly transposed the public procurement directives by allowing arrangements between public bodies to fall outside those directives. The court re-stated their view that arrangements between public authorities were subject to the public procurement regime.

- *Commission v Germany* (Case C–126/03)—where Germany was held to have breached the directives in the case of the actions of the City of Munich. The council had won a long-term contract for the treatment of waste from a separate entity which was a waste authority. The council subsequently sub-contracted part of that contract to a private sector firm without competition. The court decided that the public procurement rules should have been followed twice. Munich should have won the contract in a competition set up by the waste authority and then awarded its sub-contracts through another public procurement exercise.

Financial and Proprietary Controls

8.12   Chapter 7 introduced the complex framework set up to control companies and formed by Pt V of the Local Government and Housing Act 1989 and the Local Authorities (Companies) Order 1995 (SI 1995/849) as amended. Overall, Pt V lays down a number of definitions which determine whether a company is "controlled" or "influenced." This is then supported by the 1995 Order which applies two further tests to determine whether the company is then "regulated" or "unregulated." If a company is controlled it will be regulated; and if influenced it may well be regulated.

Regulated companies are treated very much as if they are the local authority and are therefore subject to financial and proprietary controls. The financial controls on regulated companies were significantly amended by the Local Authorities (Capital Finance) (Consequential, Transitional and Savings Provisions) Order 2004—SI 2004/533). That 2004 Order repealed the relevant regulations in the 1995 Companies Order so that all companies are brought within the prudential controls. The proprietary controls remain, and therefore the Pt V framework and the Local Authorities (Companies) Order 1995 are still relevant, in part at least.

Under the framework set out in Pt V controlled companies are largely those where the authority or a group of authorities own more than 50 per cent of the voting rights, and the company would therefore be a subsidiary of the local authority within the meaning in s.736 of the Companies Act 1985. Influenced companies are those where the authority has an involvement, but it is not sufficient of itself to control the company. This is largely those companies where the voting rights of the authority or its associated persons are between 20 per cent and 50 per cent. Where the control over voting rights is below 20 per cent (for example it is only an investment stake) the company cannot be regulated. Within the 20 per cent–50 per cent banding another criterion must be met before a company is influenced relating to less formal controls which may be brought to bear on its operations by the authority. This would happen, for example, if more than half of the company's business was with the authority (when it would be dependent on that business and undue influence could be brought to bear). This is a so called "business relationship test".

Under the Local Authorities (Companies) Order 1995 a company will be treated as regulated if it falls into one of three groups:

- A controlled company (*i.e.* majority voting); or

- An unlimited company or an IPS company which is influenced by the local authority (20 per cent–50 per cent voting plus business relationship) or

- A company limited by shares which is influenced by the local authority (20 per cent–50 per cent voting plus business relationship) and which meets either or both of two further tests. The first is that the authority could exercise a "dominant influence" over the company (*i.e.* force it to act in a manner which was not necessarily in its best interests—see Sch.10A, para.4 of the Companies Act 1985). The second and alternative is that, if the authority were itself a registered company, it would have to prepare group accounts in respect of the company in question.

Part V of the 1989 Act is a framework and the Secretary of State has wide order making powers in s.70(1) to regulate, forbid or require the taking of action by a company under the control of or subject to the influence of a local authority. This means that the complex mechanism which the authors have tried to simplify and explain above remains in place. The proprietary controls introduced by the Local Authorities (Companies) Order 1995 also remain in place (see below); but further controls could yet be introduced under the Pt V framework.

The Financial Controls under the Prudential Accounting Framework

All companies have to comply with the Companies Acts and are required **8.13** to draw up their financial accounts to show a true and fair view as determined by generally accepted accounting practice. Local authority accounts are prepared in accordance with the CIPFA/LASAAC Code of practice on local authority accounting (the Accounts Code) and it is important to be aware that these accounting requirements differ from generally accepted accounting practice.

From April 1, 2004 the Accounts Code will require all local authorities that have 'material' interests in a company to produce Group accounts that will take and recognise the local authority's share of the results and assets and liabilities of the company. The amounts recorded in the group accounts for the company will depend upon its exact relationship with the authority. If the company is jointly owned with a private sector company (*i.e.* a joint venture company) its accounts are likely to require consolidation into the controlling entity's accounts (*e.g.* whichever has the majority share holding, the local authority or the private sector partner).

The issue of whether a company is regulated under the Local Authorities (Companies) Order 1995 is relevant only for propriety matters. The designation will not impact on the treatment under the prudential code regime. The requirement under the Prudential Code for Capital Finance in Local Authorities (CIPFA 2003) is that "Where the authority has interests in companies or other similar related entities, the authority needs to have regard to its financial commitments and obligations to those companies/ entities." This means that all companies are treated on the same basis regardless as to whether they are regulated or not. When assessing affordability and prudential indicators local authorities are expected to have regard to liabilities that may arise. The Prudential Code draws authorities' attention to the requirements for group accounting in the Accounting Code but places no additional responsibilities upon local authorities in its regard.

Any trading company will require private sector auditors to be appointed to audit the accounts. The authority's own internal and external auditors may also look at the authority's expenditure and income on the trading company, as well as the financial information on the company which appears in the authority's accounts. The council's auditor may look to the company's own auditors for assurances in this respect. If there is a JVC with private sector involvement; the level of access to the JVC records should be covered in a shareholders' agreement.

The Proprietary Controls

8.14   The Trading Guidance reminds authorities that they will wish to "have regard to the accountability and governance framework for the company" (at para.44). It mentions the *Combined Code—Principles of Good Corporate Governance and Code of Best Practice* (updated 2003); produced by the Hempel Committee and giving a broad framework for corporate and internal controls. In many ways this governance framework will lay down a stricter code that the formal proprietary controls introduced by the Local Authorities (Companies) Order 1995.

The formal controls introduced by the 1995 Order are summarised in Figure 8.4 below.

Figure 8.4—The Proprietary Controls under the 1995 Order

- state on company stationery that the company is controlled or influenced by a local authority, giving the name of the relevant authority or authorities;
- limit the remuneration and allowances paid to directors who are members of the local authority to the amounts payable for comparable local authority duties, or as travelling and subsistence allowances;
- avoid publishing party political material;
- remove any director who becomes disqualified for membership of a local authority (otherwise than through being employed by a local authority or controlled company);
- provide information to the relevant local authority's internal and external auditors about the affairs of the company;
- provide information to Members of the relevant local authority about the company's affairs, if a Member reasonably requires it for the proper discharge of duties (unless disclosure would amount to breach of statutory requirements or an obligation owed to any person;
- provide financial information to the relevant local authority which it needs for accounting purposes.
- In addition, controlled companies must also obtain the Audit Commission's consent to the appointment of the company's auditor.
- In addition, controlled companies which are not arms length companies must make minutes of any general meetings of the company available for public inspection for a period of 4 years after the meeting (unless disclosure would be in breach of any statutory requirement or obligation owed to any person).

Stationery and publications

Under reg.4, the fact that the company is controlled or local authority influenced needs to be mentioned on all official publications and business stationery, including cheques, receipts invoices and the like. **8.15**

Payment to Directors

Regulation 5 limits the amount which may be paid to directors who are also local authority councillors. **8.16**

Prohibition on Political Activities

The prohibition on dissemination of political materials is equally applicable to a regulated company as to the local authority under s.2 Local Government Act 1986 (see reg.5). **8.17**

Audit requirements

8.18   Regulations 6 and 9 provide obligations to ensure that the affairs of the company may be reported to the authority's own auditor and persons authorised by the Audit Commission. The consent of that body is necessary to the first auditor of the company.

Information

8.19   Under reg.7, any council member of the controlling or influencing company is entitled to information about the registered company to permit him/her to proper discharge their duties.

THE GENERAL GOVERNANCE FRAMEWORK

The Council As Shareholder

8.20   The authority will need to decide the degree of active involvement (*i.e.* the extent of the governance) it wishes to have in the company. They will need to protect the interests (and investment) of the authority while providing the necessary degree of autonomy to those who are responsible for managing the company.

Normally the trading vehicle will be a company limited by shares. Through its shareholding, an authority may be involved in a number of ways: voting at general meetings, exercising rights for approval or rights or veto over those matters the shareholders have agreed to withdraw from the remit of the Board of Directors. The advice from the ODPM is that: "If (the authority) is not to be the sole shareholder, it should enter into a shareholders' agreement with the other shareholders and the company covering matters such as:

- The allocation, transfer and disposal of shares;
- The rights to be attached to different classes of shares;
- "golden shares" under which a particular shareholder can reserve the right to veto, fundamental changes, for example changes to the business objectives, the business plan, or the appointment of the managing director . . . .;
- Exit and termination plan.

(at para.55 of the Trading Guidance).

8.21   Generally speaking, shareholders do not tend to be involved directly in the running of a company and matters are very much left to the Board of Directors. However, it is possible to ensure that certain actions of the

Board are subject to shareholder control. These matters should generally be kept to a minimum, however, it is an effective form of control and, at least in its early days, it is likely that any authority will wish to exercise its control in a fairly hands-on manner.

The authority will therefore need to consider:

- Those matters (if any) to be reserved to shareholders, and

- Those matters (if any) over which it has veto rights.

The types of matter which may be subject to control or limits for example a requirement that the Board was unanimous or a requirement for shareholder referral could be:

- An obligation to approve any contractual agreements to be entered into (for example contracts in excess of a certain financial limit);

- An agreement as to the business direction of the company;

- Future expenditure commitments;

- Dividend/profit distribution policy;

- Exit provisions;

- Approval of the Business Plan each year.

It should be noted that veto powers generally represent "negative" control. If there is any form of "positive" control, or excessive veto, this is likely to be regarded as a "dominant influence" for the purposes of Pt V of the 1989 Act as described above.

The Role Of The Board Of Directors

Responsibility for the supervision and management of a company and its **8.22** day to day business will lie with its Board of Directors, except for those matters which UK company law reserves to shareholders (for example the right of shareholders exercising 51 per cent of the vote to remove a director), or are specifically reserved by the company for approval by shareholders. A decision will need to be made as to whether the role of the Board is to be:

- Actively involved in all managerial decisions of the company; or

- Operating in more strategic/supervisory role.

The outcome of this decision will influence the composition and structure of the Board, as will any decision on the importance of the classification of the company under the Local Authorities (Companies) Order 1995 (see above). If the Board is to have an active executive role, then it will need to include individuals with the appropriate skills base, and the authority will need to see whether it has those with the requisite expertise (presumably drawn from officers of the council). If, however, the Board is to have a supervisory role, reviewing overall strategy and key decisions, it could consist mainly of Members.

Guidance on the position of nominees to a trading company board is provided at paras 50–53 of the ODPM's Trading Guidance.

A director's duties are summarised below when considering the possibility of a conflict of interest.

Conflicts Of Interest

8.23   Figure 8.5 summarises the duties that a company director has, which will be relevant to local authority trading companies.

Figure 8.5—A director's duties may be summarised as:

- Comply with statutory duties (*e.g.* under the Companies Act 1985);
- Act in good faith in the interests of the company (fiduciary duty);
- Act within the powers granted by the Memorandum and Articles of Association;
- Seek to avoid conflicts of interest;
- Comply with the duty of commercial confidentiality to the company.

The primary obligation of any director of the company will be to the company; that is they should always act in the best interests of the company not the body which has chosen them. As a shareholder, the authority's interests will always be relevant, because a director must always act in the best interests of shareholders, balancing longer and shorter term objectives. However, the interests of the company are wider than the director will owe to other stakeholders, for example, employees and creditors.

If a conflict of interest arises, it is most likely to occur where a service contract being performed by the company for the authority is not progressing smoothly. These difficulties can be ameliorated by, for example, reserving more matters to be decided by the shareholders rather than the Board or preventing a director from voting in any issue in which a conflict may arise. Many local authority members are directors of companies owned by the authority and do not find any practical difficulty in managing potential conflicts of interest.

The ODPM's Trading Guidance reminds authorities of the need to consider the Code of Conduct, which will be based on the model code issued by the ODPM in November 2001. This will require registration of financial and other interests and care with personal interests. (See paras 45–47).

Directors' Fees

Paragraph 54 of the ODPM's Trading Guidance draws attention to the **8.24** need to fix fair remuneration and makes mention of the use of "remuneration committees" within the private sector. It states: "Any authority considering paying members for their responsibilities in respect of the company should do so in the context of the normal arrangements for members' allowances."

Personal Liability of Directors

As it is likely that some or all of the directors of the company will be **8.25** council members or employees, insurance may need to be taken out by the company in relation to their liabilities as a director. There is the possibility of personal liability in certain circumstances, and para.48 of the ODPM's Trading Guidance instances: "breach of duty, wrongful trading, fraudulent trading, breach of disqualification order and other specific liabilities such as corporate manslaughter" as examples of these risks. The position of indemnities and guarantees is considered in some detail in Ch.12, and the guidance advises both that guidance should be given to nominated directors and some protection is available through indemnification that the company provides insurance to protect against such risks.

Additional Risks

A company will also be responsible for taking out appropriate insurance **8.26** to cover its commercial activities.

Any authority will need to consider the implications of providing guarantees or warranties or indemnifying a company against any risks which are in excess of the risks that it is currently exposed to by the operation of the services which were previously performed by the authority itself. This may trigger State Aid rules, which are described below.

STAFFING, PERSONNEL AND EMPLOYMENT ISSUES

Paragraph 58 of the ODPM's Trading Guidance reminds authorities that **8.27** employees of the new company can only come from four sources. These are:

- Recruitment;

- Transfer from within the authority;

- Secondment from the authority;

- Taking over the staff from another entity; for example via the purchase of another business.

Staffing issues are considered in more detail in Ch.12, and the guidance draws attention to the impact of TUPE (at para.56); and to the *Code of Practice on Workforce Matters in Local Authority Service Contracts* (Annex D of ODPM Circular 03/2003 of March 2003 at para.58). General recruitment advice is provided at paras 59–61 and advice on transfer of staff at paras 62–64 of the Trading Guidance.

FUNDING AND OTHER ASSISTANCE TO THE COMPANY

8.28 The Trading Order states, at reg.2(3) that the parent authority must recover the costs of "any accommodation, goods, services, staff or other thing that it supplies" to its trading company. Full cost recovery is likely also to be relevant to avoid State Aid restrictions (see below). The legal power of local authorities to provide services to trading companies is covered at para.34 of the ODPM's Trading Guidance.

In order to operate, make inward investment (for example in new ICT) and be able to run a successful commercial operation; any company will require sufficient funds. The timing, amount and origin of these funds will need to be agreed as part of the negotiations in setting up the company. The ODPM's Trading Guidance recommends authorities that: "any financial assistance, in cash or in kind, given by the local authority that establishes or participates in it, should be for a limited period, against the expectation of returns later. Any assistance should therefore be provided under a formal agreement with the company. The agreement must be entered into for a commercial purpose." (At para.65). The power for the authority to make this investment would normally be the power in s.111 of the Local Government Act 1972 (*i.e.* incidental powers) linked to the power to trade (s.95 of the Local Government Act 2003). That power must be exercised properly, with fiduciary duty and State Aid rules in mind.

Funds may be raised in a number of ways, both initial start up funding and future grants or loans. These include:

- Issue of shares (equity);

- Loans from shareholders;

- Borrowing from third parties (*e.g.* banks); and

- Grants.

The assets which a local authority is able to contribute or make available to a company at start-up include staff, buildings, vehicles and other equipment, and intangible assets for example intellectual property rights. These assets represent the investment made in exchange for shares. These assets will need to be identified to assist entry and exit strategy and may need to be provided under contract. Services provided to a company (for example payroll and personnel) would be services provided to a private sector company and may themselves be considered local authority trading.

The Trading Guidance reminds authorities of the risk of on-going liabilities, and that while liability may be limited by shares or guarantee, there may be recourse by third parties to any guarantee given or demand for services. The guidance warns: "In considering structures, the authority should ensure that it takes appropriate steps to avoid automatically assuming responsibility for any aspects of an unsuccessful company. This should include the actual provision of services." (at para.69).

The authority can set the company up as a limited recourse company, and this may be advisable under the prudential finance regime discussed above. However, it should be noted that there will always be a "reputation" risk where the links to the authority are transparent; and this will be a requirement under the proprietary obligations of the Pt V of the Local Government and Housing Act 1989 regime. If the authority's name is linked to the company, it will find its own reputation harmed if it walks away from a failing trading venture, even if this is a legal possibility.

The position of local authorities providing services to trading companies is covered at para.34 of the ODPM's Trading Guidance.

STATE AID AND COMPETITION LAW

As a local authority is developing a company, there is the potential for **8.29** the local authority to breach State Aid rules or for the company to breach Competition law. There is also the political impact on local businesses if the authority is seen to be setting up a rival company. This means that there are both legal issues and political issues to consider. This is a specialist area of law where external advice is likely to be necessary.

In summary, the State Aid rules are intended to ensure that market forces may operate freely across Europe with no unwarranted interference through the State (national government) or an organ of the State (such as a local authority).

The following criteria must be fulfilled in order for State Aid issues to arise in respect of any measure:

- The aid must be paid through (directly or indirectly) use of state resources;

- The aid must have the potential to affect trade between member states of the EU;

- The measure granting aid must have the effect of distorting competition by conferring a benefit as an undertaking.

In relation to the need for an effect on "intra community trade" the commission and the European Court of Justice have traditionally interpreted this concept fairly widely. It does not matter that the firm or company concerned never intends to operate outside of the UK; the issue is whether the goods or services in which the company is trading are themselves potentially subject to intra community trade.

In outline, an authority must consider whether or not any support given to a company confers a benefit which is not generally enjoyed by other companies. In applying these criteria the Commission has recognised the so called "market economy investor principle" (MEIP) which provides that if the State is acting in the same way as private investors would (for example charging the same rates as a private sector investor would) then no unlawful benefit is conferred.

State Aid principles can be applied to a number of potential measures for the provision of assistance by the authority to the company. Typical examples of the types of assistance that may be provided, and which may breach State Aid rules are:

- A local authority loan money on terms more favourable than generally available commercial rates;

- Grant funding;

- The provision of guarantees or indemnities;

- Other assistance, *e.g.* premises, ICT equipment, vehicles etc. which are provided at a subsidised rate.

8.30   If State Aid issues arise, the assistance to be provided will need to be approved in advance by the European Commission through (a) it approving a formal notification, or (b) the assistance being compatible with an existing approved notified scheme, or (c) the assistance being compatible with one of the State Aid block exemptions issued by the Commission. One form of block exemption is aid to small and medium sized enterprises (SMEs), another is aid for enterprises entrusted by the State with a "public service mission."

The company may need its own advice in relation to competition law issues which are governed largely by the Competition Act 1998, the

Enterprise Act 2002 and various EC Treaty Provisions (for example Arts 81 and 82). These prohibit matters such as predatory pricing or the formation of cartels.

State Aid advice is provided at para.77 and Annex C of the ODPM's Trading Guidance; and assistance may be found on the DTI's web-site: *www.dti.gov.uk/europe/stateaid*. Competition Law advice is provided at paras 80 to 84 of that guidance; it draws attention to further advice being available from the Office of Fair Trading's web-site: *www.oft.gov.uk*.

BUSINESS PLANNING

It is regarded as good practice for a comprehensive business plan to be written at the outset of the formation of any company. This is covered in the ODPM's Trading Guidance at Annex B and in more detail in Ch.10. The business plan will need to be updated on a regular basis once the company is formed (*e.g.* annually). The business plan will identify precisely how the company will operate, the extent to which it is permitted to look for wider markets and the policies and practices it will adopt in the delivery of its contracts. **8.31**

EXIT STRATEGIES

Exit provisions will be needed to enable the authority to realise its investment in the company (and thereby extract value) and to protect its investment if the company fails to perform in accordance with the agreed objectives. The key issues to be considered are: "when does exit occur?" and "how does it occur?". These are matters, which will be effectively within the shareholder's control. **8.32**

When exit occurs and how the exit is managed could be covered in the company's constitution (Memorandum and Articles of Association). There are two basic scenarios when, generally a shareholder would need to exit the company:

- *Voluntary*, either voluntary sale of shares or where the shareholders consent to winding up;
- *Compulsory* events which compulsorily give rise to a sale of shares or winding up (for example insolvency).

In addition, the authority must consider the implications of a change of CPA status which places the authority in a category in which it can no longer trade through a company. The actual contracts performed by the company will not themselves be affected; it will be the local authority linkage which must be examined. The CPA linkage is discussed in Ch.7; this explains that the Trading Order makes transitional provisions (at reg.3) which permit the continuation of existing activities for a two year time period.

The manner of exiting an arrangement normally means one of two choices also:

- Share sale to third party; or

- Winding up of the company.

Agreeing exit provisions for a wholly owned company is not difficult although the impact on staff is a key consideration. If, however, there are more than one shareholders this may be more problematic. If it is intended to cease trading and wind up the company, the impact on existing contracts must be considered. Share sales offer a possible exit route as in a share sale the business will continue, although with a different owner. The authority will then need to decide both what happens to the assets (are these sold with the business) and how to value the business.

TAXATION

8.33   Taxation matters are covered in more detail in Ch.11. The taxation treatment of any company will need to be assessed, and this may involve both direct taxation (corporation tax) and indirect taxation (VAT). Advice is normally sought to ensure that a company is set up on a manner, which is tax efficient, for example to minimise the stamp duty implications on any transfer of property. The ODPM's Trading Guidance refers to the National Advice Service for VAT on 0485 010 9000, and web-site: *www.hmce.gov.uk*; which allows access to the leaflet: VAT Notice 700/1 *"Should I be registered for VAT?"*. See para.78 of the guidance.

CONCLUSION

8.34   The use of the company model offers exciting possibilities for those who wish to embark on commercial, risk based trading activities. Nevertheless, the legal, financial and practical issues are significant and the authority will wish to take advice on those issues, either from its own staff or from appropriate external advisors.

CHAPTER 9

COMMERCIAL TRADING IN PRACTICE

INTRODUCTION

This Chapter outlines the practical use of two different commercial **9.1** trading companies and therefore supports the material within Ch.7 and Ch.8. As the authors have commented elsewhere in this work, the powers within the Local Government Act 2003 are in their infancy. It is likely therefore that attention will turn first to the use of the charging power under s.93 and it may well be that pure commercial trading vehicles will be rare, at least for a few years following the introduction of the 2003 Act.

The two practical examples chosen represent different approaches. The first example is of a wholly owned local authority company. The motivation for its establishment was that the future needs of that host authority for the skills and expertise of the personnel concerned are now limited. The second example is of an authority setting up a joint venture company with a private sector firm. That company has been established to undertake work partially for the authority but with a view to trading more widely. The second example is of a rather more ambitious vehicle which needed significant inward investment, hence the linkage with a private sector firm.

An authority needs to be clear about some basic issues before it considers the use of a commercial trading company model. These issues are likely to be developed and to feature in the Business Case which is a requirement under the Trading Order (see Chs 7 and 8):

- The type of Pt V company (share based company, guarantee company or Industrial and Provident Society's Act company) and the legal power to participate in a company for the purposes sought and whether it would be acting lawfully in exercising this power;

- The extent to which the authority wishes to control or influence the company, either as shareholder or by appointing directors;

- The manner in which the company will be funded and the extent to which it is reliant on the authority itself for those funds;

- The extent to which involvement in the commercial trading company will expose the authority to additional risks and whether these should be protected by commercial insurance;

- The extent to which council members or officers, who are also directors, would have any conflict of interest in those different roles.

Some of the preliminary legal and financial issues which are likely to arise and upon which advice may be necessary are outlined in Figure 9.1 below. Other figures within the text provide practical guidance. These are offered in the form of questions for those considering a commercial trading company. The practical illustrations offered in the text have also been chosen to illustrate other areas upon which guidance may be needed.

Figure 9.1
Some Preliminary Questions for those Considering a Trading Company

General:

- Why set up a company—what are its underlying objectives?

- What is likely to be the impact on local businesses?

- What is the type of company structure most effective for achieving the objective?

- How widely will the company be able to operate? Will its remit be limited by geography or type of work it could undertake?

- How long is the company intended to operate? What is the exit strategy?

- How will the authority seek to maintain its control/influence of the company? What impact will this have in terms of shareholding and/or directors?

- What is the value of assets which may be transferred into the company and how will this be reflected in the shareholding?

- How many shareholders will be involved?

- Have all necessary consents been obtained (central government consent is generally necessary for any NHS or other central government participation)?

- What will the name of the commercial trading company be? Is that name available?

- Have domain names been reserved in that name?

Staffing Issues:

- Will the company be able to recruit its own employees?

- Will the employees be seconded from one or more the shareholders?

- What terms and conditions will the employees enjoy?

- Is any form of employee participation or incentive plan proposed?

Financial Issues:

- How is the company to be financed? If funds are to be raised externally, what are the likely requirements of the funders in relation to seeking guarantees from the shareholder(s)? How will this impact in State Aid and accounting terms?

- Are all the risks of the enterprise being borne by the company itself or will some be assumed directly by the shareholder(s)? How much responsibility is a shareholder willing to accept for the losses to the business and for liabilities to third parties? How are these risks likely to impact in State Aid and accounting terms?

- How are profits to be extracted or losses dealt with?

- How will the company be taxed and how will dividends be taxed on receipt? Does the structure chosen provide the best tax treatment for the company and the shareholder(s)?

- How will the activities of the shareholder(s) to be treated for accounting purposes? Will the trading company be a subsidiary or subsidiary undertaking?

THE EXAMPLE OF A WHOLLY OWNED COMPANY

Introduction

The authors have come across a number of situations where an authority has undertaken a Best Value review of a service area and has come to the conclusion that the needs of the authority have changed and that it simply does not have the in-house work to support the level of staff which it has on its payroll to undertake work of that type. Those authorities are therefore faced with a number of choices; one of which is re-deployment and another **9.2** is to consider making staff redundant. A number of authorities are now looking at the trading powers within s.95 of the Local Government Act 2003 as an opportunity to take a different direction.

One such authority had a number of consultants on its payroll; all of whom provided a valuable service to the authority but who were under utilised in the authority's own work. This was because the services concerned were of a specialist nature and the authority's own needs had changed over the years. Following a Best Value review the authority considered a range of options. Re-deployment was not considered a viable option because the staff had a high level of expertise and the only jobs available, within the authority, were of an entirely different nature. Having sought to avoid redundancy if at all possible it came up with two preferred options (following staff consultation). These were outsourcing to a private sector firm or setting up a company and trading well beyond the boundaries of the authority.

The authority did undertake an outsourcing exercise but found that there was a lack of market interest in taking over the services concerned because of their specialized nature; and the lack of guaranteed work from the host authority. They therefore decided to set up a company to permit trading activity.

It should be noted that the restrictions outlined in Ch.8 of the need to compete for work because of the impact of the EU public procurement regime were not considered material in this case. This is because very little work was anticipated from the authority and the value of consultancy contracts anticipated to be let by the host authority were below the EU threshold of £153, 376 (at 2004/05 levels).

Key Practical and Commercial Issues for this Company

9.3   The authority had undertaken a degree of market research and had assessed that there was likely to be sufficient work for the company to trade profitably; although it was not expected to grow significantly. It assessed matters such as the likely competition, the risks to be faced by the company and the investment needs.

The tools used were those explored in Ch.3 on strategy and Ch.10 on practical implementation. Officers who were to move to the company undertook a SWOT analysis and considered that there was a need to build upon existing skills and experience. Their target market was to be primarily private sector firms which were working with local authorities. The actual local government market was seen as a secondary target market.

The authority sought commercial advice on the preparation of both a Business Case (to support its investment decision) and on the Business Plan to be adopted by the company. The Business Plan was to be updated on a yearly basis. The main commercial aspects related to the funding and assets; and the extent and manner in which these were made available in the light of State Aid concerns (see Ch.8).

Funding was agreed as a mix of share capital; borrowing (limited) and initial start up grant.

Finally, taxation advice was given in respect of stamp duty (on the transfer of land and assets), corporation tax and VAT.

Key Legal Issues Considered for this Company

Setting up the Company

The authority knew that the setting up of a company may be undertaken **9.4** quickly and at little significant cost. This is because companies may be formed "ready made" from a number of suppliers; although most authorities will wish to purchase a bespoke company from a firm of commercial lawyers. This allows the type of company to be tailored to the needs of the authority and avoids buying a company which has a "history"; albeit a company which has never traded. However, before rushing to set up the company the authority concerned wished to obtain proper legal advice to make sure it utilised the most suitable company model. The advice given covered a range of issues outlined below.

Legal Advice Sought

Legal advice was sought as follows: **9.5**

- The terms and conditions under which employees would work for the company, and whether those staff would be seconded or transfer via TUPE across from the authority;
- A share-incentivisation scheme for selected employees and the most tax efficient way of making those benefits available;
- The terms and conditions upon which assets would be made available; both tangible assets and intellectual property (which was the know-how of the council);
- The accounting treatment of the company in the accounts of the authority;
- The legal terms and conditions under which the company would be trading with third parties, particularly the risks and liabilities which the company could undertake as the contracting party:

Advice on the Memorandum and Articles

- Whether standard Articles governing the internal running of the **9.6** company were suitable;
- Whether extra protection was to be provided via a shareholders' agreement under which certain matters would be remitted to the

shareholders for agreement and not left to the directors. These included:

- o scope of business;
- o disposing of any assets;
- o acquiring land or property;
- o incurring expenditure or taking on liabilities not previously approved in the Business Plan;
- o giving guarantees;
- o undertaking litigation.

- Those matters over which the shareholders would have veto rights.

- Those matters in which the shareholders would have to be unanimous.

Advice on Directors' duties

9.7   As the directors were to be drawn partially from the authority itself, advice was prepared on directors duties both under the Companies Act 1985 and also the fiduciary duties owed to the company. This included advice on the Code of Conduct for Members and the linkage to the Council's own Standards Committee. This also involved advice on indemnities for officers and Members.

Figure 9.2
Some General Regulatory Issues

- How does company impact on competition in the relevant markets and what restrictions if any are to be accepted by the shareholders?

- Is the commercial trading company likely to be considered to be in receipt of "State Aid" which distorts or threatens to distort trade?

Conclusion on the In-House Model

9.8   This model seems to be well suited to those authorities whose needs have changed over the years. The authors are aware of examples relating to the provision of asbestos removal, sale of local authority developed computer software, archeological services and specialist engineering services. In all cases the common theme seems to be that there is a wish to serve a market which lies beyond the public sector and beyond the local authority's own boundaries. There is also only limited availability of work from the host authority (and therefore the Business Plan is not conditional on securing host authority work) and limited need for capital investment (the businesses are largely "people" rather than "asset" based).

THE EXAMPLE OF A JOINT VENTURE COMPANY

Introduction

This authority was aware that there were a number of public sector **9.9** bodies (primarily within the education sector), who would prefer to have their business support services (for example payroll and finance) to be delivered by those with specific experience of public service delivery. It realised that there was a business opportunity and that it could undertake trading activity with public bodies under s.1 of the Local Authorities (Goods and Services) Act 1970. However, it also realised that to be able to compete in that market with existing players it would need both commercial expertise and financial investment. The authority already had considerable borrowings, and was looking to make substantial investment in its own services particularly in the area of new ICT systems for the authority. It had no monies available to invest in this new project.

It therefore undertook some market soundings to see whether any private sector company would be willing to work as its partner to generate profits for the authority from third party work. The authority would supply useful know-how and skills and the private sector would offer the commercial knowledge and the necessary capital to operate a business.

The authority realised quickly that the type of private sector companies that it was interested in working with, would only consider this opportunity if presented with a proper business case to support the necessary financial longer term investment. That business case would have to show the commercial viability of the model; and particularly how the new venture could borrow money and repay it without full recourse back to either the local authority or the private sector company. In colloquial terms, the venture would have to have a reasonable prospect of being able to stand on its own two feet.

It should be noted that the restrictions outlined in Ch.8 of the need to compete for work because of the impact of the EU public procurement regime were not considered material in this case. This is because the authority was outsourcing the likely work which the company could undertake through a service contract which would be awarded to the company as part of the procurement arrangements (see below). This meant that there was very little future work to be anticipated from the authority; although minor new contracts of a value below the EU threshold of £153, 376 (at 2004/05 levels) were possible.

After considering a number of options the authority determined that it would seek to meet its own ICT investment needs by outsourcing some of its own work. However, it would make it a pre-condition that any bidder for the work would have to be prepared to set up a joint venture company (JVC) in which the authority would hold shares. That company would be offered a long duration service contract provided this afforded a cost effective solution to the council. That is, the outsourcing itself would have to offer proper value for money compared with an in-house solution. There was no point in the authority paying an excessive price for its ICT services just to give the company a profit; some of which (after tax) would be ploughed back into the local authority. However, if the company had a service contract it could borrow against this income stream, and use this capital to generate third party work and, ultimately pay a proportion of those profits back to the authority.

Procurement Issues

9.10   One of the complicating issues in this arrangement was the need to procure a private sector company to undertake the authority's work as well as to be a shareholder and investor in the JVC. Whether or not any joint venture succeeds is unlikely to depend on the vehicle or precise structuring of the commercial trading company, although it is important to have a suitable framework which does not impede the progress of the enterprise. What is far more important is choosing a suitable partner and having trust and confidence in that partner.

The setting up of a company does not of itself trigger any EU procurement requirements; it is the awarding of contracts which triggers that regime. It was therefore necessary to use a procurement exercise to choose a partner, and to make it clear that a pre-condition of being awarded the work was a willingness of that partner to set up a commercial trading company in an agreed form. In this case, the private sector partner set up the company and the authority took shares in that commercial trading company.

The EU regime was triggered because a contractual arrangement needs to be put in place between the authority and the commercial trading company. The authority wished to procure services from the commercial trading company through a contractual relationship with the company. It therefore needed to award that contract to the commercial trading company in compliance with the regime. The authority made known its requirements at four key stages in the procurement process:

- Procurement strategy; The authority determined that the setting up of a commercial trading company was a requirement which must be complied with; but it did allow for variant bids (*i.e.* bidders could suggest other models of service delivery);

- The advertisement stage; The wishes of the authority for a commercial trading company was disclosed; allowing potential partners to become self-selecting, depending on their willingness (or otherwise) to participate in JVC;

- Selection Process; Bidders were short-listed, partly on the basis of track record (technical capacity) and ability to deliver the overall project. Experience in operating JVC companies was relevant in this assessment;

- Evaluation of Bids; Bidders were chosen and bids evaluated, partially on an assessment of the partnership model, *i.e.* the structure of the commercial trading company proposed.

Figure 9.3
Some General Contractual Issues for JVCs

- Will the trading company be treated as a contracting entity which needs to procure its own goods and services under the EU procurement regime?

- Will the local authority shareholder be able to supply goods and services to the company and will this be regulated as "trading" with the private sector?

- Will any shareholder be able to derive extra profit from supplying goods and services to the company or will all contracts be treated as being "at arm's length"?

- How will these obligations be policed by the shareholders?

Key Practical and Commercial Issues for this Company

Staffing Issues

One of the main issues for the authority related to the treatment of staff. **9.11** It was decided, during negotiations with interested parties that a secondment model would meet the requirements of all stakeholders. This allowed the workforce to remain employed by the authority but to participate in the development of the company. It is anticipated that some staff may be recruited directly by the company as its third party work expands.

Taxation

The taxation treatment of the company required analysis to consider the **9.12** tax treatment of both direct taxation (corporation tax) and indirect taxation (VAT). Advice was given to ensure that the JVC was set up on a manner which is tax efficient, for example to minimise the stamp duty implications on any transfer of property.

> **Figure 9.4**
> **Some Confidentiality Issues for JVCs**
>
> ● What information will a shareholder learn about the other's busi-
>   nesses as a result of this venture and to what extent is it going to be
>   covered by confidentiality obligations?
>
> ● To what extent does each shareholder need intellectual property
>   licenced by the other?
>
> ● Who will own the intellectual property generated by the company?
>   Will the shareholders partners be able to use it?
>
> ● How will the company be treated for the purposes of the Freedom of
>   Information Act 2000?
>
> ● To what extent can directors of the company release information to
>   their appointing shareholders?

Key Legal Issues Considered for this Company

Vires of Setting up the Company

9.13   The company was set up before s.95 of the Local Government Act 2003
was enacted and therefore initially used the powers within s.2(1) of the
Local Government Act 2000 (the wellbeing power). The authority was
comforted by the government's recognition of the use of the power for
company participation in the draft guidance (*Working with Others to
Achieve Best Value* (DETR/ODPM Consultation Paper of 2001). Nevertheless, this reminds authorities of the important limitation on the exercise of
this power: "provided they are satisfied that the primary purpose behind
the formation of, or participation in, a particular company is likely to
achieve the promotion or improvement of the economic, social or environmental wellbeing of the authority's area" (At para.3.12).

Having set the company up in this manner; the authority is reconsidering
whether its Memorandum and Articles need changing to make clear that it
has the power for wider commercial trading under s.95 of the Local
Government Act 2003.

Structuring the Company

9.14   The authority were attracted to the flexibility of the company model and
the ability to control the company through ownership of shares; with
different classes of shares carrying different voting rights. At the time the
company was set up, companies of this type were classified under the

regime laid down in Pt V of the Local Government and Housing Act 1989 and the Local Authorities (Companies) Order 1995 (SI 1995/849 as amended). As this was before the advent of the prudential accounting regime; classification had important limitations, particularly in terms of borrowing of the JVC.

The authority therefore took a minority stake of below 20 per cent to ensure that it was not deemed to have "control" over the JVC. This classified the company as a "minority interest company" and its borrowing was not linked to that of the authority. Instead it protected its rights through "veto" rights over key decisions, through a "golden-share" arrangement protected by a complex shareholders' agreement.

In the light of the changes to the law by the prudential accounting regime (also introduced by the Local Government Act 2003), the authority is considering its shareholding as it is now able to hold a majority of the shares without automatically triggering the requirement for the company's borrowings to be covered by the capital finance regime. Under the prudential regime; the authority has to consider the level of recourse to the authority of the company and make prudential arrangements for this. As Ch.8 reveals, the current arrangements which were introduced on April 1, 2004 offer considerably more flexibility for JVC arrangements.

All companies are subject to generally accepted accounting practice. The way in which the results and assets and liabilities of a commercial trading company are recorded in the accounts of an authority will depend upon its exact relationship between the bodies. A company's accounts are likely to require consolidation into the controlling entity's accounts (in this case, those of the private sector "partner").

Figure 9.5
Some general management issues for JVCs

- What sort of Board and management structure will be required? Certain issues will be matters for the Board of directors but other issues will be reserved to shareholders for their approval—which matters fall into which category?

- Is the JVC to be deadlocked, *i.e.* both parties having equal number of shares, and representation at board level or will the one partner have a majority and therefore control. Will the minority partner be given "veto" voting rights over certain key issues? If so, which are these?

- How are shareholder disputes to be resolved?

Conclusion on the JVC Model

9.15   As well as the commercial success of the arrangement; three key advantages have been identified for this model. These are: "partnership" delivery; financial transparency and longer term stability.

The use of the JVC model has enabled the authority to be involved in the working relationship with the private sector partner in a number of different ways. This is outside of its role as client in the commercial relationship. In its role as shareholder it is able to vote at general meetings, exercise rights of approval or rights or veto over those matters which have been reserved to it; it holds directorships within to the Board of Directors (although it could have chosen only to attend the Board in the capacity of observer). This has given tremendous flexibility in the structure of the JVC partnership; and also means that a council is able to change its role as the partnership evolves.

The use of the company vehicle has offered significant clarity and transparency in terms of the success (or failure) of the partnership. Open book disclosure is truly possible leading to greater accountability. This level of disclosure is not possible with a contractual co-operation agreement. With the company model the shareholders have a forum to discuss how profits are to be dealt with, for example paid in dividends to the shareholders or plough back into service delivery, or divert into other schemes.

The JVC model has acted as a focus for economic regeneration by creating a major new commercial entity within the council's area. As it is possible to change shareholders, it does mean that a change of partner is possible without necessarily winding up the company. That is, on expiry of the current service contract a new procurement exercise could lead to a new partner to whom the shares of the first partner may be sold. This arrangement means that the third party contracts which the company has entered into are not affected and it also leads to longer term job security for those employed by the company as their employer does not change.

CONCLUSION

9.16   At the end of 2004, there were very few examples of local authority trading companies operating. This is to be expected as the powers within the Local Government Act 2003 have only recently been introduced. As discussed in Ch.8 one of the major factors which seems to inhibit authorities from setting up trading companies is the need for that company to compete against others to undertake work because of the impact of the EU public procurement regime. For differing reasons; that limitation was not considered material in either case as explained in the text.

The two examples given here represent very different approaches and motivations. It may be seen that the JVC model is more complicated to deliver than a purely in-house model; however, both have their advantages and disadvantages. It is hoped that these examples will provide a practical illustration of the scope of the s.95 trading power.

Part Three

Practical Implementation

CHAPTER 10

PRACTICAL IMPLEMENTATION ISSUES

INTRODUCTION

The decision to charge or trade has now been taken, as described in **10.1** Ch.3, and the relevant activities authorised by the council. This decision will have included the determination as to whether a local authority wants to avail itself of commercial trading powers under s.95, or engage in charging activity for civic benefit under s.93.

Attention then turns to the practical implementation issues that arise in order to put any such decision into effect. Obviously, what implementation issues there are will depend on the council's strategy. Throughout this chapter, a distinction is made between s.93 and s.95 as the issues will be different.

It is also worth pointing out that legal rules at this part of the process are relatively scarce. Both s.93 and s.95 of the Local Government Act 2003 have specific legal rules associated with them (for example the requirement under s.95 of the Local Government Act 2003 and the Trading Order to have a business case) and each is supported by guidance from the ODPM (see Appendix 2) to which the local authorities must "have regard;" however, leaving aside these basic legal areas, the key areas in implementation are financial, administrative and commercial. It is these issues that are considered in this chapter.

The extent of the implementation activity required by any local authority at this stage in the process depends on whether it is s.93 charging or s.95 commercial trading that is planned and also the scale of the activity. In general, whilst a local authority would be expected to have properly analysed the market before engaging on an extensive commercial trading venture, it may well be enough for it to "take a view" from internal knowledge on who is doing what in the marketplace in relation to a marginal charging scheme. Essentially, it all comes down to risk management, which is one of the areas specifically examined below.

It is important to emphasise that it would be extremely unfortunate for a local authority to properly go through its strategic planning work, as described in Ch.3, and then get the implementation matters discussed in this chapter all wrong. An example might be of an authority that decides it might not want to commercially trade under s.95, but simply wants to obtain a little more civic benefit by charging for some discretionary services. If it then fails to define the "service" for s.93; does not put in place an appropriate accounting regime to track the costs and income; and does not get legal advice on whether an alternative charging power is available in any particular instance, it can still all go wrong. At one end of the spectrum are legal errors that could render the council's activity *ultra vires* and void, through to the other end of the spectrum where the consequence is just plain inconvenience in having to sort out a mess after the event. Either way, there is no reason why any local authority should find itself in this position if it follows a number of simple steps as examined below.

An over-arching issue to mention in this instance is whether a single person should oversee a council's charging and trading activity. It would be possible to appoint a Director of Trading who would have this function, though many local authorities might see this as unnecessary and something that would not fit within their current managerial arrangements. The authors have therefore suggested that the council needs to set down a policy framework which has the role of controlling charging and trading activity, whether there is a single person overseeing that or not.

This chapter examines all of the practical implementation issues, including business and financial issues, risk analyses, analysing the market and management and organisational issues. It concludes by looking at the risk of challenge, which is another area most local authorities would want to consider.

THE BUSINESS PLAN

10.2   If a local authority is contemplating commercial risk based trading under s.95 of the Local Government Act 2003, then there is a statutory requirement for a business case. This is provided by the Local Government (Best Value Authorities)(Power to Trade)(England) Order 2004. However, as noted in Ch.3, the *business case* has a different function from the *business plan*. As the Trading Guidance points out at para.37:

"There is a distinction to be drawn between the business case and the business plan:

- the *business case* assesses the risk involved in the proposed trading enterprise and decides whether or not it should proceed. It starts the process of business planning;
- the *business plan* sets out the objectives of the business, how they are to be achieved and standards met, adjusts it in the light of

experience in changing circumstances. It is a comprehensive analysis of the business situation at a particular point in time."

As noted above, these provisions relate to s.95 and commercial risk based trading. However, every charging or trading activity needs proper authorisation and proper planning. As such, this advice is as valid in relation to s.93 as it is for s.95. In simple terms, the business case refers to the legal authorisation and justification for the activity—thereby making it a strategic planning issue—whereas the business plan is more a practical implementation issue.

Figure 10.1 illustrates three of the main purposes that the ODPM believes a business plan serves.

Figure 10.1
Purposes of a Business Plan

- To demonstrate to members, potential investors and the company board that the business is a viable enterprise, with an identified market, an achievable set of business objectives, and an adequacy of managerial and other necessary skills and experience;

- To assure potential clients the business is well run and has the capacity and resources to ensure reliability and quality;

- As an internal management tool to ensure that all parts of the business work together towards common and consistent goals, and that these goals are based on sound analyses, assumptions and are consistent with local authority objectives.

The objectives in Figure 10.1 are directed towards the company route, as it is taken from the Trading Guidance. However, many of the areas mentioned are equally valid in relation to charging activity.

The following areas should be covered in any charging or trading business plan:

- Powers; the local authority will need to ensure that it has addressed the powers issue and it is clear the powers on which it relies. For commercial trading, s.95 of the Local Government Act 2003 and the Trading Order are all that is required by way of powers, save for that which creates the activity in question as a local authority function. For s.93 business plans, it will also be necessary to make a reference to the powers that are relied upon, to which s.93 will attach;

- The business area; there will have to some identification of the nature of the activity that is to be engaged in, with some reference to how that impacts on the council itself;

171

- Any assets and equipment required to deliver services in this area;

- What staffing would be required to deliver services;

- Likely recipients of the service or clients/customers;

- The charges that will be levied for the services, how these will be calculated and elements of income, expenditure and profit;

- Capacity; whether the activity can be undertaken using existing capacity or whether growth is required;

- Benefits to other parts of the local authority's activities *e.g.* economies of scale.

10.3   There is no doubt that for s.95 commercial trading activity, a comprehensive business plan document will be required. It is more likely that a company venture will concentrate on a single or narrow area, rather than being established as a general trading company. An example might be a local authority that has a UPVC window manufacturing factory, which it sets up as a s.95 company. Here, whilst a comprehensive business plan would be required, it would focus on the market in relation to the manufacture and sale of windows specifically. Whilst there is no reason why a local authority cannot set up a general trading company, this seems less likely bearing in mind the necessity for detailed supporting documentation to the venture.

In business planning terms, s.93 offers a different set of issues. Whilst any s.95 activity is likely to be significant (or else it would not justify the costs of establishing a company), s.93 charging activity may be marginal in its nature. If this is the case, then it would be unsurprising if there was no business plan at all. However, the authors would always advise that some sort of business plan is necessary, however brief. This raises an issue that recurs throughout the consideration in this chapter of the various practical implementation steps: that is to what extent is it worth undertaking the work for relatively minor and disparate discretionary services? The answer, in the view of the authors, is to set up a corporate system, perhaps utilising a template suite of documents, which have to be completed in relation to each discretionary service. By keeping these documents proportionate to the activity in question, the local authority can ensure that the proper steps have been gone through and also that a needlessly bureaucratic system is avoided. In relation to the business case, for example, such a system might require at least one A4 sheet with template headings, giving the areas that need to be covered. This would then be completed for each activity undertaken (such as those described in Ch.6) with the necessary detail.

Taking the example of the grounds maintenance for the RSL, and bearing in mind the matters mentioned above that should be included in the business plan, that A4 sheet would contain details of the grounds maintenance work, who the RSL is that is receiving the service, how the service would be provided (whether by existing capacity or new capacity), whether new assets or equipment are required, what would be charged for the service and so on. It should be pointed out that the local authority has to have this information because without it it would have no prospect of ensuring that income and expenditure are properly balanced under the duty in s.93(3) of the Local Government Act 2003. The authors simply suggest, therefore, that there is an official way of recording this information as part of the legal and financial audit trail. In relation to discretionary charging, of course, issues of powers and income/expenditure balancing are likely to be of greater significance.

As part of the council's business planning activity, it needs to record the strategic direction agreed for the business and discussed in Ch.3.

If the council is engaging in commercial activity and establishing a trading company for this purpose, the business strategy might be to develop the company's activities to deliver income of £X per annum or to have a capital value of £Ymillion by a certain date. This strategy would deliver either income generation to support the council tax or a capital value that can subsequently be realised by the council via a sale of the company's shares.

The business strategy may also cover the direction of the business over the longer term, for example whether diversification into new markets is envisaged, development of new products or merger with other players in the marketplace.

For s.93 services, this strategy includes the civic benefit that is to be obtained from providing the discretionary service and its general impact on the community.

THE RISK ANALYSIS

In embarking on any major commercial trading venture, a risk analysis **10.4** would really be an essential document in support of that venture. However, a minor risk analysis will also assist in discretionary charging activity too, and could well be included as part of the suite of documentation mentioned above.

The basic components of any analysis of risk will be as follows:

- Identifying risk—what are the risks that may occur?
- An estimation of the risks—what is the likelihood of this happening?
- Quantifying the consequences of a risk happening—what will this mean?
- Ascertaining the costs of a risk occurring—what will it cost?
- Identifying the party on whom the burden of risk will fall—who will bear this responsibility?

It can therefore be seen that the components of a risk analysis are relatively straightforward and such an exercise can be major or minor in its scale. Once the various data has been identified, the council can produce a risk matrix and from that develop a risk management strategy. If major commercial transactions are considered, such as PFI or PPP schemes, risk analyses of this nature are critically important. This is because risk has a directly proportional effect on value for money. In other words, if a council tries to allocate responsibility for a risk to a party that does not control it, then that party will require substantial extra payment to take that risk. The art in balancing the value for money curve is to ensure that the party that has the influence over the risk, controls it for no extra payment. In simple terms, the risk on completing building the school on time is on the builder and that company should bear that risk without any extra payment as the completion of the building work is entirely within its gift.

PPP and PFI schemes are mentioned as risk may play a different role in relation to trading activity. Here, the issue may be whether the risks associated with engaging in any activity make it worthwhile or not. In other words, risk analysis may assist the council in deciding whether it wants to trade in this area or is better avoiding it.

Local authorities have extensive expertise in the analysis of risk already. It is therefore essential that this expertise is engaged in its charging and trading activity so that appropriate decisions can be taken. What is needed is a combination of risk management techniques (which most local authorities will have somewhere within their structure) and those with detailed technical knowledge of the relevant activity.

10.5   Looking at the example mentioned in Ch.6 for loaning art works to the private sector, the risk matrix would be prepared by a group of officers with risk management, technical (*i.e.* art gallery staff) and commercial expertise. This would take into account risks such as the art being stolen (a classic risk management issue); the recipients not paying (a commercial issue); and the inability of the art gallery to have sufficient exhibits likely to interest the corporate entities who will be the customers (a technical issue). The solutions to some of these problems may well be very straightforward, for example taking out necessary insurance arrangements to protect against theft.

Looking at the example of grounds maintenance work for the RSL, there a benefit may be gained by ensuring that the work is undertaken on the local authority's terms and conditions, which may limit liability in certain circumstances. Alternatively, the control system mentioned above might hold that a particular local authority department can only engage in £X value of work at any particular time. All of these various solutions will have the consequence of limiting risk.

As mentioned above, risk may well play a different part in relation to trading and the ultimate decision would be not to proceed with a particular scheme. An example here might be a local authority that plans to provide a discretionary service in a market where there is already over supply at local level. Here the council might decide that the combination of the risks of challenge (one of the existing contractors claiming that the council has not exercised its powers properly), political risk (members being contacted about the effect on the existing contractors) and economic risk (*i.e.* damage to the pre-existing local economy) make this proposal unviable.

The Figure 10.2 gives examples of risks that local authorities might consider in relation to charging and trading activity.

Figure 10.2
Examples of Risks

- disgruntled customers;
- problems with service delivery;
- non payment for services;
- legal challenge by current providers of similar services;
- lack of support by Local Authority staff;
- insufficient interest in and take up of the services;
- diversion from core activity

THE MARKET ANALYSIS

The council also needs to be clear what is happening in its local or the national marketplace, relevant to the activity it intends to pursue. In fact, the same goes for any charging or trading activity using existing powers (as described in Ch.4) where consideration would still need to be given to who else is in the market. However, a local authority will need to examine its marketplace for commercial trading activity under s.95 of the Local Government Act 2003 and discretionary charging under s.93 of the Local Government Act 2003 for different reasons. **10.6**

Turning to discretionary charging first, it may well be that the local authorities engage in activity best described as "gap filling" in which case it is unlikely that there will be a mature market currently in existence. In some circumstances, this will be exactly why a local authority has decided in its strategic planning, to provide such a service at all. In other circumstances, there might be other service providers around, but not providing the services in the same way or for the same client base as the council is. However, there will be a number of reasons why the local authority wants to give consideration to what else is available in the marketplace, including legal reasons (the likelihood of a challenge by an existing service provider); political reasons (including pressure on members); and the needs of the community.

Where commercial trading is contemplated the reason that a full market analysis needs to be undertaken is likely to be quite different. Here the underlying driver will be commercial, *i.e.* if stiff competition already exists in a marketplace and a local authority is about to launch its s.95 company into that arena, it is unlikely to make any significant inroads and may well fail commercially. So whilst there may be less of an issue in relation to legal matters, commercial issues will be paramount.

A market analysis can range from a professionally commissioned substantial external analysis, undertaken by a leading player offering such services, leading to a full written report and costing a significant sum; to an internal discussion/think tank, collation of local knowledge and the like. The latter might include experience the council has via its functional work of any activity (for example, trading standards complaints about the standard of minor building work undertaken in the community or social services department verifying that no service is available of a particular type to the elderly community).

Figure 10.3 summarises some of the questions that should be included in any market analysis. It is up to each local authority to determine what level of market analysis it needs and then to keep appropriate records of its findings. In the view of the authors, a full analysis would be required of a major commercial trading venture. However, if more marginal discretionary services are being offered, then the control system mentioned above could include another A4 sheet asking some fairly basic questions of what services are being provided by whom and at what cost that needs to be completed and retained as part of the legal and financial audit trail.

It may well be that findings in relation to the marketplace may need to be fed back into the strategic planning work described in Ch.3, particularly if the results of any such analysis are not those anticipated. As an example, if a local authority determines to establish its UPVC manufacturing plant as a company, believing it to be capable of delivering profits back to the council from trading generally; it may wish to reconsider this course if a market analysis demonstrates that the company would face severe competition selling to the private sector and is unlikely to succeed. In those circumstances, the council may prefer to pursue a different option, such as undertaking a trade sale of the venture for a capital sum.

Figure 10.3
The Market Analysis—Questions to be Asked

- Who is providing services now?
- How well are they doing it?
- Is there evidence of problems in service delivery?

- Is there room for new providers in the marketplace?
- Should it be us?
- What will the long term effects on the market be?

USER SURVEYS

When describing the market analysis above, the authors look at the issues **10.7** from the position of service providers who might already be delivering services of a similar type to those proposed to be delivered by the council. However, there is another way of looking at this, and that is from the perspective of users themselves, which is likely to predominately mean members of the public.

An understanding of the user base of any council services is essential to the local authority and closely linked to its own aims and objectives, community leadership and the achievement of Best Value. This point was picked up by the Audit Commission in its paper *The Price Is Right? Charges for Council Services* published in September 1999. It states:

"An understanding of the user is essential, not just to get the best out of charging, but also to develop and improve any service. The Best Value regime makes it clear that services cannot be developed in isolation from the user." (At para.44).

Chapter 3 looked at the policy issues in relation to charging as one of the strategic areas that needs consideration as part of planning. However, a user survey might also be a practical implementation step that an authority needs to consider. User surveys can be extremely useful in giving the council vital information on the level of charge that will be acceptable and what motivates users of the services. Used in conjunction with other data, councils can take much more effective decisions on all areas of charging policy, including discretionary charging. An example might be given in relation to opening hours for leisure facilities. If the council's swimming pool normally opens at 8.00am and closes at 7.00pm, it could devise a discretionary service scheme using leisure powers under s.19 of the Local Government (Miscellaneous Provisions) Act 1976. Under the scheme, charges would be levied for extended opening hours, say from 6.00am to 8.00am in the morning and 7.00pm to 10.00pm in the evening. There would be no purpose in offering such a service if there was no demand for it and a user survey would assist with this. Furthermore, if the council were able to determine what type of person would use such a service, this may also assist in its establishment of the charges. Put simply, if the early morning swimming is largely to be utilised by those in full time employment, rather than the under-privileged, the council may wish to levy a higher charge.

Another example might be in relation to city centre parking. There is no reason why a local authority cannot charge different amounts for different car parks, perhaps with a premium for the most centrally located, with lower charges for those a little further out from the city centre. Again, user surveys will assist in determining whether such a strategy would be successful.

An allied matter to user surveys is take-up of new services offered. If the services are taken up enthusiastically, then there is clearly a need for them; conversely, if the take-up is poor, then the authority may determine that the requirements are not there. This will also impact on how the authority balances the books under the duty of s.93(3) of the Local Government Act 2003.

PERFORMANCE LEVELS

10.8   Also relevant to the issue of implementation will be the performance levels historically achieved by the council in the provision of its own services. Whilst the s.93 power is available to any local authority (unless and until it is disapplied by the government), it is to be hoped that authorities offering services using this route would only do so if they have achieved good levels of performance in the past. If this is not the case, then there may well be problems with the recipients of the services, leading to criticism of the authority. Of course, this may well be the type of situation which prompts the Secretary of State to act to remove powers to charge.

If the authority is to engage in extensive activity then an upper quartile performance would be useful. Simply agreeing to mow a few extra lawns will be less of an issue.

The Best Value regime may help here: local authorities will have been inspected for many of the charging activities and this will clearly illustrate the standards of service being met. Furthermore, the idea of a Best Value review as a precursor to engaging in extensive new activity would be a good one. Applying the 4 C's could be an illuminating experience, for example asking the 'challenge' questions, such as why should we do this? should it be us? will it work?

A COST/BENEFIT ANALYSIS

10.9   Any local authority engaging in charging or trading activity needs to be mindful of its core aims as set down in its community strategy. These issues are discussed in Ch.3 when looking at strategic planning. However, as part of its implementation work, a local authority may well determine that some form of cost/benefit analysis would be helpful in challenging whether any proposal will meets its intended needs. It goes without saying that the other services on offer from a local authority should not deteriorate as a direct result of its engagement in commercial trading or charging for discretionary services. This would be particularly damaging to the latter, as the whole purpose of discretionary charging is to provide a service and levy a charge in order to achieve greater civic benefit. It would be deeply unfortunate if a local authority engaged in the performance of a discretionary service, successfully levying charges as appropriate, but found that its core service had suffered as a result. As core service areas will feed directly into the authority's Comprehensive Performance Assessment, such a result would be devastating.

The same could be said of commercial trading using a company. If the authority determines that this is the way to go but finds that the work involved in establishing and nurturing the company into its new marketplace is so extensive that resources are pulled off other core areas, then this would again be a very unfortunate result.

Undertaking a cost/benefit analysis will therefore enable the local authority to look at any particular activity and see if the burdens justify the benefits.

Any such analysis could really be part of the business planning exercise, rather than done separately, but should cover the following areas:

- What will be the benefit to the public of the new service?

- What will be the impact of delivering the new services on existing services?

- What economies of scale will be achievable?

- What management and other time will be necessary to launch the new services?

- How will the new services help other services the council delivers?

It goes without saying that if such an exercise throws up genuine difficulties, the council might determine that notwithstanding the fact such a new service would be useful, the benefits that it would deliver do not justify the time and effort in establishing such a service and therefore determines not to go down that route.

ECONOMIC, SOCIAL AND ENVIRONMENTAL WELLBEING CASES

Whether an authority is intending to trade commercially or sell some discretionary services, it may well be acting under wellbeing powers. These are discussed at length in Ch.4 which examines s.2 of the Local Government Act 2000. This authorises a local authority to do anything that is likely to promote or improve the economic, social or environmental wellbeing of its area. The authors particularly emphasise the fact that the power is a power of "first resort," is intended to be purposively applied and used and **10.10**

179

is the subject of very supportive guidance from the ODPM. That said, any local authority that utilises wellbeing powers still needs to properly justify their use. In order to do this, the authority has to explain exactly why an activity will promote or improve economic, social or environmental wellbeing. This involves a relatively straight forward exercise whereby a note is made of the evidence available to the council to support such a case.

Using the examples in Ch.6, the council would need to demonstrate in support of its service of loaning art works to the private sector that to do so would promote or improve wellbeing. Here, the council might say that the social wellbeing of the community will be benefited by the art works that are currently not on display anywhere being displayed in the reception areas of the corporate headquarters; furthermore, there would be an economic benefit to the council in levying the charge, thereby permitting the purchase of more art works in the future. Whatever the various reasons are for using wellbeing, these need to be recorded. This material also needs to correlate with both the community strategy and the other parts of the legal and financial audit trail. So far as the community strategy is concerned, all wellbeing powers need to be used with reference to that strategy and there should be a harmony apparent. So far as the other aspects of the legal and financial audit trail are concerned, a correlation might, for example, exist with the market analysis. If the social services department is saying that no market is available in a certain service for the elderly, than that will be evidence to support the contention that to offer that service would promote or improve the social wellbeing of elderly people in the community.

The economic, social or environmental wellbeing case should not necessarily be long but must cover the essential points. This would also include a demonstration that there is no prohibition on using wellbeing powers in accordance with s.3 of the Local Government Act 2000. This matter is also examined in Ch.4. Whilst the case here does not need to be prepared by lawyers, it should be able to withstand judicial scrutiny and not be a "sham."

MANAGEMENT AND ORGANISATIONAL ISSUES

10.11   Under this heading, the required activity will differ, depending on whether the council is proposing a commercial trading venture or more civic benefit from discretionary charging.

Turning to trading first, if the council is intending to set up a s.95 company, then the steps included in Ch.7 will need to be addressed. Obviously, the company will need staff, accommodation, assets and equipment and all of those things will be under the umbrella of the corporate entity created. But the council will still need some form of "client side" within its structure.

A variety of issues will need to be accommodated to ensure that the council's control of its trading company is appropriate. This may include matters such as:

- How does the company report to the local authority?
- What links are there between the council and the board of directors?
- How are the company's activities reported to members?
- Is an officer responsible for the council side of the company's activities?

Whilst these issues will need to be determined, the majority of the activity will be in relation to the company, rather than at the local authority.

This situation is to be contrasted with the position under charging for discretionary services. Here life is more complex as there will be no structure external to the local authority. If the activity really is only marginal in its nature, then no changes at all may be required to the management and organisation of the authority itself; there is simply an addition of a few more activities to what the council does now. In other circumstances, however, the services due to their nature or extent will need to be properly planned.

An example of a s.93 service that would need to be properly talked through in advance is that described in Ch.6, namely the loaning of art works to the private sector. In relation to that venture, the following would be required:

- A person responsible for the development and management of that service;
- Professional advice from the art gallery on which artworks to loan etc;
- Commercial advice on the market and what should be charged;
- Legal advice on powers and use of s.93;
- Financial advice on costings and accounting;
- Administrative support.

If the cost of providing this service is in six figures, it is unlikely that the **10.12** local authority could simply bolt it on to existing structures without any impact. It may well be that recruitment of new staff is required in which case decisions have to be taken as to where they will be placed and the impact of new staff and new services on the existing operations needs to be carefully considered. Leaving aside the issue as to whether a local authority appoints a director of trading or any other titled officer with responsibility for overseeing all of the charging and trading activity that goes on, each department engaging in the delivery of discretionary services for a charge needs to consider its own organisational position.

The issue about the use of s.93 of the Local Government Act 2003 is that these activities normally will be undertaken in some pre-existing part of the council, whether this be refuse collection, grounds maintenance, building maintenance or leisure. Whether any specific decisions need taking about structural changes will depend on the nature and extent of the activity. This is an issue that may well be determined as a strategic issue, as described in Ch.3.

Many local authorities might be put off by any suggestions they need to make extensive changes to their structure in order to accommodate s.93 activities. It is for this reason that the authors have emphasised the requirements for a policy framework which would enable the political management of the authority together with senior officers to control such activities. Mentioned above are the vision as planned, the risk analysis, market analysis and cases for use of the economic, social or environmental wellbeing powers. The suite of documents that will form the legal and financial audit trail may well include guidelines on recruiting staff and when organisational change should be considered.

Nonetheless, if extensive activities under s.93 of the Local Government Act 2003 are ongoing, it does raise the issue as to whether having a Director of Trading post would be useful in order to provide guidance and assistance to all the other parts of the council that will be engaging in such activity within their functional areas.

ACCOUNTABILITY

10.13   Accountability in the council's charging or trading operations will also differ according to whether it is commercial trading and therefore profit or civic benefit that is the aim. Either way, any local authority needs to supplement its management and organisational issues with further provisions on accountability. The reason for this is that the council will wish to control profit making ventures that might result in losses; but also monitor delivery of discretionary services that might be having an unintended consequence. The arrangements under accountability should ensure that there are clear lines of responsibility both on the member and officer side and that appropriate safety mechanisms are included.

Such measures might include the following:

- Designating a director of trading to over see the council's charging and trading activities;
- Alternatively, introducing a system whereby the appropriate Chief Officer takes responsibility for activity in his or her functional area

or there is a designated lead officer or manager in respect of any significant charging or trading activity;

- A business case is required by law in relation to commercial trading but the council could adopt an internal rule whereby a business case and business plan is required for all charging or trading activity over a certain financial threshold, numbers of staff involved etc;

- The requirement for a sign off by the director of legal services and/ or chief financial officer of more significant arrangements, again linked to financial thresholds or some other measure;

- Amendment to the Standing Orders or Financial Regulations of the authority;

- A requirement to report to members periodically, or where certain circumstances are triggered;

- A requirement to report to members if a loss is being made, a business plan is failing, market conditions have changed, a legal challenge has been made or other unanticipated consequences have occurred.

It is up to each local authority to determine what they want to include in their system. It goes without saying, however, that a comprehensive system is more likely to avoid challenge, be more sensitive to the needs of the community and ensure the charging and trading activity is more effectively targeted.

TACTICAL ISSUES

It was mentioned above that a local authority has to decide the scale of **10.14** its practical implementation work. It goes without saying that the scale should be proportionate to the nature and extent of its charging or trading activity and to risk.

This means that any commercial trading activity, which by its nature is risk based and likely to be extensive, would make all of the steps contained in this chapter essential.

However, where a local authority is engaging in the delivery of some discretionary services, which may be marginal to its other activities, it may "take a view" on the extent of this work that is required. A simple example in this regard is a marketplace analysis. If a local authority is to cut a few extra lawns, then it might well determine that it is unnecessary to have any external advice on the marketplace and to simply take account of the views of members (who regularly interact with the community), those engaged in the services and anyone else internally who might offer a view. The nature of the legal and financial audit trail may also be proportionate to the scale of the activity. A council may determine that a one page business plan is sufficient for a marginal activity with an insignificant value; whereas a new scheme such as loaning art works to the private sector might require a fuller business case. Above all, the authority needs to be flexible in its strategy and be prepared to take decisions as it goes along.

Tactics will also include timetabling of projects. This may be a more important issue than it at first appears. As an example, Ch.6 considers a local authority establishing a new service of loaning art works to the private sector. It would certainly not be recommended for the director of leisure services to consider such a service might be viable and to embark on the works of alteration to the art gallery mentioned under that example before the contracts with the corporate entities that will be the recipients of the service have been properly executed. This illustrates why timing will be a key factor.

The following is the sort of process that a local authority will need to pursue:

- The policy framework would be laid down by the political leadership (see Ch.3);
- Members and officers internally would be canvassed for ideas of services that would provide civic benefit and be capable of being provided by the council;
- Preliminary legal advice will need to be taken including the application of the three tests for applicability of s.93 of the Local Government Act 2003, as described in Ch.5;
- Consideration given to the marketplace, who is already providing such a service and what would the user demand for that service be?
- Develop an outline business case and a more detailed business plan;
- Seek member authority formally;
- Enter contracts where appropriate;
- Establish other aspects of the appropriate "system";
- Commence activity.

It is important to emphasise that no money should be spent pre-contract; changes to the local authority's departmental or other structures should not be undertaken before the services are being delivered; and the situation should be constantly monitored, for example to see whether there is likely to be a challenge.

RISK OF CHALLENGE

10.15   The risk of challenge will differ from area to area, service to service and local authority to local authority. In the view of the authors, however, it is inevitable that charging and trading will end up before the courts over the next few years in some form or another.

It has to be said that the risk must be higher in relation to s.95 commercial trading activities. Risk based trading, in competition with the private sector, is most likely to generate powerful and well resourced opposition. The *McCarthy and Stone* case demonstrates that where the actions of the local authority in levying a charge may impact on the business and profits of a commercial entity, it will normally have no qualms in mounting a challenge. After all, in that case Richmond-upon-Thames London Borough Council simply sought to levy a flat fee charge of £25 for a pre-planning inquiry, in order to contribute towards the officer time involved. Whilst this may have seemed relatively minor to the council, the company no doubt considered what the impact would be if every local authority across the UK introduced a similar charge. The sort of figures that might have been involved can only be the subject of conjecture but it was clearly important enough for the company to challenge the case and to continue appealing to the House of Lords after losing the case in both the Divisional Court and the Court of Appeal. What is remarkable, however, is the fact that having won the case, the precedent was created that no local authority could charge for that activity anywhere else. In relation to risk of challenge, therefore, it may not be just local issues that are applicable. It is for this reason that the legal and financial audit trail must be sound if a local authority is to withstand any such challenge.

The risk in relation to s.93 charging activity is likely to be lower, predominately because such activity is motivated by civic benefit, not profit. Often such activities will be "gap filling" in their nature and the council in delivering such services will not be in direct competition with the private sector. However, this may not be universally the case and it is still possible that challenges will be generated in relation to such activity.

Discretionary charging activity also offers much more flexibility if a local authority is faced with a challenge. If Barchester District Council is providing numerous different discretionary services across its functional areas successfully, but it emerges that in one particular area there is a private sector complainant, then it has the ability to decide whether to continue providing those services or not. Many local authorities in such a position might take a pragmatic line and, leaving aside any legal issues, might decide simply to abandon that area in order to avoid a challenge. In these circumstances it would only be if a sustained challenge across a wide variety of different areas were made that such an authority would consider it to be worth fighting a case over.

Obviously, the same cannot be said in relation to commercial risk based trading, though it is to be hoped that conflict can be avoided.

10.16 There are two main avenues of challenge, namely judicial review and a complaint to the external auditor. As well as these two main areas, a number of other areas might occur, such as actions in contract or tort, consumer law or the bringing of political pressure to bear.

Turning to judicial review first, there are a number of grounds that might be relied upon either relating to the first limb of the *ultra vires* doctrine, *i.e.* that the council did not have legal authority to engage in the activity in question; or that it has exercised whatever power is available to it outside of the requirements of public law. Judicial review cases will be familiar to local authorities and have provided the context for many of the cases referred to elsewhere in this work. In particular, the challenge of the Yorkshire Purchasing Organisation by the BEC and the challenge of Richmond-upon-Thames LBC by McCarthy and Stone were both via judicial review proceedings.

Equally likely is a complaint to the external auditor. Auditors' powers have now been consolidated into the Audit Commission Act 1998 and they remain extensive powers whereby auditors can challenge the activities of local authorities. In Ch.13 the authors mentioned the historical context of charging and trading activity and it can be seen that the Audit Commission played a substantial role in supporting the government of the time in dissuading local authorities from engaging in municipal trading activity. However, since the Audit Commission has changed to its more strategic regulation approach, it is unlikely that it would play any significant role of this nature in the powers under the Local Government Act 2003. More likely is that any complainant would be advised to take action directly through the courts using judicial review proceedings.

A whole host of other areas of challenge might arise including actions in contract or tort (for example where a local authority has breached a contractual arrangement it has made or has committed some other civil wrong such as breach of another party's intellectual property); actions in consumer law (for example under the Distance Selling Regulations—see Ch.11); or via political pressure to MPs and members from consumers, businesses, the Chamber of Commerce and so on.

The authors have mentioned above that any control system that is put in place by the authority to ensure that charging and trading activity is structured, should include provisions whereby extra care is taken if there is warning that a legal challenge might be made.

CONCLUSION

10.17 The practical implementation issues facing local authorities are not difficult but require proper application and discipline on the part of the authority. The danger is that local authorities authorise charging or trading without sufficient planning as described in Ch.3 or sufficient implementation activity as described in this chapter. If this is the case, then the consequences can be dire for the authority. The authors mentioned in *Municipal Trading* in 1990 that "bad cases make bad law" and this has been prevalent in the earlier history of charging and trading described in Ch.13. It is important that local authorities do not engage in modern charging and trading activity in a way which encourages challenge or leaves them vulnerable to legal actions. It would be particularly unfortunate if the wrong case gets before the courts, before local authorities have fully embraced these new powers and a new climate of uncertainty is created. However, if the steps in this chapter are followed, then such risks will be minimised.

CHAPTER 11

COMMERCIAL AND CONSUMER ISSUES

INTRODUCTION

This Chapter is designed as an "aide memoire" to draw attention to **11.1** some of the contextual legal issues which will need to be considered in developing a charging or trading strategy. It is not intended to be comprehensive nor is it a substitute of appropriate legal advice; its aim is rather to highlight some of the areas upon which legal advice is likely to be necessary.

In particular it needs to be remembered that authorities will be entering into legally enforceable agreements; normally these will be to provide services. Those contracts may be with other public bodies, with local citizens or with the private sector. It is commonly known that, generally speaking, there is no need for a contract to be written for it to be legally enforceable. Nevertheless most contracts are written to provide the necessary certainty as to the legal terms, so that both parties are clear on what they have to provide and what they are entitled to receive. Different formats of contracts will be required depending on the specific nature of the service and the market within which the authority is operating. A contract to provide refuse collection services to a neighbouring authority will be drafted in significantly different terms to a contract to cut the grass and hedges of an elderly local resident.

It should also be noted that certain types of services have special legislative provisions which govern their operation (for example agency agreements) or are generally covered by standard form agreements (such as building and engineering services). This Chapter does not explain any of that special legislation or specialised forms of agreement as this should be the subject of specific legal advice.

Any authority actively involved in trading activity should be equipped with standard terms and conditions which have been drafted by lawyers, whether internal or external; and the knowledge of how to use those standard terms. It should always be remembered that provided both parties are happy with the outcome of their agreement, matters will not need to be resolved by recourse to law. This Chapter outlines some of the areas of legal difficulty which lawyers will be familiar with and which impact upon standard form agreements. These may be less familiar to operational staff actually involved in charging or trading. It is intended to highlight the legal context within which the use of standard terms and conditions will be viewed if there is ever a dispute.

The Chapter commences with an outline of basic issues such as determining which terms and conditions govern the contractual relationship before drawing attention to some of the terms which may be implied into a contract by operation of law. It then outlines some of the legal issues around advertising before drawing attention to the impact of competition law. Finally it outlines the basic taxation issues to be considered.

PRE-CONTRACTUAL STATEMENTS

11.2   It is likely to be the case with any contract of any value that certain pre-contractual negotiations will take place before the contract conditions are finalised. During this time it is common for both parties to make certain "representations" which are relied upon by the other party as an inducement to enter into the contract. Those representations may relate to matters in the past (such as the past experience and track record) or matters which will impact on intended performance (such as willingness to share risks which may emerge or remedy defective work). There is a raft of law covering such matters.

In relation to past record, even an innocent misrepresentation may give rise to the right to end the subsequent contract (called rescission) or damages under the Misrepresentation Act 1967. Any representations as to how the parties will behave in a future contractual situation should be drafted as express contractual terms of the contract and the whole agreement protected by an "entire agreement" clause. A properly drafted entire agreement clause will make it clear that the full terms of the contract are written down and documented in that agreement and there is no other pre-existing document or representation which is not so reflected. This allows any disagreement to be resolved merely by looking at the single document.

DETERMINING THE TERMS OF THE CONTRACT

11.3   The contract terms are normally easy to determine as these will feature as express terms in a written document, signed or sealed by authorised officers from each contracting party. Difficulties can arise in two main circumstances; the first is where both contracting parties claim that the contract was made on their own standard terms and conditions (the so called "battle of the forms") and the second where the courts have to determine the contract terms in the absence of specific written terms covering the point in dispute.

Battle of the Forms

One of the most difficult situations which arises with the regular use of standard terms and conditions by both service providers and service users is the so-called "battle of the forms." This arises where both parties are only able or wish to contract on their own standard terms. Difficulties may arise where a provider is asked to supply a quotation for some services and these are sent out on a form which expressly incorporates its own terms and conditions; but then the user commissions the services in a letter which is written on its own stationery and which sets out the user's terms and conditions. This means there are two sets of standard terms and conditions in play. If the services are provided properly and paid for and both parties are completely happy then any differences in the actual terms and conditions of the two parties are unlikely ever to come to light. If, however, matters go wrong, both parties and their advisers will have to try and work out which terms and conditions governed the transaction. **11.4**

There are two leading cases on the "battle of the forms"; which illustrate how these problems can arise. In *Butler Machine Tool Company Limited v Ex-Cell-O Corporation (England) Limited* [1979] 1 All ER 965, the seller provided a quote stated to be on the seller's terms and conditions which were expressed to "prevail over any terms and conditions in the buyer's order." The buyer subsequently placed the order on its own stationery which contained his own standard terms and conditions. At the foot of the buyer's order was a tear off acknowledgement of the order which stated that "we accept your order on the terms and conditions stated thereon." The seller signed that acknowledgement and returned it to the buyer together with a covering letter stating that the order was being "entered into in accordance with the offer."

The Court of Appeal decided that the decisive document was the buyer's order and it was the buyer's terms and conditions which prevailed. This is because the seller had returned the buyer's tear off slip and had not made it clear that, as the seller, it was only offering to contract on its own terms and conditions. The reference in the seller's covering letter to "the offer" was interpreted as meaning the main terms such as price and quantity. Some subsequent cases have followed this approach even where there was no tear off slip. For example, *Sauter Automation Limited v Goodman (Mechanical Services) Limited* (1986) 34 BLR 81.

In *BRS v Arthur Crutchley Limited* [1968] 1 All ER 811 there had been the usual exchange of correspondence on the two different sets of terms and conditions. The court held that at that stage there was no contract at all

191

as this correspondence merely constituted a set of different offers neither of which had been accepted by the other party. However, when the seller actually delivered the goods he presented the buyer with a delivery note for signature stating that the sale was on the seller's terms and conditions. The buyer stamped that delivery note with a statement that the delivery would be accepted on the buyer's terms and conditions. This "buyer's stamp" was the last documented part of the transaction. On receipt of the stamped terms and conditions the seller then unloaded the goods. The court held that by unloading the goods, the seller had accepted the terms of the buyer. Therefore, the court held that there was a contract on the buyer's terms and conditions.

The basic and fundamental difficulty illustrated in each case is that neither party was willing to walk away from the transaction unless the final terms of the deal were agreed between the parties. The core element of any contract is agreement and if the parties do not agree they should not be contracting. If matters are not clear there are a number of possible legal outcomes:

- The contract is deemed to be on the provider's terms and conditions;

- The contract is deemed to be on the user's terms and conditions;

- The contract is deemed to be on neither party's terms and conditions—but merely those contractual terms which are imposed by law for such arrangements;

- The contract is deemed to be on a combination of both parties' terms and conditions; or

- It is accepted that there is no contract at all.

Courts often try and find the existence of a contract on one or other party's terms as shown by the cases above. However, this is not always possible. The case of *Hertford Foods Ltd v Lidl GmbH* [2001] EWCA Civ 938 was a more recent case with conflicting standard terms: where the Court of Appeal decided that neither parties' terms and conditions were incorporated.

Quantum Meruit

11.5   If the Court decides that services have actually been provided; but that there is insufficient evidence of agreement for them to conclude that there is any contract, then the doctrine of *quantum meruit* may apply. This entitles the service provider to a fair payment for its work. *Quantum meruit* is most commonly seen where one party has started to provide services to another whilst the parties are still in negotiation about the final terms of the contract and those negotiations then break down and so no contract is ever concluded. The service user has asked for the services to be provided and has benefited so it should make fair recompense for its gain. The risk for the user is that the court will only determine the fair price and that there will be no other performance obligations imposed (for example no guarantee of the work).

CONTRACTUAL TERMS IMPLIED BY LAW

It is important in a trading context for the total bargain of the parties, **11.6** that is their whole agreement, to be fully documented and agreed by both parties. If some matters are not covered, the law will step in and seek to "fill in the gaps." The manner in which those gaps are filled may not be to the liking of either party. This risk is best closed off by careful drafting of express written terms to cover every point.

It should also be noted that there are certain areas where the written agreement of the parties cannot overturn the legal position. As an example, it is impossible to exclude liability in certain circumstances because of the Unfair Contract Terms Act 1977 ("UCTA"); also certain legislation will imply terms as outlined below.

Terms implied by trade custom or usage

It is generally accepted that to ensure commercial efficacy, terms may be **11.7** implied into an written contract; where the document is silent on those issues. This is based on the presumption that, in such transactions, the parties are well aware of the particular commercial context and therefore have not needed to state all matters as they are so well known as not to need stating. However, custom or usage will not be implied where it is inconsistent with the tenor of the contract as a whole (See *AS Sameiling v Grain Importers (Eire) Ltd* [1952] 2 All ER 315).

Even if there is no local custom or usage a court may seek to fill in a gap on the basis of a previous course of dealing between the parties. This is only likely where there has been a long course of dealing.

The courts also often imply provisions as to reasonableness into contracts. This may be done in circumstances where there is uncertainty in contractual terms which would otherwise undermine a contract. The courts have implied terms such as a reasonable duration for a contract (*Jonescu v Royal Free Hospital Board of Governors* (1965) 109 Sol Jo 534) and that a right under a contract should be exercised within a reasonable time (*United Dominions Trust (Commercial) Ltd v Eagle Aircrafts Services Ltd* [1968] 1 All ER 104).

Consumer Contracts

Consumers enjoy greater protection by the law than commercial parties. **11.8** This is especially the case where consumers are required to sign standard form contracts. As well as legal controls, there are a number of bodies whose role is that of "consumer watchdog." Perhaps the best known of these is the Office of Fair Trading ("OFT") but there are a number of sponsored bodies such as the National Consumer Council. Local authorities themselves have often been active with a trading standards or consumer protection function (for example enforcement of Unfair Terms in Consumer Contracts Regulations (1999) or advice on civil claims).

The Unfair Terms in Consumer Contracts Regulations (1999) (SI 1999/2083, as amended) regulate consumer supply contracts and in particular any written terms within those contracts which have not been individually negotiated. These ensure that, for example, the terms are "expressed in plain intelligible language" (reg.7); and are not "unfair" (reg.5). Schedule 2 to the regulations contains "an indicative and non-exhaustive" list of terms which may be regarded as "unfair." The regulations have been supported by a number of Bulletins issued by the OFT which clarify the scope of the regulations.

It should not be forgotten that the Unfair Contract Terms Act 1977 will also regulate standard form contracts and that those dealing as consumers obtain extra protection over and above that afforded to "business to business" transactions (see below). In addition, it has long been a rule of interpretation by the courts that any ambiguities in contracts are likely to be interpreted in a manner which goes against the party relying on the particular drafting (the *contra proferentem* rule).

Also of interest to consumers are the Sale and Supply of Goods to Consumers Regulations 2002 which implement Directive 1999/44/EC on certain aspects of the sale of consumer goods and associated guarantees. The 2002 Regulations amend the Sale of Goods Act 1979, the Supply of Goods and Services Act 1982, the Supply of Goods (Implied Terms) Act 1973, and the Unfair Contract Terms Act 1977 to give additional rights to buyers in consumer cases. They also contain provisions on the legal status of guarantees offered to consumers and place obligations on guarantors in relation to such guarantees and apply to the supply of goods to consumers.

Terms Implied by Statute

11.9   Perhaps the most common terms which are likely to be implied by law into trading type contracts are those within the Sale of Goods Act 1979 (as amended) and the Supply of Goods and Services Act 1982. As explained above, consumers' rights obtain stringent protection; but all types of contracts may have terms implied into them.

The Sale of Goods Act 1979 (as amended)

11.10   The Sale of Goods Act 1979 implies various terms into a contract for the sale of goods. Section 8 Sale of Goods Act 1979 implies a term into the contract, in the absence of express price provisions, that the buyer will pay a reasonable price for the goods. The parties will, however, normally agree the price and this is usually seen as an essential part of the negotiation. Care should always be taken when using any sort of price provision other than actual monetary figures as vague provisions such as "a fair price" may be struck down for uncertainty. Each case will depend on its facts; and it may be possible to have a provision in which the "fair and reasonable" price is determined (in the absence of agreement) by reference to open book principles or by reference to an expert who will determine the price by reference to an objective standard.

Under s.10(1) Sale of Goods Act 1979, time for payment is not of the essence (*i.e.* the contract cannot be terminated for breach, and the seller is only compensated in damages) unless expressly stated in the agreement.

Section 13 states that, where goods are sold by description, there is an implied condition that the goods would correspond to that description. In practice goods are normally sold with by reference to an exact trade name or detailed specification which avoids this provision.

Section 14 implies terms as to quality and fitness. These are conformity to satisfactory quality (see new s.14(2B) of amended Sale of Goods Act 1979) and reasonable fitness for purpose (s.14(3)). Any express condition which provides more stringent promises than the legal standard is acceptable; but any provision which seeks to reduce that legal protection is likely to be regarded as an exclusion clause and may be struck down under the Unfair Contract Terms Act—see below.

Section 15 relates to a sale of goods by sample and implies two conditions, that, *inter alia*, the bulk will correspond with the sampling quality and that the goods will be free from defect. Again, any provision which seeks to reduce that legal protection is likely to be regarded as an exclusion clause and may be struck down under the Unfair Contract Terms Act 1977—see below.

Section 20 Sale of Goods Act 1979 provides that the goods remain at the seller's risk until property is transferred to the buyer.

Supply of Goods and Services Act 1982

The 1982 Act implies terms into any contract under which one party has agreed to supply services to another. This may take effect as a partial obligation alongside the supply of or hire of goods within the same contract. The duty is owed to the party to whom the services are provided. Wider categories of persons can, of course, have redress for example third parties may be protected under the law of negligence. **11.11**

The key terms implied by the 1982 Act are:

- *Sections 3 to 5* in relation to goods supplied as part of the services, these sections impose terms relating to quality and fitness that correspond to those governing quality within the Sale of Goods Act 1979.

- *Section 13* where the supplier is acting in the course of a business, an implied term that it will carry out the services with reasonable skill and care;

- *Section 14(1)* where the supplier is acting in the course of a business and the time for the services to be carried out is not fixed by the contract, or has to be fixed in a manner agreed in the contract or determined by the course of dealing between the parties, an implied term that the supplier will carry out the services within a reasonable time. Section 14(2) provides that the issue of what constitutes a reasonable time is a question of fact;

- *Section 15(1)* where the actual monetary consideration for the services is not determined by the contract, or is to be determined in a manner agreed in the contract or by a course of dealing between the parties, there is an implied term that the client will pay the supplier a reasonable charge. Section 15(2) provides that this is a question of fact.

Other issues are left to be determined between the parties; and there is a provision (s.16) which means that if stricter duties are imposed by other statutes; those stricter duties will apply (an example is in the case of inn-keepers). The Secretary of State has power under the Act to exclude particular categories of services from the implied terms (s.12(4)). For example, they do not apply to services rendered by a director of a company to that company when acting in the capacity of director (although other duties do apply—see Ch.8).

The Unfair Contract Terms Act 1977 (UCTA)

11.12   Terms implied into a contract may be negated or varied by agreement of the parties to the contract, or by a course of dealing between them, subject to the provisions of UCTA. This Act imposes certain limits on the extent to which liability for a breach of contract, negligence or other breach of duty can be avoided by express contractual terms.

In relation to business to business arrangements, the Unfair Contract Terms Act provides that:

- The terms implied by the statutory provisions outlined above (*e.g.* those under the Sale of Goods Act 1979 or the 1982 Act) can only be excluded or restricted, insofar as the term satisfies the requirement of reasonableness;

- A party cannot exclude or restrict his liability for death or personal injury resulting from negligence and, in respect of other loss or damages resulting from negligence, can do so only insofar as the contract term excluding such liability satisfies the requirement of reasonableness; and

- If the parties are trading on one party's standard terms and conditions, a term purporting to exclude or restrict liability for breach of contract is void save in so far as it satisfies the requirement of reasonableness. In this context an exclusion clause may be interpreted widely to include 'duty defining clauses' which operate as an exclusion (*e.g.* "the seller shall have no obligation to deliver the goods on time or at all"). This provision should not generally apply to clauses in negotiated agreements, although the case of *St Albans DC v ICL* [1996] ALL ER 481 held that an exclusion clause in a negotiated supply agreement can nevertheless be regarded as trading on one party's standard terms if the negotiations leave the exclusion clause "effectively untouched."

Where the Act makes an exclusion clause valid only insofar as it passes a test of "reasonableness," this test is that the term shall be a fair and reasonable one to be included in the contract, having regard to the circumstances which were, or ought reasonably to have been, known to or in the contemplation of the parties when the contract was made. The test looks at matters existing at the time of contracting, and the Act further provides that regard must be had to the guidelines set out in Sch.2 of the Act, which include:

- The strength of the bargaining position of the parties
- Any inducements offered to accept the exclusion clause *e.g.* a lower price
- Trade custom or a previous course of dealing between the parties
- Practicality of compliance with any specific conditions
- The availability of insurance.

In the case of those parties acting as consumers, Pt I of the Unfair Contract Terms Act largely precludes or restricts any reliance on exclusion clauses and clauses having similar effect. That is they are likely to be regarded as void and of no legal effect; unlike the situation with firms acting in the course of their normal business where such clauses are normally subject to the test of "reasonableness." It is worth noting that definition of consumer is not limited to individuals. For a firm to be acting in the course of a business within the Act the transaction must be integral to and not incidental to the firm's business. A firm purchasing goods incidental to its business may therefore be regarded as a consumer in relation to such a transaction under the Act.

ADVERTISING CONTROLS

Key Legal Requirements

11.13
- The Trade Descriptions Act 1968 makes it a criminal offence to give a false or misleading description about goods or services.

- The Consumer Protection Act 1987 makes it a criminal offence to give consumers a misleading price indication.

- The Data Protection Act 1998 governs the extent to which personal data can be collected, stored and used; this may well impact on lists kept for "mail shots" where the data may have been compiled for other purposes.

THE DISTANCE SELLING REGULATIONS

11.14   The Consumer Protection (Distance Selling) Regulations (SI 2000/2334), made important changes to the consumer protection regime in the UK. The regulations impact on contracts made at a distance between suppliers and consumers for the supply of goods and services. This is particularly relevant if goods or services are sold by over the internet, by telephone, or by fax. Breach of the regulations can lead to contracts with consumers being rendered unenforceable.

The Regulations give the consumer an unconditional right to cancel an order. They are entitled to a seven working day "cooling off" period in which to withdraw from the contract without penalty and without giving any reason. This cancellation period starts in a goods contract from the day after the date of delivery of the goods, and in a services contract from the date of conclusion of the contract, or the date when written confirmation is received if later. The seven day cooling off period may be extended to three months if the prescribed information is not given to the consumer.

The Regulations do not apply in "business to business" contracts nor where the supplier and consumer come face to face before the contract is made. There are also specific exemptions for certain categories of transaction from some or all of the Regulations *e.g.* financial services. The main purpose of the provisions is to ensure "transparency"; so that the consumer is fully aware of all the contractual terms and of their rights of redress. Certain information must be provided to a consumer in a clear and comprehensible manner prior to the contract being entered into: name and address of supplier; the main characteristics of goods or services; the price (including all taxes); arrangements for payment; delivery costs where they apply; arrangements for delivery (which must be within 30 days of their order unless the contact specifies otherwise); the right to cancel the order where appropriate; if the customer has to pay up-front, the seller's postal address; and how long the offer or price remains valid.

CODES OF PRACTICE

There are now a variety of industry groups and codes of practice. As an **11.15** example, the Advertising Standards Authority has its "CAP Code" (Committee of Advertising Practice Code) which seeks to regulate advertising and sales promotions *e.g.* 'prize draws' and competitions. Generally these codes do not have the force of law and so there is no direct legal sanction for non-compliance. However, the codes are generally designed to mirror obligations enshrined in legislation and compliance will assist in avoiding breach of the law. In addition failure to comply can lead to industry censure and adverse publicity and on occasions a refusal for media to carry the advertisement or offer. The Advertising Standards Authority is an independent body that investigates complaints in relation to advertising and promotions in the light of the codes. The key principals of the Codes are that all advertising and sales promotions should be legal, decent, honest and truthful, prepared with a sense of responsibility to the consumer and society and respect the principles of fair competition generally accepted in business.

COMPETITION LAW

Competition law is a very specialist area and one where it is unlikely that **11.16** there will be any current depth of expertise within local government legal departments; although the position may change with the growth of trading activity.

Chapter 8 draws attention to the competition issues which are provided by the State Aid rules designed to prevent national and local government from artificially subsidising private sector undertakings. Competition law has a wider application which restricts the manner in which a trading unit may operate. Depending on where the potential impact is EU wide or purely national, the relevant rules will be found in the EC Treaty or in the UK's Competition Act 1998. The OFT provides general advice: see *www.oft.gov.uk.*

EU Competition Rules

Article 81 of the EC Treaty prohibits all agreements between "undertak- **11.17** ings" which may affect trade between Member States and which have as their object or effect, the prevention, restriction or distortion of competition within the Common Market. Whilst there will almost always be an effect on inter-state trade where the parties to a services agreement are based in different Member States these same EU rules may also apply where the parties are based in the same Member State. Article 81 is designed to prevent "market sharing" between undertakings. The areas to be particularly aware of are situations where an agreement between two trading entities includes any provisions relating to the price each service provider charges to third parties, or contains an element of territorial protection (for example an exclusive territory). These are the matters which a local authority's own tendering rules are designed to protect against (the practice is commonly known as "collusive tendering" in the tendering context) and authorities should be well aware that this practice is unlawful.

Where an undertaking has a large share of a market or otherwise exercises market power, it must also be careful not to infringe Art.82 of the EC Treaty. Article 82 prohibits abuse of a dominant position within the Common Market or a substantial part of it, insofar as the abuse may potentially affect trade between Member States. This situation could exist where for example, a local authority in a remote rural location becomes the dominant supplier of services in that area (for example in vehicle maintenance). Fines may be imposed and there are no exemptions from the application of Art.82.

Significant changes were made to the EU competition regime from May 1, 2004 pursuant to Reg.1/2003.

UK Competition Rules—The Competition Act 1998

11.18 The Competition Act 1998 is modelled on Arts 81(1) and 82 EC Treaty and the Act has two limbs known as: the Chapter I and the Chapter II prohibitions.

The Chapter I prohibition applies to agreements which restrict competition within the UK and affect UK trade (rather than EU trade). In a similar manner, the Chapter II prohibition relates to abuse of dominance within the UK and will potentially apply to service contracts to the extent that one of the parties has a dominant position and any restrictions in the contract may amount to an abuse of that position. Following on from the changes to the EC Competition regime pursuant to Reg.1/2003, the UK regime was also changed to bring it into alignment.

TAX AND VAT

11.19 It hardly needs saying that dealing with fiscal issues requires specialist advice; and the outline below is merely to draw attention to the basics of the system.

Corporation Tax

11.20 Corporation tax is a tax levied on the profits of any "corporation." This means that this obligation is directly relevant to the activities of a local authority's trading company. The main legal provisions are in the Income and Corporation Taxes Act 1988 (as amended). Section 6(1) of that Act provides that: "Corporation tax shall be charged on profits of companies . . . ". "Profits" are defined in s.6(4)(a) to mean "income and chargeable gains."

The term "company" is also widely defined, this time in s.832: "company" means ". . . any body corporate or unincorporated association but does not include a partnership, a local authority or a local authority association." This wide definition would embrace the types of company which are permissible for trading by local authorities and a wide range of external bodies. However, it should be noted that there is an express exclusion of the local authority itself, therefore if profits were generated by trading with another public sector body (see Ch.4, in relation to the Local Authorities (Goods and Services) Act 1970), these would not be taxable.

Broadly speaking the obligations on companies to comply with their duties to pay corporation tax include:

- Having to work out the company's tax liability;

- Having to pay their tax without prior assessment by the Inland Revenue
  and

- The liability to pay penalties if they do not deliver a return by the statutory filing date, normally 12 months after the end of the accounting period.

Corporation Tax is due for "Accounting Periods" which are normally 12 months long. Accounting periods can, in some circumstances, be shorter than 12 months but never longer. The main corporation tax rate as at December 31, 2004 was 30 per cent. There is a small companies' rate of 19 per cent for companies with taxable profits between £50,000 and £300,000. Marginal relief eases the transition from the starting rate of 0 per cent (for companies whose profits are below £10,000) to the small companies' rate for companies with profits between £10,000 and £50,000. Marginal relief also applies to companies with profits between £300,000 and £1,500,000.

VAT

Where a trading company is set up it is very likely to need to register for **11.21** VAT. Where charging activity is involved or trading under other existing powers, the position is much more complicated and authorities will need to take their own specific advice. For general inquiries the Customs and Excise national help line number is 0845 010 9000.

VAT is a tax on expenditure which is paid by the ultimate consumer. VAT applies to supplies of goods and services made in the UK by a business; where those supplies are not exempt. Once a business is likely to be making taxable business supplies in excess of £58,000 (the level applicable on April 1, 2004—it is normally raised annually) it will need to register with HM Customs & Excise for VAT. It should be noted that the VAT registration threshold relates not to profit but to the value of goods or supplies invoiced, and therefore any trading company will need to register for VAT. Only those bodies registered for VAT can claim back the VAT paid on their own taxable supplies. There is a small business scheme for businesses which make under £150,000 value of taxable supplies in any annual VAT period, but this is unlikely to be relevant to a local authority trading company.

The issue of whether VAT is payable on charging activities is more complex that that for trading companies where the issues are clear. This is because it may not be clear whether the authority is making supplies in the course or furtherance of business. Generally, if they are then they will be subject to VAT unless they are exempt or the supplies are zero rated. There are, currently, three rates of VAT:

- A standard rate, of 17.5 per cent;
- A reduced rate, currently 5 per cent: and
- A 0 per cent rate.

The rate depends on the type of goods or services not the business.

There are special rules allowing local authorities to treat certain supplies as non-business that would otherwise give rise to a liability to VAT. These are set out in a customs notice (Customs Notice No.749) "Local Authorities and similar bodies" which should assist authorities in that determination. The notice is available on-line: see *www.hmce.gov.uk* and there is a good search engine within that site.

In theory, VAT is a pass through tax and its effect should be neutral for businesses. That is, if the charge for a taxable supply is £100; the trading company will actually charge £117.50, with the extra £17.50 being the VAT for which the business is accountable to HM Customs & Excise. If the company itself purchases taxable supplies for £117.50 it will have paid VAT and provided it is not the ultimate consumer the VAT paid may be set off against VAT owed. This means the main obligation is in record keeping and accounting. Therefore businesses will need to keep:

- A record of all standard-rated goods and services supplied or received as part of the business;
- A separate record of differently rated goods and supplies made or received: and
- A VAT account

If the VAT on sales is greater than the VAT on the company's purchases; the surplus is owed to the Customs and Excise. If the VAT on the purchases is greater than the VAT on the sales; the difference may be re-claimed.

CONCLUSION

This Chapter is not intended to be comprehensive nor is it a substitute of **11.22** appropriate legal advice; its aim is rather to highlight some of the areas upon which legal advice is likely to be necessary. It is intended to draw attention to some of the contextual legal issues which will need to be considered in developing a trading strategy.

EMPLOYEE AND MEMBER RELATED ISSUES

INTRODUCTION

This Chapter is designed as an *aide memoire* to draw attention to some of **12.1** the key legal and practical issues upon which advice may be needed in relation to employment related matters. In undertaking any charging or trading activity it is important to remember those who will actually be delivering that new activity. This is relevant in a number of different ways. Leaving aside the fact that the staff may themselves be a market for services, the staff may be an important source of ideas for new activities. Staff may also be asked to undertake different activities or to work in a different way to meet a council's requirements to carry out charging or trading. Local authorities should be experienced in delivering change management programmes and in managing more complex personnel issues.

If the authority wishes to set up a commercial trading company (see Chs 7 and 8), this will give rise to more complex issues. That new vehicle will either have to recruit staff directly or staff may be seconded from the authority or may transfer their employment under TUPE. Any contracts awarded to that trading company will need to take account of the authority's duty under the legal regime introduced by ss.101 and 102 of the Local Government Act 2003 and the guidance within the Best Value Circular (ODPM 03/2003).

That Circular guidance was updated, with an Addendum issued with a revised Annex C, in December 2003; and new guidance on performance plans and a revised Annex A in 2004. In relation to employment issues, there is extensive guidance within the Circular and in particular in two Annexes to the Circular (one relating to handling workforce matters in contracting (Annex C) and the other is the Code of Practice on Workforce Matters (at Annex D)).

Trading activity can give rise to a need to protect staff from extra risks; again leaving aside health and safety concerns (which fall outside of the scope of this book), there is a need to consider any increased legal risks and the ability of the council to indemnify or otherwise protect staff against those risks. The provisions introduced in 2004, provide the final section to this Chapter.

MANAGING CHANGE

12.2   Depending on the scale of charging and trading activity, changes to working patterns may be necessary. The key to managing change is proper communication. Even if there are no formal organisational changes, there may be new set of expectations concerning roles, responsibilities, relationships and behaviours. If a trading company is set up, there will be additional legal issues such as pensions and TUPE to deal with. If change is managed well, the resultant synergies can radically improve performance; if managed poorly, organisational and relationship fractures will undermine any new activity and performance will falter.

In larger scale change, it will be necessary to undertake a change management programme. The key features of the programme should include open and on-going communication, two-way consultation, a clear vision and strong leadership. It is important for it to be people orientated and designed around the individual. Formal two-way communication mechanisms should be established alongside individual, more informal arrangements that can operate on a one-to-one level with various professional representatives (*i.e.* HR professionals and Trade Unions).

Involving stakeholders

12.3   An important feature of successful staff management is ensuring that stakeholders own developments within the organisation. Involving stakeholders in the design of the service and its future ensures the sharing of ideas and concerns between those leading change and those responsible for delivery. It avoids decision making being too centralised and creates an environment where staff will be more willing both to suggest and accept change.

Examples of mechanisms and initiatives that are used to facilitate good communication are as follows:

- Seminars and away-days for staff and members;
- Trade union and staff representative consultative mechanisms;
- Newsletters;
- Regular reporting and presentations to members;
- Use of the internet and intranet through the development of websites and electronic mail; and

- Regular team meetings (staff meetings, staff briefings) attended by partnership representatives that include employee representatives.

Setting up a new Trading Company

If the authority has chosen to set up a new legal entity to undertake trading activity; a greater level of communication is likely to be necessary. A range of key issues are likely to require discussion with stakeholders. **12.4**

Core values

Operating in a commercial company is different from operating within a local authority environment as both have different cultures. It should not be assumed that because a company is 100 per cent owned by the local authority that it will have identical core values to the council. **12.5**

The authority will wish to explore with stakeholders the potential for a clash of values between the public sector and the private sector. The core values of the new trading company will need to be developed and it is important that areas of "best fit" are identified, explored and developed.

Policies and procedures

An early decision will need to be made (in consultation with trade unions and employee representatives) on an appropriate set of employment policies and procedures to be adopted by the new trading company. Whilst it may be assumed that these will always mirror those of the host local authority; this decision is not one to be taken lightly. It should not be forgotten that the company will be operating at arm's length from the host local authority and within a very different commercial environment. The decision as to the most appropriate policies and procedures needs to be taken in the light of the future development of the company: if staff are expected to move between the council and the new organisation easily then harmonisation is probably necessary. However, if future staff needs are to be met by recruitment from other private sector organisations then this may not be the best solution. In any event, it should be remembered that the local authority itself will be bound by the statutory guidance provided by the Code of Practice—*Workforce Matters in Local Authority Service Contracts* (ODPM 2003) (see below) which requires new joiners to be offered equivalent terms and conditions of existing incumbents. **12.6**

Contracts of Employment—Protecting Commercial Confidentiality

Unless a secondment model is adopted (see below) there is unlikely to be total synergy in contracts of employment with those used by the council. Even though there may be a considerable degree of similarity; the two **12.7** employers are set up within different legal environments and for different purposes. As an example, issues such as confidentiality exist in both the public sector and the private sector but these have their origins in different legal provisions. The employment contract may need to include provisions which are not typically found in public sector contracts. As an example, within the private sector some employees are subject to a restrictive covenant which is an agreement which aims to restrain an employee's actions after his or her employment has ended. This type of clause is losing favour in some quarters and being replaced by compulsory notice which is served as "garden leave." The aim in both cases is to prevent a key employee being immediately effective with a commercial rival. Restrictive covenants may be deemed to be void, unless accepted as containing reasonable restraints because these clauses are anti-competitive and in restraint of trade. A court will seek to ensure that an employer is only doing what is necessary to protect its legitimate business interests. Issues of reasonableness will mean the clause may only operate for a limited period of time or may be limited geographically (no competing business in the immediate locality).

Changes to contractual terms are likely to trigger TUPE considerations; although appropriate changes are often achievable where staff opt to adopt a new contract. Opportunities in this respect should be explored with the trade unions at an early stage in preference to ad hoc negotiations that can often lead to "cherry picking" and excess compensation to support change.

Pensions

12.8   Government policy has long been that staff should be no worse off as a result of transfers within the public sector. The Cabinet Office, *Statement of Practice on Staff Transfers in the Public Sector* (January 2000) sets out those policies relating to outsourcing or similar arrangements by central government. Some guidance in local government is provided in ODPM Circular 03/2003. Pensions are explored later in this Chapter; but it should be noted that entry to the LGPS presupposes that the workforce will be working for local authorities. A commercial trading company is only likely to be set up to enable staff to work for the private sector (see Chs 7 and 8). This may well impact on the ability of the company to retain admitted body status for the staff (see below).

Some authorities have used secondment on current terms and conditions in an attempt to overcome this problem (see below).

Collective bargaining arrangements

12.9   Collective bargaining in the public sector for pay and terms and conditions is largely undertaken at a national level. Changes to working arrangements and negotiation of new terms and conditions for new appointments to a trading company will be negotiated locally; depending on the terms and conditions of the staff. There may not be total synergy between the views of the trade unions at local and national level.

Insurance

The company will need to obtain its own insurance arrangements, for **12.10** example those for both public liability and employers' liability. Any use of the local authority insurance arrangements is likely to trigger State Aid concerns (see Ch.8) and therefore different arrangements may well be necessary. These will reflect the different risk profile the new organisation will face.

In secondment arrangements and the like, the arrangements, policies and procedures put in place for staff to follow will have to be crystal clear, well-communicated and training provided, with a full audit trail available and agreed in advance with the insurers. The key question is perhaps "will liability pass across to the host authority which supplies the staff or be accepted where it lands?"

As it is likely that the insurance arrangements will be different; this may not be a simple matter of agreeing that liability is accepted where it lands. This may involve a complex agreement on cross-liability.

SECONDMENT

Introduction

Secondment is the process whereby an employee is lent or hired out to **12.11** another employer to work, at least partially, under the direction of that other employer. Secondment arrangements within the public sector have long been a feature of local authority life with specific power to permit secondment to another local authority (or Health Authority, Special Health Authority or NHS Trust) within s.113 of the Local Government Act 1972. However, it was not until comparatively recently that local authorities started seconding staff to private sector firms. The first major example within the local government context was the strategic partnership arrangement between BT plc and Liverpool City Council, with local authority employees being seconded to a newly formed joint venture company to perform a wide range of professional support services to the Council. This major PPP exercise was written up as a case study by the 4ps in 2002.

Secondment has also been used in connection with PFI schemes in the NHS with the secondment of staff performing soft services such as facilities management (catering, portering, domestic services and cleaning), rather than those performing "hard FM services" (estate management and maintenance).

The Inland Revenue rules mean that secondment is only practicable for periods of up to ten years. Secondment gives rise to a number of other legal and practical issues and these are outlined below.

Legal Issues

Vires

12.12   Part I of the Local Government Act 2000 contains wide new general powers of wellbeing and is discussed in context within Chs 2 and 4. Prior to the 2000 Act, there were barriers to the development of secondment arrangements; although sometimes limited arrangements would be made to facilitate a transfer (for example, temporary secondment of invoice clerks until the contractor had set up its own support arrangements). The legal basis for these temporary arrangements was s.111 and s.112 of the Local Government Act 1972; although the reliance on s.111, particularly as the power to charge, was always controversial (see Ch.13).

Secondment came to the fore with PFI arrangements where the public sector body would agree with the PFI contractor that the local authority or NHS Trust could second staff to the Special Purpose Vehicle (SPV) performing the PFI contract. In the context of local government, s.2(4)(f) of the Local Government Act 2000 gives the example that the wellbeing power includes "the provision of . . . staff . . . to any person." This removed any doubt about the power to second staff to the private sector. However, s.3(2) of the Act prohibits a local authority from using the wellbeing power to raise money (whether by precept, borrowing or otherwise). This meant that (in the absence of the charging power within s.93 of the Local Government Act 2003 as discussed in Ch.5); authorities had a general problem with finding a charging power. Three solutions tended to be adopted:

- Use of s.111 of the Local Government Act 1972 as the charging power (*i.e.* it is incidental to the performance of the function, see Ch.4);

- Seek to have any SPV recognised as a public body under the Local Authorities (Goods and Services) Act 1970. This was done in the Liverpool PPP arrangement to remove vires concerns and allowed the council to "trade" freely with the SPV;

- Simply not to charge for the secondment arrangement. This commercial arrangement was determined within the context that the local authority charging to act as a sub-contractor to an SPV (which would itself incorporate that charge within its own charges and pass them back to the authority) lacked commercial sense. Any costs would therefore fall outside any unitary charge so that the contractor is only paid for its own directly employed staff and for investment and the like.

With the advent of s.93 of the 2003 Act, charging has become considerably simpler (see Ch.5).

The impact of TUPE

As discussed below, TUPE applies by operation of law, rather than the **12.13** intention of the parties. As a result, it is not normally for the parties to determine the application of TUPE, and this can create problems for secondment arrangements since TUPE may by law apply against the wishes of all parties. Against that, and from a practical point of view, if all the stakeholders want there to be secondment and wish to treat the arrangement as a secondment, the "fall back" legal position will become largely irrelevant until and at such time as a dispute develops.

This matter was discussed in the case of *Celtec Ltd v Astley* (EAT 293/00), a case concerning the agreed secondment of civil servants to TECs (Training and Enterprise Councils). In 1990, there occurred large-scale secondment of civil servants from the former Department of Employment to the newly created TECs. By 1996, the TECs wished to employ their own staff and the secondment practice ceased. The issue arose as to the date from which continuity of employment with the TECs should be calculated. Was it from the date of original secondment, or was it from 1996 when the TECs employed their own staff? The court held that the relevant transfer took place in 1990, on the basis that that was the date on which the undertaking was "controlled by" the TECs.

This case seems to have introduced unnecessary uncertainty into arrangements that were agreed by all the parties, including those employees. In practice, the legal application of TUPE will depend on the actual structure of the projected arrangement for example who retains control and ownership of the assets, what is the duration of the secondment, what services are the local authority staff performing and the like. The outcome of case law on TUPE is difficult to predict, and there is a risk that any "secondment" which is not carefully structured could be deemed to be relevant transfer for the purpose of TUPE. Particular care needs to be taken, and advice sought, where a whole service is transferred to a new entity. In this case, even though the arrangement may be called a secondment, practically speaking there may be no way back for secondees.

Contractual Issues

The contractual relationship between the parties will need to accommo- **12.14** date a number of practical management and control issues. These may be summarised as having responsibility for:

- Making sufficient staff available to perform the services, and for additional staff or replacement staff;

- Line management (sickness absence reporting and the like);

- Work allocation (impact of new technology/new work practices);

- Disciplinary, grievance arrangements;

- Discrimination claims; and

- Performance reviews, training and staff development.

VAT

12.15   As a general rule, secondments (or "supplies of staff") will be supplies subject to standard rate VAT. This means that if a local authority seconds a member of staff to another organisation ("the customer"), the supply it makes, even if the fee is only an amount equivalent to the salary and other employer costs, will be subject to the addition of VAT. If the customer is able to reclaim that VAT, the overall effect is neutral, barring cash-flow implications which may arise from any timing differences between paying the VAT to Customs and Excise and receiving payment from the customer. If the customer cannot reclaim VAT then the cost of the secondment is effectively increased by 17.5 per cent.

Practical issues

Day-to-day supervision

12.16   The new day to day working arrangements will need to be resolved to ensure a smooth start for the new company and avoid ongoing friction that may damage its commercial viability. The following main options are available:

- Secondment from the host authority; or

- External appointment.

The attitude of managerial staff to the new venture may well influence the attitude of the rest of the workforce. It is important that secondees demonstrate sufficient motivation to take the new organisation forward in a positive way. The hidden message to the rest of the staff can be that senior management are not fully committed to the new company and this is demonstrated by the fact that they are not prepared to put their own careers on the line to transfer to that venture and to make it a success. Whilst it may be tempting to recruit new mangers from outside the host authority; there may be a significant financial impact to this type of arrangement. Another, perhaps less obvious, difficulty is the need to ensure that the 'culture and core values' of the organisation are clear and shared by all. If the company is managed by those perceived to be "outsiders"; there is less opportunity to develop a shared culture.

Working practices—implied contract conditions

Sitting outside the main body of the contract may be a raft of other **12.17** "custom and practice" issues that have never been embodied in the main contract but which may need to be clarified and set alongside comparative issues in partner organisations. If these are long established they may have as much weight as a written contractual term so a unilateral withdrawal of them could result in employee-relations problems and potential legal action. Legal advice is necessary at an early stage, both to identify potential "implied contract conditions" and if there is to be any attempt to change these.

Custom and practice may include such an issue as to whether it is possible to have a radio on, during working hours in the workplace. This may be accepted practice in certain working environments but frowned upon in others. If these issues are not identified as potential problems and dealt with sensitively they are likely to cause problems and may even undermine the whole partnership.

Health and Safety

The approach to health and safety at work must be an holistic one given **12.18** that the Health and Safety Executive will look firstly at the body responsible for setting the policy when investigating any failures of Health and Safety policies in the workplace.

FIXED TERM EMPLOYEES

As part of the employment reforms the government introduced the Fixed **12.19** Term Employees (Prevention of Less Favourable Treatment) Regulations 2002 (SI 2002/2034) implementing the EU Directive on Fixed Term Work. The Regulations came into force on October 1, 2002 and provide:

- That fixed term employees must not be less favourably treated than comparable permanent employees on the grounds of their fixed term status unless this is objectively justified;

- That the use of successive fixed term contracts should be limited to four years unless their further use can be objectively justified.

STAFF TRANSFER ISSUES—THE FRAMEWORK UNDER THE LOCAL GOVERNMENT ACT 2003

Introduction

12.20 A new legal framework in relation to staff transfers and pensions was imposed as part of the Local Government Act 2003. These provisions will govern any staff transfers from the host authority to the trading company or any contractual arrangement entered into between the trading company and a third party local authority which could give rise to any staff transfer. The changes owe their origin to the government's March 2002 review of the operation of Best Value Review (the "Byers review"). Following that review, the government announced details of a package of reforms; including a commitment to introduce into local government, parallel provisions to the *Cabinet Office Statement of Practice on Staff Transfers in the Public Sector* and the annex to it, *A Fair Deal for Staff Pensions*. It also made clear that the Office of the Deputy Prime Minister would draw up a Code of Practice on the treatment of new recruits ("new joiners") working on local authority contracts alongside transferred staff. These two initiatives are discussed below.

The Local Government Act 2003

12.21 The Local Government Act 2003 contains two sections dealing with staff transfer matters (ss.101 and 102). Section 101 imposes a legal obligation to deal with staff transfer matters "in accordance with directions". The directions are issued in the form of statutory instruments that will "instruct" a local authority how to behave. The Act also provides that the government may support those directions by guidance. The Act, the directions and the guidance, together make up the legal framework. Section 102 provides a similar legal framework for pensions.

The aim of the legislative package within the Local Government Act 2003 is to introduce some much-needed clarity into the rights of employees in a transfer situation. Previously some employees had their TUPE rights supported by the main service contract but others did not. In the light of this inconsistent approach some employees were forced to rely on TUPE itself. TUPE rights are considered below and TUPE itself is one of the most complex areas of employment law. The aim of the change is that all employees affected by a transfer situation should be clear as to their rights, without needing to resort to the courts to explain those rights to them. This should avoid arguments over such matters as whether or not TUPE applies in a given situation.

This area is particularly relevant to public/public arrangements of an administrative nature where TUPE would not normally apply by operation of law (*Henke v Gerneide Schierke Vervaltungsgemeinschaft Brocken* (1997)).

Although the provisions in the Act are law, as at the end of 2004 there were no directions although the government had commenced a consultation exercise with the intention that the directions would be issued during the summer of 2005. Nevertheless, in the light of ODPM Circular 03/03 local authorities have undertaken these responsibilities and currently:

- All contracting activities by best value authorities which could give rise to TUPE obligations are conducted on the basis that the staff have the right to transfer and that terms and conditions will be preserved other than in exceptional circumstances.

- In all contracting activities by best value authorities, local authority employee transferees, already having the benefit of pension fund membership or right of access to the scheme, are being offered either retention of those arrangements, normally membership of the Local Government Pension Scheme (LGPS), or, in other circumstances, a broadly comparable scheme (as defined in the annex to the Cabinet Office Statement). Rights accrued up to point of transfer are protected within the Scheme, and will be index linked going forward where individuals decide not to transfer them. The transfer option will be either internally to the LGPS where the new employer has entered into an admission agreement or externally to the new employer's broadly comparable scheme.

Enforcement of staff issues via the service contract

The authority is expected to enforce its new statutory obligations through the service contract, and this is expected to include the agreed alternative dispute resolution (ADR) arrangements.   **12.22**

The Social Partners have agreed an appropriate dispute resolution mechanism for *Code-related issues—see http://www.lg-employers.gov.uk/people/hr—procurement/adr.html*

Authorities will need to reflect on what employee obligations need to be enforced through the contract and how to draft those contractual provisions (see the joint 4ps, IDeA and Employers Organisation guidance: *Code of Practice on Workforce Matters in Local Authority Service Contracts—Contract Clauses—2004*).

The Code of Practice

The *Code of Practice on Workforce Matters in Local Authority Service Contracts* (2003) was published before the new Act as Annex D of The Best Value Circular (ODPM 03/2003). Practical guidance is available from the Employers Organisation, the ODPM and the Audit Commission. The Code gains its legal status from the Best Value legislation (the Local Government   **12.23**

Act 1999) and is statutory guidance that is designed to secure Best Value and ensure the fair treatment of those who are "new joiners" in a contracting situation.

The Code states that contractors should:

- Offer employment to new staff on fair and reasonable terms and conditions that are, overall, no less favourable than those of transferred employees, and

- Offer reasonable pension arrangements to new staff, with minimum levels set out in the Code.

The Code refers specifically to "contracting-out of services" (para.4) and its scope will therefore embrace any arrangements of a contractual nature. The Code is therefore relevant to the contractual relationship between the local authority and its trading company; provided that company offers services to the host authority or to any other local authority. The Code will also apply whether this is the "first" outsourcing (a transfer from the authority to its trading company) or a subsequent *i.e.* "second generation" outsourcing (for example, from one private sector service provider to the trading company).

The Code is not relevant where services are provided in-house or where staff are seconded to and "managed" by the trading company; as clearly in those instances the local authority continues to be the employer. However, the trading company will need to consider the fact that it is likely to be considered as a "reference" employee both by other private sector firms and it may have to adopt flagship employment practices through the direction of its host authority. Therefore it may not have the commercial freedom of other companies in offering "new joiners" significantly different terms and conditions than any seconded employees.

The statutory guidance in the Code does not replace the existing legal framework of TUPE and the like (see below); instead it gives better rights than those provisions.

New joiners

12.24 New joiners are those recruited to work alongside the transferred workforce on an authority's contract. Those staff are to be offered "terms and conditions which are, overall, no less favourable than those of transferred employees." The trading company, as employer, will be required to consult (in a "genuine dialogue") with trade unions or other employee representatives on the package of terms and conditions to be offered to new joiners.

In the case of pensions, new recruits must be offered "reasonable pension arrangements." Paragraph 8 of the Code makes it clear that pension arrangements are to be treated separately from the normal benefit package; therefore, in outline the authority will need to consider the issues differently. A package of (non-pension) terms and conditions which are "overall, no less favourable" than transferred employees must be provided. In addition, a "reasonable pension" must be offered. Three options are explained in para.10 of the Code, each of which could satisfy the definition of "reasonable." In outline these are:

- Membership of the LGPS where the employer has admitted body status within the scheme and makes the requisite contributions;

- Membership of a broadly comparable employer pension scheme (either final salary or money purchase and, where money purchase, the employer must as a minimum match employee contributions up to 6 per cent); or

- A stakeholder pension scheme, under which the employer must as a minimum match employee contributions up to 6 per cent.

The Code refers to Cabinet Office *Statement of Practice on Staff Transfers in the Public Sector* and annex: A fair deal for pensions. This can be downloaded from: *www.cabinet-office.gov.uk/civilservice/2000/tupe/ stafftransfers.pdf*.

The concept of comparing and contrasting job roles and associated terms and conditions of employment is not a new one: the Equal Pay Act has been in force since the mid 1970s. Legislation to protect part-time and fixed-term workers is also in force and can involve a similar inquiry. What is unique, however, is for the obligation to make the judgement to be placed on a non-judicial body. The point here is that under, for example, the Equal Pay Act, it is for an employment tribunal to make the appropriate judgements. Under the Code, it is for the local authority to ultimately decide whether its service provider partner is complying with its contractual obligation to provide new joiners with "terms and conditions overall no less favourable than those of transferred staff." This can be a very difficult judgement call to make, though the local authority could make this easier by the use of appropriately worded contractual provisions.

Sub-contracting by the trading company

The Code provides that if transferred staff are transferred a second or subsequent time to a sub-contractor, then the primary obligation will remain with the main contractor. Effectively, any local authority contracting with the trading company will probably seek to secure a position where no sub-contracting takes place without their consent and for that consent not to be withheld unreasonably when certain requirements are met. These requirements could embrace Code compliance.   **12.25**

Monitoring

12.26   The authority will require monitoring information to ensure that the trading company is discharging its contractual obligations to transferred staff and new joiners. Local authority monitoring must honour the principles of proportionality and confidentiality.

Authority failure to comply with Code

12.27   The application of the Code is subject to review by the Audit Commission and appointed auditors, through the audit of the Best Value Performance Plan. The authority must confirm that all its Best Value contracts comply with these legal obligations, and that measures are in place to ensure compliance by service providers. Auditors may receive information from transferred employees, trade unions and other interested parties regarding these obligations. The sanctions for non-compliance are those that generally apply within the Best Value regime.

TUPE RIGHTS

12.28   TUPE is a reserve right and as such should not be an issue in the light of the *Code of Practice on Workforce Matters*, as discussed above, In outline it provides the following rights and responsibilities; in a staff transfer from A to B:

- Staff who are employed by A "immediately before the transfer" automatically become the employees of B from the time of the transfer, on the terms and conditions pursuant to the contract of employment they previously held with A;

- B inherits A's rights and liabilities in relation to those individuals;

- Collective agreements, made by or on behalf of A with a trade union recognised by A, are inherited by B;

- Where A recognises a union in respect of employees in the undertaking to be transferred and, following the transfer, the undertaking transferred maintains an identity distinct from any other undertaking owned by B, B must recognise the union in respect of those employees;

- Occupational pension scheme rights, in so far as they relate to old age, invalidity or survivors, do not pass from A to B;

- A must inform recognised trade unions about the consequences of the transfer, and B must provide A with sufficient information in this regard;

218

- In certain (most) circumstances, it may be necessary for A or B to consult with recognised trade unions or elected employee representatives concerning the transfer;

- Dismissal of any employee (whether before or after the transfer) for any reason connected with the transfer is automatically unfair unless the reason is "an economic, technical or organisational reason entailing changes in the workforce" in which case the dismissal can be "fair" if reasonable in the circumstances.

PENSIONS

This whole issue of public sector pensions is an area subject to on-going **12.29** review by government and the latest position should be checked with HR professionals or through the ODPM website.

The LGPS

The LGPS is a significant public service pension scheme with approx- **12.30** imately 3 million members in England and Wales. The LGPS was set up by statute under powers conferred on the Secretary of State by s.7 of the Superannuation Act 1972. Its benefits levels are therefore set by legislation and are defined and guaranteed in law. The benefits are set out in statutory instruments and may therefore be varied from time to time. Currently, the benefits are detailed in The Local Government Pension Scheme Regulations 1997 (SI 1997/1612) as amended.

The LGPS is available to local government employees under age 65, and to certain employees of other organisations that have been permitted to participate in it (either as resolution bodies or as admission bodies). Teachers, police and fire fighters are not allowed to join the LGPS and have separate pension schemes as mentioned above.

Although the LGPS is prescribed as one scheme, it is administered, structured and funded on the basis of more than 80 separate administering authorities in England and Wales, each with its own fund.

Broadly Comparable or Admitted Body Status?

The underlying principle enshrined in s.102 of the Local Government Act **12.31** 2003 is that, except in exceptional circumstances, transferring staff should continue to have access to a broadly comparable occupational pension scheme under which they can continue to earn pension benefits through future service. For transferring local authority staff, this means one of two things:

1) The new employer provides a "broadly comparable" pension scheme. Under the LGPS, this means a scheme which has been

certified as such by any qualified actuary or the Government Actuary's Department in accordance with good professional practice or GAD in accordance with the Government Actuary's Statement of Practice *Assessment of broad comparability of pension rights*, or

2) The new employer enters into an Admission Agreement to enable the staff to remain in the LGPS.

Broadly Comparable Pension Schemes

12.32   In respect of the provision of a broadly comparable scheme, a formal assessment is made by a professionally qualified actuary in accordance with proper professional practice or by GAD in line with the Government Actuary's Statement of Practice. This assessment relates only to service after transfer. There are two methods of assessment, either an 'individual assessment' or a 'passport.'

In an 'individual assessment' the pension scheme offered by the new employer is compared with the LGPS (or other relevant public service pension scheme), specifically in respect of the actual staff who will be transferring as part of the specific transfer. Once broad comparability is achieved and agreed, the new scheme will be certified as broadly comparable, but only for that specific transfer.

With a 'passport', the pension scheme offered by the new employer is compared with the LGPS (or other relevant public sector pension scheme), as it applies to all possible categories of membership. Once broad comparability is achieved and agreed, the new scheme will be certified as broadly comparable for any transfer of members from that scheme. The passport is periodically reviewed, but will essentially remain in force until there are changes to the scheme.

Although a pension scheme may be certified as being broadly comparable, this does not mean that it will provide redundancy-related pension benefits equivalent to those provided under the LGPS. It was the understanding of the Government Actuary that such benefits would transfer under TUPE. This view appears to have been supported by the European Court of Justice in *Beckmann v Dynamco Whicheloe Macfarlane Limited* (C-164/00). The Government Actuary recommends that where a TUPE transfer takes place, a local authority should seek its own legal advice to ensure that these benefits are protected.

A certificate of broad comparability does not cover discretionary benefits payable for severance arrangements or early termination. The Cabinet Office Statement specifies that there should be appropriate arrangements to protect redundancy and severance terms of staff. Local authorities should decide what approach they wish to take for these benefits, bearing in mind the need to be able to retain the ability to be able to exercise the discretion on a case by case basis up to completion of the transfer.

Admission Body Option

Service providers under most local authority contracting exercises may be **12.33** eligible to participate in the LGPS as 'transferee admission bodies.' However, eligibility to participate in the LGPS should be checked with the relevant administering authority in advance.

Admission of non-local authority employers to the LGPS takes place by means of a formal, contractual admission agreement, drawn up between the interested parties. Under the terms of the regulations, the effect of such a step is that:

- Eligible employees of the admitted body can fully participate in the Scheme and so can be described as pensionable employees; and

- The regulations governing the Scheme treat employees of an admitted body exactly the same way as if they were employed by a Scheme employer. The admitted body must therefore take such actions as required of LGPS employers as defined in the regulations. For admission status and membership status to continue, the admitted body must adhere at all times to the Scheme regulations, including, of course, the specified terms of their individual admission agreements.

The administering authority will be able to provide a specimen admission agreement that it requires the parties to enter into. Admission agreements with transferee admission bodies must contain certain prescribed clauses. These are complex legal documents and specific advice will be necessary. The Admission agreement may well contain provisions requiring the new admitted body to provide suitable indemnities and a bond to protect the scheme from any financial failure of the admitted body.

Bonds and Indemnities provided by the Admission Body

When contractors were first permitted to enter into admission agree- **12.34** ments it was a standard requirement of the LGPS Regulations that a bond or indemnity had to be put in place. The position has now changed and the onus is on the relevant authority to undertake and individual assessment based on the risks of business failure of the admission body. The level of risk and subsequent need of the indemnity or bond must be actuarially assessed. That level will be determined by factors such as the number of members covered by the admission agreement and their salaries, length of service, ages etc. Any risk of business failure should be monitored throughout the period of contract; and therefore the level of bond may change.

221

Working for the Private Sector after Transfer?

12.35   Another prescribed clause in an admission agreement with a transferee admission body is a representation and warranty from the transferee admission body to the administering authority and to the local authority which is transferring the staff (if different) that all the transferee admission body's employees (or class of employees) who are specified as members are employed in connection with the services, assets or function referred to in the relevant contract or arrangement.

If an employee of the new employer ceases to be employed in connection with the services, assets or function referred to in the relevant contract or arrangement, then he will cease to be eligible to be an active member of the LGPS. However, the expression 'employed in connection with' is not defined in the LGPS Regulations and its meaning is therefore open to interpretation. Some local authorities, however, do specify a minimum percentage of time to be spent on contract work that need not be for the out-sourcing authority. Clearly an employee may be partially working directly on local authority work and partially on work for third parties whilst remaining within this definition. In the absence of specific case law or guidance on the point it would seem sensible to have an assessment, at least on an annual basis of the work which transferred staff are undertaking and if no work has been undertaken in connection with the strategic services contract for the authority during the previous twelve months to consider whether or not that employee is eligible to remain an active member of the LGPS.

INDEMNITIES FOR OFFICERS AND MEMBERS

12.36   In the light of the fact that certain Officers and Members may be undertaking different duties in relation to trading activity; attention must turn to how those individuals may be protected by the authority in respect of any greater risk to which they are exposed. A typical example may be an individual who becomes the director of a trading company and therefore faces increased duties and potential sanctions (for example those for wrongful trading).

The original legal position in relation to indemnities relies upon two statutory provisions. The first is s.265 of the Public Health Act 1875, which provides an immunity from suit for all officers and members acting on behalf of a local authority, provided that they are acting in a "bona fide" manner. It also provides that they will be indemnified in costs for defending any such action. Whilst the original provision only applied to that particular Act, it was subsequently extended by the Local Government (Miscellaneous Provisions) Act 1976 to cover all functional areas of local government.

However, s.265 does not cover an officer or member when they have acted negligently (see the case of *Bullard v Croydon Hospital* [1953] AER

596); where the conduct is reckless as to the consequences; where criminal acts are involved; or where the council has acted *ultra vires*. There are therefore substantial gaps in the protection afforded by this section. Moreover, s.265 will also not be available to permit the bringing of defamation proceedings.

Greater protection may be provided by suitably drafted contractual indemnities (the power for the authority to grant these is in s.111 of the Local Government Act 1972 when attached to the relevant statutory provision which permits the function). However, in the light of the increasing range of duties undertaken by Officers and Members; further provisions were included at s.101 of the Local Government Act 2003, to make a statutory instrument offering greater protection. An ODPM paper entitled *Providing Indemnities to Relevant Authority Officers and Members* (ODPM July 2004), led to the relevant regulations: the Local Authorities (Indemnities for Members and Officers) Order 2004 (SI 2004/3082).

The main areas of assistance are in relation to: negligent actions by an Officer or Member; where the Officer or Member is serving on an outside body (this has proved problematic in the past as it can be argued that they are not acting on the Council's behalf); and where the authority has unwittingly acted *ultra vires*. However, the new provisions do not apply where the actions are reckless, fraudulent or criminal and do not authorise the taking of defamation proceedings.

The authority is able to provide greater coverage through a contractual indemnity attached to the contract of employment, but care will be needed to ensure that the authority is acting lawfully in granting a wider indemnity; otherwise that indemnity will be *ultra vires* the authority (see Ch.2).

CONCLUSION

Local authorities should be experienced in delivering change manage- **12.37** ment programmes and in managing more complex personnel issues. This Chapter highlights a number of areas in which personnel issues may arise in the context of undertaking any charging or trading activity. The key development to be expected is the "directions" which will be issued in relation to s.101 and 102 of the Local Government Act 2003. These are expected in 2005. In practice however authorities are already complying with the relevant legislation in advance of the completion of the legal framework.

Part Four

Context and History

CHAPTER 13

AN INTRODUCTION TO LOCAL GOVERNMENT AND THE HISTORY OF THE TRADING DEBATE

INTRODUCTION

This Chapter is intended to assist those who are new to local government **13.1** or to the issue of trading within local government. It commences with an outline of local government structures and continues by looking at the relationship between local government and central government before examining the history of the trading debate.

This Chapter therefore seeks to place the issue of charging and trading within its wider context. This is more relevant, perhaps, than at first meets the eye as the context covers not only the formal public policy devised and implemented by central government, but also impacts on the regulatory environment and provides the background to judicial decisions in relevant cases. In relation to charging and trading, this context has been particularly significant to any local authority engaging in charging and trading activity in getting a 'feel' for how the activity might be regarded across a number of fronts.

In order to set out this context it is necessary to start by looking at the legal position enjoyed by local authorities, placed in the constitutional context in which local government itself operates. The central government/ local government divide is a fault line running throughout this book but its importance is explained in this Chapter. Having realised that powers emanate from Parliament and are provided to local authorities via legislation, it is necessary to look at the types of local authority that are the recipients of those powers. These not only vary, but are the subject of continual reform and development. The manifestation of the regional government debate is a good example of recent developments in this area. Regional government itself is but a strand of a wider decentralisation policy which is inextricably tied up with local government powers.

It is also necessary to look at issues surrounding the regulation of local government as these have also changed and provide a different context to that previously in existence. There have been changes not only to the mechanisms of control, for example the transition from the old Compulsory Competitive Tendering regime under the former government, through Best Value to the new Comprehensive Performance Assessment. Moreover, the regulatory bodies, principally the Audit Commission, have also changed. The new regime of 'strategic regulation' for the Audit Commission is a radical step to ensure that it is still in tune with the reforms facing local government itself.

In the development of powers over time within the framework mentioned above, there have been noticeable changes in how powers are given, whether they are given to local authorities, how widely they are drawn and interpreted. An analysis of this subject matter reveals that there are different eras with different characteristics, from the early, perhaps liberal, days of the early twentieth century; through problem years in the 1980s and 1990s where powers were removed and restrictive interpretations were imposed; to the modern renaissance post-1997 where the government has delivered general powers of community initiative to support its wider local government reforms.

This contextual material, perhaps enables some consideration of the future direction of the trading debate and the extent to which it is dependent on the particular political party in power and what further twists and turns might be expected if governmental change comes about.

THE STRUCTURE OF LOCAL GOVERNMENT

13.2 The evolution of modern local authorities was consolidated towards the end of the nineteenth century with the creation of county councils as the upper tier of local government and urban districts and rural districts as the lower tier. Separate arrangements prevailed in areas which had county borough status and also in London. Development thus far had been haphazard to say the least and as Tony Byrne notes in his work *Local Government in Britain*, "the structure was the product of a continuing patching up exercise: it was not purpose built."

In the period before the Second World War, local government was in a period of ascendancy. Powers and duties were being transferred from other bodies such as school boards, boards of guardians and public assistance committees which had hitherto provided services of a public nature. Furthermore, central government was assuming new powers itself and devolving these onto local authorities. For example, town and country planning and major public housing schemes. During this period, the bedrock of local government was strengthened by new Acts of Parliament which conferred new powers each specific to a particular new function. All different types of powers and duties were involved from adoptive measures, private and local Bills, agency powers and those where input was to be divided between the different tiers of local government. This evolutionary approach, based on a very large number of individual Acts of Parliament has led to commentators referring to the statutory framework of local government as "a patchwork quilt".

In the period after the Second World War; functions were removed from local authorities and given to more specialist bodies. As an example, the provision of water, gas and electricity supplies were removed from local authorities. Prior to 1945, a number of local authorities exercised water functions; by the Water Act 1945 water supply was transferred from some local authorities to water boards; the Water Act 1973 transferred the function to regional water authorities; followed by the Water Act 1989 transferring the function to private water companies within a government regulated environment. Other examples are that new towns were placed in the hands of appointed boards, construction of motorways made the responsibility of the Ministry of Transport rather than local authorities and the Countryside Commission charged with the preservation and enhancement of the environment.

By the time the late twentieth century had arrived, the system of local government had become somewhat more settled, with the standard two tier system applying in rural areas (with the county council exercising strategic functions and the district councils exercising local functions); local governance in London being provided by 32 local councils and the Common Council of the City of London, with the Greater London Council performing the county council role; five Metropolitan Counties existing whereby the Metropolitan County Council had slightly different strategic roles to shire counties, sitting alongside Metropolitan Borough and City Councils exercising most functions. The Local Government Act 1985 abolished the Metropolitan County Councils—and the GLC with them—leaving the 36 metropolitan authorities and the 33 London Boroughs as unitary authorities. In a further reorganisation process in the 1990s more than 80 unitary authorities were created, largely by making larger district and city councils unitary and thereby cutting them out of their previously existing shire county areas.

The issue of strategic governance in London dominated local authority life in the capital for some time, until the Greater London Authority Act 1999 created the GLA and this development was seen to be innovative as the new strategic body was to have an elected mayor. Underneath the strategic Greater London Authority, there are the specialist authorities of Transport for London, the Metropolitan Police, the London Fire and Emergency Planning Authority and the London Development Agency.

It would be both premature and misleading to suggest that local government structural reform has now come to an end. In Labour's second Parliamentary term, the Deputy Prime Minister John Prescott pushed forward with an initiative to create regional government in England, leading to a referendum on an elected regional assembly for the North East region. Had this gone forward, then the government had promised to reorganise local government below it into a unitary structure, thereby preserving three levels of government (central government, regional government and local government, as opposed to central government, county council and district council). As it turned out, the vote by the public was heavily against the creation of a regional assembly and these plans were subsequently abandoned.

13.3 The relevance of the type of local authority or public body concerned lies in the particular nature of the powers that will be available to it. The starting point is with the unitary authorities, whether those be the ones created in 1995 to 1997, metropolitan authorities or London Borough councils, as these are able to exercise all relevant powers available to local government. By contrast the exercise of powers in the two tier system by counties and districts is dependent on the nature of the different authorities. County councils exercise functions on a county-wide basis which are more geared to wider administration enabling economies of scale to be achieved, technical and financial resources to be available and a holistic view taken. Accordingly, county councils deal with education, social services, leisure services, county planning, highways, consumer protection and waste management. Other services are better dealt with on a much more local level and district councils deal with housing, local planning, environmental health, refuse collection, leisure services and licensing.

It can therefore be seen that certain functions (for example education or environmental health) are dealt with only at one level or the other. Other functions are dealt with jointly with county councils undertaking certain elements and the district council undertaking others; a good example of this is town and country planning where the county council develops structure plans and the district council local plans. Some powers may be exercisable by either the county or the district and leisure services are a good example of this. The legal framework of powers available to an authority to undertake its functions will therefore differ.

In the case of the Local Government Act 2003, a different legal division was introduced between authorities. The power to undertake trading through commercial companies is limited to the better performing authorities under the CPA classification; although charging powers are granted more widely.

As Ch.2 explains, the legal basis for charging and trading is to identify legal authority for that action. This is otherwise known as *capacity* and is the first limb of the *ultra vires* doctrine explained in that Chapter. In that context, it is necessary to consider each local authority as a unique entity with its own statutory framework although (outside of single purpose authorities), it will share this framework with other local authorities of the same type.

THE RELATIONSHIP BETWEEN CENTRAL AND LOCAL GOVERNMENT

The relationship between central and local government is underpinned **13.4** by the absence of a written constitution. As a result of this, the position of local authorities is determined by other conventions and historical developments. The starting point is the doctrine of Parliamentary sovereignty, which essentially means that Parliament is the supreme body and has the power to pass legislation without restriction. In effect, Parliament can provide legislation containing positive powers enabling local authorities to undertake activities and it can also include limitations and restrictions on those powers to control how those powers might be exercised.

Not only has this constitutional settlement become more problematic, with the continual erosion of the position of local government by a succession of over dominant central government administrations, but it also shows that the UK is out of step with its European counterparts. The work of Clarke and Stewart has shown that this gives local authorities in those jurisdictions greater confidence to focus on the leadership of a particular area, rather than seeing themselves as simple deliverers of services. Their paper *Community Governance, Community Leadership and the New Local Government* (Joseph Rowntree Foundation, 1998) stated:

> "The dominant European model has different roots. In many countries the existence of local government was written into the constitution. This means that while the legislator can change local government, there are major constraints. Such constitutional provisions expressed the idea of local self government and so a different meaning—the community governing itself. The council then becomes the means for this. The concept has deep implications."

Clarke and Stewart conclude that, unlike their British counterparts, European councils have less of a preoccupation with the performance of services and more with community leadership:

> "It means that a local authority gains its identity through the community rather than from the services it provides. One result has been that European authorities have always been more ready to deliver services in a variety of ways, using collaboration between authorities, private and public companies, and voluntary organisations. There has been little of the British instinct that, given a task to do, it is the local authority's responsibility to get on and do it itself."

The European Charter of Local Self Government was originally a focal point for efforts to improve the constitutional position of local government in this country. It was adopted in 1997. The purpose of the Charter is to promote local self-government and to allow local authorities to manage their own affairs. The scope of self government is the pivotal element of the Charter. It is stated in Art.4 that the basic powers and responsibilities of local authorities should be prescribed by the constitution or by statute. Powers given to local authorities should be full and exclusive and local authorities should exercise full discretion over them. However, the whole document is to be construed on the basis of the legal system in operation in each relevant country. As an example, Art.2 indicates that "the principle of local self government shall be recognised in domestic legislation, and where practicable in the constitution . . ." As the United Kingdom has no constitution, it complies with this. Article 4 requires "the basic powers and responsibilities of local authorities (to be) prescribed by the constitution or by statute . . ." However, there is no requirement to have a single legislative instrument for this purpose, therefore the plethora of miscellaneous and haphazard Acts that have grown up in the UK over time, have to suffice for this purpose. Furthermore, "Powers given to local authorities shall normally be full and exclusive. They may not be undermined or limited by another central or regional authority except as provided for by the law . . . ." Obviously, with Parliament being supreme in the UK, this is provided for by the law in this country, and so the powers available to local authorities are not full and exclusive by any manner. This means that the UK broadly complies with the Charter, but it is an arguable point whether it meets the spirit of it.

Regulation and Inspection of Local Government

13.5   The regulation of local government has also changed as time has gone on. In the earliest days, the *ultra vires* doctrine was the main tool by which local authority actions were constrained. As Chapter 2 explains, if a local authority acts beyond its powers, then its actions are *ultra vires* and void. In these early days, central government interference in the direct performance of services was unheard of and certainly not the norm. However, as time went on central government became more prescriptive about what local authorities should be doing and developed a range of controls to underpin that interest.

The controls are often politically driven, for example the Compulsory Competitive Tendering regime in the mid 1980s which supported a privatisation agenda favoured by the Conservative government of Margaret Thatcher. CCT was eventually abolished and replaced by the Best Value regime, introduced by the Local Government Act 1999. This provided the legal duty in s.3 of the Act to make arrangements to secure "continuous improvement" in the performance of functions. This was supported by the potential to intervene directly in the running of a local authority which breached the legislation; through the mechanism in s.15 of the Local Government Act 1999.

The government overlaid the Best Value regime with its new policy, the idea of a comprehensive performance framework. This was based on the twin elements of 'carrot and stick,' with the latter being provided by the power to direct local authorities to act in a certain way and the former represented by 'freedoms and flexibilities' for those better performing authorities. The Comprehensive Performance Assessment is the subject of extensive research and commentary and will not be dealt with here. Suffice to say, however, that it operates on the basis of a self-assessment by the authority itself and is then comprised of an independent corporate assessment and assessment in relation to services by the external inspectors of the Audit Commission. As such, the CPA represents the latest government thinking in regulating local authorities and their activities. It is also relevant to charging and trading in the sense that the s.95 powers to engage in commercial trading via a company, described in Ch.7 have been linked to the CPA classifications. Accordingly, only an authority featuring in the categories of *excellent, good* or *fair* will be able to avail itself of those powers; those in *weak* or *poor* will be denied the opportunity to trade commercially.

The CPA is only one of a number of measures under which central government agencies review and inspect the performance of local government. Pressure has grown in recent times for a reduction in those inspections; on the basis that this diverts attention away from the delivery of services. In response, the Audit Commission published a paper *Strategic Regulation: Minimising the Burden, Maximising the Impact* in December 2003. This paper sets out a new approach which is that regulation should be proportionate to risk and performance, and regulators should be able to demonstrate that the value of their work outweighs the costs associated with it. The new approach was manifested in a three year inspection holiday for those authorities classified as *excellent* under the CPA and a commitment to bring the various inspection activities of different bodies more closely together.

Government Control through the Drafting of Statutes

The modern tendency is to draft "framework legislation" under which **13.6** the government of the day is able to issue subordinate legislation—thus allowing the flexibility to react to changing circumstances.

Whilst this form of drafting has practical advantages; it has also attracted criticism because of the argument that this impacts, in effect, like a delegation of power from Parliament to government Ministers. As an example, when the Local Government Bill was going through the House of Lords in 1992, the government intended to give the secretary of state power to make "such modifications of Part 1 of the 1998 Act as he thinks fit . . .". Lord Simon of Glaisdale raised in the House of Lords debate the constitutional objection to this provision, known as 'Henry VIII' provisions. He said:

"It was so called because it is a power similar to that given to Henry VIII by the Statute of Proclamations to amend by ministerial decree an Act of Parliament." That is what this provision does. That became a matter of contention between Parliament and the executive for 150 years. The right of Parliament to legislate was in a famous phrase, "the cause for which Hampden died in the field and Sydney on the scaffold." It was by their efforts and the efforts of others that the matter was resolved in favour of Parliament in 1688 and 1689."

As a result of the eloquence expressed by Lord Simon in this debate, the House of Lords voted in favour of an amendment withdrawing the power sought to be given to the minister. However, subsequent Bills also sought to go down this route and eventually provisions reached the statute book in the form of s.16 of the Local Government Act 1999 on Best Value which permit the secretary of state to both grant new powers to local authorities that do not currently exist and to modify or exclude powers already given by Parliament. This very much fits in with current governmental thinking on how statutes should be drafted and managed, but offends a historical Parliamentary principle. Something of a compromise was reached in these circumstances by requiring the order containing the relevant ministerial provisions to be approved by both Houses of Parliament under the positive resolution procedure.

THE ROLE OF THE COURTS IN CONTROLLING TRADING

13.7 Whilst the doctrine of *ultra vires* has not always existed for local authorities, in the nineteenth century the powers of local authorities were vague with little constraint over what could be done. Accordingly, Blackstone wrote in 1758 that municipal corporations could do all the acts of a legal person and were not subject to the *ultra vires* doctrine. This legal freedom, if it ever existed, was removed by the provisions of the Municipal Corporations Act 1835 which established that the authorities could only expend money on matters statutorily empowered. Since that time, the doctrine has been an important feature of local government law. At first the doctrine was used only in relation to single purpose statutory corporations (see for example, the case of *Baroness Wenlock v River Dee Co* (1885) 10 App. Cas 354); but it was soon used to control local authorities for example in *Attorney General v London County Council* [1907] AC 131.

The *ultra vires* doctrine has two limbs, namely *capacity* and *exercise of powers* and these are considered in Ch.2. Capacity is a matter of the scope of the powers given by Parliament and is therefore largely controlled by the government of the day; although disputes on construction are determined by the Courts. The need to exercise a power in a valid manner, without abuse is a matter which is largely judged before the Courts and where the judiciary have played a significant role in the trading debate.

A purposive interpretation was given to the construction of powers; in an early company law case on the *ultra vires* doctrine in the case of *Attorney General v Great Eastern Railway Company* (1880) 5 App. Cas 473. Lord Selborne in delivering a classic judgment stated:

> ". . . the doctrine ought to be reasonably and not unreasonably under-stood and applied, and whatever may fairly be regarded as incidental to, or consequential upon, those things which the legislature has authorised, ought not (unless expressly prohibited) to be held, by judicial con-struction, to be *ultra vires*."

Those who were seeking to restrict the flexibility given to local author-ities often relied upon the second limb of exercise of powers to challenge the activities of the relevant authority. Somewhat of a milestone judgment was delivered in the case of *Roberts v Hopwood* [1925] AC 578. In this case the House of Lords made various statements which compared the duty of a local authority in relation to its ratepayers' money to the duty of a trustee in relation to money held on trust. This case was the one of the first to discuss the concept of a fiduciary duty of a local authority, which is another important doctrine which permeates the case law on municipal activities.

The facts of the *Roberts v Hopwood* case illustrate the way in which the common law can develop, by way of judicial policy. Under s.62 of the Metropolis Act 1855, the corporation could pay its workforce such wages as they "may think fit." This wide discretion obviously meant that it was difficult to challenge the authority on the basis of acting beyond its powers, those powers themselves being so widely drafted. The council wished to act as a model employer and therefore paid wages on a uniform basis across a range of employees, and at rates higher than those prevailing in the area.

The councillors were challenged not on the absence of a power but on the basis of abuse of their powers. The court commented: "They (the councillors) took an arbitrary principle and fixed an arbitrary sum which was not a real exercise of their discretion."

Clearly the motive behind the exercise of the power was implicitly **13.8** political and this was a factor criticised by the court. The *Roberts v Hopwood* case is considered to be a milestone because of the extension of the *ultra vires* principle not only to the lack of capacity but also to the related concept of abuse of that power. Unless one reads the phrase 'may think fit' very narrowly the councillors clearly had the capacity to pay wages well above the norm. However, the court felt that the council members had not considered the relevant issues as they should have done and were therefore making a gift of ratepayers' money to council employees. They had no powers of philanthropy and in these circumstances that gift was a sum of money which properly belonged to the electorate. The value of the gift was represented by the overpayment of wages above the norm prevailing in the area. This case is also an illustration of the principle of the court's careful control over the spending of money by local authorities.

The actual consideration of "trading" has also come before the courts over the years. Even in the period before the Second World War, authorities were behaving innovatively in the exercise of their powers. As an example, in *Attorney General v Smethwick Corporation* [1932] 1 Ch 562 where comments were specifically made on the issue of trading. The facts of the case reveal that Smethwick wished to set up an in house printing, stationery and bookbinding facility incidental to their library and education functions. As indicated earlier, the courts had developed a doctrine whereby they interpreted statutes as authorising not only matters expressly covered but also acts "reasonably incidental" to the express acts. This principle later received Parliamentary confirmation in s.111 of the Local Government Act 1972 which is considered in Ch.4. Smethwick Corporation was seeking to utilise its common law incidental powers, to operate an in house facility for printing and similar matters.

Whilst upholding the action of the authority, Lord Hanworth, Master of the Rolls, made some adverse comments on the practice of municipal trading. He said:

"I agree with (counsel for the auditor) that the corporation could not start a printing business in the sense in which those terms would generally be understood. They cannot cater to the public or endeavour to trade and make a profit. But is it to be said on the other hand, that they must not have any printing done on their own premises? If that can be done and it saves the ratepayers money, is not that wise? This is quite a different case from *Roberts v Hopwood*, the decision in which is beside the point. It appears from the facts that the corporation have exercised their discretion within the area trusted to them, and under these circumstances it seems impossible to hold that they are not authorised to take the further steps which prudence dictates and modern mechanism renders possible."

There are three issues to note from this case. The first is that the council were held to be able to use their incidental powers because they had no specific power to set up a printing facility; those powers being incidental to the specific statutory power relating to the functions of education and libraries. Secondly, they had to exercise their function "within the area entrusted to them." This means it was not an unlimited discretion but constrained by the specific wording of the statute which deposed those powers, *i.e.* they could not trade with the public at large. Finally, they had to act as "prudence dictates." In other words they could not act unreasonably or abuse those powers, for example, by acquiring plant and machinery well in excess of the requirements for their own use. These three controls still apply today in the area of charging and trading. The case is also an example of the judiciary commenting expressly that "trading" itself is not a lawful activity for a local authority. This has remained the position until the Local Government Act 2003, which officially recognised that commercial trading was a legitimate activity; provided it was undertaken in the manner permitted by s.95 of that statute.

The judicial opposition to "trading" received significant publicity with the House of Lords case of *Hazell v Hammersmith and Fulham LBC* [1992] 2 AC 1. This was a case where the authority entered into a series of interest rate swaps to take advantage of fluctuations in the money market. It eventually entered into 562 swaps with a total value in excess of £6 billion at a time when its own annual budget was in to the order of £45.5 million. Earlier, in the Court of Appeal, the authority claimed that its activities were part of a financial planning exercise. However, the Court of Appeal indicated that the manner in which the activity was being conducted amounted to speculation rather than prudent debt management. "As time went and the pattern of the council's activity became established, the inference that it was engaged in trade (or speculation) becomes even clearer." ([1990] 2 WLR 1038 at p.1073).

MOVES TO ABOLISH THE *ULTRA VIRES* DOCTRINE?

Although the ultra vires doctrine has been part of the bed-rock of local **13.9** government law for centuries there have been a number of moves to abolish the doctrine. In the recent past, the matter was considered by the Legal Risk Review Committee which was established on April 29, 1991 under the chairmanship of Lord Alexander. The aim was to identify areas of obscurity and uncertainty in the law affecting financial markets. The committee was particularly concerned by the impact of the judgement in *Hazell v Hammersmith and Fulham LBC* [1992] 2 AC 1. In this respect, the remit of the committee was unashamedly financial in its perspective and in particular in its consideration of the role of third party financial institutions dealing with local authorities. Indeed, the *ultra vires* doctrine was not the only aspect of this area of the law which was considered, although over half the submissions made to the Committee dealt with the uncertainties created by *ultra vires*.

Various suggestions were made for remedying the situation in relation to *ultra vires*. In the end, the Committee recommended that the *ultra vires* doctrine should be abolished altogether and the area governed by a simple legal rule. Paragraph 28 of Appendix 1 to the consultation paper states:

"The most logical approach would be to abolish the rule completely and enact a general principle that all corporations and similar bodies, whatever their objects, should have the same capacity as natural persons of full age."

Ironically enough, conferring on local authorities such powers would, remove them entirely from legal restriction, except in cases where activities undertaken were in breach of the civil or criminal law. In this regard, even the most hopeful local authority commentators considered such a suggestion unachievable at the time.

The Audit Commission disagreed with the recommendation of the Alexander Committee that the *ultra vires* doctrine should be abolished. The Commission emphasised the position of the local authority council tax payer rather than the financial institution seeking to do business with local authorities. The Commission drew attention to important distinctions to be drawn between local authorities and companies; which in their view indicated that the former should not escape the rigours of the *ultra vires* doctrine as the latter have done. These are the fact that there is a public interest in the extent of local authority's powers, local authorities are established by statute and cannot go into liquidation and most importantly of all, that the activities of local authorities are funded by compulsory taxation upon those who have no option but to pay. The Audit Commission therefore invited the government to clarify the law so as to remove the underlying difficulties which resulted in the *Hammersmith and Fulham* case.

The in-coming Labour party that was elected to government in 1997 decided not to abolish the *ultra vires* doctrine. Instead it gave authorities a much wider general power to act on behalf of the interests of its local community. These powers of community initiative were intended to permit innovative action and to be a useful power of first resort. The power is contained in the Local Government Act 2000 which permits a local authority to do anything that is likely to promote or improve the economic, social or environmental wellbeing of its area. This power is considered fully in Ch.4 and is an important legal foundation for a wide variety of local authority activities.

The reason the government chose general powers of community initiative as opposed to powers of general competence were summarised by Hilary Armstrong MP in the Parliamentary debate on the Local Government Bill that became the Local Government Act 2000. She stated:

"The power of wellbeing, which gives the power to respond to the environmental, economic and social needs of the area, expresses what some have called the power of general competence, but in a way that makes the responsibilities of local government clear. It is not local government's responsibility to engage in foreign policy or in issues that lie outside the scope of its public's concerns about what can be effectively achieved locally. Local people do not want local government to take over the powers of central government; they want it to respond effectively to their wishes.

The clause begins to express those objectives more clearly. I must tell the honourable gentleman that we did an enormous amount of work on the power of general competence, but all the academics and advisers from the LGA and its previous incarnations felt that such a power would not make much progress with the *ultra vires* problems. We reached the decision to work on the power of wellbeing because it would make clearer the objectives that the principal authorities can and should spend money on achieving. Local authorities can talk about whatever they like. In a free society, no-one can stop them from doing that. In fact they could probably do what they like, as long as they do not spend public money on it. The clause and the power will enable authorities to set local priorities and take decisions about how they wish to respond to those priorities."

A SOFTENING OF ATTITUDES TOWARDS TRADING BY LOCAL AUTHORITIES

The attitude of the government and other significant players to local authority trading activity may be divided into two distinct phases with the watershed being 1995. Before that date the attitude was almost universally hostile; after that date, there has been a gradual shift to acceptance of the principle, although within a regulated environment. **13.10**

1980–1995

The modern debate on trading came to the fore with the advent of the Compulsory Competitive Tendering (CCT) regime introduced by the former Conservative government in the 1980s. That regime required local authorities to market test certain in-house services against the private sector in a formal tendering exercise. With the legal duty to tender such services came the potential for one local authority to bid for the services of another and the rise of so-called "cross-boundary tendering." This was predictable, bearing in mind the new pressure to make a return on capital on in-house services and a greater pressure to be competitive. Cross-boundary tendering brought into sharp focus whether the local authorities did have the power to undertake large service contracts for each other, involving commercial risk, or not. **13.11**

The spectre of local authorities working for each other and undermining the government's flagship policy forced external auditors to give consideration to the true extent of local authority powers and to determine whether this practice was permissible. The position of the Audit Commission was spearheaded by its in house solicitor, and supported by Counsel as appropriate. In 1989, an opinion was obtained, indicating that the practice of cross-boundary tendering was unlawful and would leave local authorities open to challenge from their external auditors. There followed a period of uncertainty in relation to the full extent of local authority powers and many local authorities were dissuaded from entering any form of arrangement that could be described as trading, for fear of challenge. Other local authorities who were more confident in their interpretation of powers did enter agreements during this period and achieved outcomes which are now hailed as exemplary to other authorities.

The Audit Commission's solicitor also cast doubt on the ability of local authorities to charge for the provision of discretionary services. As a result of this uncertainty, the Local Government and Housing Act 1989 included at s.150 a specific provision empowering the secretary of state to make regulations to permit charging by local authorities for a number of services. The power was widely drawn and covered activities where there was no current power or duty to impose a charge. In accordance with the (by then) traditional way of statutory drafting, the provisions were brief with supporting regulation-making powers. The government produced the first set of regulations, the Houses in Multiple Occupation (Charges for Registration Schemes) Regulations in 1991 (SI 1991/982) which enabled local housing authorities to levy charges for dealing with notifications in respect of HMO's and applications for registration as part of an overall scheme of management.

The issue of charging also came before the courts; for example in the case of *R. v Richmond upon Thames LBC ex parte McCarthy and Stone Developments Limited* [1992] AC 48 where the council as local planning authority had sought to levy a charge for pre-planning enquiries. After a long fight through the courts, the House of Lords held that as the holding of pre-planning enquiries was calculated to facilitate or be conducive or incidental to the function of determining planning applications, but the levying of the charge was unlawful as it was incidental to an activity that was itself incidental to the core function. Accordingly, the House of Lords held that levying the charge was *ultra vires*. This case drew legal powers to levy charges into the same uncertainty as had existed for some years in respect of general municipal trading.

By the mid-1990s, the position of local authorities in relation to their use of powers and duties had deteriorated significantly. A hostile government had continually emphasised the message of *ultra vires*, supported by the Audit Commission. This created a climate of fear which was fuelled by the risk of litigation before a judiciary, which was considered to be unsympathetic to any innovative behaviour by local authorities.

1995–2005

13.12   The tide turned in the mid-1990s for two reasons. The first was that for the first time in many years, a case before the courts was decided favourably in terms of the interpretation of powers, and secondly a fresh counsel's opinion had been obtained by the government in relation to the process of reorganisation arising from devolution in Wales.

The Local Government (Wales) Act 1994 had been proposed by the government to create a Welsh Assembly and deliver devolution. However, a number of legal issues arose out of the proposals, requiring counsels' opinions to be obtained. Some of these opinions differed in their approach to powers, leading the Department of the Environment in February 1995 to consult Stephen Richards QC, then Treasury Counsel, to advise on the extent of the Local Authorities (Goods and Services) Act 1970 following uncertainty that had arisen on the legal position of educational institutions.

In a considered and lengthy opinion of February 19, 1995 Stephen Richards QC indicated that the 1970 Act was to be broadly construed and would permit local authorities to engage in trading for profit and take on staff for the purposes of their trading activities. The DoE was taken aback by the answer, leading some to assume that this was not the answer it had anticipated or necessarily wanted. In any event, it provided Stephen Richards with voluminous new material and asked him to reconsider his view. In a second opinion on June 12, 1995 he confirmed his view that the 1970 Act should be construed purposefully. This was a major development in local government. Having been provided with comprehensive legal advice suggesting that the stance the DoE had taken for some years was misguided, the government had to act and provided guidance to local authorities, relaying to them this new position on the interpretation of the 1970 Act.

This changed approach by the government was followed in December 1996 by a sympathetic ruling in a trading case. This was *R. v Yorkshire Purchasing Organisation ex parte British Educational Supplies' Association* (1997) (95 LGR 727 and *The Times*, July 10, 1997). In the case, a joint committee set up by a group of Yorkshire authorities was involved in widespread trading activity using the Local Authorities (Goods and Services) Act 1970. By the time of the case, the YPO employed 373 full time staff, had an annual turnover of £130 million and sold to non members more than £2 million worth of goods a year. It also had a full array of catalogues and undertook its activities in a fully commercial manner.

The activities of YPO received a sympathetic hearing. The Court of Appeal said that the 1970 Act empowered local authorities to trade for profit and that they could purchase supplies necessary for those trading operations. It even confirmed that speculative trading was permissible with local authorities and other public bodies under that legislation. This case is considered in more detail in Ch.4.

Despite these advances in the mid-1990s, the government remained hostile and the Audit Commission did not desist from its constant reminders as to what local authorities could or could not do, based on restrictive interpretations of the law.

In order to publicise the trading debate, Gordon Prentice MP published **13.13** a Private Members Bill in 1996 which would have had the effect of clarifying the legal powers of local authorities. Whilst Gordon Prentice fronted the Bill, it was largely promoted by the Association of Direct Labour Organisation (now APSE), with much of the drafting undertaken by the authors. The purpose of the Bill—entitled *The Local Authorities (Trading and Competition Powers) Bill* (Bill 119) was to clarify trading powers. Essentially, the Bill worked on the basis of sweeping away all of the uncertainties that had arisen in relation to trading (mostly forwarded by restrictive legal views from the Audit Commission) so that there could be no doubt, for example, that local authorities could use the Goods and Services Act without spare capacity; that supplementary activities to trading purposes would also be authorised; providing specific charging powers and confirming that different trading powers exist in parallel. It also provided that the government could regulate the activity by subordinate legislation. This would preserve to the Secretary of State the ability to exclude certain categories of goods from trading, prevent any particular authority from using the provisions, restrict the geographical area over which they might apply, apply terms and conditions to agreements or to include an income cap. Notwithstanding the fact that the terms of this Bill had been very carefully crafted to try and give local authorities the advantage of removing the uncertainties, whilst preserving control on the part of the government, it did not receive formal governmental approval. Accordingly, whilst the Bill passed its first reading on May 1, 1996, it did not survive the subsequent Parliamentary process.

In May 1997 the Labour party came to power after 18 years in opposition. It set about implementing a major reform programme for local government known as the Modernisation Agenda. This included improving central/local relations and seeking to encourage and develop a "mixed economy" of service provisions. The twin pillars on which the Modernisation Agenda were based were Best Value and the governance changes to the decision making processes of local authorities. These plans were set out in the White Paper, *Modern Local Government: In Touch With the People,* published by the government in 1998.

The DETR commissioned a legal study of local authority powers which was published in November 2000. The report, Law *Relating To Local Government—Research Report,* was written by Colin Crawford, Stephen Sauvain QC, Andrew Coulson and Michael Clark. They commented:

"... not only are authorities struggling to continue to provide the services under increasing financial constraints, but that the uncertainty puts at risk initiatives which are not only seen as desirable by the authority but which the government also encourages, such as the development of CCTV schemes, coordinated social and health service provision. New mechanisms such as Anti Social Behaviour Orders and accreditation schemes are also seen as at risk." (see Ch.6 of the Report).

This paper contained chapters on both charging and trading and it is interesting to note that this appears to be one of the earliest—if not the founding—paper seeking to draw that distinction.

This was followed in April 2001 by a consultation paper entitled: *Working With Others To Achieve Best Value—s16 Of The Local Government Act 1999—A Consultation Paper On Changes To The Legal Framework To Facilitate Partnership Working* (DETR April 2001). The purpose of the consultation was to seek views on changes necessary to the law to promote partnership between Best Value authorities and other organisations in the public, private and voluntary sectors. It canvassed issues such as forming and participation in local authority companies, providing a wider range of goods and services to partners, whether public or private, providing financial assistance to other bodies, including pooling budgets and joint commissioning. Many of these proposals were particularly relevant to municipal trading.

In implementing the second main pillar of the reform agenda, namely the changes to governance arrangements in local authorities, the government also included important new powers of community initiative. These featured in the Local Government Act 2000 and provided the much vaunted powers of economic, social and environmental wellbeing. The drafting of these powers mirrored the wide drafting of s.16 of the Local Government Act 1999 and gave local authorities an important *general* power to promote or improve the wellbeing of their areas (see Ch.4). Despite the breadth of these powers, during the debate in Parliament government Ministers gave the clear message that nothing in the Bill that became the Local Government Act 2000 would change authorities' ability to trade in goods and services.

13.14 In support of the wellbeing powers, the government had commissioned background research from legal specialists. Their report (*Law Relating to Local Government—Research Report* DETR) was published in November 2000. The research had the three main objectives of undertaking a desk based review of the current state of the law; investigating the empirical basis for the debates surrounding statutory constraints on councils; and to draw together practical lessons and guidance on the legislative framework. The published report advised the government that "it is important to distinguish between charging and trading." Whilst it would recognise that these overlap in policy and practical terms, the authors of the report consider that they were different in two important ways, namely:

"First, the level of a charge must be related to the cost of provision. The maximum sum to be recovered must be the total cost of provision of the service being provided, although it is possible to have differential rates within the overall scheme. The making of a profit would take the activity into the realms of trading.

Secondly, while both charging and trading can be authorised expressly by legislation the courts have held that trading cannot be conducted generally by implication from, or as incidental to, the whole range of local authority powers."

This distinction between charging and trading was subsequently mentioned by the government in its consultation paper entitled *Working With Others To Achieve Best Value—Section 16 Of The Local Government Act 1999—A Consultation Paper On The Changes To The Legal Framework To Facilitate Partnership Working* (DETR March 2001). It was also found in the new White Paper *Strong Local Leadership—Quality Public Services* (DTLR September 2001). This paper charted the second phase of the Modernisation Agenda and led to the Local Government Act 2003. In particular, the White Paper raised the possibility of greater "freedoms and flexibilities" for better performing authorities and the genesis of the Comprehensive Performance Assessment. So far as trading is concerned, it was immediately apparent that the highest performing councils would have freedom to trade more widely across the range of their services, whereas those poor and weak performing would not.

The White Paper indicated that the government now intended to "go further than the proposals in the consultation paper (that is the *Working With Others* paper mentioned above) and provide wider powers to trade for all authorities, where this helps achieve Best Value and delivery of public services." The White Paper led to the Local Government Act 2003.

The provisions of the Local Government Act 2003 are fully considered in Pt 2. That Act provided official government recognition that commercial trading was possible, within defined limits and that charging for discretionary services was to be available to all authorities.

CONCLUSION

13.15 In conclusion, therefore, the debate over local authority powers and their ability to engage in projects to deliver charging and trading outcomes has had a satisfactory conclusion. Whilst the *ultra vires* doctrine does still exist, new general powers of community initiative ameliorate its effect. It is fair to say that in the early to mid 1990s, it seemed distinctly unpredictable that any improvement in the operation of the powers system would be forthcoming but local authorities have welcomed the later developments. This process reached full circle with the granting of new specific powers to engage in charging and trading in the Local Government Act 2003.

Part Five

Charging and Trading in Scotland, Wales and Northern Ireland

CHARGING AND TRADING IN SCOTLAND, WALES AND NORTHERN IRELAND

INTRODUCTION

This book is predominantly directed towards the position in England and   **14.1**
Wales where the Local Government Act 2003 applies. Even then, the
situation in Wales is slightly different in that the Welsh Assembly Government adopts many of the roles undertaken in England by the UK
government. Notwithstanding this, however, the majority of the provisions
are the same.

This is not the same in either Northern Ireland or Scotland. Northern
Ireland has its own historical position which has significance to the
performance of all local authority functions. Accordingly, what local
authorities in that region can achieve in charging and trading is much more
limited.

In Scotland, there is also devolution, although the Scottish Parliament
has greater powers than the Welsh Assembly. In this region, there is wholly
separate legislation governing many aspects of local government, including
Best Value, performance management and charging and trading.

This chapter therefore seeks to briefly explain the position in relation to
Northern Ireland, Wales and Scotland for the benefit of the people in those
areas. Predictably, this can only be a brief exposition, otherwise it would
lead to a "book within a book." Figure 14.1 briefly summarises the position.

Figure 14.1
**Summary of the Legal Position in Relation to Charging and Trading in
Northern Ireland, Wales and Scotland**

- In Northern Ireland the Local Government Act 2003 does not apply
  and there are devolved arrangements, although these are in their

infancy. In effect, as there is no wellbeing power in Northern Ireland and Best Value is slightly different, the "old law" position applies in relation to charging and trading;

- In Wales the Local Government Act 1999 and 2000 apply, including the concepts of Best Value and community leadership. However, the Welsh Assembly takes the place of the UK government and the Welsh Assembly Government takes the place of the Office of the Deputy Prime Minister. It should be noted that there is no CPA in Wales;

- In Scotland, the Local Government Act 2003 and other powers that are relevant do not apply. The Scottish Parliament has passed the Local Government in Scotland Act 2003, which has introduced Best Value and community leadership as statutory provisions for the first time, as well as including a new charging and trading regime.

CHARGING AND TRADING IN NORTHERN IRELAND

Introduction

14.2   Northern Ireland, whilst part of the UK, has a particularly troubled recent past. This is particularly relevant when looking at local government powers in general and therefore has an equal relevance to the subject of charging and trading as examined in this book.

Whilst the Local Government Act 1972 bestowed extensive new powers on local authorities in England, Wales and Scotland, at the same time, Northern Ireland local government was moving in the opposite direction. The Local Government (Northern Ireland) Act 1972 took away powers from local authorities in the region, leaving them with responsibility for only a smaller number of areas such as environmental services, leisure, recreation and a limited input to economic development. It is particularly striking that the 26 local authorities that currently make up local government in Northern Ireland spend a total of only £340 million out of a total public expenditure budget of over £7 billion.

Following the commencement of the troubles, the area of Northern Ireland has been ruled directly by central government in England. Furthermore, a series of large quangos was set up in relation to key areas such as education, housing and health and Next Steps agencies also run a number of other areas. Notwithstanding this, somewhat dismal, picture, matters might be about to change in Northern Ireland. In 1998 the Belfast Agreement was made offering Northern Ireland a new way forward. Under this arrangement, devolved government institutions were established, including the Northern Ireland Executive and Assembly. The Assembly has been suspended by the UK government on a number of occasions when problems have flared up; however it is hoped that power sharing can be agreed in Northern Ireland and the Assembly will ultimately take full responsibility for government in the region.

Below central government level, the local government landscape has a completely different complexion to that elsewhere in the United Kingdom. After the Belfast Agreement was made it was agreed to have a Review of Public Administration. The Review was formally established in June 2002, with the brief to develop "options for reform which are consistent with the arrangements and principles of the Belfast Agreement, within an appropriate framework of political and financial accountability." This Review has been ongoing for a number of years but is likely to lead to a new settlement in terms of the central/local government balance.

The Review resulted in a public consultation document in 2004 which sought to consult widely on future proposals for local government. The consultation document proposed five possible models which were summarised in the *Municipal Journal* of May 6, 2004 as follows:

- Status quo: this model envisages no change to the overall structure of public administration;

- Centralised: under this model all major services would be delivered directly by government departments;

- Regional and sub-regional public bodies: a range of public bodies, operated either regionally or sub-regionally, would deliver public services;

- Reformed status quo with enhanced local government: while keeping the main features of the current system, local government would be given new responsibilities;

- Strong local government: major public services would be the responsibility of a smaller number of new councils. (See Colin Knox and Paul Carmichael *Northern Ireland: The Way Ahead*).

Not surprisingly, local authorities see this as a potential new start for them following a disastrous three decades in which their powers have been severely curtailed. There are currently 26 district councils in Northern Ireland and a number of the options mentioned above would see them gaining substantial new powers and being placed more on a footing with local government in England, Wales and Scotland. Indeed, in a recent report, Scotland and Northern Ireland's expenditure were compared with local authorities in Scotland controlling 36.6 per cent of public expenditure; whereas local government in Northern Ireland was responsible for a mere 3.4 per cent of expenditure.

Local authorities may well face a reorganisation into unitary authorities, which would have the effect of reducing their number but increasing their power. Also relevant here would be services currently under the control of major quangos, particularly roads and education.

It goes without saying that such is the limited amount of local government expenditure that there are many fewer opportunities in relation to charging and trading than are relevant to authorities elsewhere.

Local Government Powers in Northern Ireland

14.3   As mentioned above, local authorities in Northern Ireland enjoy far fewer powers than their counterparts on the mainland. This was because major powers were stripped away from them in 1972. Obviously, this has an impact on their ability to engage in charging for discretionary services and commercial trading.

The following are the key points to note about powers in Northern Ireland:

- The Local Authorities (Goods and Services) Act 1970 does apply, as elsewhere in the United Kingdom;

- Local authorities in Northern Ireland do have Best Value, although not under the Local Government Act 1999, which is the legislation which introduced Best Value for England and Wales or the Local Government (Scotland) Act 2003, which introduced it for Scottish local authorities. Instead, there is the Local Government (Best Value) Act (Northern Ireland) 2002. This is considered below and was introduced by the Northern Ireland Assembly. However, it is less extensive than Best Value elsewhere;

- Local authorities do not have wellbeing powers as the Local Government Act 2000, applicable in England and Wales, does not apply in Northern Ireland. This is particularly significant to charging and trading, bearing in mind the regularity with which this power of first resort is cited by local authorities in order to justify such activity. Prior to the wellbeing provisions being enacted, local authorities often relied on economic development powers (previously in the Local Government and Housing Act 1989, s.33). In Northern Ireland there remain separate economic powers in the Local Government (Miscellaneous Provisions)(Northern Ireland) Order 2002. Whilst an important development, this falls short of the power of wellbeing both in its range and in the limited specific powers attached to it. Those powers do permit the acquisition, management and disposal of land but this is not comparable with the extremely broad capabilities offered by the wellbeing powers. In particular, the ability to join with others in partnership is lacking;

- The Local Government Act 2003, which introduced a new power to charge for discretionary services and new powers of commercial trading in England and Wales, does not apply in Northern Ireland. This is mentioned in a recent consultation paper on conferring trading powers under s.95 of the Local Government Act 2003 on Welsh Local Authorities. This considers the position in Scotland and Northern Ireland and at para.7 it is confirmed that "there is currently no general legal basis on which local authorities in Northern Ireland may engage in trading activity." (see *Local Authority Trading Powers—A Welsh Assembly Government Consultation Paper* December 2004).

Charging and Trading in Northern Ireland

The absence of applicability of the provisions in the Local Government **14.4** Act 2003 is particularly significant for Northern Ireland, bearing in mind the coverage of those provisions and their likely usage by local authorities elsewhere for charging and trading activities. This means that there are no specific powers in existence to authorise charging or trading in Northern Ireland. Effectively, this means that local authorities in Northern Ireland must rely on the "old" law position whereby they have to identify a power to authorise a particular activity and then implement that power within the public law framework. This is, in effect, the same position that local authorities in England, Wales and Scotland were in prior to the enactment of the 2003 Act. However, it is worthy of note that the pre-existing powers available to local authorities in Northern Ireland are narrower than those applicable elsewhere, as described above.

In effect, of the three categories of charging and trading permissible, the following would be the position:

- *Public To Public;* here the availability of the Local Authorities (Goods and Services) Act 1970 is particularly useful. This will be a key power enabling local authorities to enter into agreements for specified purposes with other local authorities and other public bodies. It should be noted that the 1970 Act is as originally legislated, *i.e.* the extra freedoms available following the amendment of the Act in Scotland would not be available in Northern Ireland;

- *Public To Private;* here a local authority would have to identify a power has being available and implement it lawfully. The only other area that might be relevant is spare capacity;

- *Trading With Members Of The Public;* again, here a local authority would need to identify an available power and exercise it reasonably. Spare capacity might also assist a local authority in this area.

The old compulsory competitive tendering regime did apply in Northern Ireland, although again in a slightly different form. The Local Government

(Miscellaneous Provisions) (Northern Ireland) Order 1992 was subsequently repealed by the new Best Value provisions as described below. However, local authorities have continued to operate past CCT contracts for blue collar services via extensions to those arrangements or under new Best Value arrangements.

Best Value In Northern Ireland

14.5   The Local Government (Best Value) Act (Northern Ireland) Act 2002 was passed by the Northern Ireland Assembly and came into operation on April 1, 2002. The focus of the legislation is the same as the Local Government Act 1999 in England and Wales, namely the introduction of a regime of Best Value. Both Acts have the same interpretation of what is meant by Best Value and specify a requirement to make arrangements for continuous improvement in the way in which functions are exercised, having regard to a combination of economy, efficiency and effectiveness.

However, the Northern Ireland Act is much shorter, containing only three sections. There are no requirements for local authorities to conduct Best Value reviews of their functions; to prepare a Best Value Performance Plan; or in relation to inspection of compliance with the Act. The consultation provisions are different and there are no regulations about the keeping of accounts by Best Value authorities included in this Act.

Nonetheless, the broad thrust of the Act is the same as in England and Wales, *i.e.* to place a duty on local authorities to make arrangements to secure continuous improvement in the way in which their functions are delivered. This may assist district councils in Northern Ireland in making the case for charging and trading activity. Whilst not confirming any specific charging or trading powers, local authorities seeking to achieve these aims will use the securing of Best Value as one of the necessary elements of the authorisation.

Should new specific powers be required for charging and trading, then powers to introduce these is already available. Section 3 of the Local Government (Best Value) Act (Northern Ireland) 2002 states:

(3)(1) If the Department thinks that a statutory provision prevents or obstructs compliance by councils with the duty imposed by s.1(1), the Department may by order make provision by modifying or excluding the application of the provision in relation to councils;

(2) The Department may by order make provision conferring on councils any power which the Department considers necessary or expedient to permit or facilitate compliance with the duty imposed by s.1(1);

(3) In exercising a power conferred under sub section (2) a council shall have regard to any guidance issued by the Department.

It can be seen that this power is similar to that given in s.16 of the Local Government Act 1999. It gives the government the power to introduce new powers to enable the council to form a whole range of partnership models and to amend or remove any unidentified barriers to the delivery of Best Value in Northern Ireland. However, this power has not yet been used and no guidance has been issued under it. Bearing in mind that no order can be made under s.3 of the 2002 Act unless a draft has been laid before and approved by resolution of the Northern Ireland assembly, it is unlikely that there will be any movement for some time, bearing in mind the Assembly is suspended.

Conclusion

The situation in Northern Ireland in relation to charging and trading is therefore unique, but unsatisfactory nonetheless. It is to be hoped that the Review of Public Administration, which is scheduled to publish a detailed series of proposals in 2005, delivers a new settlement for local authorities whereby they are granted further powers more in line with local government in the rest of the United Kingdom. In the interim, the effect of this legal scenario on charging and trading is likely to be significant and less activity of this nature will be undertaken. **14.6**

TRADING AND CHARGING IN WALES

Introduction

In Wales the development of Government policy on local government has taken place in the context of the development of the partnering relationship between the National Assembly for Wales and local government. The key facets of that relationship are the Partnership Scheme and Partnership Council which the National Assembly for Wales has established in accordance with the Government of Wales Act 1996 and the policy agreements (equivalent to LSPs in England) which each of the 22 unitary authorities have entered into with the National Assembly. **14.7**

The Partnership Council comprising representatives of local government (including town and community councils, fire and national parks authorities) and the Welsh Assembly Government meets on a quarterly basis. It has established an important role in debating and assisting in the development of policy in Wales.

The Partnership Scheme issued in December 2000 sets out the Assembly's approach to support local government and the framework within which they both should operate (including the role of the Partnership Council). It states amongst other things that the Assembly would within the framework of primary legislation seek to empower local authorities to ensure the delivery of the wide range of services to local communities directly and through encouraging voluntary and business enterprise.

Freedom and Responsibility in Local Government

14.8   For Welsh local government the equivalent to the English white paper *Strong Local Leadership—Quality Public Services* is the policy statement *Freedom and Responsibility in Local Government*. The differences in policy (particularly the adoption by the National Assembly of the Wales Programme for Improvement as explained below) between these papers provides ample evidence (if any was required) of an increasing divergence of government policy with regard to local government in Wales, through the Welsh Assembly Government, from that in England.

Whereas the English White Paper refers to proposals to give greater freedom to trade and to charge for discretionary services (referring to the previous consultation document *Working with Others to achieve Best Value*) the Welsh policy statement says little on the subject. It merely states that the Welsh Assembly Government would work with the UK Government to take forward legislation under s.16 of the Local Government Act 1999 to remove legal obstacles to local authorities achieving continuous improvement and in particular to remove the constraints in the Local Authorities (Goods and Services) Act 1970 to give greater freedom to trade.

It is understood that the Assembly presently sees these objectives as having been achieved by the coming into force of the Local Government Act 2003 and there is no intention therefore at the present time to pursue specific statutory amendments.

Importantly the policy statement did not contain the provisions from the English White Paper concerning the role of the Comprehensive Performance Assessment. Instead it reiterated its proposals for a system of self/peer assessment which was locally owned with involvement of audit and inspection agencies being proportionate to the risk involved and with the objective of assisting improvement. No classifications or tables similar to that proposed for the CPA process were to be involved.

This issue takes on an additional importance in the context of the Government's position on commercial trading by local authorities under s.95 of the Local Government Act 2003. As already stated in Ch.6 the Government has stated its intention to allow only authorities in the *excellent, good* or *fair* categories under the CPA to trade using the powers for commercial trading contained in the Local Government Act 2003. There is no specific power (as for English authorities under s.100 of the Local Government Act 2003) to differentiate in the granting of the "trading powers" on the basis of categorization of performance of authorities. Nevertheless s.122 of the Act does enable any regulations under the Act to be made which make different provision for different cases or areas.

The Wales Improvement Programme

14.9   This alternative approach to best value had been endorsed by the Partnership Council on October 15, 2001 and draft guidance had been issued in December 2001. Subsequently the guidance was contained in

Circular 18/2002 issued by the National Assembly in June 2002 (which replaces the earlier circular guidance on Best Value in Wales).

The approach comprises the following elements:

- Whole authority analysis of fitness to achieve continuous improvement across its corporate and service functions. It will be led by the authority itself but will include some external and independent perspectives (including external auditors and other Inspectorates) and must identify the areas where the authority most needs to focus improvements. There is no prescribed tool or methodology to be used. Further specific reviews may be identified as being necessary.

- Risk assessment. This will need to be agreed between the authority and its regulators. It will examine potential or actual risk factors including the scale of the risk and the scale of benefit likely to be achieved by any change. This provides the focus on areas to be covered by the Improvement Plan.

- Improvement Plan. This will report the key findings of the whole authority assessment and risk assessment and identify how those findings are reflected in its future work programme. It will constitute the statutory best value performance plan and could form part of a Policy Agreement with the Assembly.

- Regulatory Plan. This also will take into account the whole authority assessment and the risk assessment. It will be developed in consultation with the authority and provide a programme of audits and inspections by statutory inspectorates to ensure effective co-ordination and planning. There is no automatic requirement for an inspection following a review and inspection arrangements will change as a result of the emphasis on joint working to support improvement.

- Public Summary. This is the summary of the Improvement Plan required to be published by the authority setting out the authority's performance to date in key areas and results of actions taken to improve and actions planned and targets set.

There is no intention to categorize the performance of the authority in the same way as under the CPA procedures for English authorities and this is reflected in the fact that s.100 of the Local Government Act 2003 (requiring the Audit Commission to categorize authorities by reference to their performance) refers only to English local authorities.

The Local Government Act 2003

The Local Government Act 2003 applies in Wales, unlike in either Scotland or Northern Ireland. However, there are some differences, as the role of the Deputy Prime Minister in England is replaced by the Welsh Assembly Government and the Welsh Assembly in Wales. **14.10**

Looking at the law, all of the principal sections of the Local Government Act 2003 apply in Wales including s.93 conferring power to levy a charge for discretionary services and s.94 which confers power to disapply s.93; s.95 giving the power to grant local authority powers to commercially trade and s.96, which enables conditions to be imposed; and also s.97 giving power to modify enactments, though this is a little different.

The way that the system works, s.124 of the Local Government Act 2003 states that the "appropriate person" means the Secretary of State in relation to England and the National Assembly for Wales in relation to Wales. This is essentially the only differentiation that needs to be made, as charging and trading applies to Best Value authorities which as defined by the Local Government Act 1999 includes local authorities and other public bodies in Wales.

Having determined that the National Assembly for Wales is the appropriate person, the principal sections of the 2003 Act become clear. This is because under s.93, for example, where the power to levy charges for discretionary services is given by the Act directly, it is the "appropriate person" that has the ability to issue guidance; in relation to s.95, it is the appropriate person who can issue the order giving the power to local authorities to trade and under s.96 it is the appropriate person who can impose conditions. In effect, wherever the Secretary of State has a power then that power in Wales is conferred on the Assembly. The only difference here is in relation to s.97 on modifying enactments, as explained below.

Notwithstanding the fact that the basic provisions apply, there are still differences, in particular in relation to commercial trading under s.95, and these are explained below and illustrated in Figure 14.2.

Charging and Trading Before the Local Government Act 2003

14.11   Here, the position in Wales was identical to that in England. Most of the principal powers that local authorities would have used to undertake work for one another, the private sector or members of the public would be the same as in England. The principal power here is the Local Authorities (Goods and Services) Act 1970 but a number of other Acts conferring charging or trading ability (for example, the Civic Restaurants Act 1947, the local Government (Miscellaneous Provisions) Act 1976 etc.) all apply in Wales. One interesting point is that in Wales the government is still conferring new designated bodies under the 1970 Act. As an example, the Local Authorities (Goods and Services)(Public Bodies)(Wales) Order 2004 (SI 2004/2878 (W.248)) conferred a designated body status on PBS 2003 Limited. This enabled Rhondda Cynon Taff County Borough Council to provide catering and grounds maintenance services to PBS 2003 Limited which is a PFI company. As mentioned in Ch.2 it is unlikely that the Secretary of State in England will issue any more orders under the 1970 Act.

Charging for Discretionary Services in Wales

Section 93 of the Local Government Act 2003 confers the power directly **14.12**
onto Best Value authorities to levy a charge for the provision of discretionary services which they have power elsewhere to undertake.

The only difference in relation to this part of the Act is that under s.93(6)
it is the Welsh Assembly that has the power to issue guidance on the use of
the s.93 power. The National Assembly for Wales issued this guidance
*General Power for Best Value Authorities in Wales to Charge for Discretionary
Services—Guidance on Power in the Local Government Act 2003* in February
2004. The guidance is reproduced in Appendix 2, but to all intents and
purposes is identical to the guidance for England.

In relation to s.94 of the Local Government Act 2003—the power to
disapply the s.93 power—this is given to the Welsh Assembly too.

By the end of 2004, there was no evidence that the 22 local authorities in
Wales were using the powers to charge for discretionary services any more
than their counterparts in England.

Commercial Trading in Wales

The situation in relation to the conferring of commercial trading powers **14.13**
on local government in Wales is slightly different. The starting point is the
same, *i.e.* the power conferred by s.95 for the appropriate person to give the
powers to local authorities is conferred on the Welsh Assembly, just as this
role is operated by the Secretary of State in England. However, where the
Deputy Prime Minister has already exercised these powers within England,
no order had appeared by the start of 2005 in Wales. Instead, the Welsh
Assembly Government issued a consultation paper seeking the views of
those in and around local government on the conferring of such a power.
The consultation exercise commenced in December 2004 and ended on
February 7, 2005. The consultation paper was called *Local Authority
Trading Powers—A Welsh Assembly Government Consultation Paper*. It is
available from the Welsh Assembly Government web site on
www.wales.gov.uk.

Notwithstanding the fact that these provisions have not yet come in, the
consultation exercise illustrates the general view being taken of the power
by the Welsh Assembly and it is likely that a very similar power will be
conferred on local government in Wales, as it has in England. However,
there will be some important differences as explained below.

The consultation paper recounts the legislative context in which the
Local Government Act 2003 is conferred; it differentiates the difference
between charging and trading—as the authors have in this book—and also
compares the position in Wales to that elsewhere. In England, the s.95
order is already made; in Scotland different legislation applies and, as
mentioned above, the Local Government Act 2003 does not apply in
Northern Ireland and the "old law" position applies.

It is mentioned that the Local Government Act 2003 does not automatically grant trading powers to Welsh local authorities; it deliberately gives the discretion to the Welsh Assembly to determine whether it would be appropriate to do so. However, para.2 of the consultation paper indicated that, "the Assembly Government believes that, in principle, there are compelling reasons for conferring the power." These include the policy of giving freedoms and flexibilities to local government in Wales, bestowing further flexibility on authorities' ability to deliver services and to maximise efficiency. Accordingly, "the Assembly Government therefore proposes to invite the National Assembly for Wales to confer the power to trade on the terms . . . ." set out in the consultation paper.

Who Can Trade?

14.14   The power to trade is proposed to be given to all Best Value authorities in Wales, which includes three fire and rescue authorities, three national park authorities and 22 unitary councils.

It is not proposed to give the trading power to police authorities.

Some issues are raised by conferring trading powers on single purpose authorities, who do not enjoy the full functional coverage that the unitary authorities do. No doubt this will be covered in any subsequent order made by the Welsh Assembly Government under s.95.

Relevance of the CPA?

14.15   As mentioned above, the Comprehensive Performance Assessment does not apply in Wales. Accordingly, it is not possible to link commercial trading activity to local government performance in such a direct manner. Notwithstanding this, the Welsh Assembly has not taken the view that trading powers should be linked to performance, preferring the broader approach offered by the Wales Improvement Programme.

Safeguards on Trading Activity?

14.16   The Welsh Assembly Government proposes to impose similar safeguards to those in effect in England. Accordingly, each local authority or body exercising the powers would be required to provide a comprehensive business case and require full approval of the authority for that business case before trading operations can begin.

The other safeguards that apply in England would also apply in Wales, in particular the imposition of EU Competition law and State Aid. The consultation paper refers to the Regulatory Impact Assessment undertaken by the government in England which concluded that "the impact of local authority trading on the private sector, and in particular the risk of private sector suppliers losing significant amounts of business, would be relatively slight. We have no reason to suppose that would differ in Wales." However, the effect on the market of trading via companies can only be assessed in the light of full compliance with EU and State Aid principles.

Another safeguard that will be imposed, relating directly to the last point, is that where an authority gives assistance to its trading company, it must recover the costs of so doing from the company. This would include recovery of the full costs of any support or services provided and would prevent continuing subsidies being given to a trading company.

So far as accounts and audit are concerned, the same provisions as apply in England would be applicable, namely that s.18 of the Local Government Act 2003 allows companies controlled and influenced by a local authority to be brought within the new capital controls. However, these currently rely on definitions in Pt V of the Local Government and Housing Act 1989, until definitions based on accounting practice are completed by CIPFA. The Welsh Assembly intends to follow exactly the same line as the government in England in adopting such generally accepted accounting definitions instead of the legal definitions in Pt V of the 1989 Act.

The government in Wales proposes to amend the statutory guidance on the Wales Programme for Improvement so as to require authorities to include in their improvement plans a summary of the uses to which trading powers have been put.

Withdrawal of the Trading Power?

The position in Wales, being slightly behind the government in England, **14.17** has the benefit of seeing how the English provisions have bedded down. Accordingly, the comments in paras 13 to 15 of the consultation paper demonstrate an awareness of difficulties that might arise with trading companies that have been raised in the debate.

It gives a number of examples of circumstances where the power may be withdrawn including:

- Sustained and serious trading losses which call into question the overall financial health of the authority;

- Clear evidence of an authority's non trading services (especially those which it is obliged to provide) suffering a significant drop in standards because of undue emphasis being placed on trading operations;

- Major irregularities in trading accounts or lack of proper management controls;

- Breaches of the bar on continuing subsidy to local authorities or Competition or State Aid law.

It is the second of these that is particularly significant and a point that has been raised by the authors when looking at the s.95 provisions. It is for this reason, that the authors have suggested that a local authority needs to be very clear on what it is trying to achieve with the commercial trading powers and ensuring that it has considered all relevant matters that will affect those aims.

Figure 14.2 illustrates some of the similarities and differences between the operation of the trading power in England and in Wales.

Figure 14.2
Differences and Similarities between England and Wales in Commercial Trading

Similarities

- Section 95 applies as in England;
- There is still the power to confer the power on local authorities via an Order rather than an automatic right to the power;
- In Wales you still need a local authority company;
- The council cannot subsidise the company and must recover the costs of help given;
- A full business case is required, with approval by the authority;
- EU Competition law and State Aid applies just the same
- Accounting issues, in relation to off/on balance sheet are the same

Differences

- The Welsh Assembly Government, not the Office of the Deputy Prime Minister is the "appropriate person";
- The s.95 Order has not yet been made in Wales;
- There will be slightly different coverage—in Wales the s.95 powers are likely to include national parks, for example;
- There is no CPA in Wales and operation of the trading powers is not directly linked to local authority performance;
- Instead, there is a link with the Welsh Programme for Improvement (WPI), which is Best Value based.

Power to Modify Enactments

14.18   Section 97 of the Local Government Act 2003 gives the Secretary of State in England the power to modify enactments. In particular, it permits the Secretary of State, where an enactment "prevents or obstructs" Best

Value authorities charging for a discretionary service or commercially trading, it can "amend, repeal, revoke or disapply the enactment." (see s.97(1)). Section 97(2) also confers on the Secretary of State a power to amend, repeal, revoke or disapply an enactment which "makes provision for, or in connection with, power to charge for the provision of a discretionary service."

Here, the position in relation to Wales is different. Instead of simply granting these powers to the Welsh Assembly, they are reserved to the Deputy prime Minister. However, under s.97(7), where exercising the power, the Deputy Prime Minister must not make any provision relating to Wales, unless he has consulted the National Assembly for Wales. Furthermore, he must not make any provision in relation to legislation made by the National Assembly for Wales without its specific consent.

Conclusion

The position in Wales is therefore very similar to that in England and is **14.19** likely to run in parallel. As mentioned above and below, the situation in Northern Ireland and Scotland is much different.

Commentators will no doubt watch with interest the development of charging and trading powers in Wales. Not least because of the absence of a CPA link to commercial trading. In this way, a similar situation exists to that whereby commentators will watch where the absence of a requirement to have a trading company in Scotland makes any difference.

CHARGING AND TRADING IN SCOTLAND

Introduction

The Local Government in Scotland Act 2003 received royal assent in **14.20** February 2003 and the trading provisions within that Act came into force on April 1, 2003 (see SSI 2003/134). The Act is a major piece of local government legislation for Scotland and includes provisions on three key areas, namely: Best Value, community planning and economic, social or environmental wellbeing.

The enhanced powers to trade in Scotland are expressly linked to Best Value and are found within the Part 1 of the Act; which is the section relating to Best Value and Accountability. Sections 10–12 are the key provisions; although s.10 relaxes the restrictions formerly contained with regard to taking into account non-commercial considerations. The Act itself was supported by Explanatory Notes which were prepared by the Scottish Executive and which assist in understanding the legislative provisions, though do not themselves have legal effect. Unlike the English and Welsh trading regimes, the main power for trading is an enhanced power under the Local Authorities (Goods and Services) Act 1970. This Act has been expressly amended in Scotland to provide a wider power to trade than that formerly available.

In outline the legal framework for trading therefore comprises the existing powers which existed before the enactment of the 2003 Act, as modified by the new provisions within the 2003 Act; together with express new powers within ss.11 and 11A of that Act.

THE LEGAL PROVISIONS

The Section 11 Power to Trade

14.21   Section 11 of the 2003 Act re-writes large sections of the Local Authorities (Goods and Services) Act 1970. The origins of that Act are summarised in Ch.4 and it will be recalled that within England and Wales, the Act identifies a specified list of public bodies with whom authorities are able to trade. Section 11 makes significant amendments to the 1970 Act and the new provisions are summarised in the Explanatory Notes as follows:

"Section 11—Relaxation of restrictions on supply of goods and services etc by local authorities

23. Section 11 amends the Local Authorities (Goods and Services) Act 1970 (c.39) ("the 1970 Act") to provide a new framework for the provision of goods and services by local authorities to individuals and other organisations.

24. Goods and services can be provided under a trading agreement to anyone the local authority chooses, although the well being of the area or persons within the area must be considered. Subsection *(1M)* of the 1970 Act provides that before entering into any agreement under subsection (1) of the 1970 Act, local authorities should have regard to whether doing so will be likely to promote or improve the wellbeing of its area, persons within that area or both. In this subsection "wellbeing" has the same meaning as it has in section 21.

25. Where the agreement is with another local authority the local authority can build its capacity for the purpose of supporting the agreement and the income it makes is not subject to restriction.

26. Where the agreement is with other public authorities or bodies, contractual partners where the provision is intended to support services provided to the authority through a pre-existing contract; or to bodies serving a public purpose where the provision is to support that public purpose, the local authority must trade from its own surplus capacity in staff services, property and facilities, although the income it makes is not subject to restriction.

27. Where the agreement is with other trading partners than those described above, the local authority must trade from its own surplus capacity in staff services, property and facilities, and the income it makes will be subject to financial limits set by the Scottish Ministers as provided by subsection *(1D(b))*. Subsections *(1D)* and *(1E)* provide that the financial limits also apply to dividend income and profit share income derived from a local authority's interest in a company which has trading agreements to which, if the local authority itself were a party, the financial limits would apply.

28. Such limits, which, according to subsections *(1F)* and *(1G)* of the 1970 Act, can be set to cover all trading operations or different amounts for different trading operations, will be set by order after consultation and subject annulment in pursuance of a resolution of the Scottish Parliament. The Scottish Ministers will have the power to approve exclusion from the relevant limit of income generated by a particular agreement entered into an authority. It is expected that such approvals will be offered only according to clear and explicit criteria."

The first thing to note about s.11 is that this is a completely different route to permit trading type activity from that undertaken in England or Wales. It is a matter of some interest that the Scottish Parliament decided to go down such a completely different avenue and, as has subsequently transpired, not one without its own dangers and complications. Nonetheless, this is the avenue that has been chosen north of the border and commentators will watch with interest how well it fares.

14.22 Local authorities in Scotland have already raised concerns about the interpretation of these provisions. Bearing in mind the fact that the Scottish Parliament has taken a piece of English legislation (*i.e.* the original Local Authorities (Goods and Services) Act 1970) and has changed it, it has been argued that the Act prior to its amendment by the Scottish Parliament should have its original legislative meaning, as interpreted by the courts. It was mentioned in Ch.4 that the Court of Appeal judgment in the case of *R. v Yorkshire Purchasing Organisation ex part British Educational Suppliers Limited* (1998) ELR 195 specifically held that the 1970 Act did not rely upon spare capacity and that local authorities could recruit staff, purchases assets and equipment etc to undertake agreements that had been reached. Notwithstanding this, the explanatory notes produced by the Scottish Executive have indicated that in some circumstances a local authority may only use spare capacity, and this flies in the face of the settled interpretation of the Act in England and Wales. It is also interesting to note that the Office of the Deputy Prime Minister indicated that s.95(4) of the Local Government Act 2003 specifically required any local authority engaging in commercial trading to do so via a company, due to issues in relation to EU competition law and state aid. Bearing in mind this advice from the ODPM, it is surprising that the Scottish Parliament has decided to go a different way and that there is no requirement of any local authority to establish a company in relation to this type of activity. Again, it is early days in the life of the legislation and it is not possible to say at this stage whether this will provide difficulties later on.

Whereas in England and Wales, local authorities are expected to act in accordance with Best Value and wellbeing principles, there is no specific link between the trading activity and specific legislation. Here the legislation is different with subsection (1M) of the amended Act indicating that before entering an agreement the local authority in question should have regard to wellbeing issues.

Perhaps more importantly, there was a distinction drawn in Scotland between public sector and non-public sector trading. This is where the issue about capacity building comes to the fore as the explanatory notes produced by the Scottish Executive suggest that it is acceptable to take on new capacity in relation to public to public trading, but not for public to private trading or for trading with wider bodies with functions of a public nature. As mentioned above, this view is contentious and not supported by local government in the region as it appears to offer a regressive rather than progressive position. Taken at face value, it would undermine a wide range of related activity including the ongoing implementation of effective community planning and delivery frameworks, the drive towards greater efficiencies in the pooling of resources and the ability to jointly deliver linked services and objectives.

Another major difference between this legislation and that south of the border is that there is a regulation making power permitting the Minister to set a financial limit on the income generated from specific trading activities. Ministers in England steered away from this particular instrument of control, believing it to be difficult to manage. Notwithstanding the fact that the legislation was passed in 2003, the Scottish Ministers have yet to impose any financial limit.

The final major difference between these provisions and those in England is that trading in Scotland is all linked to the requirement to maintain proper trading accounts as provided by s.12 of the 2003 Act and as described below.

The Section 11A Power to Trade

14.23   Section 11A is a stand-alone power to undertake construction activity, an area which is expressly excluded from the 1970 Act (see Ch.4). The Explanatory Notes explain the provision as follows:

"Section 11A—Special provision for local authority contracts for construction of buildings or works

29. Section 11A provides that a local authority may enter into agreements with any person for the construction or maintenance of any buildings or works. Such agreements are governed by any regulations made under the power provided at subsection *(2)*.
30. Subsection *(3)* provides that specific reference can be made in the regulations issued under this section to any code of practice or other document for the purposes of extending the scope of the regulations to cover such codes or documents. This means that such codes or documents will in effect have the same legal standing as the regulations.
31. Subsections *(6)* and *(7)* provide that such regulations shall be made after consultation and are subject to annulment in pursuance of a resolution of the Scottish Parliament."

It has been necessary to insert a separate and further specific power to trade in construction related activity, bearing in mind the fact that this is expressly excluded from the Local Authorities (Goods and Services) Act 1970. It was mentioned above that the Scottish provisions and guidance refer to the Compulsory Competitive Tendering regime, which has only relatively recently been abolished north of the border. Of course, under the CCT regime the provisions in relation to "construction or maintenance" work which were governed by the Local Government (Planning and Land) Act 1980 spring to mind.

However, a new specific agreement has been incorporated into the Act via s.11A which allows local authorities to enter into new agreements for the construction of buildings and works, albeit subject to additional controls by the government. As detailed, Ministers have the power to set financial limits on income related to any such new activity.

Trading Accounts

Section 12 provides part of the regulatory framework which is a **14.24** requirement to keep proper accounts for the trading activity. Section 12 is linked to the general duty to follow proper accounting practice within s.14 of the 2003 Act. The Explanatory Notes explain the provisions within Section 12 as follows:

"Section 12—Trading operations and accounts

32. Section 12 provides that where proper accounting practice (as specified in section 14) states that a local authority should keep and publish a trading account for an activity, that activity should be budgeted for so that over a three year period on a rolling basis the revenue of the activity at least equals the expenditure."

It was mentioned above that the requirement to keep trading accounts is completely different to the regulation of trading activity in England and Wales. This harks back to the old CCT days where either a break even or a rate of return on capital employed had to be achieved by each local authority undertaking construction or maintenance work or other defined activities.

Here, the legislation has been amended to require that not only proper accounts be kept in respect of all trading activity of significance; but also, that over a three year period on a rolling basis, the activity should break even. Whilst this new provision is more user friendly than the old rules (for example the three year rolling basis of calculation) it provides an extra burden for those local authorities engaging in such activity in Scotland.

It is obviously crucial to decide what is significant and what is not significant trading activity, and this is explained further below.

In England, there is no requirement to keep separate accounts in respect of trading activity under the Local Government Act 2003; however, there is a requirement to keep a separate account under the Local Authorities (Goods and Services) Act 1970, although that will only be relevant to public to public trading because of the overall legal regime applying in that area.

Guidance and Regulations supporting Trading in Scotland

14.25   As at February 2005, the Scottish Executive had not commenced its consultation on guidance on s.11 of the 2003 Act; nor on the guidance and regulations necessary to implement s.11A of the 2003 Act. However, the Best Value Task Force produced an advisory note: *Local Government in Scotland Act 2003: Trading Advisory Note* (2004) which will be useful for those undertaking trading activity. That guidance does not have statutory force and is intended to be supportive of the main Task Force guidance; *Local Government In Scotland Act 2003—Guidance By The Best Value Taskforce On s.1(1)—The Duty To Make Arrangements To Secure Best Value.* (2003).

HOW WILL TRADING IN SCOTLAND OPERATE?

Introduction

14.26   In the absence of statutory guidance and publication of regulations, the following section is necessarily speculative and up to date guidance on particular schemes must be sought from appropriate legal advisors.

The first point to note is that the trading provisions are part of the overall modernisation agenda and are designed to be supportive of Best Value and the legal framework provided by competition law and state aid as detailed earlier in this book (see Ch.8). As the Task Force Guidance reminds authorities: "For the avoidance of doubt, the policy intention is not to allow local authorities unfettered opportunities to expand trading simply to increase turnover and employment; with the added flexibilities and freedoms created by Local Government In Scotland Act 2003 goes a commensurate duty of responsibility to account for trading in an open and transparent manner." (see Background).

Featured below is a more detailed example of how the Scottish trading provisions will operate, supported by the new legislative provisions described above.

Public Trading

The changes to the Local Authorities (Goods and Services) Act 1970 **14.27** replace the previous grouping with whom trading may be undertaken and gives a series of definitions of bodies with which trading activity (to varying degrees) is to be permitted. These include:

- Other local authorities;
- Public authorities or bodies;
- Persons providing goods or services to authorities;
- Persons, whilst not being of a public body, has functions of a public nature.

There are clear links with an authority's community partners and the ability to trade between organisations. However, also specified clearly in the above is the possibility and potential for reciprocal trading with bodies such as PPP contractors, which are providing services to the authority or are engaged in works of a public nature. This opportunity was clarified by the Local Government Committee of the Scottish Parliament in its consideration of the legislation, and represents a clear route to engaging public services in such schemes where this proves to be of best value to the authority and its partners. The new revisions also empower local authorities to trade goods and materials in support of trading agreements.

The revision of the Local Authorities (Goods & Services) Act 1970 should also encourage authorities to examine linkages with other elements of the new Act such as the power to advance wellbeing and the new prudential borrowing regime.

Whilst all of the above new flexibilities are welcome, it is clear that the purpose of the Act is not to encourage any monopoly of provision by any sector. In addition, specific areas of the trading framework regarding income generated from 'commercial services' activity will be subject to set statutory limitations.

For example, income from other local authorities, public sector bodies, or generated via agreements in support of a public purpose (including a local authority's own) will not count. However, specific limits will be established for income from private sector trading (where the provision of goods and services will not further the public works of the trading partner). It is possible that a percentage of net turnover may be applied to govern external type works subject to such limitation, however, again the legislation does provide for exceptions by consent from Ministers where for example, the contextual environment within which an authority operates requires a greater degree of such activity, for example, a shift via stock transfer towards a greater percentage of works of a capital nature.

Regulations on these statutory limits have yet to be laid, however, it is likely that discussion will be ongoing.

The new trading environment must be viewed in the context of the specific statutory guidance relating to competitiveness, trading and the discharge of authority functions currently being developed in relation to the Act. The Scottish Executive circulated for open consultation in Scotland in March of 2003 a document that was entitled *Local Government in Scotland Act 2003—Guidance Approved By The Scottish Ministers on s.1(1)—The Duty To Make Arrangements To Secure Best Value.* Under the title of "Required Best Value Arrangements" it was indicated that an authority that secures Best Value will be able to demonstrate:

Competitiveness, Trading And The Discharge Of Authority Functions

14.28

- It is conscious of being publicly funded in everything it does; it has regard to obligations under the state aid rules; and it is aware of the need to conduct its business in a manner which demonstrates appropriate competitive practice;

- Account is taken of the potential economic impact of the authority's activities (particularly new activities) on the local business community and others;

- The power to advance well being is not used to raise money, beyond imposing reasonable charges for the work undertaken;

- Where the authority's activities count as entering into an agreement to supply goods and services, the Local Authorities (Goods and Services) Act 1970 is observed;

- The requirement to keep trading accounts under proper accounting practice is observed where appropriate to the authorities' activities, in order to provide a transparent audit trail.

The Best Value Taskforce published its own guidance giving further details and explanations in relation to these provisions. The document *Local Government in Scotland Act 2003—Guidance By The Best Value Taskforce On S1(1)—The Duty To Make Arrangements To Secure Best Value* at Ch.6, it is said that the above-mentioned five bullet points mean:

1. That service plans and business plans explicitly justify the nature and scale of work for which trading operations are required;

2. That the authority is responsive to the interests of stakeholders such as the business community, the voluntary and independent sectors and suppliers, who feel that the authority listens to their views;

3. That the results and implications of such analysis are fed back to managers engaged in planning to ensure that they take such factors into account;

4. That where proper accounting practice and good management require it, trading accounts are prepared and disclosed;

5. That the transparent and fair allocation of all shared costs is ensured.

External Trading

The Best Value Taskforce Guidance *Local Government In Scotland Act* **14.29** *2003—Trading Advisory Note* reminds councils that they will be required to consider the nature and purposes of their various activities, whatever their history, to see which come within the definition of trading activities. It may be helpful for Councils to recognise that a major reason for Trading Accounts to be kept and published is to establish that Councils are not undertaking work of a significant scale for the general public or other bodies at taxpayers' risk and expense when this same work could be better provided by others, nor that they are seeking to profit in any significant way from their tax exempt status in their trade to private individuals.

Indeed, in reviewing their services under this guidance, Councils should consider the following issues:

- External trading should not be undertaken simply for its own sake nor to perpetuate historical practice. Councils should have clear, explicit reasons for work of this nature, which justify the associated balance of risks and rewards;

- Legitimate reasons for undertaking trading outside the Council could include the following:

    — Reduced cost to the Council by sharing of overheads;
    — Makes use of surplus capacity;
    — Shared gains of joint working through the Community Planning process;
    — Reduced costs to partners be they public, private or voluntary;
    — Limited local alternatives or market failure;

- — Contributes to the Council's corporate goals in a way which cannot be better provided by an alternative provider (key links to the Power to Advance Wellbeing);
- — Creation of critical mass of business to allow desired standards of technology etc. to be justified;
- — Provides contribution to local economy which contributes to sustainable development;
- — Provides a degree of local market regulation.

- Dependant upon the scale in question, Councils must be mindful to a degree of the impact that their trading could potentially have on businesses that contribute to local employment and the local economy. Clearly, the spirit of wider trading freedom within the Local Government in Scotland Act 2003 is to remove unhelpful restrictions on sensible partnership working and enhance joint initiatives, not to encourage a monopoly of provision. Such assessments must form a core part of any decision-making process with clear linkage to the aims identified previously. The result of this appraisal may be two-fold: it may alter the selected option or indeed, help re-enforce its need and suitability.

Trading Accounts in Scotland

14.30   Section 12 of the Act provides the critical support framework to the new trading environment as it governs both the introduction of the new three year break even targets for 'significant' trading activities and introduces the new accounting framework which will be utilised to identify and govern such undertakings. In addition, when viewed with the repeal of CCT, it also introduces the concept of new service structures focussed towards the delivery of Best Value, operating under a single trading account thanks to the removal of specifically defined activities.

This raises the question as to which is the trading activity of the council that is deemed to be of significance and therefore subject to above break even target and disclosure requirements, or subject to specific tests, is the activity deemed not to be of significance and therefore not subject to the above?

The reference to accordance with proper accounting practices provides a statutory basis for the Best Value Accounting Code of Practice (BVACOP) which will used to be fully adhered to. It should be noted that should the activity be deemed not to be significant, BVACOP provides that the authority should keep an internal trading account for specific governance purposes but this will not need to be externally published.

The questions therefore are:

- What do we mean by trading operations under the new legislation and which are likely to be deemed as significant?

- What tests can be utilised to assist in this definition?

- With no more defined activity restrictions, what can we now do to enhance service delivery structures?

Fortunately, detailed guidance has been produced to assist in these considerations. The latest guidance on the tests of significance and the application of proper accounting procedures for local authority trading are contained within *A Best Value Approach to Trading Accounts—A Guidance Note for Local Authority Practitioners* (June 2003), which has been jointly produced by CIPFA Directors of Finance Section and LASAAC (Local Authority (Scotland) Accounts Advisory Committee).

Indeed the document suggests that in addition to carrying out the trading operations and significance test on past CCT services, authorities should also consider their application in areas such as:

- Letting of Industrial Estates and Other Investment Properties

- Provision of Car Parking

- Printing Services

- Market Undertakings (Double Glazing factories etc)

- Professional and Support Services

- Crematoria

- Ports

- Civic Halls

- Theatres and Museums

- Home Care Services

- Residential Homes

- Specialist Educational Support Services

- Housing Management

The document, which is expected to be eventually contained within the revised BVACOP's guidance for Scotland, sets out a series of tests for defining as to whether or not a trading activity should be deemed as significant and therefore subject to the tests of s.12 of the Act.

It states:

"The test of what is a trading operation will be a matter for individual authorities and should be based on a careful consideration of a wide range of services, and not simply on their past status as CCT or non CCT activities. The test is likely to be based on whether the service meets both the following criteria:

(i) the service is provided in a competitive environment—*i.e.* the user has discretion to use alternative providers; and

(ii) the service is provided on a basis other than straightforward recharge of cost—*i.e.* users take the service on the basis of quoted lump sums, fixed periodical charges, or rates, or a combination of these."

(*see* page 10, *A Best Value Approach to Trading Accounts*, CIPFA/ LASAAC).

The above comments, whilst still subjective, do assist local authorities to a degree in identifying works which are clearly of a trading type nature although arguably (i) above could be applied to a wide range of non-regulatory functions, and (ii) is open to change as authorities re-structure their approach to accounts in line with the new requirements of the legislation and the drive towards Best Value.

Trading Operations & the Test of Significance

14.31 As previously stated and regardless of any specific service nature, local authorities have always had the power to establish internal trading accounts to monitor services if they believed their existence would be of benefit to the authority. The new requirements of the Act have not changed this situation, merely provided greater flexibility to authorities away from the previous prescriptive approach of defined activities. The test of significance is of key importance, as the outcome will dictate whether the activity will be required to break even over a three-year cycle and publicly disclose its trading performance. To aid identification in this area a series of tests are contained within the CiPFA/LASAAC document, two of which are shown below in Figure 14.3 and Figure 14.4.

Figure 14.3	
TEST OF SIGNIFICANCE CRITERIA	
Financial Criteria	**Non Financial Criteria**
The size of the turnover of the trading operation, relative to the Council's net revenue budget.	The importance of a trading account to demonstrating service improvement and achievement of targets.

Financial Criteria	Non Financial Criteria
The risk of financial loss to the authority is exposed to in carrying out the operation.	The risk of service or reputational loss the authority is exposed to in carrying out the operation.
	The service areas likely to be of interest to its key stakeholders and their needs.

(page 28, *A Best Value Approach to Trading Accounts*, CIPFA/LASAAC)

Figure 14.4

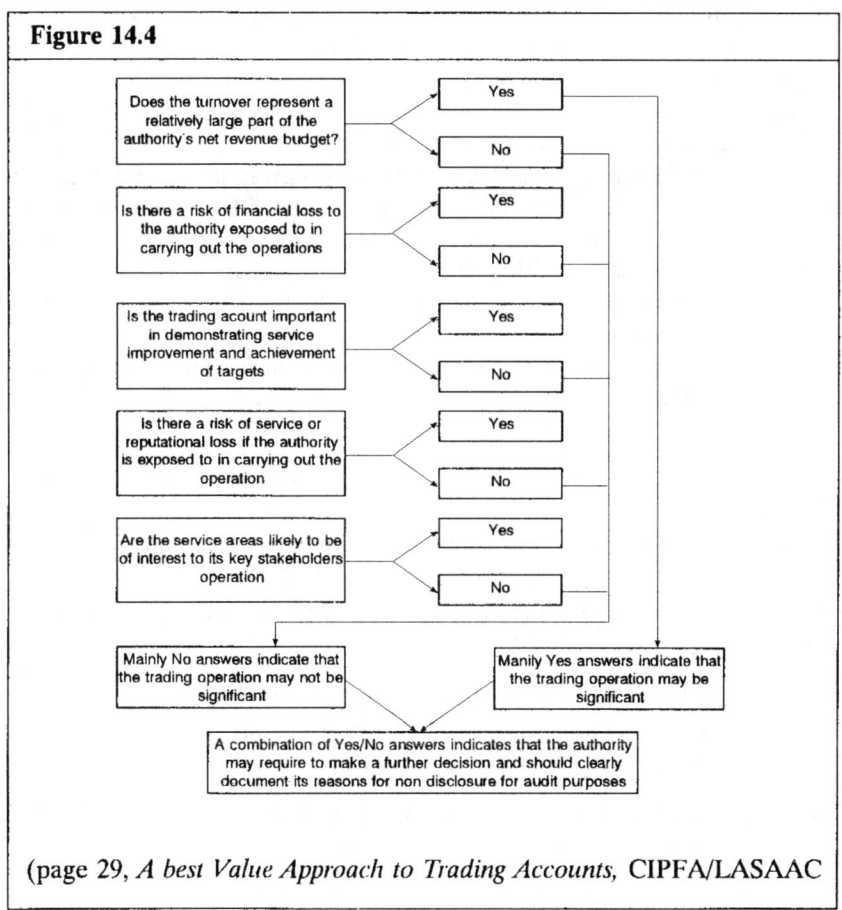

(page 29, *A best Value Approach to Trading Accounts,* CIPFA/LASAAC

It is likely that whilst councils may take distinct views on the results of **14.32** the above tests to their own specific service areas (including both CCT and Non-CCT services) a common theme will be the development of new service structure groupings under a single trading account operation, helping to improve working arrangements through the consolidation and integration of services. For example, councils maintaining a single trading account for a unified facility management service which may contain both 'hard' and 'soft' services. It is also likely that such functions due to their increased size and scope, may likely be deemed significant and therefore subject to the requirements specified in s.12 of the legislation. This would also most likely be the case for combined property services functions or environmental service resources.

The intention of the Local Government in Scotland Act 2003 is to remove barriers to innovation, but within a legislative framework that secures Best Value, including accountability for the use of public assets and public funds. For avoidance of doubt, the intention is not to allow local authorities unfettered opportunities to expand trading simply to increase turnover and employment: with the added flexibility and freedoms created by the Act goes a commensurate duty of responsibility to account for trading in an open and transparent manner.

It is neither desirable nor possible to set down prescription with regard to trading activities. Decisions will be made by individual Councils on the organisation and delivery of their services, and Councils will have to examine their choices to determine which result in a requirement to maintain and publish trading accounts. The CiPFA/LASAAC Guidance will assist with this task.

Figure 14.5 compares the trading provisions in Scotland with those in England and Wales.

Figure 14.5
Comparison of Trading Provisions in Scotland and England

- The position in Scotland is completely different to that in England and Wales;

- The Local Government Act 2003 does not apply in Scotland and Best Value, wellbeing and related provisions are contained instead in the Local Government in Scotland Act 2003;

- In England, a distinction is made between charging and trading by the law, in Scotland there is no such distinction;

- Scotland has a financial limit to control trading activity, England does not;

- England requires a company in order to engage in commercial trading, Scotland does not;

- In England, the power in s.95 of the Local Government Act 2003 to engage in commercial trading is freestanding;
- In Scotland the trading power is specifically linked to wellbeing.

Conclusion

Scotland has taken a truly different route to England and Wales in relation to charging and trading. This has not been without difficulty and there are some elements of the Scottish regime which have still as yet to be resolved. However, it is laudable that the Scottish Parliament has done things in its way and has introduced provisions with a truly Scottish look and feel to them.

CONCLUSION

It is significant that in all the different areas of the United Kingdom **14.33** (save for Northern Ireland), provisions have been introduced in relation to trading. It will be interesting to compare the development of some of these areas, particularly where one area has chosen one route and another has chosen another route. The best example of this is perhaps the area of the Goods and Services Act, where the Scottish Parliament chose to extend its provisions to permit wider trading, where the Parliament in England chose to introduce a completely new set of provisions in the Local Government Act 2003. Over time it is certain that commentators will be able to analyse which has met its need better.

Either way, however, trading has reached the statute book throughout the UK and it is up to the local authorities that benefit from the powers to show what can be achieved using them.

Part Six

Conclusion

CHAPTER 15

CONCLUSION

The powers given by the Local Government Act 2003 to charge for **15.1** discretionary services and to permit authorities to engage in risk based commercial trading were still in their infancy when this book was completed. These powers are revolutionary, bearing in mind the history of charging and trading (see Ch.13) and have been sought by local authorities for some time. The powers were introduced by the government to meet a range of perceived needs. These may be summarised as:

- The wish of authorities to act in an entrepreneurial manner;
- The wish of authorities to deliver a wider range of services and to offer a wider range of choice to service users;
- The drive to create income (cashable savings) or to reduce costs through greater efficiency (non-cashable savings);
- The wish to correct market failures, for example to provide services where the market is unwilling or unable (for commercial reasons) to do so;
- The wish to explore partnership working in its widest sense.

These powers were warmly welcomed. But the question was asked at the end of 2004 (when the charging power had been in force for a year and the trading power for over six months) as to whether the new powers were being used?

The work that the authors have done with local authorities; including training courses and conferences, specific legal advice and helping to develop strategies, has given an interesting insight into how local authorities were viewing the powers. By that time, very few—if any—authorities were using s.95 to authorise the establishment of a company to trade; and perhaps more surprisingly, only a few pioneers were really getting to grips with s.93 and realising the potential for levying charges across a wide range of discretionary activity.

The view of the authors accords with some early surveys conducted on use of these powers; although more will be known when the much more extensive research currently being undertaken by INLOGOV is published. In the *Local Government Chronicle* of December 3, 2004, the front page commentary lamented the "pitifully little use of new powers to charge and trade, after demanding them for more than two decades." It based this on a survey of almost 250 councils by the Local Government Association, which concluded that 76 per cent of local authorities had no plans to use the discretionary charging powers and 80 per cent no plans to use the commercial trading powers.

This is a curious situation, considering the context in which local authorities found themselves in late 2004. So much attention had been paid to the Gershon review, the requirement to make substantial efficiency savings; pressure on resources through the finance settlement; and even more pressure to deliver on core service areas as evidenced by the CPA classifications. Bearing these areas on mind, it is very surprising that authorities did not look very quickly at what these powers might do to help them.

The authors have their own views on this situation.

Firstly, there is no doubt that a degree of ignorance and confusion exists as to the scope of these powers; particularly at the higher levels within certain authorities. Whilst some authorities have made themselves familiar with the powers, others have not. There remain across local government, pockets of confusion over how the provisions work and what they cover, the terminology used and uncertainty about what activities will be permissible. It is hoped that this book will have assisted authorities in overcoming those uncertainties.

Secondly, there can be no doubt that the government's decision to graft on to the pre existing legal landscape new powers in the Local Government Act 2003 has not been without consequence. Despite the government's genuine desire to make things simpler, if a new power is introduced in a complex area, on the basis that it will not apply if other powers exist, then by definition those involved need to have some knowledge of the pre existing situation in order to know this is the case; this by definition undermines the intention to simplify.

Thirdly, it is necessary to see why s.95 has not been welcomed more wholeheartedly. Section 95 is intended and appropriate only for major "risk based" commercial trading, characterised by the motive of profit. It does not therefore sit easily with the prevailing culture of the public sector. Whilst many in local government are happy to act efficiently; few are willing to embrace the dominant culture of the bulk of the commercial sector. It is a big step to take on board the ethos of the private sector; even though there are many examples of ethical businesses. It has been recognised that it will be difficult for a new trading entity to retain a wholly public sector ethos but then compete with the rest of the private sector, in the absence of either a direct or indirect subsidy from the parent local authority (which is forbidden by the State Aid rules—see Ch.8). In the view of the authors, most local authorities want to work in the public sector; but just act more efficiently and across a wider area of users.

There are also practical and legal considerations. The council has to set up a specific trading company for this purpose, as described in Ch.7. Although the technical step of setting up a company is not too difficult or expensive; the ongoing legal and practical issues are significant. The power is limited to better performing authorities under the CPA and the establishment of the company is surrounded by other requirements, including the preparation of a business case considering matters such as risk and reward. Even those steps specifically required by law are supplemented by other practical requirements, such as staffing and resourcing the company, finding the work, engaging in risk management and putting in place detailed financial arrangements to meet the fiscal regime. It is fair to say that many local authorities are disappointed when they appreciate the impact of the legal and commercial environment which they will have to deal with.

This effort would be palatable if the company was guaranteed to perform the existing functional work from the authority; but becomes less attractive where the company is treated equally with other private sector companies who are invited to bid for work. Many authorities have been disappointed to realise that the EU public procurement regime prevents authorities from awarding higher value contracts without competition; even to a wholly owned commercial trading company. Chapter 8 confirms that this requirement is necessary to meet EU law, and that case law exemptions based around a narrow reading of the *Teckal* case are unlikely to assist in getting round this requirement. Mention is also made in that Chapter of the associated problems under EU competition law, particularly State Aid rules.

Fourthly, It is also likely that some "snap" judgements have been made. In particular, many local authorities seemed to decide early on that s.93 is of limited value and will not deliver efficiency savings; the consequence of this seemed to be that they must go down the commercial trading company route to deliver efficiencies. The authors feel the need to challenge that assumption immediately. As Ch.5 illustrates, far from being a minor cost recovery tool, s.93 could be described as a panacea, despite the fact it has to be operated within a statutory framework. the examples given in Ch.6 demonstrate powerfully what can be achieved by using this power.

The problem with s.93 seems to be one of perception. Whilst it is true **15.2** that s.93 is not designed for the generation of income; it does assist in spreading costs which would otherwise only fall on the authority itself. Whilst it might be easy to be superficially dismissive about cost sharing, authorities need to focus on the value and civic benefit of their discretionary activities, not their use for income generation or profit. The work of the authors in this area has thrown up a whole range of different activities where non-cashable efficiency benefits may be achieved; without any set up costs, with no requirement for either a company or a high CPA rating, and at very little risk.

Differential pricing is the real key. This means that a local authority can levy a charge for a service and provided the overall income is met by expenditure; no "profit" will be made. It is permissible for a local authority to invest in new equipment, to defray part of those costs by using the equipment for third party usage and to charge some people the full cost, others a reduced cost and provide the services to further groups free of charge. In effect, this means that a substantial amount of income derived from third party usage can be mopped up by expenditure, thereby delivering enhanced civic benefit which assists the council in a number of ways. All of the examples in Ch.6 demonstrate this benefit to one degree or another.

Fifthly, there is a degree of inertia or unwillingness to be the first in local government to try something new. Acting in an entrepreneurial manner does not come easy to the bulk of authorities. Whilst there are a number of notable exceptions who are pathfinders; the bulk of authorities seem to be waiting for others to be in the vanguard so that they can follow in a well proven path.

In conclusion; what seems clear to the authors is that there is no option of "staying the same" but earning profits under the new regime. The 2003 Act seems to push local government down a route in which it either undertakes some charging activity using s.93 and obtains civic benefit and efficiency savings (though non-cashable); or it changes into a s.95 company, accepts the ethos of the private sector and recognises that the primary purpose is to generate a profit which the parent authority can then spend as it wishes (normally by subsidisation of the Council Tax).

If local authorities do genuinely wish to find their own "third way"; and to set up and run a trading company with a public or a private sector ethos this will be in many ways the hardest feat of all. Whilst the authors wish those authorities well, and have confidence that some at least will be successful; it is their view that a local authority would have to be very successful at s.95 trading to replicate the civic benefit that can be achieved using s.93. If a company is set up and starts trading it may take several years of hard work to get to a turnover of £500,000 per annum from outside the authority. Following the deduction of costs and leaving an appropriate investment in the company to let it grow—and of course paying the dreaded corporation tax—there is unlikely to be sufficient profit left to the council to fund a single teacher's post. Compare that with small amounts of charging activity going on across a complete range of functions and offering a small amount of civic benefit in each; it starts to become clear why so many local authorities have not been tempted to set up a commercial trading company just yet, until they have taken full advantage of the other powers, particularly s.93.

Many who have examined the provisions in detail now take the view that s.93 is in fact the power that local authorities sought for so long. What many local authorities wanted to do was not to set themselves up as a private sector organisation and be the private sector but to have more freedom to undertake work for a wider group than just their only local authority; and to retain that public sector ethos, whilst acting more efficiently. The ability to recover a cost for this type of work, or to provide it free to those who need the services to obtain wider civic benefit was the aim.

What is clear is that government has authorised three routes which may be followed: the use of existing powers; the new charging power added to existing discretionary powers or full commercial risk based trading via a company (assuming the CPA classification allows). It will be very interesting to revisit the use of the powers after a few years to see which path they have chosen.

APPENDICES

Appendix 1—Legislation and Statutory Instruments   16.1

The Local Government Act 2003   16.2
The Local Government Act 2003, sections 93–97 on charging and
trading
Statutory Instruments under the Local Government Act 2003   16.3
Statutory Instruments under the Local Authorities (Goods and
Services) Act 1970   16.4

Appendix 2—Guidance on Charging and Trading   17.1

Government Guidance

- General Power for Best Value authorities to charge for
  discretionary services—guidance on the power In The Local
  Government Act 2003—ODPM—November 2003 (The
  'Charging Guidance')   17.2

- General Power For Local Authorities To Trade In Function
  Related Activities To A Company—Guidance On the Power
  In The Local Government Act 2003—ODPM July 2004 (The
  'Trading Guidance')   17.49

- General Power For Best Value Authorities In Wales To
  Charge For Discretionary Services—Guidance On The Power
  In The Local Government Act 2003—National Assembly For
  Wales February 2004 (The 'Welsh Charging Guidance')   17.65

**Appendix 3—Miscellaneous Documentation in Relation to
Charging and Trading**   18.1

- Complete list of public bodies under the Local Authorities
  (Goods and Services) Act 1970   18.2

Legislation and Statutory Instruments   16.1

The Local Government Act 2003   16.2

- The Local Government Act 2003, sections 93-97 on charging and trading

s.93 Power to charge for discretionary services

(1) Subject to the following provisions, a best value authority may charge a person for providing a service to him if—

- (a) the authority is authorised, but not required, by an enactment to provide the service to him, and

- (b) he has agreed to its provision.

(2) Subsection (1) does not apply if the authority—

- (a) has power apart from this section to charge for the provision of the service, or

- (b) is expressly prohibited from charging for the provision of the service.

(3) The power under subsection (1) is subject to a duty to secure that, taking one financial year with another, the income from charges under that subsection does not exceed the costs of provision.

(4) The duty under subsection (3) shall apply separately in relation to each kind of service.

(5) Within the framework set by subsections (3) and (4), a best value authority may set charges as it thinks fit and may, in particular—

- (a) charge only some persons for providing a service;

- (b) charge different persons different amounts for the provision of a service.

(6) In carrying out functions under this section, a best value authority shall have regard to such guidance as the appropriate person may issue.

(7) The following shall be disregarded for the purposes of subsection (2)(b)—

    (a) section 111(3) of the Local Government Act 1972 (c. 70) (subsidiary powers of local authorities not to include power to raise money),

    (b) section 34(2) of the Greater London Authority Act 1999 (c. 29) (corresponding provision for Greater London Authority), and

    (c) section 3(2) of the Local Government Act 2000 (c. 22) (wellbeing powers not to include power to raise money).

(8) In subsection (1), "enactment" includes an enactment comprised in subordinate legislation (within the meaning of the Interpretation Act 1978 (c. 30)).

s.94 Power to disapply section 93(1)

(1) The appropriate person may by order disapply section 93(1)—

    (a) in relation to particular descriptions of best value authority or particular best value authorities;

    (b) in relation to the provision of a particular kind of service by—

        (i) all best value authorities,
        (ii) particular best value authorities, or
        (iii) particular descriptions of best value authority.

(2) The power under subsection (1) includes power to disapply for a particular period.

s.95 Power to trade in function-related activities through a company

(1) The appropriate person may by order—

    (a) authorise best value authorities to do for a commercial purpose anything which they are authorised to do for the purpose of carrying on any of their ordinary functions, and

    (b) make provision about the persons in relation to whom authority under paragraph (a) is exercisable.

(2) No order under this section may authorise a best value authority—

    (a) to do in relation to a person anything which it is required to do in relation to him under its ordinary functions, or

    (b) to do in relation to a person anything which it is authorised, apart from this section, to do in relation to him for a commercial purpose.

(3) An order under this section may be made in relation to—

    (a) all best value authorities, particular best value authorities or particular descriptions of best value authority;

(b) all things authorised to be done for the purpose of carrying on a particular function, particular things authorised to be done for that purpose or particular descriptions of thing authorised to be so done.

(4) Power conferred by an order under this section shall only be exercisable through a company within the meaning of Part 5 of the Local Government and Housing Act 1989 (c. 42) (companies in which local authorities have interests).

(5) A best value authority on which power is conferred by an order under this section shall be treated as a local authority for the purposes of Part 5 of the Local Government and Housing Act 1989 if it would not otherwise be such an authority, but only in relation to a body corporate through which it exercises, or proposes to exercise, the power conferred by the order.

(6) In its application by virtue of subsection (5), section 70(1) of the Local Government and Housing Act 1989 (c. 42) (power to make provision about what a company under the control, or subject to the influence of, a local authority does) shall only apply in relation to the doing for a commercial purpose of the thing to which the order under this section relates.

(7) In this section—

"best value authority" does not include—

(a) a police authority established under section 3 of the Police Act 1996 (c. 16),

(b) the Common Council of the City of London in its capacity as a police authority,

(c) the Metropolitan Police Authority, or

(d) the London Development Agency;

"ordinary functions", in relation to a best value authority, means functions of the authority which are not functions under this section.

s.96 Regulation of trading powers

(1) The appropriate person may by order impose conditions in relation to the exercise by a best value authority of—

(a) a power to do anything for a commercial purpose, or

(b) a power to do anything for such a purpose through a company.

(2) In exercising such a power as is mentioned in subsection (1), a best value authority shall have regard to such guidance as the appropriate person may issue.

(3) An order under this section may be made in relation to—

(a) all best value authorities,

(b) particular best value authorities, or

(c) particular descriptions of best value authority.

(4) In this section, "best value authority" does not include—

    (a) a police authority established under section 3 of the Police Act 1996,

    (b) the Common Council of the City of London in its capacity as a police authority,

    (c) the Metropolitan Police Authority, or

    (d) the London Development Agency.

(5) In subsection (1)(b), "company" has the same meaning as in Part 5 of the Local Government and Housing Act 1989.

s.97 Power to modify enactments in connection with charging or trading

(1) If it appears to the Secretary of State that an enactment (whenever passed or made), other than section 93(2) or 95(2), prevents or obstructs best value authorities—

    (a) charging by agreement for the provision of a discretionary service, or

    (b) doing for a commercial purpose anything which they are authorised to do for the purpose of carrying on any of their ordinary functions, he may by order amend, repeal, revoke or disapply the enactment.

(2) The Secretary of State may by order amend, repeal, revoke or disapply an enactment (whenever passed or made), other than section 93, which makes in relation to a best value authority provision for, or in connection with, power to charge for the provision of a discretionary service.

(3) The power under subsection (1) or (2) to amend or disapply an enactment includes power to amend or disapply an enactment for a particular period.

(4) An order under this section may be made in relation to—

    (a) all best value authorities,

    (b) particular best value authorities, or

    (c) particular descriptions of best value authority.

(5) An order under subsection (1)(b) may be made in relation to—

    (a) all things authorised to be done for the purpose of carrying on a particular function,

    (b) particular things authorised to be done for that purpose, or

    (c) particular descriptions of thing authorised to be so done.

(6) An order under subsection (1)(b) may not be used to authorise a best value authority to do in relation to a person anything which it is required to do in relation to him under its ordinary functions.

(7) In exercising the power under subsection (1) or (2), the Secretary of State—

    (a) must not make any provision which has effect in relation to Wales unless he has consulted the National Assembly for Wales, and

    (b) must not make any provision in relation to legislation made by the National Assembly for Wales without the consent of the Assembly.

(8) The National Assembly for Wales may submit proposals to the Secretary of State that the power under subsection (1) or (2) should be exercised in relation to Wales in accordance with those proposals.

(9) Subject to subsection (10), no order shall be made under this section unless a draft of the statutory instrument containing the order has been laid before, and approved by resolution of, each House of Parliament.

(10) An order under this section which is made only for the purpose of amending an earlier order under this section—

    (a) so as to extend the earlier order, or any provision of the earlier order, to a particular authority or to authorities of a particular description, or

    (b) so that the earlier order, or any provision of the earlier order, ceases to apply to a particular authority or to authorities of a particular description,
       shall be subject to annulment in pursuance of a resolution of either House of Parliament.

(11) In this section—
"discretionary service", in relation to a best value authority, means a service which the authority is authorised, but not required, to provide;
"enactment" includes an enactment comprised in subordinate legislation (within the meaning of the Interpretation Act 1978 (c. 30));
"ordinary functions", in relation to a best value authority, means functions of the authority which are not functions under section 95.

Statutory Instruments under the Local Government Act 2003   **16.3**

- The Local Government (Best Value Authorities)(Power to Trade) (England) Order 2004 (SI 2004/1705)

- The Local Government (Best Value Authorities) (Power to Trade) (England) (Amendment No.1) Order 2004 (SI 2004/2307)

- The Local Government (Best Value Authorities) (Power to Trade) (England) (Amendment No.2) Order 2004 (SI 2004/2573)

Statutory Instruments under the Local Authorities (Goods and Services) Act 1970

- Statutory Instruments defining public bodies under the Local Authorities (Goods and Services) Act 1970

16.4 *List of Statutory Instruments under the Local Authorities (Goods and Services) Act 1970*

1. Local Authorities (Goods and Services) (Public Bodies) Order 1972 (SI 1972/853)
2. Local Authorities (Goods and Services) (Public Bodies) Order 1975 (SI 1975/93)
3. Local Authorities (Goods and Services) (Public Bodies) Order 1981 (SI 1981/1049)
4. Local Authorities (Goods and Services) (Public Bodies) Order 1990 (SI 1990/433)
5. Local Authorities (Goods and Services) (Public Bodies) Order 1992 (SI 1992/2830)
6. Local Authorities (Goods and Services) (Public Bodies) Order 1993 (SI 1993/2097)
7. Local Authorities (Goods and Services) (Public Bodies) Order 1994 (SI 1994/37)
8. Local Authorities (Goods and Services) (Public Bodies) (No. 2) Order 1994 (SI 1994/1389)
9. Local Authorities (Goods and Services) (Public Bodies) (Meat Hygiene) Order 1995 (SI 1995/2626)
10. Local Authorities (Goods and Services) (Public Bodies) (The Julie Rose Stadium) Order 1996 (SI 1996/2534)
11. Local Authorities (Goods and Services) (Public Bodies) (Sports Councils) Order 1996 (SI 1996/3092)
12. Local Authorities (Goods and Services) (Public Bodies) (Trunk Roads) Order 1996 (SI 1996/342)
13. Local Authorities (Goods and Services) (Public Bodies) (Trunk Roads) (No.2) Order 1996 (SI 1996/1814)
14. Local Authorities (Goods and Services) (Public Bodies) (English Heritage) Order 1997 (SI 1997/1835)
15. Local Authorities (Goods and Services) (Public Bodies) (Greater London Enterprise Limited) Order 1997 (SI 1997/809)
16. Local Authorities (Goods and Services) (Public Bodies) Order 1997 (SI 1997/101)
17. Local Authorities (Goods and Services) (Public Bodies) Order 1997 (SI 1997/2095)
18. Local Authorities (Goods and Services) (Public Bodies) (Trunk Roads) (No.1) Order 1997 (SI 1997/204)
19. Local Authorities (Goods and Services) (Public Bodies) (Trunk Roads) (Amendment) Order 1997 (SI 1997/849)
20. Local Authorities (Goods and Services) (Public Bodies) (Trunk Roads) (No.2) Order 1997 (SI 1997/850)
21. Local Authorities (Goods and Services) (Public Bodies) Order 1998 (SI 1998/308)
22. Local Authorities (Goods and Services) (Public Bodies) (No.2) Order 1998 (SI 1998/868)
23. Local Authorities (Goods and Services) (Public Bodies) (No.3) Order 1998 (SI 1998/1123)

24. Local Authorities (Goods and Services) (Public Bodies) (No.4) Order 1998 (SI 1998/1574)
25. Local Authorities (Goods and Services) (Public Bodies) (No.5) Order 1998 (SI 1998/2956)
26. Local Authorities (Goods and Services) (Public Bodies) (No.6) Order 1998 (SI1998/3095)
27. Local Authorities (Goods and Services) (Public Bodies) (No.1) Order 1999 (SI 1999/421)
28. Local Authorities (Goods and Services) (Public Bodies) (No.2) Order 1999 (SI 1999/1754)
29. Local Authorities (Goods and Services) (Public Bodies) Order 2000 (SI 2000/63)
30. Local Authorities (Goods and Services) (Public Bodies) (No.2) Order 2000 (SI 2000/1027)
31. Local Authorities (Goods and Services) (Public Bodies) (Scotland) Order 2000 (SSI 2000/207)
32. Local Authorities (Goods and Services) (Public Bodies) (Scotland) (No.2) Order 2000 (SSI 2000/403)
33. Local Authorities (Goods and Services) (Public Bodies) (England) Order 2001 (SI 2001/243)
34. Local Authorities (Goods and Services) (Public Bodies) (England) (No.2) Order 2001 (SI 2001/691)
35. Local Authorities (Goods and Services) (Public Bodies) (England) (No.3) Order 2001 (SI 2001/1823)
36. Local Authorities (Goods and Services) (Public Bodies) (England) (No.4) Order 2001. (SI 2001/ 3347
37. Local Authorities (Goods and Services) (Public Bodies) (England) Order 2002 (SI 2002/522)
38. Local Authorities (Goods and Services) (Public Bodies) (Wales) Order 2002 (SI 2002/1729)
39. Local Authorities (Goods and Services) (Public Bodies) (England) (No.2) Order 2002 (SI 2002/2244)
40. Local Authorities (Goods and Services) (Public Bodies) (England) (No.3) Order 2002 (SI 2002/2624)
41. Local Authorities (Goods and Services) (Public Bodies) (England) Order 2003 (SI 2003/354)
42. Local Authorities (Goods and Services) (Public Bodies) (England) (No.2) Order 2003 (SI 2003/1018)
43. Local Authorities (Goods and Services) (Public Bodies) (England) (No.3) Order 2003 (SI 2003/2069)
44. Local Authorities (Goods and Services) (Public Bodies) (England) (No.4) Order 2003 (SI 2003/2558)
45. Local Authorities (Goods and Services) (Public Bodies) (England) Order 2004 (SI 2004/485)
46. Local Authorities (Goods and Services) (Public Bodies) (England) (No.2) Order 2004 (SI 2004/2475)
47. Local Authorities (Goods and Services) (Public Bodies) (Wales) Order 2004 (SI 2004/2878)

Guidance on Charging and Trading

General Power for Local Authorities to Trade in Function Related Activities Through a Company

Guidance on the Power in the Local Government Act 2003

Office of the Deputy Prime Minister
Eland House
Bressenden Place
London
SW1E 5DU
Telephone 020 7944 4400
Web site www.odpm.gov.uk

Further copies of this publication are available from:
Office of the Deputy Prime Minister Publications
PO Box 236
Wetherby LS23 7NB

Tel: 0870 1226 236
Fax: 0870 1226 237
Textphone: 0870 1207 405
Email: odpm@twoten.press.net

or online via the Office of the Deputy Prime Minister's web site.
ISBN 1 85112 723 2

Printed in Great Britain on material containing 75% post-consumer waste and 25% ECF pulp.

July 2004

Reference no. 04 LGF 02424

CONTENTS

17.1

Introduction   17.2

  Scope Of The Guidance   17.3
  Sections 95 & 96 of the Local Government Act 2003   17.4
  The Statutory Instrument   17.5

Background   17.6

Context for Trading   17.7

Charging and Trading   17.8

Relationship with Local Authorities (Goods and Services) Act 1970 and Local Government Acts 2000 and 2003   17.9

Comprehensive Performance Assessment   17.10

  Re-Categorisation under CPA   17.11
  Position of Consortia   17.12

Trading Through a Company   17.13

  Restrictions on Power to Trade   17.14
  Local Government Capital Control System   17.15
  Providing Services to Trading Companies   17.16

Preparing to Trade   17.17

Making a Business Case and Business Planning   17.18

  Making a Business Case   17.19
  Organisational Issues   17.20

Trading Through a Company   17.21

  Structure   17.22
  Governance Framework   17.23
  Conflicts of Interest   17.24
  Personal Liability for Directors   17.25
  Nominees to Trading Company Board   17.26
  Directors Fees/Remuneration   17.27
  Shareholding   17.28
  Staffing, Personnel and Employment Issues   17.29
  Recruitment Issues   17.30
  Transfer of Staff   17.31
  Local Authority Assistance to Companies   17.32
  Transparency   17.33
  Procurement   17.34
  State Aid   17.35
  Taxation   17.36
  Human Rights Act   17.37

**Anti-Competition Legislation and Competition with
Local Businesses**   **17.38**

   Competition Law   **17.39**

Exit Strategy   **17.40**

Annex A   **17.41**

Preparing to Trade   **17.42**

Annex B   **17.43**

Business Case arid Business Plan   **17.44**

Annex C   **17.45**

State Aid   **17.46**

Annex D   **17.47**

Acknowledgements   **17.48**

Introduction

1. The *Local Government Act 2003* ('the Act') received Royal Assent on 18 September 2003. Section 95(1) of the Act provides power for the Secretary of State, or (in relation to authorities in Wales) the National Assembly for Wales, to make an order enabling best value authorities (with certain exceptions) to trade in any of their ordinary functions. The Act is available from The Stationery Office and can be found on The Stationery Office Website: http://www.hmso.gov.uk/acts/acts2003/20030026.pdf. **17.2**

SCOPE OF THE GUIDANCE $\qquad$ 17.3

2. The purpose of this guidance is to provide assistance to local authorities in England on trading through a company in anything that they are authorised to do for the purpose of carrying on their ordinary functions. Now that the relevant order has been made under sections 95 and 96 of the Act—the *Local Government (Best Value Authorities) (Power to Trade) (England) Order 2004* (S.I. 2004/1705), ('the Trading Order') this guidance explains how, in the view of the Secretary of State, issues in relation to trading may be handled. This is statutory guidance issued under section 96(2) of the Act, to which authorities are required to have regard.

3. This guidance should not be taken to constitute legal advice or to provide a comprehensive view of the law.

SECTIONS 95 & 96 OF THE LOCAL GOVERNMENT ACT 2003

4. The Act contains new powers for best value authorities to trade in function-related activities through a company and also provides for the regulation of these trading powers. Section 95 provides power for the Secretary of State, to make an order enabling best value authorities (with certain exceptions[1]) to trade in any of their ordinary functions through a company. Orders made under the power may relate to all best value authorities or to particular best value authorities, or descriptions of best value authority. This enables the scope of the trading powers to be related to an authority's performance categorisation under the Comprehensive Performance Assessment regime ('CPA'). The Trading Order is framed by reference to descriptions of authority which, by virtue of an order made from time to time under section 99(4), of the Act are of a particular category. The *Local Authorities (Categorisation)(England)*

---

[1] See section 95(7) of the Act for the best value authorities that are not included within the scope of the power.

Order 2004 (S.I. 2004/1704) is the first order made under that provision which categorises English local authorities according to their performance.

5. Section 96(1) provides an order-making power to impose conditions on the exercise of any trading power by a best value authority, including where this is undertaken through a company.

17.5 THE STATUTORY INSTRUMENT

6. The Trading Order made under sections 95 and 96 of the Act provides, in respect of English local authorities, powers to trade in function-related activities through a company.

The Local Government (Best Value Authorities) (Power to Trade) (England) Order 2004

In summary, the Trading Order:

- applies only to best value authorities which are local authorities within the meaning of section 1(2) of the Local Government Act 1999 and by virtue of such order, as may be made from time to time under section 99(4) of the Act, are within one of the following categories—'excellent', 'good' or 'fair'. (This Order does not apply to authorities referred to or specified in article 1(3) of the Order, when acting in their capacity as fire authorities).

It provides that:

- a best value authority is authorised to do for a commercial purpose, anything which it is authorised to do for the purpose of carrying on any of its ordinary functions

- before exercising the power, a best value authority is required to prepare a business case in support of the proposed exercise of the power which must be approved by the authority

- a best value authority shall recover the costs of any accommodation, goods, services, staff or any other thing it supplies to a company in pursuance of any agreement or arrangement to facilitate the exercise of the power

- where a best value authority ceases to be a best value authority to which this Order applies anything which that authority is in the process of doing at the time the Order ceases to apply to that authority, may be completed by that authority; and any agreement or arrangement shall cease to have effect at the end of the period of 2 years from the date of the Order ceasing to apply to that authority

---

7. The Trading Order does not apply to best value authorities that are not local authorities. However, it is intended to consider in due course, whether a further order should be made to confer the trading power on the wider family of best value authorities. The grant of powers to other best value authorities will only be made if it is clear that the powers are necessary, ie existing powers are insufficient. The intention also is that the grant of powers, as with local authorities, will be related to performance assessment.

Background 17.6

8. The *Local Authorities (Goods and Services) Act 1970* governs the way in which local authorities are allowed to 'trade' with other **public** bodies. It authorises local authorities to enter into agreements with public bodies for the provision of goods, materials, and administrative, professional and technical services, for the use of vehicles, plant and apparatus, and for the carrying out of maintenance. There is also a power for the Secretary of State to designate by order that any person(s) exercising functions of a public nature shall be a public body for the purposes of the Act.

9. The Consultation Paper, *Working with Others to Achieve Best Value: Section 16 of the Local Government Act 1999—A Consultation Paper on Changes to the Legal Framework to Facilitate Partnership Working* (DETR, March 2001), proposed to provide a new power alongside existing powers to enable best value authorities to provide a full range of goods and services to others working in partnership with them. The Local Government White Paper, *'Strong Local Leadership—Quality Public Services'* (DTLR, December 2001) went further than the earlier Consultation Paper, proposing to provide wider powers to trade for all authorities where this helps achieve best value and the delivery of public services.

10. The powers under the Act enable local authorities to trade with private bodies and persons for profit (i.e. charges fixed at more than cost recovery). In the case of local authorities in England (which fall within the definition of a best value authority), the powers have been introduced as part of a new package of freedoms and flexibilities following the CPA. The powers are available to councils assessed as 'fair', 'good' and 'excellent' in the CPA. They are not available to councils assessed as 'weak' or 'poor' in the CPA. The power to trade is only exercisable through a company. This will help to ensure a level playing field with the private sector.

Context for Trading 17.7

11. Trading will help create a dynamic and entrepreneurial public sector that will increase diversity and choice in the delivery of public services. Trading should encourage local authorities to extend and improve the range of services they offer and will introduce new players into the market. Trading with a wider range of bodies should help to increase the scope for partnership working and provide business opportunities for the private sector.

12. Trading activity needs to contribute towards Best Value in the related function. Local authorities can only set up trading arms in **function-related** activities. Authorities need to be clear that they have the power to engage in an activity before they trade in it.

13. Surpluses on commercial operations under the section 95 trading power (i.e. post tax surpluses) would be available to individual

authorities to use as they see fit. Trading should be conducted on a fully transparent basis and authorities should not distort markets through the provision of inappropriate subsidies to trading companies.

17.8 Charging and Trading

14. Sections 93 and 94 of the Act provide a new power for best value authorities to charge for discretionary services. Discretionary services are those services that an authority has the power but not a duty to provide. An authority may charge where the person who receives the service has agreed to its provision. This new power to charge does not apply where the power to provide the service in question already benefits from a charging power or is subject to an express prohibition from charging. Best value authorities are required to have regard to any guidance that may be issued by the Secretary of State. Guidance has already been published, *General Power for Best Value Authorities to Charge for Discretionary Services—Guidance on the Power in the Local Government Act 2003* (ODPM, November 2003). This Guidance is available on the ODPM Website: www.local.odpm.gov.uk/guidprop.pdf.

15. The charging and trading powers are separate and may be exercised separately. The essential difference between charging and trading is that charging for discretionary services is limited to cost recovery whereas trading (through a company) permits the making of a profit. There are 4 main differences in the powers:

Differences Between Charging And Trading

(i) charging relates only to discretionary services, whereas the power to trade is for all services

(ii) all best value authorities can use the power to charge whereas the power to trade is available only to councils rated 'fair', 'good' or 'excellent' under the CPA

(iii) charging is limited to the recovery of the cost of providing the service whereas trading can be at a profit

(iv) the power to trade is only exercisable through a company

---

17.9 Relationship with Local Authorities (Goods and Services) Act 1970 and Local Government Acts 2000 and 2003

16. The *Local Authorities (Goods and Services) Act 1970* has served local government well. Authorities have made extensive use of these powers to provide goods and services to other authorities, both to make use of surplus capacity and to secure the benefit of economies

of scale. However, the 1970 Act restricts the type of services provided and the bodies with whom an authority can trade. The new trading powers contain no such restrictions.

17. Section 2(1) of the *Local Government Act 2000* ('the 2000 Act') permits local authorities to engage in a range of activities including the provision of staff, goods, services and accommodation to any person, in connection with their power to promote the economic, environmental and social wellbeing of their area. This power is constrained by section 3(2) of the 2000 Act which prevents authorities from exercising their 'wellbeing' powers simply in order to raise money.

18. As a result of section 95 of the Act, activities under section 2(1) of the 2000 Act, such as the provision of goods and services can now be traded, that is made available at a commercial rate in connection with a wellbeing purpose. An activity undertaken in connection with the exercise of the wellbeing function is to be regarded as something which local authorities are 'authorised to do for the purpose of carrying on any of their ordinary functions' (see section 95(1)(a) of the Act). The authorisation to trade conferred by the Trading Order amounts to an entirely separate free-standing and specific primary power which can be used in conjunction with the wellbeing power. There is no basis for regarding the restrictions on raising money provided in section 3(2) of the 2000 Act as having any application to the exercise of the trading power for the following reasons:

- the effect of the prohibition on raising money in section 3(2) is to prevent local authorities from using the wellbeing power primarily to raise money—in short, 'revenue raising' or commercial purposes' are not purposes which in themselves fall within the scope of the section 2(1) wellbeing power;

  however

- Section 95 trading is a separate power which authorises 'function-related' commercial activities and so may be exercised in conjunction with an activity or service whose primary purpose is to achieve the promotion of wellbeing.

Trading in 'Well-Being' Function-related Activities (Illustration)

1) The wellbeing function is an 'ordinary function' for the purpose of section 95(1)(a)
2) A local authority makes a decision to carry out an activity or provide a service which it considers is likely to promote or improve the economic, social or environmental wellbeing of its area
3) The Trading Order will authorise that authority to do those things for a commercial purpose where the authority is categorised as 'fair' and above. The power to trade in wellbeing function-related activities is a primary power specifically conferred by the Trading Order. The local authority cannot be acting in breach of the restriction on raising money in section 3(2) of the 2000 Act, quite simply because it is not, and indeed cannot be, trading under the wellbeing powers.

---

19. Existing *public to public* trading activities under the *Local Authorities (Goods and Services) Act 1970* ('the 1970 Act') will remain. These will operate in parallel with the section 95 trading power. Applications from bodies seeking public body designation under section 1(5) of the 1970 Act will not receive Ministerial approval where it appears that the body seeking the designation is largely a local authority sponsored vehicle designed perhaps to avoid the statutory framework in sections 95 and 96 of the Act, or to facilitate quasi private trading opportunities for local authorities categorised as 'weak' or 'poor' under CPA. The powers contained in the Trading Order are primarily concerned with *public to private* trading.

20. There are also powers permitting trading, other than the 1970 Act viz

   - *Civic Restaurants Act 1947*
   - Section 145 of the *Local Government Act 1972* (Provision of entertainments)
   - Section 19 of the *Local Government (Miscellaneous Provisions) Act 1976* (Recreational facilities)
   - Section 38 of the *Local Government (Miscellaneous Provisions) Act 1976* (Power to provide computers and computer facilities and making use of spare capacity)
   - Orders made under section 150 of the *Local Government & Housing Act 1989* (ie HMOs Charges for Registration Schemes, Recovery of Costs for Public Path Orders, Charges for Land Searches and Charges for Overseas Assistance and Public Path Orders)

There may be other powers as well. These powers remain unaffected because the purpose of section 95(2)(b) is to preserve existing trading powers.

17.10   Comprehensive Performance Assessment

17.11   RE-CATEGORISATION UNDER CPA

21. As the power to trade is limited to authorities categorised as 'excellent', 'good' and 'fair' under the CPA, if an authority is re-categorised as 'poor' or 'weak' under CPA, it will no longer be able to exercise the power to trade under the Trading Order. Such a re-categorisation will not render unlawful the performance of any obligations under trading contracts already entered into by the authority whilst it had those powers. The transitional provisions in the Trading Order provide that existing trading by local authorities re-categorised under CPA as 'poor' or 'weak' may continue for up to 2 years maximum, after which trading shall cease if the authority fails

to regain 'fair', 'good' or 'excellent' status. 'Fair' authorities should therefore exercise caution before entering into trading arrangements if they have any reason to believe they might drop into a lower CPA category. This would be an appropriate item for consideration and evaluation in the business case before trading begins.

22. The Trading Order provides that any "agreement or arrangement entered into for the purpose of facilitating the exercise of *(the trading power)* shall cease to have effect at the end of the period of two years beginning with the date on which this Order ceases to apply to the authority". As the trading power is exercised by the authority, any agreement or arrangement entered into by the authority will cease to have effect (and be incapable of performance) from the expiry of the relevant second anniversary (but will not be void). This provision will apply to any agreement which the authority may have entered into with the trading company (eg for the supply of works, goods or services) and also any other arrangement entered into by the authority with the trading company (which will include the acquisition of shares, giving of grants and secondment of employees etc). Any other agreements or arrangements entered into by the trading company outside of the agreements or arrangements with the authority will remain unaffected. Any rights, liabilities and obligations which may have accrued under an agreement or arrangement prior to the relevant second anniversary will still be capable, in law, of being enforced.

23. There are a number of practical consequences that arise from the potential loss of the power to trade through CPA re-categorisation:

- authorities need to take into account the potential loss of the power to trade in the contractual relationships which they may enter into. For example, authorities may wish to include '**break clauses**' to extricate themselves from agreements and other arrangements, since otherwise there may be a claim for breach of contract against the authority;

- the inclusion of such break clauses in an agreement may result in a loss to the trading company. As a consequence, the authority will need to agree the extent of any **compensation** which should be payable in such circumstances. The levels of any such compensation should be included in the original contract (or at least a formula for calculating the level of compensation) as the authority's bargaining position will be weak at the time of exercising the break clause. In doing so the authority should have regard to the nature of the company as a trading entity doing business with others and accruing creditors whilst also having regard to their fiduciary duties to council tax and ratepayers. Authorities will need to build any assumptions for compensation into the business planning;

- authorities will also need to take into account the potential loss of the powers to trade in the arrangements which they enter into. In particular, authorities will need to have regard to shareholdings, loans and other financial arrangements which will cease to have effect. As with agreements, authorities will need to include provision for '**exiting**' such arrangements. As a consequence, authorities will need to determine (well in advance of the expiry of the relevant second anniversary) whether they should dispose of their shareholding in the trading company or sell the business as a going concern and/or put in place arrangements to wind up the trading company;

- if the authority has the power to secure the winding up of the trading company and wishes to choose this route as the exit strategy (particularly if the trading company is wholly owned by the authority, but less so if the trading company has other shareholders) then the authority will need to have included 'break clauses' in the agreements or arrangements which the trading company has with third parties. Such provisions will result in the payment of **compensation** but will enable the venture to be wound up. When the agreement and arrangements have been terminated and any compensation due has been paid, the trading company can be wound up and assets distributed after payment of outstanding debts (which will invariably include redundancy costs).

If the shares are not sold, nor the company wound up during the two year transition period, then the shareholding and other agreements associated with the venture will cease to have effect beyond the two year deadline.

24. Where the trading company has third party shareholders (whether a joint venture or otherwise), then similar exit arrangements will need to be put in place. These will primarily be the sale of shares by the authority, probably subject to a right of first refusal in favour of existing shareholders (or an option for other shareholders to purchase). These arrangements should be reflected in the Shareholders Agreement and the Articles of Association of the trading company with provisions or a formula for an agreed valuation of the shares to avoid the authority being in a poor bargaining position at the time of sale. To cover the situation where there may be no buyer for the shares during the transition period, the authority may need to consider the inclusion of a '**put option**' (i.e. a right for the authority to require the other shareholders to purchase its shares at, say, a 'fair' value to be determined in accordance with a pre-agreed mechanism which would be contained in the Shareholders Agreement or in a separate option agreement).

25. Another possibility is for the trading company to issue a class of redeemable shares to the authority, on terms that the shares are redeemable out of profits (i.e. there must be profits) at the option of

the authority in the event that the local authority's trading powers were suspended. The redemption price could again be a price to be determined in accordance with a pre-agreed mechanism. (Note that section 159(A) of the *Companies Act 1985* provides that the price must not be determined in accordance with any person's direction or opinion—it would need to be a pre-set mechanism, based on the last audited accounts). Once the shares were redeemed, the local authority's equity interest in the company will be at an end. For this option to be practicable, the shares would need to be issued as redeemable (i.e. non-redeemable shares cannot be re-classified as redeemable after issue).

26. The options for the authority on re-categorisation (and not returning to a 'fair', 'good' or 'excellent' CPA rating by the end of transition period) are to dispose of its shareholding or to sell the business as a going concern and/or to wind up the trading company. This is because at the end of the two-year transition period the arrangements comprising the shareholding will cease to have effect, and it will not be practicable for the authority to retain a legal or beneficial interest in the shareholding. There are various arrangements which authorities may consider but they will need to take their own advice as to whether these are possible within the terms of the Trading Order. Such may include:

- a temporary suspension of the rights attaching to the authority's shares (i.e. the right to vote, right to appoint directors, the right to income, etc). Ordinarily, it would be possible in principle to write such provisions into the Articles of Association of the trading company (similar 'dis-enfranchisement' provisions are commonly included in, for example, private equity (or 'buy out') articles for managers/directors who cease to be employed pending compulsory sale of their shares). The suspended rights would be reinstated once the trading power had been restored. However, as all arrangements in connection with the trading will cease to have effect so would any 'suspension of rights';

- the establishment of a trust. Should the shareholding be transferred to a third party to hold on trust for the authority, then as the authority will be the beneficiary of the various rights under the shares this arrangement would similarly cease to have effect at the end of the transition period;

- a purchaser could be sought for the shares in the trading company with the authority acquiring an option to purchase exercisable upon the authority's CPA rating being regained. If such an agreement or arrangement is entered into pursuant to the authority's trading powers then such will also cease to have effect at the end of the transition period.

17.12   **POSITION OF CONSORTIA**

27. Existing public to public trading activity by consortia under the 1970
Act will be unaffected by the provisions. The section 95 trading
power is capable of being exercised jointly by local authority
members of a consortium, where the constituent members have
individual assessments under the CPA of 'fair', 'good' or 'excellent'.
Where individual members are assessed under the CPA as 'poor' or
'weak', and the remaining consortium members wish to exercise
section 95 trading, it will be necessary for the local authorities
concerned to review the membership of the consortium to exclude
the 'poor' or 'weak' members from the consortium arrangement as it
applies to the exercise of the section 95 trading power.

17.13 Trading through a Company

17.14   **RESTRICTIONS ON POWER TO TRADE**

28. Section 95 of the Act enables Best Value authorities to provide on a
commercial basis, anything that is related to a function of the
authority or is ancillary, conducive or facilitative to the exercise of
that power. The power is widely drawn to include all functions,
whether express, implied or incidental. This would therefore cover
any functions carried out under section 111 of the *Local Government
Act 1972* (incidental functions). Sub-section 111 (3) does not inhibit
the use of these powers, as the power relied on to trade is section 95,
and not section 111.

29. Whilst the power to trade is widely drawn it is subject to restrictions,
principally:

● the power must be exercised through a company (within the
meaning of Part 5 of the *Local Government and Housing Act
1989*);

● the trading must be function-related;

● the power cannot be used to authorise trading in anything which
an authority is statutorily obliged to do in relation to a person;

● Section 95 trading may also be regulated through the imposition
of conditions by order, under section 96 of the Act;

● only authorities categorised as 'excellent', 'good' or 'fair' may
exercise the section 95 trading power;

● this power cannot be exercised by any Police Authority, the
London Development Agency, or authorities when acting in
their capacity as fire and rescue authorities;

● any company established for the purposes of carrying out trading
under this section, in which a local authority has an interest,
shall be subject to the rules about controlled, influenced,

310

regulated and minority interest companies provided by Part 5 of the *Local Government and Housing Act 1989* and the *Local Authorities (Companies) Order 1995 (*)*.

(*) NB Part V of the *Local Authorities (Companies) Order 1995* has been repealed by the *Local Authorities (Capital Finance) (Consequential, Transitional and Saving Provisions) Order 2004* which came into force on 1 April 2004.

30. In deciding whether and how to exercise the trading power, authorities must still have regard to their own procedural rules, Wednesbury principles of reasonableness, proper purposes and fiduciary duty. A business case and risk analysis will be required. Local authorities will not be able to delegate some formal decisions and determinations to companies, unless they are covered by an Order under the *Deregulation and Contracting Out Act 1994.*

LOCAL GOVERNMENT CAPITAL CONTROL SYSTEM 17.15

31. Part 1 of the *Local Government Act 2003* introduces a new system of local government capital expenditure controls for financial years beginning on, or after, 1 April 2004. The new system requires local authorities to determine for themselves how much they can afford to borrow, and to stay within the limits they determine (sections 2 and 3). Authorities are required to have regard to CIPFA's 'Prudential Code for Capital Finance in Local Authorities' in making their determinations. The Government retains a reserve power to impose limits on borrowing either nationally or for individual authorities (sections 2 and 4).

32. Section 18 of the 2003 Act allows companies controlled or influenced by a local authority to be brought within the new capital controls by regulations. The current wording of this section relies on definitions of 'company', 'control' and 'influence' contained in Part 5 of the *Local Government and Housing Act 1989*. However, Ministers made clear in the Parliamentary debates on the Bill for the 2003 Act that they wished to replace these definitions with more up to date definitions based on generally accepted accounting practice. However, this is to wait until CIPFA has included more robust provisions on group accounting in the *Code of Practice on Local Authority Accounting*. Once CIPFA has completed its revisions, ODPM intends to use the powers under section 117 of the 2003 Act to substitute the accounting definitions for the current reference to Part 5 in section 18.

33. Therefore, when an authority sets its own limits in accordance with section 3 and the Prudential Code, it sets them purely for the authority—the borrowing it itself is to undertake, considering its own revenue account resources available to service the borrowing. But the Prudential Code (in paragraph 31) says—*"Where the authority has*

interests in companies or other similar related entities, the authority needs to have regard to its financial commitments and obligations to those companies/entities". In other words, if there is any obligation to pay amounts to a company or a risk that a company will call on the authority's resources, that will reduce the resources available to service debt and hence will reduce the borrowing limits. Any transactions of such companies that have an impact on the authority's finances will have to be taken into account in assessing the affordability of any proposed borrowing by the authority. However, whilst the Prudential Code currently does not operate on a group basis, if ever a national limit were to be imposed under section 4, it would be the intention to make regulations under section 18 to apply the limit to local authority groups rather than just to the core authority.

17.16   PROVIDING SERVICES TO TRADING COMPANIES

34.   Based upon ordinary principles, an authority has the power to do anything reasonably incidental to its express powers. The power to trade in function-related activities under section 95(1) is an express power. Accordingly, if for example it appeared to an authority that the arrangements for the carrying out of function-related trading would be most appropriately handled by a 'company', the authority would be able to establish a company for that purpose under its subsidiary powers. Local authorities may wish to extend to companies carrying out function-related trading, assistance of whatever kind they think appropriate, including providing staff and other support services. There are several different ways in which local authorities can provide services to the companies through which they trade. Providing such assistance is incidental to, or part and parcel of, the power to enter into an arrangement with a company for the purpose of exercising the power to trade. Accordingly, the following ancillary and express powers may also be used in connection with a company involved for the purpose of exercising the power under section 95:

- power to certify agreements related to the company under the *Local Government (Contracts) Act 1997* (ie long-term contracts for services or other agreements providing finance in connection with such contracts);

- power to enter into shareholders agreements before and after the establishment of the company;

- power to enter into agreements with the company for the supply of, works, goods and services (by and to the company), the transfer and secondment of staff, the provision of premises, and the exercise of intellectual property and other contractual rights;

- any consequential activity;

- power to hold, buy, or sell shares and receive dividend payments;

- discretionary services provided under section 2 of the 2000 Act, for which a charge could be made under section 93 of the Act.

35. Because the power to trade is subject to a restriction requiring it to be exercised through a company, it follows that the authority has the requisite power to enter into arrangements with a company in order for the trading power under section 95 to be exercised. It is not necessary therefore, for the company to be expressly designated as a public body under the *Local Authorities (Goods and Services) Act 1970*, in order for the authority to be able to provide it with staff, goods etc, for the purpose of exercising the power to trade.

Preparing to Trade   17.17

36. Local authorities will need to be prudent, in particular, about putting council tax payers' money at risk. It is for this reason that the Order requires authorities to prepare a detailed business case before embarking on trading under these powers, and to have the business case approved by the council, or in the case of authorities operating executive arrangements, by the executive, before trading starts The council may wish to discuss these proposals with their auditor to check the auditor is satisfied with the arrangements the council has made for managing the risks in the process. Local authorities remain bound by European legislation, domestic law, general administrative legal principles such as Wednesbury reasonableness, and their fiduciary duty. A number of steps need to be considered by authorities when preparing to trade. These are set out at **Annex A**.

Making a Business Case and Business Planning   17.18

37. There is a distinction to be drawn between the business case and the business plan:

- the **business case** assesses the risk involved in the proposed trading enterprise and decides whether or not it should proceed. It starts the process of business planning;

- the **business plan** sets out the objectives of the business, how they are to be achieved and standards met adjusted in the light of experience and changing circumstances. It is a comprehensive analysis of the business situation at a particular point in time.

MAKING A BUSINESS CASE   17.19

38. There are a number of steps that should be undertaken to make a business case and produce a business plan. These are set out in **Annex B** along with an outline of a possible Business Plan. The

Annex also includes extracts from *Developing a Successful Business Plan—a Ten Step Guide* (PricewaterhouseCoopers, 1997) which authorities may find helpful. The business plan is not an end in itself—it is a means of ensuring business success. Business planning is much more than an annual event of producing the business plan. For example, if unforeseen circumstances occur, elements in the plan may be in need of revision.

17.20   **ORGANISATIONAL ISSUES**

39.   The organisational model for the business venture will need to be considered and defined at an early stage. Although an authority may want to establish a company for the purpose of using it as a vehicle for function-related trading, it does not have to proceed in that way. It may equally trade through a company in which it has not been directly involved in setting up for this purpose. A local authority need not establish its own company, nor are the commercial purposes necessarily just those of the authority. It would be possible for a local authority to agree with an established commercial company to trade through it on a contractual basis to mutual benefit. Whatever an authority chooses to call or establish as their trading body, it has to fit the description of 'companies' under Part 5 of the *Local Government and Housing Act 1989*. Definitions of a company in Part 5 include:

     (a)   a company limited by shares;

     (b)   a company limited by guarantee and not having a share capital;

     (c)   a company limited by guarantee and having a share capital;

     (d)   an unlimited company;

     (e)   a society registered or deemed to be registered under the *Industrial and Provident Societies Act 1965*.

Any of these forms may comprise a company for the purposes of section 95. However, it seems most likely that the company form taken will be a company limited by shares which provides more flexibility to trading companies, particularly with regard to distributions of profit and raising risk capital. The choice will have a fundamental impact on how people are employed, and the skills and numbers required.

40.   All of the options listed above have a different legal status which will impact on how they are run, managed and financed. Depending on the model chosen, the operation will need to be open to an appropriate level of scrutiny. The authority's section 151 Officer, and probably the authority's Monitoring Officer, will need to be involved to different extents at different stages of preparation.

41.   A trading company will be a separate legal entity from a local authority. It will derive its legal authority from its Memorandum of

Association and the Companies Acts. Its directors and officers will derive their authority from the articles of association and the law relating to companies. The objects of the company will be defined in its memorandum and articles of association. They should be drawn carefully to ensure they cover all potential trading activity. Table A of the *Companies Act 1985* contains model articles of association for a trading company which are normally used as a base by most companies and adapted to specific circumstances.

Trading through a Company 17.21

STRUCTURE 17.22

42. A company may be limited by shares or by guarantee. A trading company is likely to be limited by shares. Other vehicles such as companies limited by guarantees (with or without share capital), are unlikely to be appropriate for a trading company as these are more appropriate for a not-for-profit company which may also be registered as a charity. An unlimited company is unlikely to offer the level of protection the local authority would want. However special vehicles which can be created in this framework, such as Industrial and Provident Societies, may offer a more flexible approach suitable for some circumstances.

43. The company will be run by its board of directors answerable to the membership in accordance with the articles of association. A board of between 3 and 8 directors is most likely to be practical. The participating local authority should be represented on the board, and its level of representation and voting rights are likely to be proportionate to its shareholding. The members or officers who are appointed directors will participate directly in the activities of the company, and are answerable to the company and have the powers and duties of company directors whilst they do so. Other local authority members and officers may become involved if, by agreement, they are given the right to attend board meetings as observers. They cannot participate in decision-making, though, and must avoid so doing for fear of becoming shadow directors.

GOVERNANCE FRAMEWORK 17.23

44. Authorities will need to have regard to the accountability and governance framework for the company. They may wish to refer to 'The Combined Code—Principles of Good Corporate Governance and Code of Best Practice', originally published by the Stock Exchange in June 1998 (updated 2003). It was produced by the Hampel Committee and superseded the work of Cadbury and Greenbury. It gives a broad framework for corporate and internal controls. Reference may also be made to guidance produced by the Strategic

315

Partnering Taskforce (ODPM), which can be found on the ODPM website: http://www.odpm.gov.uk/ssdp.

17.24   CONFLICTS OF INTEREST

45.   Local authority members and officers should be aware of potential conflicts of interest when carrying out their roles for their authorities, or when acting as directors of trading companies. The conduct of local authority members is governed by their authority's code of conduct. That code must include, as a minimum, the mandatory provisions of the model code of conduct, issued by ODPM in November 2001.

46.   Members must register certain financial and other interests as set out in the Code of Conduct. Members should have regard to the specific categories of interests set out in the Code but should note that these include naming any company for which they are a remunerated director and also membership of or a position of general control or management in any company or industrial and provident society. The Code of Conduct for members sets out the circumstances in which a member should regard himself as having a 'personal interest' in any matter. These include any matter relating to any interest which the member is obliged to register. Members who consider they have a personal interest in any matter should declare that interest if the matter is discussed at a meeting of the authority. In addition, a member with a personal interest also has a prejudicial interest if the interest is one where a member of the public, if he or she knew all the relevant facts, would think that the interest was so important that it would be likely to prejudice his judgement of the public interest. A member with a prejudicial interest in a matter being discussed must withdraw from the meeting. Members themselves must decide whether or not they have personal or prejudicial interests in particular issues.

47.   A Director's principal duty is to the company, but any members that are elected as directors are still bound by relevant codes of conduct, in so far as they do not conflict with their legal obligations under company law. In addition when voting as a director on company matters, regard must be had to any rules on declaring interests as set out in the Memorandum and Articles and any restriction in those on voting in certain circumstances. If the company is set up by the authority specifically to take advantage of section 95 it may be considered advisable to adopt similar rules on interests to those contained in the Code of Conduct as members will be familiar with these and it will ensure consistency amongst all directors.

17.25   PERSONAL LIABILITY FOR DIRECTORS

48.   Company directors may incur personal liability, for example in respect of breach of duty, wrongful trading, fraudulent trading,

breach of a disqualification order and other specific liabilities such as corporate manslaughter. It is good practice for the company to insure against this risk. It is advisable for directors to check the company's indemnity policy and good practice for authorities to issue guidance to their nominated directors on the responsibilities and liabilities of being a director of a company. Such guidance should cover matters such as a director's duties to act in the best interests of the company, provision and use of information, duty to employees and the fiduciary duty to creditors, as well as warning of the potential for personal liability. Local authorities may be able to indemnify members and officers against this personal risk. However, any such indemnity will generally only cover actions taken honestly and in good faith.

49. The 2000 Act contains a power at section 101 to make provision by Order enabling local authorities to indemnify their officers and members. The Government proposes to bring forward an Order which is intended to clarify the position which will be in addition to any existing powers that authorities have relied upon.

NOMINEES TO TRADING COMPANY BOARD   17.26

50. The authority will need to consider whom they should nominate to be on the board of the company. For an authority operating executive arrangements, the responsibility for making decisions about the company, including who should be their nominee or nominees, may be made by either the executive or the full council depending on the circumstances. A member of the executive might find him or herself in a position where their position on the board of the company might lead to their having a personal and prejudicial interest in a matter the executive was dealing with which might restrict their ability to take decisions on the executive. If a nominee is an officer of the authority, the authority or executive, as the case may be, may want to consider whether they should be the Chief Executive, or where there is more than one nominee whether the Chief Executive should be one of the nominees.

51. A successful company will be one that works alongside the authority in delivering joint objectives. The authority will have to consider how to balance the need to assist the company to achieve its trading objectives with the principles of transparency, accountability and probity. Where the business of the company has moved to being more significant, an authority should consider the benefits which the appointment of independent (or non-executive) directors could bring to the business.

52. The managing director will probably be an employee of the company, but in exceptional circumstances may be seconded from the local authority or another shareholder. Arrangements must be established to ensure that the managing director has no conflict of

interest. If it is a local authority secondee the authority may wish to set up arrangements for appropriate information use and confidentiality to ensure that the council and the company can be satisfied their position is not weakened by the secondment.

53. The company's articles of association will set out the internal operation of the company, e.g. shareholding, voting rights, the appointment of directors, the operation of the board, declarations and conflicts of interest, indemnities/insurance cover and financial regulations.

17.27   DIRECTORS FEES/REMUNERATION

54. Local authorities will wish to give consideration to the remuneration and rewards of the directors and management. Private sector companies often have remuneration committees that determine pay levels and whether other incentives, such as share options and employee share option plans should be in place. Any authority considering paying members for their responsibilities in respect of the company should do so in the context of the normal arrangements for members allowances.

17.28   SHAREHOLDING

55. Either the local authority will be the sole shareholder, or it may, initially or later, allocate or sell shares to others. If it chooses to exercise its powers under section 95 through a company previously established by others to achieve different commercial objectives, it will need to satisfy itself that its own commercial objectives will be satisfied through this particular company. If it is not to be the sole shareholder, it should enter into a shareholders agreement with the other shareholders and the company, covering matters such as:

- the allocation, transfer and disposal of shares;
- the rights to be attached to different classes of shares;
- 'golden shares' under which a particular shareholder can reserve the right to veto fundamental changes, for example changes to the business objectives, the business plan, or the appointment of the managing director. Local authorities should make full use of this principle to safeguard matters which are fundamental to the purpose for which they are establishing the company, but need to take care that they do not change the status of the company for the purposes of Part 5 of the 1989 Act;
- exit and termination provisions.

17.29   STAFFING, PERSONNEL AND EMPLOYMENT ISSUES

56. Whether the trading company is established as a company for direct service provision using existing employees, or as a joint arrangement

with another local authority (also using existing employees), the company will be a separate legal entity. Local government employees may be transferred to the company. This may amount to a transfer under the *Transfer of Undertakings (Protection of Employment) (Regulations) 1981* (as amended) ('TUPE') or it may be subject to Directions made under section 101 of the 2003 Act. Whether or not there is a TUPE transfer depends on the facts of the individual case.

57. It is the responsibility of local government to promote a well-trained and motivated workforce. Local authorities should consult their employees and recognised trade unions or staff representatives throughout, with full disclosure of information on all matters affecting the workforce. Full, effective and continuous communication is key to managing transfers well.

58. However, if the decision is to establish an organisation, which is separate from the local authority which has created it, there are a number of issues associated with employing people to deliver services. Employees for the new enterprise can only come from one of four sources, which are:

   (i)   recruitment from the local/national market place;

   (ii) transfer of staff from within the local authority;

   (iii) secondment of staff from the local authority;

   (iv) another arrangement, e.g. taking over the employees of another existing business through a merger/take-over/purchase of that business.

Depending on the facts, in the case of ii) iii) and iv) above TUPE may apply. However this is dependent on the particular circumstances regarding the establishment of the local authority trading company and/or arrangements regarding secondment of staff to a commercial company through which the local authority is trading. In the case of ii) *the Code of Practice on Workforce Matters in Local Authority Service Contracts* (Annex D of ODPM Circular 03/2003 published 13 March 2003) concerned with new joiners to an outsourced workforce, will also apply.

RECRUITMENT ISSUES   17.30

59. Any recruitment exercise needs to determine the duties and responsibilities of new employees and the skills, knowledge and experience, which will be required. Appropriate salaries will need to be established and it may be useful to evaluate the jobs through a recognised mechanism. At the same time, the other terms and conditions will need to be established, including hours to be worked, pay arrangements, flexibility of working hours/patterns and arrangements, leave entitlement, sick pay arrangements, statutory/ best practice policy requirements and pension arrangements/ entitlement.

60. For a new limited company these terms and conditions may be the same as existing local authority terms and conditions, and existing staff may transfer across with appropriate safeguards. If terms and conditions in the new company are unrelated to local government terms remember that, if the aim is to attract some local government employees in to the business to take advantage of their specific knowledge or expertise, then the attractiveness of the offer, particularly in relation to pensions, will vary for potential employees.

61. There is a need to comply with existing employment legislation, for example:

- Race Relations, Sexual Discrimination, and Disability Discrimination legislation;
- Working Time Directive;
- National Minimum Wage legislation;
- Employer's Liability and Public Liability Insurance requirement;
- Statutory Sick Pay/Maternity Pay/Paternity and Adoption Leave;
- Time off for Dependants;
- Health and Safety.

17.31   TRANSFER OF STAFF

62. Where existing local authority workers are transferred to the new business, which is seen as separate from the work of the local authority, the expectation would be that their existing terms and conditions will be protected under the *Transfer of Undertakings (Protection of Employment) Regulations, 1981* (as amended) (TUPE), or under Directions to be made under section 101 of the Act, unless there are exceptional circumstances. In particular, this means that all their contractual entitlements are protected whilst they continue to carry out the work which previously formed a part of the working practices of the local authority, and throughout their employment with the new employer, unless their terms and conditions are changed for a reason other than the transfer. This is also the case for any employee transferred from one business to another.

TUPE Regulations

These aim to ensure that:

the contract of employment between the existing employer and its employees, with their rights and liabilities are transferred automatically to the new employer

it would be automatically unfair to dismiss employees in connection with the transfer, unless this is for specific and defined reasons

collective agreements in place with the existing employer are transferred to the new employer

the existing employer is obliged to inform and consult with employee representatives whose members are affected by the transfer.

---

63. It is anticipated that DTI aim to go out to public consultation on new TUPE Regulations in late summer 2004. However the issue of occupational pension entitlements and their protection in the event of a TUPE transfer is already being addressed through provisions in the Pensions Bill, currently before Parliament. Under best value, local authorities have been exhorted to follow the policy set out in the Cabinet Office *Statement of Practice on Staff Transfers in the Public Sector* and the Annex to it, *A Fair Deal for Staff Pensions* (January 2000). Whilst this has no statutory basis, it does provide certainty and clarity to staff transfers in the public sector including in relation to pension entitlements. The *Code of Practice on Workforce Matters in Local Authority Service Contracts* (Annex D of ODPM Circular 03/2003) is intended to ensure that new joiners to transferred out workforces are offered terms and conditions which are, overall, no less favourable than those of transferred staff. These best value duties in relation to staff transfers are equally relevant to the transfer or secondment of staff as part of setting up trading companies under section 96.

64. Sections 101 and 102 of the Act confer new powers on the Secretary of State to require best value authorities in England, when engaged in contracting-out exercises, to deal with staff matters in accordance with directions. The background to this is the commitment made as part of a package of workforce measures following the Review of Best Value to make statutory within local government, the provisions in the Cabinet Office *Statement of Practice of Staff Transfers in the Public Sector* and the Annex, to it, *A Fair Deal for Staff Powers*.

LOCAL AUTHORITY ASSISTANCE TO COMPANIES 17.32

65. If a trading company is established for commercial purposes, then necessarily it will seek to make a profit. Any financial assistance, in cash or in kind, given by the local authority that establishes or participates in it, should be for a limited period, against the expectation of returns later. Any assistance should therefore be provided under a formal agreement with the company. The agreement must be entered into for a commercial purpose. The agreement may provide for grants, loans or guarantees. Before entering into such an agreement, the local authority should satisfy itself that it will achieve its objective, and the company should satisfy itself that it will meet its objective in terms of its business plan. In addition the usual rules on vires, Wednesbury reasonableness and fiduciary duty apply. Also the conditions in the Trading Order and the requirements of competition legislation need to be met.

66. Under the conditions provided in article 3(3) of the Trading Order a local authority must recover the costs of any accommodation, goods, services, staff or any other thing it supplies to a company in pursuance of any agreement or arrangement to facilitate the exercise

of the power. Each authority making use of the new power to trade will need to establish a robust methodology for assessing the costs to the authority of providing assistance to a trading company.

Authorities are free to decide what methodology to adopt. They may however find it helpful to draw on existing and familiar principles as set out in the CIPFA *Best Value Accounting Code of Practice*. One option would be to use the Code's definition of 'Total Cost'. As an alternative, authorities may wish to consider adding to total cost an appropriate contribution for Corporate and Democratic Core (CDC) and Non-Distributed Costs (NDC), as those terms are defined in the Code, as part of the costs of provision. The Code offers guidance on practice authorities might adopt and is amended from time to time to take account of changes in requirements.

67.   A local authority which establishes a trading company should expect to receive income from that company either in the form of dividend payments or through the growth in value of its shares or other investments in the company, which it can subsequently realise. Income from a trading company may be applied in any area of the local authority's activities to support expenditure, subsidise services, or reduce local taxation.

68.   The local authority will only be responsible for debts and losses of a limited liability company to the extent of the nominal value of its shareholding, and, more significantly, to the extent of any guarantee or contractual arrangement that it has entered into. If there is no such guarantee or agreement, the local authority would not be under any obligation to meet the company's debts, and if it wished to do so it would have to satisfy itself that it had the legal power and that it was exercising that power properly.

69.   However there are other risks if the company cannot meet its debts, if that company provides services that would otherwise be provided by the authority. This might arise in the context of insolvency or where the company is unable to deliver on any contracts with the authority which may give rise to losses or liability on the authority in respect of any failure by the company to deliver. In considering structures, the authority should ensure that it takes appropriate steps to avoid automatically assuming responsibility for any aspects of an unsuccessful company. This should include the actual provision of services.

17.33   TRANSPARENCY

70.   It is important that trading companies can operate on an equal footing with their competitors, but it is equally important that they are not used as a device for inhibiting legitimate public access to information about local government and local government services. The local authority should ensure that its own internal auditors have access to information held by the company and its subsidiaries.

71. The local authority should ensure that its overview and scrutiny committees are able to exercise their powers in relation to the discharge of local authority functions under the relevant legislation. When a local authority (or a committee or executive) meets to consider the affairs of the trading company, such matters may be exempt from disclosure to the public if they fall within Schedule 12A of the *Local Government Act 1972* (as provided in section 100A(4) of the 1972 Act). Matters listed in Part I of the Schedule are exempt from disclosure if the local authority so provides by resolution, although Part II of the Schedule qualifies a number of the exemptions. However, in the interests of openness, transparency and accountability a local authority will want to consider whether it would be in the public interest for discussions to take place in public. In January 2005 local authorities will be subject to the disclosure requirements set out in the *Freedom of Information Act 2000* ('the FOIA'). These requirements may mean that some matters that currently do not have to be disclosed to the public, will have to be disclosed if it is considered to be in the public interest to do so.

72. The *Data Protection Act 1998* ('DPA') requires data controllers to register with the Information Commissioner. A data controller is an individual or a body which determines the purposes for which, and the manner in which, information about individuals (i.e. personal data) is to be processed (which includes obtaining, holding, using, storing, altering and disposing of personal data). Where the company is simply a data *processor* in respect of local authority data (in other words it does not determine the manner in which and the purposes for which the data are to be processed), then it does not need to register with the Information Commissioner, but the local authority would need to have in place a processing contract with the company, the basic terms of which are prescribed in the DPA. It is very likely that a trading company if it processes personal data will need to notify the Information Commissioner under the DPA 1998 especially if it employs staff, keeps client lists etc. For example, processing includes collection, organisation, retrieval, alteration, storage and disclosure and destruction of data which means that it is likely that a company would be covered by the provision.

73. The FOIA will apply to the local authority and the authority may consider that there should be an agreement in place with the company to ensure that information which is held by the trading company on behalf of the authority, which the authority is under an obligation to disclose, can be easily accessed. A distinction needs to be drawn between the local authority dealing with or through a separate private company, which would not be subject to FOI requirements, as it would not be a 'public authority' and a company which the local authority set up to trade in an activity related to one of its functions. Where a person (including a legal person, e.g. a company) or body provides under a contract with the local authority any service the provision of which is a function of the authority, such

a person or body may be designated a 'public authority' for purposes of FOI requirements, by order under section 5(1)(b) of the FOIA. There is a possibility that a company carrying out contracted out services could be designated a public authority in its own right and subject to the section 1 obligation.

74. The local authority should consider appointing a 'contract officer' and/or 'contract member' with primary responsibility for liaison between the company and the authority, and for access to information about it. It might wish to place limitations on these individuals to ensure that they are fully accountable to the authority as a whole and to ensure that the Section 151 Officer/Monitoring Officer countersigns major decisions about the company's operations.

75. The authority or, where they are operating executive arrangements, the executive should view the company's audited accounts and reports on the activity and trading position of the company. The authority should also approve the business plan and see the accounts at least annually but are likely to require more frequent reports.

17.34 PROCUREMENT

76. The EU procurement rules may apply where the authority provides services, supplies or staff to the trading company, where the authority buys services, supplies or staff from the company or where the company itself buys services. It is likely that the procurement rules will apply to procurement by the company, if the company has been established to meet needs in the general interest, does not have an 'industrial or commercial character', and is wholly or mainly funded by a body (such as a local authority) to which the rules apply, or is subject to management supervision by such a body, or has more than half its membership or board of directors appointed by such a body. The company should not become a means for avoiding normal good practice in local authority procurement, certainly so far as probity and anti-fraud measures are concerned. It should adopt a formal procurement policy.

17.35 STATE AID

77. If the State (this includes local authorities) provides aid that affects trade between Member States and distorts competition (through conferring a benefit) this could contravene the EC prohibition on the granting of state aid. Although there is no definition of state aid, Article 87(1) of the Treaty establishing the European Communities sets out four elements—all of which must be satisfied if a measure is to constitute state aid. These are given, with some further information in **Annex C**. If the four tests are met, or if there is a risk that they are met, then there is an obligation to notify the European Commission, before measures are put into effect. If there are

advantages of any kind then authorities need to examine this issue. Some types of aid, such as 'de minimis' aid, are covered by block exemption regulations published by the Commission. These provide an exemption from the need to pre-notify the Commission, provided all the requirements set out in the relevant regulation are met. As the rules governing state aid are not straightforward, it is essential to consider at the earliest possible stage whether a measure will present problems and to obtain specialist advice.

TAXATION

17.36

78. Local authorities should plan ahead and understand that local authority companies will be subject to taxation, especially VAT and corporation tax. Further information about corporation tax may be obtained from the tax office that deals with the company's affairs or alternatively from the tax office that deals with the local authority's affairs. Local authorities must consider the VAT implications of establishing a trading company. The limited company as a normal trader is not entitled to recover tax under the special VAT rules that apply to local authorities (section 33 of the *Value Added Tax Act 1994*). Therefore, the normal VAT rules apply to that company. Any queries about the VAT affairs of the trading company should be referred to the National Advice Service on 0845 010 9000, and HM Customs and Excise's website www.hmce.gov.uk. All public notices can be found on Customs' website. However, local authorities may find the following guidance useful: VAT Notice 700/1 *'Should I be registered for VAT?'*.

HUMAN RIGHTS ACT

17.37

79. If any company set up under these provisions is held to be carrying out the function of a public authority they shall be bound by the *Human Rights Act 1998* (see *Donoghue v Poplar HARCA*). In that case the company set up by the local authority to own and manage certain of its housing stock was held to be carrying out the functions of a public nature in respect of accommodation provided for the authority's nominated tenant.

Anti-competition Legislation and Competition with Local Businesses

17.38

80. The requirement to use companies for trading under section 95 places local authorities in the same position as any other commercial undertaking as to the need to meet costs and make a profit. If local authority trading operations were to prove successful, there could be some impact on local markets especially small businesses. The successful development of larger trading operations by local

authorities however, could reasonably be expected to lead to new economic opportunities as well as possible disadvantages for small businesses, as suppliers or in specialist markets.

17.39   **COMPETITION LAW**

81.   The *Competition Act 1998* introduced two prohibitions which reflect Articles 81 and 82 of the EC Treaty respectively. The Chapter I prohibition covers agreements between undertakings that have the object or effect of distorting competition in the United Kingdom, or a part of the United Kingdom. The Chapter II prohibition makes unlawful conduct by one or more undertakings which amounts to an abuse of a dominant position in a market in the United Kingdom.

82.   Authorities should consider any proposed charging and trading activities very carefully against the requirements of competition law, consulting their own lawyers as necessary. Trading by local authorities may be subject to the provisions in the *Competition Act 1998* and/or Articles 81 and 82 of the EC Treaty.

83.   Whether or not a local authority may be considered an undertaking with respect to a particular activity (and therefore subject to competition rules), depends on whether the activity is 'an economic activity', a term which has a complex legal meaning. Neither the legal status of the trading body (i.e. being a company or not) nor the way in which it is funded are determinative on this. Therefore, the new provisions do not make a significant difference in local authorities' obligation to abide by competition rules. Guidelines on the two prohibitions and additional guidance on when a public body may be an undertaking can be found at www.oft.gov.uk

84.   Local authorities who, having read the guidance, are still unsure about whether they may be considered undertakings with respect to an activity and whether that activity may infringe competition rules, are urged to seek legal advice.

17.40   Exit Strategy

85.   There are likely to be two circumstances in which authorities would require an exit strategy from trading. The first relates to the loss of the power to trade as a result of a CPA review which places them in a category that is unable to trade. Transitional provisions in the Order permit the continuation of existing trading activities an authority is already involved in, subject to time limits. The second relates to where an authority either fails in a trading operation or decides that it wishes anyway to withdraw. Both situations may have implications for staff involved.

ANNEX A:

Preparing to Trade

A number of steps need to be considered:

Preparing to Trade

Market Analysis—Initial opportunities for trading are most likely to arise in the context of existing service provision. This will be because local authorities understand the market and know what is involved in delivering that service. Before a local authority commits to any business venture there is a need to confirm if there is either an existing demand or a strong potential demand for service or product. Analysis should be undertaken by researching customers, products and competition. This will result in a better understanding of the competitive position, the chance to spot opportunities, risks being reduced, and, better decision making.

Customer Research—This will identify the numbers and types of people whom might become customers. 'Profiling' customers enables authorities to locate the 'ideal' customers for the product or service. The aim is to understand as much as possible about customers' behaviour, needs, expectations and buying patterns. The more precisely a market niche is identified, the more selling opportunities there are likely to be.

Service/Product Research—This looks at what is being sold, how it compares with other services or products and how it might be developed or refined. If the service is not new and if there is little difference in product/service between competitors, then another approach may need to be found, eg more convenient, after-sales service.

Competition Research—The level and strength of competition indicates how difficult it will be to gain a share of that market. Identifying similar products and potentially similar customers will highlight whether there is a gap in the market. A detailed analysis of competitors' strengths and weakness will demonstrate whether there is a place for the product or service.

Risk Analysis—Researching customers, products and competition will provide information that will enable an evaluation of risks to be undertaken, in context. Risks may arise in the internal environment (eg staff, internal customers, office technology, wages, finance); the microenvironment (eg external customers, distributors, suppliers, competitors), and, the macroenvironment (eg political, economic, socio-cultural and technological factors).

Carrying Out Analysis and Research—a research brief should specify the information needed to evaluate the target market and the opportunity to gain entry. Possible sources of information about the target market include the Internet, Trade Associations, the local library, local Business Link, Chamber of Commerce or Enterprise Agency. The range of information needed includes:

- market data: what is the size and growth rate of the market? Who are the potential customers? Consider both local and national markets.

- competitive data: who are direct competitors? What are their services and prices?

- internal data: what information is already available to assess the strengths and weaknesses of your service/product and its core capabilities?

- what is the future outlook for the service/product?

NB Desk research involves data already available, for example, economic trends and specific industry sector reports. Field research requires the collection of information directly from potential customers. Examples include market surveys, telephone questionnaires and focus group research. Professional market research companies can be used to carry out this research. The cost of using a company needs to be balanced against the type of information needed.

17.43 ANNEX B:

Business Case and Business Plans

17.44 A. Making a Business Case

There are a number of steps that should be undertaken to make a business case and produce a business plan:

Business Case and Business Plan

- The following should be undertaken:

- an analysis of current activities, including resources, costs and standards of the business.

- an assessment of risks faced and how significant these risks are (there are commercial models on the market to help quantify the risk to a business).

- conduct a strengths/weakness/opportunities/threats (SWOT) analysis against the general objective of reducing risks and achieving business success. Some of the questions raised may only be answered by conducting research. Consider dependencies, a range of scenarios and draw up contingency plans.

- consider options to exploit strengths·and opportunities, correct weaknesses and reduce threats. Assess options in terms of priorities, practicalities (in terms of resources and time) and financial viability.

- check against factors determining long term trends—political, economic, demographic, social, technological, legislative and environmental factors.

- create a customer/service matrix, identifying current and new areas for both dimensions.

- subject the intended pattern of activity to a further SWOT check and amend if necessary.

- taking account of the likelihood of risk occurring.

- if risks are too high, then do not proceed.

From this analysis and research:

- define your trading activities.

- set business objectives, levels, standards and performance criteria.

- decide on costing and charging policies and systems.

- define resource requirements in terms of staff and operational resources.

- outline start up costs and investment required.

- identify sources of finance.

- produce a co-ordinated action programme.

- produce a master budget.

- define monitoring, evaluation and revision processes.

PURPOSES OF A BUSINESS PLAN

The business plan has at least 3 purposes:

Purposes of A Business Plan

- to demonstrate to members, potential investors and the company board that the business is a viable enterprise, with an identified market, an achievable set of business objectives, and an adequacy of managerial and other necessary skills and experience
- to assure potential clients the business is well-run and has the capability and resources to ensure reliability and quality
- as an internal management tool to ensure that all parts of the business work together towards common and consistent goals, and that these goals are based on sound analyses, assumptions and are consistent with LA objectives

---

B. Possible Business Plan

Overview

A brief statement of the fundamental features of the business, its nature, size, what it aims to do for whom, what makes it unique and those features that will give it particular credibility and point to its viability.

Summary

The summary can include background information and be written so that it can be used on its own. The important elements will be:

- the fundamental purpose and character of the business including the mission statement and core values.
- primary or core objectives. What does the business hope to achieve over the next one to three years?
- business history.
- summary of all key elements of the plan.
- a statement highlighting the advantages of the business to an investor.

Management and Staffing (see also 'Organisational Issues' below)

- a description of staffing—managerial, professional/technical, administrative and external suppliers of advice, information or services. Overall numbers and the names, qualifications and experience of key staff.
- an analysis of what the business needs in terms of skills and experience and any planned action to ensure these needs are met. This might include planned recruitment, training initiatives, staff (re) deployment or redundancy.

Products/Services

- a description of what the business produces and to what standard.
- what skills and processes are involved? Processes will include performance and quality management, including success criteria, and protective measures such as copyrights, licence rights and insurances.

Markets and Marketing

- market analysis—who are the current and potential customers and competitors?
- marketing—how does the business promote itself?
- marketing strategies—how might the business develop?

Action Programme for the Development of the Business

What needs to be done to ensure that the plan's objectives are met?

- an action programme to meet the requirements of clients, reflect demographic or other trends

- description of how the business may need to develop if it is to respond effectively to a changing business environment eg organisational structure, systems and skills

- intangible issues, such as image and reputation.

Operational Resources

A qualitative as well as quantitative evaluation of resources—other than staffing and finance (considered in other section(s)—needed to fulfil the operational objectives of the business. These will include premises, transport, ICT systems, other plant and equipment and information (including market intelligence, databases and proprietary knowledge).

Finance

Effective financial control will be essential to avoid business failure. This section will include the essential elements of accountancy processes and financial factors and targets (normally over a three year period) including estimates of expenditure and income, charging policies, cash flow, capital programmes and financing and budgets.

Performance Review and Revision

Systems for monitoring progress against the plan, comparing performance against targets and success criteria and of reviewing the plan itself. There are various types of review and revision—frequent monitoring and running adjustments, reactions to unpredicted occurrences and comprehensive annual review and revision. Systems may be described to monitor expenditure, income and other budgetary control, output returns, non-productive time, employee absence and turnover and analysis of customer complaints and of customer opinion surveys. There should be frequent reporting to the Board. Consideration might be given to the appointment of independent directors.

Risk Assessment and Sensitivity Analysis

All projects are subject to uncertainty and a degree of risk, e.g. inflation, fluctuations in demand etc, which is why it is essential to build a risk management assessment into the financial projections. Sensitivity analysis will help to determine the most robust options. By identifying the main variables and uncertainties in a project, assessing their cost implications, including any losses of income, and reviewing the potential range of feasible outcomes, sensitivity analysis should establish which options will be able to offer the flexibility to cope with change while still retaining an ability to deliver the required option. Risk and uncertainty will never be eliminated and so any assessment should also identify the planned management responses for dealing with each of the main risk factors.

Supporting Appendices

This may include profiles of key partnership players, market research studies, technical specifications, detailed organisation charts, legal documents such as copies of contracts, agreements, leases etc.

C. Developing a Successful Business Plan—Guide by PricewaterhouseCoopers

In 1997, Pricewaterhouse published, *Developing a Successful Business Plan—a Ten Step Guide*—Pricewaterhouse (1997). These extracts are reproduced by permission of PricewaterhouseCoopers.

STEP 1—CAPTURE THE INTEREST AND IMAGINATION OF THE POTENTIAL INVESTOR

Articulate the key investment criteria of the opportunity
- What does the business do?

- What is its key markets?

- Key selling points/critical success factors

- Barriers to entry

- Competitive advantage

Identify risks and how they will be managed:
Outline the strategic objectives
- Plans for developing new products

- Identify new target markets

- Detail plans for implementing this strategy

Briefly state business's qualifications
- What is the business's past success record?

- What abilities do management bring to the venture?

Present your financial projections summary
- How much growth is expected?

- What earnings are projected?

- Relate financial projection to the strategic objectives

- Over what period of time will these be achieved?

- Present an overview of sensitivities

Indicate the amount, form and use of finance
- How much finance is required?

- What will the money be used for?

STEP 2—YOUR CAPABILITY TO OFFER GENUINE INSIGHT

Provide a history of the development of your business
- Date and form of incorporation

- Major acquisitions and disposals, creating the group in its current form

- What are the major accomplishments of your business?
- What setbacks have you met?

Describe the industry in which you operate

- What is the size of the industry?
- Who are the major participants in the industry? (Competitors? Market leaders? Suppliers?)
- What factors are important to success in your industry?
- If available, what do published forecasts say about the future growth and profile of the industry?
- What fashions, legislation or environmental trends affect your industry?
- What barriers to entry exist?
- How do macroeconomic issues effect the industry?
- Discuss trends in corporate activity in the sector and prices paid for business (this helps investors formulate and evaluate exit potential)

STEP 3—ANALYSIS THAT'S SHARP ENOUGH CUT THE COMPETITION

What is the state of your market?

- Show that a market exists for your products or services
- Show you understand market forces and have the abilities and resources to supply and market effectively
- Offer a realistic estimate of potential market share based on sound assumptions
- Give a concise, realistic appraisal of the competition—use charts if they will get the information across more effectively (including SWOT analyses)
- Don't knock your competitors unjustifiably—show how you can achieve sales goals despite competition

Describe your customers

- Who are they? (Individuals? Manufactures? End users?)
- Where are they located geographically?
- How sensitive are they to price, quality and service?
- Who buys or expresses an interest in the your product?
- Expand on how you will approach entry to market advertising expenditure, direct marketing etc.

- Remember your gain in market share lost by a competitor.
- What is the competitive edge of the business?
- Outline the geographical focus of your selling effort.

STEP 4—WILL THIS PRODUCT DOUBLE THEIR MONEY?
Present the product well
- Use charts, photographs or drawings if you think they will help
- Describe advantages clearly and avoid too much technical information
- Consider use of an appendix for highly technical explanations

Describe it succinctly
- What need does it fulfil and how does it relate to the market place?
- What features make your product unique? (Cost? Technology? Versatility?)
- Is it patented or copyrighted?
- How is your product perceived in the industry?
- Compare prices of competing product.

Describe product development
- How fully developed is it? (Working model? In production? In use?)
- What needs to be done next—will finance be used on product development?
- Are there opportunities to expand the product line?
- Are additional specialist staff required to continue the development?

Consider brand issues
- Discuss intellectual property protection
- How valuable is your brand in the market?
- What impact will branding have on the success of the product?
- How much will the branding costs be—is it a worthwhile investment?

Discuss competitive products on the market
- How do they compare in quality and feature with your product?
- Articulate your own pricing policy
- Why do customers buy competitors' products?
- What pricing strategies are pursued for these products?
- Is it normal to pay commissions or offer other discounts?

STEP 5—. . . YES IT DOES RUN LIKE CLOCKWORK

Describe the production process

- How will critical elements be controlled? (Bottlenecks? Quality? Delivery?)

- To what extent are you dependent on key factors? (Suppliers? Materials? Skilled Labour?) How are these issues being addressed/are they available?

- What make or buy decisions are involved?

- What raw materials are required?

- What is your relationship with suppliers?

- What is the production capacity? Is it sufficient for the future?

- Discuss contractual relationships with suppliers

- Discuss quality assurance procedures

- Discuss approach to solutions of production problems

- Are there any key processes that give you a competitive advantage?

Evaluate your plant and equipment needs

- What are your facilities and equipment needs?

- What future additions will be required for expansion and how much will they cost?

- Outline the ongoing capital maintenance requirements

- Is there a need to rely on sub-contractors?

- Outline capital expenditure needs going forward

- Discuss potential for asset financing opportunities

What are your needs for premises?

- What are your existing premises and where are they located?

- Are the existing premises suitable for your needs?

- Do you need additional premises?

STEP 6—YOUR CUE TO BLOW YOUR OWN TRUMPET

Identify Key management personnel and their backgrounds

- Who are the key managers and what have they accomplished in the past?

- What are their goals for the organisation?

- Is there a balance of skills among the members of management (marketing, research, finance, administration)?

Be frank

- Openly discuss the strengths of current management
- Indicate what additional skills will be required as the venture grows
- Include full profiles of key individuals and an organisation chart in appendices
- Highlight industry expertise
- Highlight previous roles where money was invested by institutions
- Individual weaknesses should not be identified—team weaknesses should be considered and ways of addressing them identified

Discuss the structure of the organisation

- How are responsibilities distributed?
- Try to demonstrate that management isn't a one-man show
- What additions to management are anticipated?
- Show how the board will function

Describe the role of any outsiders in the venture

- Are there to be any non-executives on the board of directors?
- What skills will they bring to the organisation?

Discuss personnel requirements

- What are your employee needs?
- Discuss any particular trade skills needed
- What are your labour costs, including benefits?
- How will you attract sufficient, suitably qualified employees?
- What is the state of your industrial relations?
- Financial commitment from management will be expected.

STEP 7—THIS IS HOW WE'RE GOING TO GET THERE

Show how the strategy will work

- How does the new strategy relate to the existing strategy?
- The strategy should build on specific competitive advantages
- Ensure internal consistency
- Co-ordinate figures with those in other Sections
- Show that the timings are realistic
- Why has it not been done before?

Outline the strategy in respect of:

- Capital expenditure program

- Staff Recruitment

- Product testing

- Contacting distributors or licensing product

- Marketing

- Selling

- Accounting functions

- Obtaining and processing orders

- Protecting competitive advantage

Timetable or identify key points

- Expected completion dates

- Milestones

STEP 8—. . . AND ALL THE FIGURES ADD UP

Clarity and presentation

- Show the careful thought that the financial projections and the assumptions have been given

- Document your assumptions explicitly making reference to market intelligence and market share projections (this may be best in an appendix)

- Include a commentary on the financial projections

- Avoid too many spreadsheets—be clear and concise—but use appendices where necessary

Include historical statements

- If possible include audited financial data for the past two to five years and relate projections to historical information

Present financial projections

- Prepare projected income, cash flow and balance sheets for the next three to five years (monthly for 1st year, quarterly thereafter—if practical)

- Model the impact of capital expenditure, fixed costs and R&D on the cash flow

- Include a break-even/sensitivity analysis, identifying the split between fixed and variable costs

- Include and identify as such a contingency element (but do not be too prudent so as to diminish management equity share)

- Explain the dynamics of profit to cash flow conversion
- Identify key value drivers and the impact these drivers have on profit and cash flow
- Model realistic/practical sensitivities

STEP 9—I JUST COULDN'T PUT IT DOWN

Get the basics right
- Punctuation, spelling and grammar should be 100% correct
- Make sure the document is checked through for errors by several people

Make it readable
- Keep it in the style of one writer
- Edit vigorously to cut waffle and present ideas more sharply. Keep paragraphs short (a few sentences each)
- Only use jargon if there is no other way of expressing yourself.
- Explain technical terms and issues clearly.
- Give the argument a clear logical flow

Present it well
- Avoid design gimmicks
- Avoid extravagant production techniques
- Number pages
- Ensure overall clarity
- Differentiate headings from sub headings
- Don't cram more than 350 or so words onto a page
- Use appendices to contain more detailed material where appropriate

STEP 10—EVERY LAST ITEM ADDS

Supporting your case
- Profiles of key management personnel (including track record and brief CV)
- Market research studies
- Photographs or drawings of the product
- Detailed technical specifications/patents
- Organisation chart
- Letters of commitment from potential customers and suppliers

- Plant layout
- Press coverage about your business and its operating environment
- Detailed financial models

ANNEX C:

State Aid

1. If the State (this includes local authorities) provides aid that affects intra-Community trade and distorts competition by favouring certain undertakings or the production of certain goods, this could constitute unlawful state aid. As a broad indication, the giving of a loan at a rate of interest below the Commission threshold (i.e. at a non commercial rate), equity investment on less favourable terms than the private sector (eg in terms of risk and reward), grant funding, guarantees, provision of vehicles, facilities etc, free of charge could all amount to unlawful state aid. In practice the test of whether a measure affects intra-community trade is very easily satisfied.

2. It is particularly important to be aware of the situations in which state aid may be an issue, as the European Commission has the power, in cases of unlawful aid, to halt payments and to order repayment of aid already paid, with interest. Not only is this politically embarrassing, but it is also potentially very disruptive and damaging to the recipient of the aid in question.

3. There is no definition as such of state aid. Article 87(1) of the Treaty establishing the European Communities ('the TEC') sets out four elements all of which must be satisfied if a measure is to constitute state aid. These are:

   - The aid must be granted by the state or through state resources;

   - The aid favours certain undertakings or the production of certain goods;

   - The aid affects trade between Member States; and

   - The aid will distort, or has the potential to distort competition.

4. It is often very difficult even to establish, in any case, whether these four elements are met. Although there is no definition of aid in the $_T$EC, examples of aid might include subsidies, loans on preferential interest rates, guarantees on especially favourable terms, provision of goods or services on preferential terms and indemnities against operating losses.

5. Other rules set out both within the TEC and within separate guidelines, frameworks and regulations produced by the Commission may apply to a measure—taking it outside the Article 87(1) elements, or exempting it altogether, provided always that specific requirements are fulfilled. Special rules apply to particular sectors and to aid for particular purposes, for example, aid for training, for small or medium-sized enterprises, or for enterprises entrusted by the state with a 'public service mission'. These rules are complex and even if

the criteria for their application are satisfied, notification of the measure in question to the Commission may still be mandatory.

6. As the rules governing state aid are not straightforward, it is essential to consider at the earliest possible stage whether a scheme will present problems and to obtain specialist advice. If the Commission has to be notified, this is a long process and can take many months. The earlier the issue of state aid is addressed, the more likely a solution can be found: whether through re-structuring a scheme to avoid problems, or by obtaining Commission clearance in sufficient time for its implementation.

7. Queries on the interrelationship between local authority trading and the state aid rules can be directed to the state aid team in ODPM. Useful guidance is also contained in the DTI booklet 'European Community State Aid', which is available on the DTI Website: **http:// www.dti.gov.uk/europe/stateaid**.

ANNEX D:

Acknowledgements

The Office of the Deputy Prime Minister sincerely thanks all the members **17.48** of the 'local authority trading working group' which was established to identify key issues for local authority trading, for their contributions and assistance in the development of this guidance.

MEETINGS

1. The working group met on—

- 28 May 2003
- 27 September 2003
- 8 December 2003
- 9 February 2004.

MEMBERSHIP

2.

Joint Chair	Cllr Paul Bettison	Leader, Bracknell Forest Borough Council
	Geoffrey Tierney	Local Government Efficiency & Modernisation Division, ODPM
Members	Cllr John Browning	LB of Bexley
	Tony Eccleston	Bracknell Forest BC
	Graham Symonds	Bracknell Forest BC
	Mark Odell	Doncaster MBC
	Gareth Moss	East Staffordshire DC
	Cllr David Finch	Essex CC
	Andrew Hudson	Essex CC
	John Tilsley	Essex CC
	Cllr Nick Chard	Kent CC
	Cllr Mike Snelling	Kent CC
	Kevin Harlock	Kent CC
	Cllr Richard Marbrow	Liverpool CC
	Graeme Creer	Liverpool CC
	Cllr Mavis Smitheman	Manchester CC
	Ruth McNeil	Manchester CC

Peter North	Manchester CC
Rodney Lund	Manchester CC
Chris Malyon	New Forest DC
Sonja Bauer	Newham LB
Helen Sidwell	Newham LB
Cllr John Baskerville	Norfolk CC
Peter Hawes	Norfolk CC
Graham Jermyn	Norfolk CC
Cllr Kevan Lim	Suffolk CC
Andy Severy	Suffolk CC
Cllr David Davis	Surrey CC
Phil Walker	Surrey CC
Keith Beaumont	LGA
David Evans	LGA
Emma Varley	LGA
Paul O'Brien	APSE
Ben Taylor	Audit Commission
Andrew Davies	National Assembly for Wales (LGM)
Alan Aisbett	ODPM (Strategic Partnering Taskforce)
John Layton	ODPM (Strategic Partnering Taskforce)

Other	Graham Fletcher	ODPM (LGF)
Participants	Wendy McGregor	ODPM
	Jacqueline Miller	ODPM
	Melvin Hughes	ODPM
	Jimi Adeleye	ODPM
	Xavia Morbey	ODPM
	Chuka Iwobi	ODPM

The Rt Hon Nick Raynsford MP, Minister for Local and Regional Government attended the 2nd meeting of the Group.

General Power for Best Value
Authorities to Charge for
Discretionary Services —
Guidance on the Power in the
Local Government Act 2003

1.   The Local Government Act 2003 (the 2003 Act) received Royal **17.49**
     Assent on 18 September 2003. The 2003 Act includes a general
     power for Best Value Authorities (as defined in section 1 of the
     Local Government Act 1999) in both England and in Wales to
     charge for discretionary services. This power comes into force two
     months after Royal Assent on 18 November 2003. The Local
     Government Act 2003 is available from The Stationary Office and
     can be found on The Stationary Office website:
     http://www.hmso.gov.uk/acts/acts2003/20030026.pdf.

2.   This guidance is issued under the power at section 93(6) of the 2003
     Act. Best Value Authorities must have regard to the advice it
     contains when charging for discretionary services under the power at
     section 93 of the 2003 Act. This guidance applies only to England.
     Separate guidance will be issued for Wales.

3.   The charging power in the 2003 Act is available to all Best Value
     Authorities and is not linked to an authority's Comprehensive
     Performance Assessment (CPA). This guidance offers advice on:

     ●   The scope of the general power to charge for discretionary
         services;

     ●   Authorities having benefit of the power;

     ●   Discretionary services;

     ●   The limitation to cost recovery;

     ●   Calculating the costs and setting the charge;

     ●   The Competition Acts and the effect on local businesses; and on

     ●   Use of the power to remove the power to charge and amend
         existing legislation.

4.   This Guidance is available on the ODPM web site (web link:
     www.local.odpm.gov.uk/guidprop.pdf). It applies only to the general
     power to charge for discretionary services contained in the 2003 Act.
     It does not apply to charges levied under other legislation through
     which an authority has a power to charge. Where an authority has
     benefit of a separate power to charge for a discretionary service
     (either now or in the future), that power will remain in force and the
     new general power to charge for discretionary services at section
     93(1) of the 2003 Act will not be available (see section 93(2) of the
     2003 Act).

5.   Charges made under the power to charge at section 93 of the 2003
     Act are limited to cost recovery. Any authorities wishing to engage in
     commercial activity with the private sector in their discretionary
     services will need to rely on other powers such as the trading powers
     bestowed under section 95 of the 2003 Act.

17.50 Trading Powers in the 2003 Act

6. Section 95(1) of the 2003 Act provides power for the Secretary of State, or (in relation to authorities in Wales) the National Assembly for Wales, to make an order enabling best value authorities (with certain exceptions) to trade in any of their ordinary functions. The new powers will be introduced as part of a new package of freedoms and flexibilities following CPA and will be commenced by Order. The intention is that the new power will be available to councils judged 'fair', 'good' and 'excellent' in the CPA. The power to trade conferred by these provisions is only exercisable through a company within the meaning of Part 5 of the Local Government and Housing Act 1989 ("the 1989 Act") (companies in which local authorities have interests).

7. Section 96 of the 2003 Act provides an order-making power to impose conditions on the exercise of any trading power by a best value authority, including where the trading activity is undertaken through a company. Best value authorities are required to have regard to guidance issued about the exercise of their trading powers. Guidance on the trading powers contained in sections 95 and 96 of the 2003 Act will be issued separately.

17.51 Key Features of the Charging Power in the Local Government Act 2003

8. The general power to charge for discretionary services provided in the 2003 Act[1] (at sections 93–94 & 97–98) has a number of key features:

- Authorities are under a <u>duty</u> (set out on the face of the Act) to secure that, taking one year with another (see paragraphs 21 and 24), the income from charges do not exceed the costs of provision.

- Authorities must already have the power to provide the service. This includes discretionary services provided under well being powers in the Local Government Act 2000.

- The recipient of the discretionary service must have agreed to its provision and to pay for it.

- Applies both in England and Wales.

- Does not apply to services which an authority is mandated or has a duty to provide.

---

[1] The Local Government Act 2003 can be found on The Stationary Office website: http://www.hmso.gov.uk/acts/acts2003/20030026.pdf.

- Does not override any (existing or future) provisions in primary or secondary legislation which:

  — Expressly prohibits an authority from charging for a discretionary service; or

  — Confers a power to charge for a discretionary service.

- Charges may be set differentially, so that different people are charged different amounts. Authorities are <u>not</u> required to charge for discretionary services. They may provide them for free if they so decide.

- A reserve power (section 94) to allow the Secretary of State to disapply the new charging power.

- Powers at sections 97–98 would allow the Secretary of State to modify or exclude the application of an enactment that confers power on an authority to charge for a discretionary service or that restricts their ability to charge for a discretionary service.

Which authorities will be able to use the power to charge for discretionary services in the 2003 Act? 17.52

9. The new powers for charging for discretionary services are available to all <u>best value authorities</u> and are <u>not</u> subject to the <u>Comprehensive Performance Assessment</u>. There are 552 best value authorities in England and in Wales. Authorities by type of authority are as set out below:

35	Counties
33	London (Inner & Outer Boroughs)
36	Metropolitans
68	Unitary
238	Districts
42	Police[2]
33	Fire[3]
11	National Parks & Broads
6	Passenger Transport
6	Joint Waste
41	Best Value Town & Parish Councils
3	Greater London Authority Family[4]

[2] Includes the Metropolitan Police.
[3] Includes the London Fire and Emergency Planning Authority.
[4] Includes the Greater London Authority, Transport for London and the London Development Agency. The Metropolitan Police and the London Fire and Emergency Planning Authority are grouped with the police and fire authorities respectively.

17.53 # What are Discretionary Services?

10. Discretionary services are those services that an authority has the power, but is not obliged, to provide. For example Authorities have the power under various statutes to offer a range of advisory services, such as trading standards and fire safety, but do not have a clear power to charge. The Local Government Act 2000 gave authorities a general power to promote the economic, social and environmental well being of local communities (see paragraph 14). This power gives authorities very broad discretion to provide additional services, but does not provide a clear power to charge. There are, therefore, a variety of services that an authority can provide. Through the new power to recover via a charge the costs to an authority of providing a service, the Government aims to encourage authorities to provide more wide-ranging and new and innovative services for their communities.

> ## DISCRETIONARY SERVICES OFFERED BY AUTHORITIES
>
> Local authorities are currently involved in a wide range of discretionary services that include discrete areas of activity and examples of extensions to statutory services.
>
> Some of the discretionary services most frequently offered are large scale, well-established and are often regarded as part of the mainstream activities of the local authorities. For example, many authorities are major suppliers of leisure services, including sports, recreation and parks and countryside facilities, museums, galleries, theatres and concert halls. One metropolitan authority is now extending its galleries service by offering works of art on loan to local businesses and residents.
>
> Extensions to statutory services include range of advisory services linked to planning and development control. These are not a statutory requirement, but can make an important contribution to the operation of the statutory services. Local authorities have chosen to enhance their Social Services support by offering assistance to vulnerable young people and their families in the home, and supporting elderly residents leaving hospital. A district council in the South East of England is committing significant resource to providing key worker housing, going beyond its specific responsibilities as a housing authority.

11. Services that an authority is mandated or has a duty to provide are not discretionary services and will not benefit from the new power at section 93 of the 2003 Act. However additions or enhancements to such mandatory services above the level or standard that an authority has a duty to provide may be discretionary services.

12. To be able to make use of the new power to charge for a discretionary service, authorities must have an existing power to provide that service. Under ordinary legal principles, an authority has

power to do anything reasonably incidental to its express powers. In circumstances where an authority wishes to charge, for example for works or supplies, the authority will need to satisfy itself that the enactment which authorises provision of a particular service would also permit the provision of anything reasonably incidental to that service. Where an authority is relying on subsidiary powers under section 111(1) of the Local Government Act 1972 to authorise the provision of a service to facilitate the discharge of a specific function, then the authority may charge under section 93(1) of the 2003 Act for that function related service by virtue of the dis-application at section 93(7)(a) of the 2003 Act.

13. Where a power to charge for a particular service is provided elsewhere in legislation (either currently or in the future) that power takes precedence and the new power to charge in the 2003 Act does not apply. Similarly where there is an express prohibition in legislation that prevents authorities from making a charge for a service that prohibition will remain in force and the new power to charge will not be available.

Wellbeing   17.54

14. Local Authorities[5] have wide powers to provide discretionary services including powers in the Local Government Act 2000 (section 2) to do anything they consider likely to achieve the promotion or improvement of the economic, social and environmental wellbeing of their areas. For the purposes of the new power to charge in the 2003 Act, the prohibition on raising money in relation to their power to promote wellbeing is to be disregarded (see s3(2) of the 2000 Act and s.93(7) of the 2003 Act). A similar provision at s.34(2) of the Greater London Authority Act is also to be disregarded. This dis-application of the prohibition on raising money fulfils the commitment to provide a general power to charge for services provided under wellbeing powers—see paragraph 69 of the guidance issued in March 2001 about the "Power to Promote or Improve Economic Social or Environmental Well-Being".

Limitation to cost recovery   17.55

15. By providing a power to charge for discretionary services the Government's aim is to encourage authorities to provide those sorts of services they would otherwise decide not to provide (or improve) at all because they cannot justify or afford to provide them for free or to improve them. The aim is not to provide a new source of income for authorities, but to allow them to cover their costs.

[5] In relation to well-being powers, in England a Local Authority means a County, District or London borough council, the Common Council of the City of London in its capacity as a local authority and the Council for the Isles of Scilly; in Wales it means a county or a county borough council.

16. The 2003 Act therefore provides that for each discretionary service for which a charge is made using the new power, authorities should be under a duty to secure that, taking one year with another, the income from charges for that service does not exceed the costs of provision.

17. The requirement to take one year with another recognises the practical difficulties local authorities will face in estimating the charges. It establishes the idea of balancing the books over a period of time (which may be a number of years—see paragraphs 21–23) without having to have detailed prescription either on the face of the Act or in secondary legislation. Any over or under recovery that resulted in a surplus or deficit of income in relation to costs in one period should be addressed by an authority when setting its charges for future periods so that over time income equated to costs (see also paragraph 26).

17.56

Calculating the Costs of Provision and the Charge

18. Each Authority making use of the new power to charge will need to establish a robust methodology for assessing the costs to the authority of providing each discretionary service. Authorities are free to decide what methodology they wish to adopt. They may however find it helpful to draw on existing and familiar principles as set out in the CIPFA Best Value Accounting Code of Practice (the Code). One option would be to use the Code's definition of Total Cost. As an alternative, authorities may wish to consider adding to Total Cost an appropriate contribution for Corporate and Democratic Core (CDC) and Non-Distributed Costs (NDC), as those terms are defined in the Code, as a part of the costs of provision.

19. The Code offers guidance on practice authorities might adopt and is amended from time to time to take account of changes in requirements.

20. Any capital and investment costs necessary to establish a new service or to improve or extend an existing service are legitimate costs of providing the service. Consistent with standard local government accounting practice, to the extent that these costs are charged to revenue, they can be set against income in calculating whether the cost ceiling rule has been met.

21. Section 93(3) of the 2003 Act places authorities under a duty to secure that, taking one financial year with another, the income from charges does not exceed the costs of provision. The Government recognises that when establishing a new service, authorities may have limited information initially upon which to base their assessment of the costs they expect to incur and thus the charge that should be made for a particular service. This provision is intended to allow an authority flexibility in the setting of the charge for each kind of

service so that over a period of time (which may be a number of years—see paragraphs 22–23) the charges made for that particular service do not exceed the costs incurred by an authority in providing that service.

22. Authorities will wish to establish a period over which it would be appropriate to gather information or make estimates to calculate the cost of providing a particular kind of service and therefore the charge that should be levied. This period may also be the period over which an authority would expect to compare income with costs for the purposes of complying with the duty at section 93(3) of the 2003 Act (see paragraph 16–17). The period adopted may differ both between services within an authority and between authorities. The 2003 Act does not specify a period over which charges should be calculated; this is left to authorities' discretion.

23. Initially Authorities may find it useful to consider assessing the cost of providing a service, the projected take-up of that service and thus the charge that should be made, over a period of not less than 1 year and no more than 3 years. For services that require capital investment it may be appropriate to specify a longer period.

Setting the Charge   17.57

24. The 2003 Act allows authorities to set the level of the charge for each discretionary service as they think fit within the restriction that the income from charges for each kind of service must not exceed the costs of its provision as described at paragraphs 18–23 above. By virtue of section 93(4) of the 2003 Act, authorities are to secure that for "each kind of service" the income from charges does not exceed the costs of provision. This provision allows authorities to compare the charges for and income from similar or related services together and so offers some flexibility to group services together when assessing compliance with the duty imposed by section 93(3) of the 2003 Act.

25. Should they so wish Authorities may continue to provide a service for free. Equally they may decide not to make a charge at all for a new discretionary service or to charge different amounts to different groups of recipients. The general charging power recognises that in certain circumstances authorities may wish to offer certain services at a reduced charge or for free, for example to the disabled, the unemployed or those in receipt of benefit, while making a charge based on the cost of providing the service to other recipients. Differential charging for local authorities' discretionary services is already well established, through, for example, discount cards for leisure services. These principles could be applied more widely for services where the general charging power applies.

17.58 # Use of estimates and later adjustments

26. Authorities should use the best available information about the expected cost for each service over the period (see paragraphs 21–23) adopted by the authority for assessing the cost of that particular service. There may, however, be circumstances where an authority inadvertently recovers more than its costs and thus generates a surplus. Where surpluses or deficits of income in relation to costs result from the use (particularly initially) of estimated income and expenditure information or from unexpectedly high or low uptake for a service, such surpluses or deficits should be taken into account when setting charges in the following period (see paragraph 17) so that taking one year with another income does not exceed costs and the authority complies with the duty.

17.59 # Obtaining the Recipients agreement

27. Under the new power, authorities will not be able to require a person to pay for discretionary services that they do not wish to receive or use. The new power will operate on the basis that the discretionary service is offered at a charge and that anyone who requires the service agrees to take it up on those terms.

17.60 # Preparing to Charge

28. When offering any new services at a charge or introducing a charge for existing services, authorities are advised to make appropriate administrative arrangements. These might include the following matters:

- Terms and conditions for the provision of the service;

- Information about charges e.g. discounts; annual increases;

- Billing/payment arrangements (including third parties).

29. Providing discretionary services and in particular advisory services may take authorities and their officers outside the coverage of their existing professional liability insurance. Authorities are therefore advised to review the cover provided by their professional liability insurers in connection with their duties on behalf of the authority and to ensure that they are properly insured in this respect for any new services they propose to offer. A proportion of any such insurance costs would be a legitimate element of the costs of the service in question.

30. When considering the introduction of charges for advisory services authorities will wish to take a view as to whether the charges will improve overall levels of regulatory compliance. Consultation with local businesses and other interested parties may inform their consideration.

The Competition Acts and effect on local businesses   17.61

31. Authorities need to ensure that when using the general charging power conferred by the 2003 Act they fully comply with other complementary legislation such as the Competition Acts. Otherwise they risk being investigated and taken to court for non-compliance and may incur significant associated costs.

32. When considering whether to charge for services using the general charging power, authorities are advised to consider the likely impact on local businesses and may wish to consult with them and other interested parties.

Use of power to remove the power to charge   17.62

33. The Government expects to use the power at section 94 to remove the power to charge for discretionary services from particular authorities or in respect of particular services only exceptionally. However this section means that the Government could take action for example in the event of unfair competition.

34. The Secretary of State could remove the power to charge in circumstances where an authority was found to be making a commercial return on charges levied under section 93, where the authority otherwise had no power to trade on a commercial basis (i.e. the power in section 95 had not been extended to the authority in question—see paragraphs 6–7)).

35. The power might be dis-applied in respect of a particular service, where it might be deemed not in the public interest to charge for that service.

36. Any orders under section 94 of the 2003 Act to remove the power to charge would also contain transitional provisions (under section 123 of the 2003 Act) that would take into account any existing charging arrangements affected by the withdrawal of the power.

Use of powers to amend existing legislation   17.63

37. Once authorities begin to use the proposed new powers to charge, it may become clear that there is certain legislation in place that in some way restricts a best value authority's ability to charge for the provision of a discretionary service. The provisions at sections 97 and 98 will allow modification of any such enactment following rigorous scrutiny in both Houses of Parliament. These powers are similar to those in the Local Government Act 2000 in relation to the promotion of economic, social and environmental well being.

17.64   Other issues

38.   The implications of the European Court of Justice's ruling in the case of *European Communities v Italian Republic*[6] are to be noted in the context of charging for services. The case relates to concessionary rates for access to local museums, monuments, galleries etc. In its judgement the Court held that the state is not permitted to grant concessionary rates for access to cultural sites for its own nationals only. Similar principles apply to sites controlled by local authorities (since the state is held responsible for its municipal and decentralised authorities) and to concessions based on residency rather than nationality which was held to be another way of favouring nationals over non-nationals.

> Office of the Deputy Prime Minister
> November 2003

---

[6] EC Court Judgement—62001J0388 Judgement of the Court (Sixth Chamber) of 16th January 2003. Commission of the European Communities v Italian Republic.

NATIONAL ASSEMBLY FOR WALES

General Power for Best Value Authorities in Wales to Charge for Discretionary Services— Guidance on the Power in the Local Government Act 2003

1. The Local Government Act 2003 (the 2003 Act) received Royal Assent on 18 September last year. The Welsh Assembly Government worked closely with the Office of the Deputy Prime Minister to ensure that Welsh interests were adequately reflected in this Act. The 2003 Act includes a general power for Best Value Authorities in both England and in Wales to charge for discretionary services. Best value authorities are defined in section 1 of the Local Government Act 1999, and the term "best value" also refers to the Wales Programme for Improvement as it applies to Welsh local authorities. This power came into force two months after Royal Assent on 18 November 2003. The Local Government Act 2003 is available from The Stationary Office and can be found on The Stationary Office website:
http://www.hmso.gov.uk/acts/acts2003/20030026.pdf.

2. This guidance is issued under the power at section 93(6) of the 2003 Act. Best Value Authorities must have regard to the advice it contains when charging for discretionary services under the power at section 93 of the 2003 Act. This guidance applies only to Wales. Separate guidance has been issued for England.

3. This guidance offers advice on:

   - The scope of the general power to charge for discretionary services;
   - Authorities having benefit of the power;
   - Discretionary services;
   - The limitation to cost recovery;
   - Calculating the costs and setting the charge;
   - The Competition Acts and the effect on local businesses; and
   - The use of the power to remove the power to charge and amend existing legislation.

4. This Guidance is available on the Assembly's web site (web link: www.Wales.Gov.UK). It applies only to the general power to charge for discretionary services contained in the 2003 Act. It does not

apply to charges levied under other legislation through which an authority has a power to charge. Where an authority has benefit of a separate power to charge for a discretionary service (either now or in the future), that power will remain in force and the new general power to charge for discretionary services at section 93(1) of the 2003 Act will not be available (see section 93(2) of the 2003 Act).

5.   Charges made under the power to charge at section 93 of the 2003 Act are limited to cost recovery. Any authorities wishing to engage in commercial activity with the private sector in their discretionary services will need to rely on other powers, such as the trading powers bestowed under section 95 of the 2003 Act.

17.66   *Trading Powers in the 2003 Act*

6.   Section 95(1) of the 2003 Act provides the Welsh Assembly Government with a power to make an order enabling authorities under the Wales Programme for Improvement to trade in any of their ordinary functions. The intention is that the new power will be available to those Welsh authorities that have been assessed as eligible to trade via their performance under the Wales Programme for Improvement. The power to trade conferred by these provisions is only exercisable through a company within the meaning of Part 5 of the Local Government and Housing Act 1989 ("the 1989 Act") (companies in which local authorities have interests).

7.   Section 96 of the 2003 Act provides an order-making power to impose conditions on the exercise of any trading power by a best value authority, including where the trading activity is undertaken through a company. Best value authorities are required to have regard to guidance issued about the exercise of their trading powers. Guidance on the trading powers contained in sections 95 and 96 of the 2003 Act will be issued separately.

17.67   *Key Features of the Charging Power in the Local Government Act 2003*

8.   The general power to charge for discretionary services provided in the 2003 Act[1] (at sections 93–94 & 97–98) has a number of key features:

- If authorities decide to charge for discretionary services, they will be under a duty (set out on the face of the Act) to secure that, taking one year with another (see paragraphs 21 and 24), the income from charges does not exceed the costs of provision.

- Authorities must already have the power to provide the service. This includes discretionary services provided under well being powers in the Local Government Act 2000.

[1] The Local Government Act 2003 can be found on The Stationary Office website: http://www.hmso.gov.uk/acts/acts2003/20030026.pdf.

- The recipient of the discretionary service must have agreed to its provision, and to pay for it.

- The power does not apply to services that an authority is mandated or has a duty to provide.

- The power does not override any existing or future provisions in primary or secondary legislation which:

  — Expressly prohibits an authority from charging for a discretionary service; or

  — Confers a power to charge for a discretionary service.

- Charges may be set differentially, so that different people are charged different amounts. Authorities are not required to charge for discretionary services. They may provide them for free if they so decide.

- A reserve power (section 94) to allow the Welsh Assembly Government to disapply the new charging power.

- Powers at sections 97–98 would allow the Welsh Assembly Government to modify or exclude the application of an enactment that confers power on an authority to charge for a discretionary service or that restricts their ability to charge for a discretionary service.

Which authorities will be able to use the power to charge for discretionary services in the 2003 Act?   **17.68**

9. The new powers for charging for discretionary services are available to all best value (Wales Programme for Improvement) authorities in Wales, which comprise:

   Unitary authorities
   Police[2]
   Fire[3]
   National Parks

What are Discretionary Services?   **17.69**

10. Discretionary services are those services that an authority has the power, but is not obliged, to provide. For example Authorities have the power under various statutes to offer a range of advisory services, such as trading standards and fire safety, but do not have a

---

[2] It should be noted that Police and Fire Authorities in Wales derive their status as best value authorities from the local government Act 1999, the operational requirements from this status are the responsibility of the Home Office and the Office of the Deputy Prime Minister respectively.

[3] The Fire and Rescue Bill currently before Parliament, provides for the transfer of responsibility for Welsh Fire Authorities from ODPM to the National Assembly for Wales.

clear power to charge. The Local Government Act 2000 gave authorities a general power to promote the economic, social and environmental well being of local communities (see paragraph 14). This power gives authorities very broad discretion to provide additional services, but does not provide a clear power to charge. There are, therefore, a variety of services that an authority can provide. Through the new power to recover via a charge the costs to an authority of providing a service, the Welsh Assembly Government aims to encourage authorities to provide more wide-ranging and new and innovative services for their communities.

DISCRETIONARY SERVICES OFFERED BY AUTHORITIES

Local authorities are currently involved in a wide range of discretionary services that include discrete areas of activity and examples of extensions to statutory services.

Some of the discretionary services most frequently offered are large scale, well-established and are often regarded as part of the mainstream activities of the local authorities. For example, many authorities are major suppliers of leisure services, including sports, recreation and parks and countryside facilities, museums, galleries, theatres and concert halls.

Extensions to statutory services include a range of advisory services linked to planning and development control. These are not a statutory requirement, but can make an important contribution to the operation of the statutory services. Local authorities have chosen to enhance their Social Services support by offering assistance to vulnerable young people and their families in the home, and supporting elderly residents leaving hospital.

---

11. Services that an authority is mandated or has a duty to provide are not discretionary services and will not benefit from the new power at section 93 of the 2003 Act. However additions or enhancements to such mandatory services above the level or standard that an authority has a duty to provide may be discretionary services.

12. To be able to make use of the new power to charge for a discretionary service, authorities must have an existing power to provide that service. Under ordinary legal principles, an authority has power to do anything reasonably incidental to its express powers. In circumstances where an authority wishes to charge, for example, for works or supplies, the authority will need to satisfy itself that the enactment which authorises provision of a particular service would also permit the provision of anything reasonably incidental to that service. Where an authority is relying on subsidiary powers under section 111(1) of the Local Government Act 1972 to authorise the provision of a service to facilitate the discharge of a specific function, then the authority may charge under section 93(1) of the 2003 Act for that function related

service by virtue of the dis-application at section 93(7)(a) of the 2003 Act.

13. Where a power to charge for a particular service is provided elsewhere in legislation (either currently or in the future) that power takes precedence and the new power to charge in the 2003 Act does not apply. Similarly where there is an express prohibition in legislation that prevents authorities from making a charge for a service that prohibition will remain in force and the new power to charge will not be available.

Wellbeing   **17.70**

14. Local Authorities[4] have wide powers to provide discretionary services including powers in the Local Government Act 2000 (section 2) to do anything they consider likely to achieve the promotion or improvement of the economic, social and environmental wellbeing of their areas. For the purposes of the new power to charge in the 2003 Act, the prohibition on raising money in relation to their power to promote wellbeing is to be disregarded (see s.3(2) of the 2000 Act and s.93(7) of the 2003 Act). This dis-application of the prohibition on raising money fulfils the commitment to provide a general power to charge for services provided under well being powers.

15. Draft guidance on the wellbeing powers for Welsh local authorities was issued in May 2001 and is available via the Assembly's web-site. An updated version of this guidance, taking account of the provisions in the 2003 Act, will be issued for consultation in the near future.

Limitation to cost recovery   **17.71**

16. By providing a power to charge for discretionary services the Welsh Assembly Government's aim is to encourage authorities to provide those sorts of services they would otherwise decide not to provide (or improve) at all because they cannot justify or afford to provide them for free or to improve them. The aim is not to provide a new source of income for authorities, but to allow them to cover their costs.

17. The 2003 Act therefore provides that for each discretionary service for which a charge is made using the new power, authorities should be under a duty to secure that, taking one year with another, the income from charges for that service does not exceed the costs of provision.

18. The requirement to take one year with another recognises the practical difficulties local authorities will face in estimating the charges. It establishes the idea of balancing the books over a period of time (which may be a number of years—see paragraphs 22–24)

---

[4] Wellbeing powers are restricted to the principal authorities in Wales.

without having to have detailed prescription either on the face of the Act or in secondary legislation. Any over or under recovery that resulted in a surplus or deficit of income in relation to costs in one period should be addressed by an authority when setting it charges for future periods so that over time income equated to costs (see also paragraph 27).

17.72 *Calculating the Costs of Provision and the Charge*

19. Each Authority making use of the new power to charge will need to establish a robust methodology for assessing the costs to the authority of providing each discretionary service. Authorities are free to decide what methodology they wish to adopt. They may however find it helpful to draw on existing and familiar principles as set out in the CIPFA Best Value Accounting Code of Practice (the Code). One option would be to use the Code's definition of Total Cost. As an alternative, authorities may wish to consider adding to Total Cost an appropriate contribution for Corporate and Democratic Core (CDC) and Non-Distributed Costs (NDC), as those terms are defined in the Code, as a part of the costs of provision.

20. The Code offers guidance on practice authorities might adopt and is amended from time to time to take account of changes in requirements.

21. Any capital and investment costs necessary to establish a new service or to improve or extend an existing service are legitimate costs of providing the service. Consistent with standard local government accounting practice, to the extent that these costs are charged to revenue, they can be set against income in calculating whether the cost ceiling rule has been met.

22. Section 93(3) of the 2003 Act places authorities under a duty to secure that, taking one financial year with another, the income from charges does not exceed the costs of provision. The Assembly Government recognises that when establishing a new service, authorities may have limited information initially upon which to base their assessment of the costs they expect to incur and thus the charge that should be made for a particular service. This provision is intended to allow an authority flexibility in the setting of the charge for each kind of service so that over a period of time (which may be a number of years—see paragraphs 23–24) the charges made for that particular service do not exceed the costs incurred by an authority in providing that service.

23. Authorities will wish to establish a period over which it would be appropriate to gather information or make estimates to calculate the cost of providing a particular kind of service and therefore the charge that should be levied. This period may also be the period over which an authority would expect to compare income with costs

for the purposes of complying with the duty at section 93(3) of the 2003 Act (see paragraph 17–18). The period adopted may differ both between services within an authority and between authorities. The 2003 Act does not specify a period over which charges should be calculated; this is left to authorities' discretion.

24. Initially Authorities may find it useful to consider assessing the cost of providing a service, the projected take-up of that service and thus the charge that should be made, over a period of not less than 1 year and no more than 3 years. For services that require capital investment it may be appropriate to specify a longer period.

Setting the Charge   **17.73**

25. The 2003 Act allows authorities to set the level of the charge for each discretionary service as they think fit within the restriction that the income from charges for each kind of service must not exceed the costs of its provision as described at paragraphs 19-24 above. By virtue of section 93(4) of the 2003 Act, authorities are to secure that for "each kind of service" the income from charges does not exceed the costs of provision. This provision allows authorities to compare the charges for and income from similar or related services together and so offers some flexibility to group services together when assessing compliance with the duty imposed by section 93(3) of the 2003 Act.

26. Should they so wish, Authorities may continue to provide a service for free. Equally they may decide not to make a charge at all for a new discretionary service or to charge different amounts to different groups of recipients. The general charging power recognises that in certain circumstances authorities may wish to offer certain services at a reduced charge or for free, for example to the disabled, the unemployed or those in receipt of benefit, while making a charge based on the cost of providing the service to other recipients. Differential charging for local authorities' discretionary services is already well established, through, for example, discount cards for leisure services. These principles could be applied more widely for services where the general charging power applies.

Use of estimates and later adjustments   **17.74**

27. Authorities should use the best available information about the expected cost for each service over the period (see paragraphs 21–23) adopted by the authority for assessing the cost of that particular service. There may, however, be circumstances where an authority inadvertently recovers more than its costs and thus generates a surplus. Where surpluses or deficits of income in relation to costs result from the use (particularly initially) of estimated income and expenditure information or from unexpectedly high or low uptake for

361

a service, such surpluses or deficits should be taken into account when setting charges in the following period (see paragraph 18) so that taking one year with another income does not exceed costs and the authority complies with the duty.

17.73   *Obtaining the Recipients agreement*

28.   Under the new power, authorities will not be able to require a person to pay for discretionary services that they do not wish to receive or use. The new power will operate on the basis that the discretionary service is offered at a charge and that anyone who requires the service agrees to take it up on those terms.

17.76   *Preparing to Charge*

29.   When offering any new services at a charge or introducing a charge for existing services, authorities are advised to make appropriate administrative arrangements. These might include the following matters:

- Terms and conditions for the provision of the service;
- Information about charges e.g. discounts; annual increases;
- Billing/payment arrangements (including third parties).

30.   Providing discretionary services, and in particular advisory services, may take authorities and their officers outside the coverage of their existing professional liability insurance. Authorities are therefore advised to review the cover provided by their professional liability insurers in connection with their duties on behalf of the authority and to ensure that they are properly insured in this respect for any new services they propose to offer. A proportion of any such insurance costs would be a legitimate element of the costs of the service in question.

31.   When considering the introduction of charges for advisory services authorities will wish to take a view as to whether the charges will improve overall levels of regulatory compliance. Consultation with local businesses and other interested parties may inform their consideration.

17.77   *The Competition Acts and effect on local businesses*

32.   Authorities need to ensure that when using the general charging power conferred by the 2003 Act they fully comply with other complementary legislation such as the Competition Acts. Otherwise they risk being investigated and taken to court for non-compliance and may incur significant associated costs.

33. When considering whether to charge for services using the general charging power, authorities are advised to consider the likely impact on local businesses and may wish to consult with them and other interested parties.

Use of power to remove the power to charge   **17.78**

34. The Welsh Assembly Government expects to use the power at section 94 to remove the power to charge for discretionary services from particular authorities or in respect of particular services only exceptionally. However this section means that the Welsh Assembly Government could take action, for example in the event of unfair competition.

35. The Welsh Assembly Government could remove the power to charge in circumstances where an authority was found to be making a commercial return on charges levied under section 93, where the authority otherwise had no power to trade on a commercial basis (i.e. the power in section 95 had not been extended to the authority in question—see paragraphs 6-7)).

36. The power might be dis-applied in respect of a particular service, where it might be deemed not in the public interest to charge for that service.

37. Any orders under section 94 of the 2003 Act to remove the power to charge would also contain transitional provisions (under section 123 of the 2003 Act) that would take into account any existing charging arrangements affected by the withdrawal of the power.

Use of powers to amend existing legislation   **17.79**

38. Once authorities begin to use the proposed new powers to charge, it may become clear that there is certain legislation in place that in some way restricts a best value authority's ability to charge for the provision of a discretionary service. The provisions at sections 97 and 98 will allow modification of any such enactment following rigorous scrutiny in both Houses of Parliament. These powers are similar to those in the Local Government Act 2000 in relation to the promotion of economic, social and environmental wellbeing.

Other issues   **17.80**

39. The implications of the European Court of Justice's ruling in the case of *European Communities v Italian Republic*[5] are to be noted in the context of charging for services. The case relates to concessionary

---

[5] EC Court Judgement—62001J0388 Judgement of the Court (Sixth Chamber) of 16th January 2003. Commission of the European Communities v Italian Republic.

rates for access to local museums, monuments, galleries etc. In its judgement the Court held that the state is not permitted to grant concessionary rates for access to cultural sites for its own nationals only. Similar principles apply to sites controlled by local authorities (since the state is held responsible for its municipal and decentralised authorities) and to concessions based on residency rather than nationality which was held to be another way of favouring nationals over non-nationals.

National Assembly for Wales
February 2004

APPENDIX 3

Miscellaneous Documentation in Relation to Charging and Trading

Table of Statutory Instruments and Acts designating public bodies for the purposes of Local Authorities (Goods & Services) Act 1970

Statutory Instruments and Acts	Name of Public Body/Authority
Local Authorities (Goods and Services) (Public Bodies) Order 1972 (SI 1972/853)	The Welsh Hospital Board
	The Commission for the New Towns
	The Lee Valley Regional Park Authority
	The County Councils Association
	The Association of Municipal Corporations
	The London Boroughs Association
	The Urban District Councils Association
	The Rural District Councils Association
	The Joint Advisory Committee on Local Authority Purchasing
	The Local Government Training Board
	The Local Authorities' Conditions of Service Advisory Board
	The Local Authorities' Management Services and Computer Committee
	The Women's Royal Voluntary Service

	The St John Ambulance Association and Brigade The British Red Cross Society Age Concern The National Citizens Advice Bureaux Council The National Marriage Guidance Council The Family Planning Association
	The National Joint Council for Local Authorities administrative Professional Technical and Clerical Services (including constituent Provincial Councils) The Joint Negotiating Committee for Justices' Clerks The Joint Negotiating Committee for Justices' Clerks Assistants The Joint Negotiating Committee for Approved Schools and Remand Homes in England and Wales The Whitely Council for New Towns Staff The National Joint Council for County Council Roadmen (including constituent Provincial Councils) The National Joint Council for Local Authorities (Manual Workers) (including constituent Provincial Councils) The National Joint Council for Workshops for the Blind The Joint Negotiating Committee for Local Authorities Services (Building and Civil Engineering) The Joint Negotiating Committee for Local Authorities Services (Engineering Craftsmen) The National Joint Council for Local Authorities' Fire Brigades The National Joint Council for Chief Officers of Local Authorities' Fire Brigades The Joint Negotiating Committee for the Probation Service The Police Council for the United Kingdom

	The Joint Negotiating Committee for Clerks of County Councils
	The Joint Negotiating Committee for Town Clerks and District Council Clerks
	The Joint Negotiating Committee for Chief Officers of Local Authorities
	The Joint Negotiating Committee for Youth Leaders and Community Care Wardens
	The Joint Committee for Water Engineers Salaries
	The Medical and (Hospital) Dental (Committee C, Public Health Service) Whitley Council for the Health Services (Great Britain)
	The Dental (Local Authorities) Whitley Council for the Health Services (Great Britain)
	The Association of Education Committees
	A Regional Hospital Board, Hospital Management Committee or Board of Governors of a teaching hospital
	A voluntary hospital within the meaning of the National Health Service Act 1946 (repealed with savings by the National Health Service Act 1977, s129, Sch.14, para.1–3, Sch.16)
	A society or individual receiving payments out of moneys provided by Parliament under s.96(1) of the Criminal Justice Act 1967 (repealed by the Powers of Criminal Courts Act 1973, s.56(2), Sch.6)
	A managing Committee of an approved probation hostel or home within the meaning of 46(1) of the Criminal Justice Act 1948 (repealed by the Powers of Criminal Court Act, s.56(2). Sch.6)
	A probation committee of after care committee constituted under s.45 of and Sch.5 to the Criminal Justice Act 1948 (repealed by the Powers of Criminal Court Act, s.56(2). Sch.6)
	A police committee or watch committee constituted in accordance with the provisions of s.2 of the Police Act 1964 (repealed by the Police Act 1996, s.103(3), Sch.9, Pt 1)

	A police authority for a combined area constituted in accordance with the provisions s.3 of the Police Act 1964 (repealed by the Police Act 1996, s.103(3), Sch.9, Pt 1)
	A New Town Development Corporation
	An Institution to which grants in aid of university education are paid out of moneys provided by Parliament
	A local council of social service
	A community relations council
	A citizens' advice bureau
	A local marriage guidance council
	A community association
	An old people's association
Local Authorities (Goods and Services) (Public Bodies) Order 1975 (SI 1975/193)	**National Bodies or Bodies Related to National Body**
	The Association of Metropolitan Authorities
	The Association of County Councils
	The Association of District Councils
	The Receiver for the Metropolitan Police District
	A Magistrates' Court Committee
	The Arts Council of Great Britain
	The Welsh Arts Council
	A Regional Arts Association
	A Local Arts Council sponsored or grant aided by a local authority
	The British Film Institute
	The Sports Council
	The Sports Council for Wales
	A Regional Sports Council
	The English Tourist Board
	The Wales Tourist Board
	A Regional Tourist Board established by the English Tourist Board or the Wales Tourist Board

	A Passenger Transport Executive
	The Royal Society for the Prevention of Accidents
	The Council for Small Industries in Rural Areas
	The Mid-Wales Industrial Development Association Development Committee
	The Eastern Border Development Association Development Committee
	The Lincolnshire Joint Development Committee
	The West Midlands Development Committee
	The Millom Development Committee
	The English Industrial Estates Corporation
	The Welsh Industrial Estates Corporation
	The Whitely Council for the Staffs of Industrial Estates Corporation
	The Joint Negotiating Committee for the Chief Executives of Local Authorities
	The Joint Negotiating Committee for Former Approved Schools and Remand Homes in England and Wales
	The Joint National Council for Local Authorities' Services (Manual Workers) (including constituent Provincial Councils)
	The Committee on Salary Scales and Service Conditions of Inspectors, Organisers and Advisory Officers of Local Education Authorities
	Educational Bodies The managers, governors or other body responsible for the management of:- (a) a voluntary aided or special agreement school (b) a special school not maintained by a Local Education Authority (c) a school or other educational establishment (including a college of education in receipt of grant under section 100(1)(b) of the Education Act 1944(a)

	(d) within the meaning of the Education Acts 1944 (This Act was repealed with savings by the Education Act 1996, ss.32(6), 582(2), (3) Sch.5, para.1, Sch.38, Pt 1, Sch.39, Pt II, para.39(1)), 1946 (This Act was repealed by the Education Act 1996, s.582(2), Sch.38, Pt 1), 1959 (This Act was repealed by the Education Act 1996, s.582(2), Sch.38, Pt 1), 1962 (This Act was repealed by the Teaching and Higher Education Act 1998, s.44(2), Sch.4), 1964 (This Act was repealed by the Education Act 1996, s.582(2), Sch.38, Pt 1), 1967, 1968 (This Act was repealed by the Education Act 1996, s.582(2), Sch.38, Pt 1) and 1971 (This Act was repeated by the Education Act 1980, ss.22(5), 38(6), Sch.7).
	The managers, governors or other body responsible for the management of an independent school which operates otherwise than for profit. The managers, governors or other body responsible for the management of; (a) residential college for adult education (b) an establishment for the further education or training of disabled persons. The Workers' Educational Association and constituent branches A Regional Advisory Council for Further Education The Welsh Joint Education Committee The Council of the Royal College of Art The Cranfield Institute of Technology A college of London University The Wiltshire Rural Music School Ltd The Wiltshire Drama Association **Social Services Bodies** The managers, governors or other body responsible for the management of:- (a) a nursery school (b) a pre-school playgroup (c) a hospital playgroup which operates other than for profit.

	The Pre-School Playgroups Association and constituent bodies
	Mudiad Ysgolion Meithrin
	The managers of a voluntary home registered under the Children Act 1948 (This Act was repeated by the Social Work (Scotland) Act 1968, ss.2(4), 3(9), 7(8), 21(3), 95(2), Sch.9, Pt 1 and the Child Care Act 1980, s.89(1), (3), Sch.4, para.9, Sch.6).
	The managers of a controlled or assisted community home provided under the Children and Young Persons Act 1969.
	The managers of a home provided by a voluntary organisation operating otherwise than for profit, for the elderly, the physically or mentally handicapped or unmarried mothers.
	The National Council of Social Service
	The Council of Social Service for Wales
	The National Association for Mental Health
	The National Society for Mentally Handicapped Children
	The Psychiatric Rehabilitation Association
	The Mental After Care Association
	The Samaritans
	The Richmond Fellowship
	The North, Western and Southern Regional Associations for the Blind and constituent bodies
	The Wales Council for the Blind and constituent bodies
	St Dunstan's for Men and Women Blinded on War Service
	The Central Council for the Disabled and affiliated bodies
	The Wales Council for the Disabled and affiliated bodies
	The North, Midland, West and South-East Regional Associations for the Deaf
	The Welsh Association for the Deaf

	The Royal National Institute for the Deaf
	The British Association of the Hard of Hearing
	The National Deaf Children's Society
	The British Deaf Association
	The management committee of a voluntary youth organisation affiliated to the National Council of Voluntary Youth Organisations.
	Trustees administering an Alms House Charity
	A housing association registered under Part II of the Housing Act 1974
	A Rural Community Council
	A Village Hall Management Committee
	The Soldiers', Sailors' and Airmen's Families Association
	The National Federation of Women's Institutes and constituent branches
	The National Union of Townswomen's Guilds and constituent branches
	Other bodies A society for the provision of smallholdings or allotments as mentioned in s.49 of the Smallholdings and Allotments Act 1908.
	Local Trustees administering allotments
	The Chiltern Mothercraft Training Society
The Local Authorities (Goods and Services) Act 1970 (s.1(4))	defines "public body" as any local authority, police authority established under s.3 of the Police Act 1996 any housing action trust established under Part III of the Housing Act 1988, any person who is a public body by virtue of ss.(5) of this section (those in SI's above), in relation to any parish council or representative body of a rural parish.
The Local Authorities (Goods and Services) Act 1970 (s.7)	states that the Great Yarmouth Port and Haven Commissioners shall be treated as a public body for the purposes of paras (a) and (b) of subsection (1) as those paras apply in relation to agreements entered into by the Broads Authority.

Local Government Planning and Land Act 1980 (s.163(1))	any urban development corporation.
Local Authorities (Goods and Services) (Public Bodies) Order 1981 (SI 1981/1049) (as amended by SI 1997/2971, art.6).	The Crown Agents for Overseas and Government Administrations.
Education Reform Act 1988 (Sch.12, para.11)	grant maintained schools.
Education Reform Act 1988 (Sch.12, para.68)	Polytechnics, colleges and schools falling within the Polytechnics and Colleges Funding Council.
Local Authorities (Goods and Services) (Public Bodies) Order 1990 (SI 1990/433)	The City Literary Institute Medway Housing Society Limited
Water Resources Act 1991 (s.4(4))	National rivers;
Water Resources Act 1991 (s.158)	also authorises arrangements to be made with local authorities.
Water Consolidation (Consequential Provisions) Act 1991	Part V of the Water Industry Act 1991. In April 1996 the NRA was replaced by the Environment Agency. The Environment Agency is a public body under the 1970 Act (see the Environment Act 1995). ss.65, 120, Sch.8, para.5, Sch.22, para.13
Local Authorities (Goods and Services) (Public Bodies) Order 1992 (SI 1992/2830)	Her Majesty's Chief Inspector of Schools in England Her Majesty's Chief Inspector of Education and Training in Wales Bethnal Green City Challenge Company Limited Bradford City Challenge Limited
	Deptford City Challenge Limited Hulme Regeneration Limited Nottingham City Challenge Partnership Limited

The Further and Higher Education Act 1992 (Sch.8, Pt II, para.71(1))	any institution within the further education sector or the higher education sector
Local Authorities (Goods and Services) (Public Bodies) Order 1993 (SI 1993/2097)	Blackburn City Challenge Partnership Bolton City Challenge Partnership Limited Community North (Sunderland) Dalton City Partnership Limited Derby Pride Limited Harlesden City Challenge Limited Hartlepool City Challenge Board Hulme Community Homes (Manchester) Limited Leicester City Challenge Limited The Newcastle West End Partnership Limited North Tyneside City Challenge Partnership Limited Stratford Development Partnership Wolverhampton City Challenge
Local Authorities (Goods and Services) (Public Bodies) Order 1994 (SI 1994/37)	Development Board for Rural Wales Welsh Development Agency
Local Authorities (Goods and Services) (Public Bodies) (No.2) Order 1994 (SI 1994/1389)	Batley Action Limited Brixton City Challenge Company Limited Douglas Valley Partnership Limited North Kensington City Challenge Company Limited Walsall City Challenge Limited Newtown South Aston City Challenge

Local Government (Wales) Act 1994 (Sch.13, para.26)	the Residuary Body for Wales.
Environment Act 1995 (Sch.8 para.5)	the National Park Authority.
Environment Act 1995 (Sch.22, para.13)	the Environment Agency and the Scottish Environment Protection Agency.
Local Authorities (Goods and Services) (Public Bodies) (Meat Hygiene) Order 1995 (SI 1995/2626)	Minister of Agriculture, Fisheries and Food for England Secretary of State for Scotland and Wales
Local Authorities (Goods and Services) (Public Bodies) (Trunk Roads) Order 1996 (SI 1996/342)	Secretary of State for the Environment, Transport and the Regions Secretary of State for Wales DBFO contractor
Local Authorities (Goods and Services) (Public Bodies) (Trunk Roads) (No. 2) Order 1996 (SI 1996/1814)	The Secretary of State for the Environment, Transport and the Regions Secretary of State for Wales
Local Authorities (Goods and Services) (Public Bodies) (The Julie Rose Stadium) Order 1996 (SI 1996/2534)	The Julie Rose Stadium
Local Authorities (Goods and Services) (Public Bodies) (Sports Councils) Order 1996 (SI 1996/3092)	The English Sports Council The United Kingdom Sports Council The Scottish Sports Council
Local Authorities (Goods and Services) (Public Bodies) Order 1997 (SI 1997/101)	Huddersfield Pride Limited

	Routes to Work (Derby) Limited
	Stainforth Development Limited Sydenham SRB Trust
Local Authorities (Goods and Services) (Public Bodies) (Trunk Roads) (No.1) Order 1997 (SI 1997/204)	a management agent and a works contractor
Local Authorities (Goods and Services) (Public Bodies) (Greater London Enterprise Limited) Order 1997 (SI 1997/809)	Greater London Enterprise Limited
Local Authorities (Goods and Services) (Public Bodies) (Trunk Roads) (Amendment) Order 1997 (SI 1997/849)	
Local Authorities (Goods and Services) (Public Bodies) (Trunk Roads) (No.2) Order 1997 (SI 1997/850)	Secretary of State for the Environment, Transport and the Regions Secretary of State for Wales DBFO Contractor
Local Authorities (Goods and Services) (Public Bodies) (English Heritage) Order 1997 (SI 1997/1835)	The Historic Buildings and Monuments Commission for England
Local Authorities (Goods and Services) (Public Bodies) Order 1997 (SI 1997/2095)	Bedford Bereavement Care Limited Wansbeck Energy Company Limited
Education Act 1997 (Sch.7, para.2)	the Qualifications and Curriculum Authority and the Qualifications Curriculum and Assessment Authority for Wales.
Local Authorities (Goods and Services) (Public Bodies) Order 1998 (SI 1998/308)	Bedford (Caldwell and Kingsbrook) Regeneration Partnership

	Bedford (Queens Park) Partnership Limited Dewsbury Partnership Limited Into Work (Sunderland) Limited Ryedale Energy Conservation Group Limited
Local Authorities (Goods and Services) (Public Bodies) (No.2) Order 1998 (SI 1998/868)	Further Education (London Region) Services (FELORS)
Local Authorities (Goods and Services) (Public Bodies) (No.3) Order 1998 (SI 1998/1123)	Newham Healthcare Trust
	Bristol Regeneration Partnership Limited West Euston Partnership Limited The Institute of Burial and Cremation Administration
Local Authorities (Goods and Services) (Public Bodies) (No.4) Order 1998 (SI 1998/1574)	Community Initiative Partnerships Hounslow Cultural and Community Services Hounslow Sport and Recreation Services
Local Authorities (Goods and Services) (Public Bodies) (No.5) Order 1998 (SI 1998/2956)	Breakthrough UK Limited (Manchester City Council) Bishops Castle and District Lifeline Company Limited (Shropshire County Council and South Shropshire District Council) Greater Nottingham Rapid Transit Limited (Nottinghamshire County Council and Nottingham City Council) Thorney Close Action and Enterprise Centre (Sunderland City Council) Twining Enterprise Limited (Richmond upon Thames London Borough Council) Manchester Care and Repair Limited (Manchester City Council

Local Authorities (Goods and Services) (Public Bodies) (No.6) Order 1998 (SI 1998/3095)	London Luton Airport Operations Limited
School Standards and Framework Act 1998 (Sch.30, para.2(1))	any Education Action Forum established in an education action zone *(subject to sub para.2 of the 1970 Act).*
Regional Development Agencies Act 1998 (Sch.7, para.3)	Regional Development Agencies
Local Authorities (Goods and Services) (Public Bodies) (No.1) Order 1999 (SI 1999/421)	The Borough of Havant Sport and Leisure Trust The Teacher Training Agency
Local Authorities (Goods and Services) (Public Bodies) (No.2) Order 1999 (SI 1999/1754)	The Academy of Youth Limited Coronation Park at Launceston, Cornwall The New Opportunities Fund The Preston and Western Lancashire Racial Equality Council Renaisi Limited
National Health Services Act 1977 (updated by Health Act 1999) s.28 NHS Act 1977 (inserted by National Health Service Reform and Health Care Professional Act 2002, s.6(2), Sch.5, paras 4 and 12(a))	Strategic Health Authority, Health Authority, Special Health Authority, Primary Care Trust and Local Health Board.
Greater London Authority Act 1999 (s.388)	the Greater London Authority, the London Fire and Emergency Planning Authority, Transport for London and the London Development Agency are now public bodies under the 1970 Act.
Local Authorities (Goods and Services) (Public Bodies) Order 2000 (SI 2000/63)	Boston Volunteer Charity (Boston Borough Council)

	Tee Valley Leisure Limited (Redcar and Cleveland Borough Council) West Cumbria Estates Management Limited (Cumbria County Council) Commission for Local Administration in England (Allerdale Borough Council)
	Manchester Commonwealth Games Limited and Manchester 2002 Limited: Barrow-in-Furness Borough Council Blackburn Borough Council Blackpool Borough Council Bolton Metropolitan Borough Council Burnley Borough Council Bury Metropolitan Borough Council Carlisle City Council Cheshire City Council Chester City Council Chorley Borough Council Congleton Borough Council Copeland Borough Council Crewe and Nantwich Borough Council Cumbria County Council Eden District Council Ellesmere Port and Neston Borough Council Fylde Borough Council Guildford Borough Council Halton Borough Council Hyndburn Borough Council Knowsley Metropolitan Borough Council Lancashire County Council Lancaster City Council Liverpool City Council Macclesfield Borough Council Manchester City Council Oldham Metropolitan Borough Council Pendle Borough Council Preston Borough Council Ribble Valley Borough Council Rochdale Metropolitan Borough Council Rossendale Borough Council St Helens Metropolitan Borough Council Salford City Council Sefton Metropolitan Borough Council South Lakeland District Council South Ribble Borough Council Stockport Metropolitan Borough Council

	Surrey County Council Surrey Heath Borough Council Tameside Metropolitan Borough Council Trafford Metropolitan Borough Council Vale Royal Borough Council Warrington Borough Council West Lancashire District Council Wigan Metropolitan Borough Council Wirral Metropolitan Borough Council
	Wyre Borough Council
Local Authorities (Goods and Services) (Public Bodies) (No.2) Order 2000 (SI 2000/1027)	Edward Harvist's Charity The Hines Trust
	Mayor of Harrow's Charity Fund
Local Authorities (Goods & Services) (Public Bodies) (Scotland) Order 2000 (SI 2000/207)	A person who has entered into a contract with the Scottish Ministers and a subcontractor of such a person under such a contract.
Local Authorities (Goods & Services) (Public Bodies) (No.2) (Scotland) Order 2000 (SI 2000/403)	Highlands and Islands Enterprise Scottish Enterprise Scottish Environment Protection Agency A National Health Service Trust A person with whom there is in force an agreement made under section 19 Enterprise and New Towns (Scotland) Act 1990 by either: (a) Scottish Enterprise for the discharge of their functions; or (b) Highlands and Islands Enterprise for the discharge their functions. A company: (a) established wholly or mainly for the purpose of providing services to a local authority; (b) of which has not less than 25% nor more than 49% of the issued share capital is held by that local authority; and (c) which has entered into a contractual arrangement with that local authority for the supply of goods and services (or either of them) to that local authority.

National Parks (Scotland) Act 2000 (Sch.2, para.11)	National Parks Authority (*Scotland only*).
Criminal Justice & Court Services Act 2000 (Sch.7, Part 2, para.44)	Local Probation Board (*only local probation boards established under section 4 of this Act*). (*Subject to s.2(2) of the 1970 Act*)
Local Authorities (Goods and Services) (Public Bodies) (England) Order 2001 (SI 2001/243) *This Order extends to England only.*	A person with whom a local education authority has entered into a contract or other arrangement for the performance of functions on the authority's behalf pursuant to direction made by the Secretary of State under s.497A(4) of the Education Act 1996. The School Development Support Agency A City Technology College, City College for the Technology of the Arts or City Academy which has entered into an agreement with the secretary of State pursuant to s.482 of the Education Act 1996.
Local Authorities (Goods & Services) (Public Bodies) (England) (No.2) Order 2001 (SI 2001/691) *This Order extends to England only.*	New Schools (Cornwall) Limited (Cornwall County Council and the provision of education services in the area of that Council) United Waste Services (South Gloucestershire) Limited (South Gloucestershire Council and the provision of waste management services in the area of that Council)
Local Authorities (Goods & Services) (Public Bodies) (England) (No.3) Order 2001 (SI 2001/1823) *This Order extends to England only.*	Thurrock Community Leisure Limited (Thurrock Borough Council) Care Plus Trust Limited (London Borough of Bexley) Paddington Development Trust (London Borough of Brent or the City of Westminster)

Local Authorities (Goods & Services) (Public Bodies) (England) (No.4) Order 2001 (SI 2001/3347) *This Order extends to England only.*	Liverpool Direct Limited (Liverpool City Council) Schools PBS Limited (Kirklees MBC)
Housing (Scotland) Act 2001 (2001 asp 10) (s.107(1))	Registered Social Landlords
Local Authorities (Goods & Services) (Public Bodies) (England) Order 2002 (SI 2002/522) *This Order extends to England only.*	A body set up by a local authority, in exercise of its powers under s.2 LGA 2000, to exercise management functions as agent of the authority under an arrangement approved by the Secretary of State under s.27 Housing Act 1985.
The Local Authorities (Goods and Services) (Public Bodies) (Wales) Order 2002 (SI 2002/1729) *This Order applies to Wales only*	The National Assembly for Wales The Care Council for Wales The National Council for Education and Training for Wales
The Local Authorities (Goods and Services) (Public Bodies) (England) (No. 2) Order 2002 (SI 2002/2244)	Kirklees Active Centre
The Local Authorities (Goods and Services) (Public Bodies) (England) (No. 3) Order 2002 (SI 2002/2624)	Active Life Limited
Water Industry (Scotland) Act 2002 (s.61)	Scottish Water

The Local Authorities (Goods and Services) (Public Bodies) (England) Order 2003 (SI 2003/354)	Swaythling Parochial Church Council York Museums and Gallery Trust South Lakeland Leisure
The Local Authorities (Goods and Services) (Public Bodies) (England) (No.2) Order 2003 (SI 2003/1018)	East Leake Schools Limited
The Local Authorities (Goods and Services) (Public Bodies) (England) (No.3) Order 2003 (SI 2003/2069)	Doncaster Dome Leisure Trust Wigan Leisure and Culture Trust Trafford Community Leisure Trust
The Local Authorities (Goods and Services) (Public Bodies) (England) (No.4) Order 2003 SI 2003/2558)	Yorkshire and Humberside Grid for Learning Foundation
The Local Authorities (Goods and Services) (Public Bodies) (England) Order 2004 (SI 2004/485)	Pyramid Schools (Cornwall) Limited Haden Building Management Limited
Local Authorities (Goods and Services) (Public Bodies) (England) (No.2) Order 2004 SI 2004/2475)	District Surveyors Association Local Authority Building Control Advisory Services Limited ("LABCAS"), being a person appearing to the Secretary of State to be exercising a function of a public nature.
Local Authorities (Goods and Services) (Public Bodies) (Wales) Order 2004 (SI 2004/2878)	PBS 2003 Limited, being a person appearing to the National Assembly for Wales to be exercising a function of a public nature.

INDEX

[all references are to chapter and paragraph number]

Accountability
implementation issues, and, 10.13
Acting in bad faith
ultra vires, and, 2.22
Activities
charging for discretionary
services, and, 5.3–5.4
Adjustments
charging for discretionary
services, and, 5.9
Administrative basis
legal basis for charging and
trading, 2.1
Administrative matters
charging for discretionary
services, and, 5.11
Admission body option
pensions, and, 12.33–12.34
Working practices
secondment, and, 12.17
Advertising controls
Codes of Practice, 11.15
distance selling, 11.14
introduction, 11.13
Appropriate persons
charging for discretionary
services, and, 5.1
commercial trading, and, 7.1
Arm's length entity
trading companies, and, 8.1
Asset availability
strategic planning, and, 3.11
Audit
trading companies, and, 8.18

Audit Commission
classification of authorities, and,
3.4

Bad faith
ultra vires, and, 2.22
"Battle of the forms"
contractual terms, and, 11.4
Best Value
charging for discretionary
services, and, 5.3
classification, and, 3.5
commercial trading, and, 7.3
Northern Ireland, and, 14.5
Blind reliance on policy
ultra vires, and, 2.19
Borrowing
trading companies, and, 8.28
'Broadly comparable' scheme
pensions, and, 12.31–12.32
Business case
generally, 8.3
introduction, 8.1
strategic planning, and, 3.15
wholly owned company, and, 9.3
Business plan
implementation issues, and,
10.2–10.3
trading companies, and, 8.31

Calculation of charges
definition of the service, 5.8
discretion, 5.8
elements, 5.8
generally, 5.7

Calculation of charges—*cont.*
methodology, 5.8
time period, 5.8
Capacity of local authority
charging for discretionary
services, and, 5.2
control by central government,
and, 13.3
introduction, 2.2
overlap between powers and
duties, 2.11
powers and duties, 2.3–2.10
Case law
legal basis for charging and
trading, 2.28–2.31
Catering for the public
drafting of the power, 4.16
introduction, 4.15
Challenge, risk of
implementation issues, and,
10.15–10.16
Change management
establishing trading company
collective bargaining
arrangements, 12.9
commercial confidentiality,
12.7
core values, 12.5
employment contracts, 12.7
insurance, 12.10
introduction, 2.4
pensions, 12.8
policies and procedures, 12.6
introduction, 12.2
stakeholder involvement, 12.3
Charging
commercial and consumer issues
and see **Commercial issues**
advertising controls,
11.13–11.15
competition, 11.16–11.18
conclusion, 11.22
introduction, 11.1
pre-contractual statements,
11.2
taxation, 11.19–11.21
terms of contract, 11.3–11.12

Charging—*cont.*
conclusion, 15.1–15.2
context
and see **Local government**
attitude to trading, 13.10–13.14
conclusion, 13.15
court's role, 13.7–13.8
introduction, 13.1
relationship with central
government, 13.4–13.6
employee and member issues
and see **Employment issues**
change management,
12.2–12.10
conclusion, 12.37
fixed term employees, 12.19
indemnities, 12.26
introduction, 12.1
pensions, 12.29–12.35
secondment, 12.11–12.18
transfer of staff, 12.20–12.28
existing powers, under
and see **Existing powers**
conclusion, 4.34
incidental powers, 4.24
introduction, 4.1
key provisions, 4.2–4.23
local legislation, 4.28–4.31
spare capacity, 4.25–4.27
specific powers, 4.32–4.34
implementation
accountability, 10.13
business plan, 10.2–10.3
conclusion, 10.17
cost/benefit analysis, 10.9
economic, social and
environmental wellbeing,
10.10
introduction, 10.1
management, 10.11–10.12
market analysis, 10.6
organisation, 10.11–10.12
performance levels, 10.8
risk analysis, 10.4–10.5
risk of challenge, 10.15–10.16
tactics, 10.14
user surveys, 10.7

Charging—*cont.*
introduction, 5.1
legal basis
    and see **Legal basis for charging and trading**
    case law, 2.28–2.31
    conclusion, 2.32
    introduction, 2.1
    ultra vires, 2.2–2.27
Northern Ireland, in
    background, 14.1
    Best Value, 14.5
    conclusion, 14.6
    introduction, 14.2
    local government powers, 14.3
    reliance on "old" law, 14.4
overview, 1.1–1.3
s.93 LGA 2003, under
    and see **Charging for discretionary services**
    examples, 6.1–6.8
    generally, 5.1–5.12
Scotland, in
    background, 14.1
    conclusion, 14.33
    introduction, 14.20
    operation of provisions, 14.26–14.32
    statutory provisions, 14.21–14.25
strategic planning
    and see **Strategic planning**
    generally, 3.23–3.24
    introduction, 3.20
ultra vires, and
    and see **Ultra vires**
    Code, as, 2.15
    express, 2.12
    incidental, 2.13–2.16
Wales, in
    background, 14.1
    conclusion, 14.19
    generally, 14.2
    introduction, 14.7
    local government powers, 14.8
    modification of enactments, 14.18

Charging—*cont.*
Wales, in—*cont.*
    "old" law position, 14.4
    statutory provision, 14.10
    Wales Improvement Programme, 14.9
Charging for discretionary services (s.93)
accountability, 10.13
activities, 5.3–5.4
adjustments, and, 5.9
administrative matters, 5.11
Best Value authorities, 5.3
business plan, 10.2–10.3
calculation of charges
    definition of the service, 5.8
    discretion, 5.8
    elements, 5.8
    generally, 5.7
    methodology, 5.8
    time period, 5.8
capacity, and, 5.2
"civic purpose", 5.1
conclusion, 5.12
contingencies, and, 5.9
cost/benefit analysis, 10.9
discretion, 5.8
discrimination against other EU nationals, 5.9
distinction from commercial trading, 5.1
dominant purpose test, 5.1
economic, social and environmental wellbeing, 10.10
enhancing services subject to a duty, 5.9
examples
    charging members of the public, 6.2–6.3
    conclusion, 6.8
    introduction, 6.1
    public to private charging, 6.6–6.7
    public to public charging, 6.4–6.5
general power, 5.2

Charging for discretionary services (s.93)—*cont.*
Guidance, 5.1
  generally, 5.1
  ODPM document, 17.49–17.64
implementation
  accountability, 10.13
  business plan, 10.2–10.3
  conclusion, 10.17
  cost/benefit analysis, 10.9
  economic, social and
     environmental wellbeing,
     10.10
  introduction, 10.1
  management, 10.11–10.12
  market analysis, 10.6
  organisation, 10.11–10.12
  performance levels, 10.8
  risk analysis, 10.4–10.5
  risk of challenge, 10.15–10.16
  tactics, 10.14
  user surveys, 10.7
introduction, 5.1
legal basis
  and see **Legal basis for
    charging and trading**
  case law, 2.28–2.31
  conclusion, 2.32
  introduction, 2.1
  ultra vires, 2.2–2.27
management, 10.11–10.12
marginal costs, and, 5.9
market analysis, 10.6
methodology, 5.8
modification of power, 5.10
Northern Ireland, in, 14.3
organisation, 10.11–10.12
nature of power, 5.2
overview, 1.1–1.3
performance levels, 10.8
policy issues, 5.6
purpose of activity, 5.1
raising money, and, 5.9
relevant activities, 5.3–5.4
restrictions on power, 5.5
risk analysis, 10.4–10.5
risk of challenge, 10.15–10.16

Charging for discretionary services (s.93)—*cont.*
Scotland, in (ss.11 and 11A)
  background, 14.1
  conclusion, 14.33
  generally, 14.20
  operation of provisions,
    14.26–14.32
  statutory provisions,
    14.21–14.25
statutory basis, 5.2
strategic planning
  and see **Strategic planning**
  generally, 3.23–3.24
  introduction, 3.20
surpluses, and, 5.9
tactics, 10.14
time period, 5.8
total costs, and, 5.9
ultra vires, and
  and see **Ultra vires**
  Code, as, 2.15
  express, 2.12
  incidental, 2.13–2.16
user surveys, 10.7
Wales, in
  background, 14.1
  conclusion, 14.19
  generally, 14.12
  introduction, 14.7
  local government powers, 14.8
  modification of enactments,
    14.18
  "old" law position, 14.4
  statutory provision, 14.10
  Wales Improvement
    Programme, 14.9
wellbeing, 10.10
Classification of authorities
charging for discretionary
  services, and, 5.3
commercial trading, and, 7.6
strategic planning, and, 3.4–3.5
Choice of charging or trading
business case, 3.15
factors
  classification of authority,
    3.4–3.5

Choice of charging or trading— *cont.*
  factors—*cont.*
    delivery of efficiency, 3.14
    introduction, 3.3
    market place, 3.6–3.9
    non-financial resources, 3.10–3.12
    specialist areas, 3.13
  introduction, 3.2
"Civic purpose"
  charging for discretionary services, and, 5.1
Civic Restaurants Act 1947
  drafting of the power, 4.16
  introduction, 4.15
Code of Practice
  transfer of staff, and
    failure to comply, 12.27
    generally, 12.23
Collective bargaining arrangements
  establishing the trading company, and, 12.9
Commercial and consumer issues
  advertising controls
    Codes of Practice, 11.15
    distance selling, 11.14
    introduction, 11.13
  "battle of the forms", 11.4
  competition
    EC rules, 11.17
    introduction, 11.16
    UK rules, 11.18
  conclusion, 11.22
  consumer contracts, 11.8
  corporation tax, 11.20
  custom or usage, 11.7
  distance selling, 11.14
  entire agreement clauses, 11.2
  implied terms
    consumer contracts, 11.8
    custom or usage, by, 11.7
    introduction, 11.6
    sale of goods, 11.10
    statute, by, 11.9–11.12
    supply of goods and services, 11.11
    unfair terms, 11.12

Commercial and consumer issues *—cont.*
  innocent misrepresentations, 11.2
  introduction, 11.1
  pre-contractual statements, 11.2
  quantum meruit, 11.5
  representations, 11.2
  sale of goods, 11.10
  statutory implied terms
    introduction, 11.9
    sale of goods, 11.10
    supply of goods and services, 11.11
    unfair terms, 11.12
  supply of goods and services, 11.11
  taxation
    corporation tax, 11.20
    introduction, 11.19
    value added tax, 11.21
  terms of contract
    "battle of the forms", 11.4
    implied by law, 11.6–11.12
    introduction, 11.3
    quantum meruit, 11.5
  unfair terms, 11.12
  value added tax, 11.21
Commercial confidentiality
  establishing the trading company, and, 12.7
"Commercial purpose"
  generally, 7.2
  introduction, 5.1
Commercial trading (s.95)
  accountability, 10.13
  "appropriate person", 7.1
  Best Value authorities, 7.3
  business plan, 10.2–10.3
  classification of authorities, 7.6
  "commercial purpose"
    generally, 7.2
    introduction, 5.1
  conclusion, 7.14
  cost/benefit analysis, 10.9
  distinction from charging
    generally, 7.12
    introduction, 5.1

Commercial trading (s.95)—*cont.*
dominant purpose test, 5.1
economic, social and
environmental wellbeing,
10.10
effect on existing powers, 7.13
establishment of companies
business planning, 8.31
competition law, 8.29–8.30
conclusion, 8.34
exit strategies, 8.32
funding, 8.28
governance framework,
8.20–8.26
introduction, 8.1
legal constraints, 8.10–8.19
prior considerations, 8.2–8.3
staffing issues, 8.24
state aid, 8.29–8.30
taxation, 8.33
type of company, 8.4–8.9
examples
conclusion, 9.16
introduction, 9.1
joint venture company,
9.9–9.15
wholly owned company,
9.2–9.8
Guidance
generally, 7.5
ODPM document, 17.1–17.48
implementation
accountability, 10.13
business plan, 10.2–10.3
conclusion, 10.17
cost/benefit analysis, 10.9
economic, social and
environmental wellbeing,
10.10
introduction, 10.1
management, 10.11–10.12
market analysis, 10.6
organisation, 10.11–10.12
performance levels, 10.8
risk analysis, 10.4–10.5
risk of challenge, 10.15–10.16
tactics, 10.14
user surveys, 10.7

Commercial trading (s.95)—*cont.*
introduction, 7.1
joint venture company
commercial issues, 9.11–9.12
conclusion, 9.15
generally, 9.1
introduction, 9.9
legal issues, 9.13–9.14
practical issues, 9.11–9.12
procurement issues, 9.10
staffing, 9.11
structure, 9.14
taxation, 9.12
vires of establishing, 9.13
legal basis
and see **Legal basis for**
charging and trading
case law, 2.28–2.31
conclusion, 2.32
introduction, 2.1
ultra vires, 2.2–2.27
legal framework
Guidance, 7.5
introduction, 7.1
Local Government Act, 7.2–7.3
Trading Order, 7.4
limitations, 7.1
local authority companies
and see **Trading companies**
establishment, 8.1–8.34
features, 7.8
legal requirement, 7.7
power to establish, 7.11
regulatory regimes, 7.9
type of vehicle, 7.10
Local Government Act 1972,
s.111, and, 7.13
management, 10.11–10.12
market analysis, 10.6
Northern Ireland, in, 14.3
organisation, 10.11–10.12
performance levels, 10.8
practice, in
conclusion, 9.16
introduction, 9.1
joint venture company,
9.9–9.15

Commercial trading (s.95)—*cont.*
practice, in—*cont.*
wholly owned company,
9.2–9.8
purpose of activity, 5.1
risk analysis, 10.4–10.5
risk of challenge, 10.15–10.16
Scotland, in
background, 14.1
conclusion, 14.33
generally, 14.20
operation of provisions,
14.26–14.32
statutory provisions,
14.21–14.25
statutory provision, 7.2–7.3
strategic planning
and see **Strategic planning**
existing private sector
company, 3.28
generally, 3.25
introduction, 3.21
joint ventures, 3.27
outsourcing, 3.26
tactics, 10.14
trading companies
and see **Trading companies**
establishment, 8.1–8.34
features, 7.8
legal requirement, 7.7
power to establish, 7.11
regulatory regimes, 7.9
type of vehicle, 7.10
Trading Order, 7.4
ultra vires, and
and see ***Ultra vires***
Code, as, 2.15
express, 2.12
incidental, 2.13–2.16
user surveys, 10.7
Wales, in
background, 14.1
conclusion, 14.19
generally, 14.13–14.17
introduction, 14.7
local government powers, 14.8
modification of enactments,
14.18

Commercial trading (s.95)—*cont.*
Wales, in—*cont.*
"old" law position, 14.4
statutory provision, 14.10
Wales Improvement
Programme, 14.9
wholly owned company
business case, 9.3
commercial issues, 9.3
conclusion, 9.8
directors' duties, 9.7
establishing the company, 9.4
funding, 9.3
generally, 9.1
introduction, 9.2
legal advice, 9.5–9.6
legal issues, 9.4
memorandum and articles, 9.6
practical issues, 9.3
taxation, 9.3
Community initiative
general powers, and, 2.6
Competition
EC rules, 11.17
introduction, 11.16
trading companies, and,
8.29–8.30
UK rules, 11.18
**Comprehensive Performance
Assessment**
charging for discretionary
services, and, 5.1
classification of authorities, and,
3.4–3.5
commercial trading, and, 7.6
control by central government,
and, 13.5
**Compulsory competitive tendering
(CCT)**
control by central government,
and, 13.5
Confidentiality
establishing the trading company,
and, 12.7
Conflict between powers
ultra vires, and, 2.11
Conflicts of interest
trading companies, and, 8.23

Consequential powers
ultra vires, and, 2.8
Construction activity
trading powers in Scotland, and,
14.23
Consultation papers
best value, and, 13.13
commercial trading, and, 7.1
Consumer contracts
implied terms, and, 11.8
Contracts of employment
establishing the trading company,
and, 12.7
Contractual terms
"battle of the forms", 11.4
implied by law
consumer contracts, 11.8
custom or usage, by, 11.7
introduction, 11.6
sale of goods, 11.10
statute, by, 11.9–11.12
supply of goods and services,
11.11
unfair terms, 11.12
introduction, 11.3
quantum meruit, 11.5
Contingencies
charging for discretionary
services, and, 5.9
Corporation tax
generally, 11.20
Cost/benefit analysis
implementation issues, and, 10.9
Council as shareholder
trading companies, and,
8.20–8.21
Custom or usage
implied terms, and, 11.7

DETR consultation papers
commercial trading, and, 7.1
Directors' liability
trading companies, and, 8.25
Directors' remuneration
governance framework, 8.24
proprietary controls, 8.16

Discretionary charging (s.93)
accountability, 10.13
activities, 5.3–5.4
adjustments, and, 5.9
administrative matters, 5.11
Best Value authorities, 5.3
business plan, 10.2–10.3
calculation of charges
definition of the service, 5.8
discretion, 5.8
elements, 5.8
generally, 5.7
methodology, 5.8
time period, 5.8
capacity, and, 5.2
"civic purpose", 5.1
conclusion, 5.12
contingencies, and, 5.9
cost/benefit analysis, 10.9
discretion, 5.8
discrimination against other EU
nationals, 5.9
distinction from commercial
trading, 5.1
dominant purpose test, 5.1
economic, social and
environmental wellbeing,
10.10
enhancing services subject to a
duty, 5.9
examples
charging members of the
public, 6.2–6.3
conclusion, 6.8
introduction, 6.1
public to private charging,
6.6–6.7
public to public charging,
6.4–6.5
general power, 5.2
Guidance
generally, 5.1
ODPM document, 17.49–17.64
implementation
accountability, 10.13
business plan, 10.2–10.3
conclusion, 10.17

Discretionary charging (s.93)—
cont.
implementation—*cont.*
cost/benefit analysis, 10.9
economic, social and
environmental wellbeing,
10.10
introduction, 10.1
management, 10.11–10.12
market analysis, 10.6
organisation, 10.11–10.12
performance levels, 10.8
risk analysis, 10.4–10.5
risk of challenge, 10.15–10.16
tactics, 10.14
user surveys, 10.7
introduction, 5.1
legal basis
and see **Legal basis for
charging and trading**
case law, 2.28–2.31
conclusion, 2.32
introduction, 2.1
ultra vires, 2.2–2.27
management, 10.11–10.12
marginal costs, and, 5.9
market analysis, 10.6
methodology, 5.8
modification of power, 5.10
organisation, 10.11–10.12
nature of power, 5.2
Northern Ireland, in, 14.3
overview, 1.1–1.3
performance levels, 10.8
policy issues, 5.6
purpose of activity, 5.1
raising money, and, 5.9
relevant activities, 5.3–5.4
restrictions on power, 5.5
risk analysis, 10.4–10.5
risk of challenge, 10.15–10.16
Scotland, in
background, 14.1
conclusion, 14.33
generally, 14.20
operation of provisions,
14.26–14.32

Discretionary charging (s.93)—
cont.
Scotland, in—*cont.*
statutory provisions,
14.21–14.25
statutory basis, 5.2
strategic planning
and see **Strategic planning**
generally, 3.23–3.24
introduction, 3.20
surpluses, and, 5.9
tactics, 10.14
time period, 5.8
total costs, and, 5.9
ultra vires, and
and see ***Ultra vires***
Code, as, 2.15
express, 2.12
incidental, 2.13–2.16
user surveys, 10.7
Wales, in
background, 14.1
conclusion, 14.19
generally, 14.12
introduction, 14.7
local government powers, 14.8
modification of enactments,
14.18
"old" law position, 14.4
statutory provision, 14.10
Wales Improvement
Programme, 14.9
wellbeing, 10.10
Discretionary language
ultra vires, and, 2.3
Discretionary services, charging for
drafting of the power, 4.33
introduction, 4.32
Discretion
charging for discretionary
services, and, 5.8
**Discrimination against other EU
nationals**
charging for discretionary
services, and, 5.9
Distance selling
advertising controls, and, 11.14

Distinction from commercial trading
charging for discretionary services, and, 5.1
Dominant purpose test
charging and trading powers, and, 5.1
Duties of local authority
distinction from powers, 2.3–2.4
introduction, 2.2
overlap with powers, 2.11

Economic, social and environmental wellbeing
implementation issues, and, 10.10
Education Act 1996, s.13
generally, 4.30
Efficiency
strategic planning, and, 3.14
Employment issues
change management
establishing trading company, 12.4–12.10
introduction, 12.2
stakeholder involvement, 12.3
collective bargaining arrangements, 12.9
commercial confidentiality, 12.7
conclusion, 12.37
contracts of employment, 12.7
establishing trading company
collective bargaining arrangements, 12.9
commercial confidentiality, 12.7
core values, 12.5
employment contracts, 12.7
insurance, 12.10
introduction, 2.4
pensions, 12.8
policies and procedures, 12.6
fixed term employees, 12.19
indemnities for officers and members, 12.26
insurance, 12.10
introduction, 12.1

Employment issues—*cont.*
pensions
'admission body' option, 12.33–12.34
'broadly comparable' scheme, 12.31–12.32
generally, 12.29
introduction, 12.8
LGPS, 12.30
post-transfer working, 12.35
secondment
contractual issues, 12.14
implied conditions, 12.17
health and safety, 12.18
introduction, 12.11
legal issues, 12.12–12.13
practical issues, 12.16–12.18
supervision, 12.16
TUPE, 12.13
value added tax, 12.15
vires, 12.12
working practices, 12.17
transfer of staff
Code of Practice, 12.23
enforcement via service contract, 12.22
failure to comply with Code, 12.27
introduction, 12.20
monitoring, 12.26
new joiners, 12.24
rights under TUPE, 12.28
secondment, and, 12.13
statutory provision, 12.21
sub-contracting, 12.25
Enhancing services subject to a duty
charging for discretionary services, and, 5.9
Entertainment provision
drafting of the power, 4.18
introduction, 4.17
Entire agreement clauses
pre-contractual statements, and, 11.2
Environmental wellbeing
implementation issues, and, 10.10

Establishing trading company
aims of business, 8.4
conclusion, 8.34
employment issues, and
    collective bargaining
        arrangements, 12.9
    commercial confidentiality,
        12.7
    core values, 12.5
    employment contracts, 12.7
    insurance, 12.10
    introduction, 2.4
    pensions, 12.8
    policies and procedures, 12.6
Industrial and Provident
    Societies Act, 8.8
introduction, 8.1
limited by guarantee, 8.7
limited by shares, 8.6
prior considerations, 8.2–8.3
type of company
    generally, 8.5
    introduction, 7.10
unlimited, 8.9
Exercise of powers
acting in bad faith, 2.22
blind reliance on policy, 2.19
examples of limitations, 2.19–2.23
improper motives, 2.21
introduction, 2.17
irrelevant considerations, 2.20
procedural impropriety, 2.23
reasonableness, 2.18
relevant considerations, 2.20
**Existing powers of charging and
trading**
catering for the public
    drafting of the power, 4.16
    introduction, 4.15
Civic Restaurants Act 1947
    drafting of the power, 4.16
    introduction, 4.15
commercial trading, and, 7.13
conclusion, 4.34
discretionary services, for
    drafting of the power, 4.33
    introduction, 4.32

**Existing powers of charging and
trading**—*cont.*
Education Act 1996, s.13, 4.30
entertainment provision
    drafting of the power, 4.18
    introduction, 4.17
Goods and Services Act 1970, s.1
    abuse of power, 4.8
    drafting of the power, 4.4
    introduction, 4.3
    limitations, 4.7–4.8
    relevant public bodies, 4.5
    services, 4.6
    surplus capacity agreement,
        4.7–4.8
Greater London Authority Act
    1999, s.30, 4.31
incidental powers, 4.24
introduction, 4.1
joint arrangements
    drafting of the power,
        4.10–4.11
    introduction, 4.9
key provisions, 4.2–4.23
leisure
    drafting of the power, 4.20
    introduction, 4.19
Local Government Act 1972,
    s.101
    drafting of the power,
        4.10–4.11
    introduction, 4.9
Local Government Act 1972,
    s.111, 4.24
Local Government Act 1972,
    s.145
    drafting of the power, 4.18
    introduction, 4.17
Local Government Act 2000, s.2
    drafting of the power,
        4.13–4.14
    introduction, 4.12
Local Government and Housing
    Act 1989, s.150
    drafting of the power, 4.33
    introduction, 4.32
local legislation
    introduction, 4.28

Existing powers of charging and trading—*cont.*
local legislation—*cont.*
local education authorities, 4.30
London, 4.31
police authorities, 4.29
Miscellaneous Provisions Act 1976, s.19
drafting of the power, 4.20
introduction, 4.19
Miscellaneous Provisions Act 1976, s.32, 4.23
Miscellaneous Provisions Act 1976, s.38
drafting of the power, 4.22
introduction, 4.21
municipal trading, and, 4.1
Northern Ireland, and, 14.4
Police Act 1996, s.25, 4.29
private sector, with
available powers, 4.8
catering for the public, 4.15–4.16
entertainment, 4.17–4.18
introduction, 4.2
leisure, 4.19–4.20
spare computer capacity, 4.21–4.22
working outside you area, 4.23
public, with
available powers, 4.11
introduction, 4.2
public sector, with
introduction, 4.2
joint arrangements, 4.9–4.11
trading with other public bodies, 4.3–4.8
wellbeing of the community, 4.12–4.14
spare capacity
introduction, 4.25
legal basis, 4.27
meaning, 4.26
spare computer capacity
drafting of the power, 4.22
introduction, 4.21

Existing powers of charging and trading—*cont.*
specific powers, 4.32–4.33
strategic planning, and, 3.17–3.18
surplus capacity agreement, 4.7–4.8
trading with other public bodies
abuse of power, 4.8
drafting of the power, 4.4
introduction, 4.3
limitations, 4.7–4.8
relevant public bodies, 4.5
services, 4.6
surplus capacity agreement, 4.7–4.8
Wales, and, 14.11
wellbeing of the community
drafting of the power, 4.13–4.14
introduction, 4.12
working outside you area, 4.23
Exit strategies
trading companies, and, 8.32
Express prohibitions
ultra vires, and, 2.4

Filling gaps in the market
strategic planning, and, 3.7
Financial control of trading companies
generally, 8.13
introduction, 8.12
Fixed term employees
employment issues, and, 12.19
Framework legislation
control by central government, and, 13.6
Functions of local authority
ultra vires, and, 2.10
Funding
trading companies, and, 8.28
wholly owned company, and, 9.3

General powers
ultra vires, and, 2.6
Gershon Review
efficiency savings, and, 3.14

Goods and Services Act 1970, s1
existing powers, and
abuse of power, 4.8
drafting of the power, 4.4
introduction, 4.3
limitations, 4.7–4.8
relevant public bodies, 4.5
services, 4.6
surplus capacity agreement,
4.7–4.8
strategic planning, and, 3.17
Governance of trading companies
additional risks, 8.26
conflicts of interest, 8.23
directors' fees, 8.24
introduction, 8.2
liability of directors, 8.25
role of Board, 8.22
shareholders, 8.20–8.21
Grants
trading companies, and, 8.28
**Greater London Authority Act
1999, s.30**
existing powers, and, 4.31
Guarantee companies
trading companies, and, 8.7
Guidance
charging for discretionary
services, and
generally, 5.1
ODPM document, 17.49–17.64
commercial trading, and
generally, 7.5
ODPM document, 17.1–17.48
National Assembly for Wales,
17.65–17.80
trading powers in Scotland, and,
14.25

Health and safety
secondment, and, 12.18

Implementation issues
accountability, 10.13
business plan, 10.2–10.3
conclusion, 10.17

Implementation issues—*cont.*
cost/benefit analysis, 10.9
economic, social and
environmental wellbeing,
10.10
introduction, 10.1
management, 10.11–10.12
market analysis, 10.6
organisation, 10.11–10.12
performance levels, 10.8
risk analysis, 10.4–10.5
risk of challenge, 10.15–10.16
tactics, 10.14
user surveys, 10.7
Implied conditions
secondment, and, 12.17
Implied powers
ultra vires, and, 2.10
Implied terms
consumer contracts, 11.8
custom or usage, by, 11.7
introduction, 11.6
sale of goods, 11.10
statute, by, 11.9–11.12
supply of goods and services,
11.11
unfair terms, 11.12
Improper motives
ultra vires, and, 2.21
Incidental powers
charging powers, 2.13–2.16
generally, 4.24
Indemnities
officers and members, and, 12.26
**Industrial and Provident Societies
Act**
trading companies, and, 8.8
Information
trading companies, and, 8.19
In-house company
business case, 9.3
commercial issues, 9.3
conclusion, 9.8
directors' duties, 9.7
establishing the company, 9.4
funding, 9.3
generally, 9.1

In-house company—*cont.*
introduction, 9.2
legal advice, 9.5–9.6
legal issues, 9.4
memorandum and articles, 9.6
practical issues, 9.3
taxation, 9.3
Innocent misrepresentations
pre-contractual statements, and, 11.2
Insurance
establishing the trading company, and, 12.10
Interest rate swaps
ultra vires, and, 2.9
Irrelevant considerations
ultra vires, and, 2.20

Joint arrangements
drafting of the power, 4.10–4.11
introduction, 4.9
generally, 2.8
strategic planning, and, 3.22
Joint venture company
commercial issues, 9.11–9.12
conclusion, 9.15
generally, 9.1
introduction, 9.9
legal issues, 9.13–9.14
practical issues, 9.11–9.12
procurement issues, 9.10
staffing, 9.11
structure, 9.14
taxation, 9.12
vires of establishing, 9.13
Joint ventures
trading powers, and, 3.27

Legal basis for charging and trading
administrative law, 2.1
case law, 2.26–2.29
conclusion, 2.30
introduction, 2.1
ultra vires
and see **Ultra vires doctrine**
capacity, 2.2–2.16

Legal basis for charging and trading—*cont.*
ultra vires—*cont.*
exercise of powers, 2.17–2.22
impact, 2.23–2.25
introduction, 2.1
Leisure powers
drafting of the power, 4.20
introduction, 4.19
Liability of directors
trading companies, and, 8.25
Loans
trading companies, and, 8.28
Local authority companies
arm's length entity, 8.1
audit, 8.18
borrowing, 8.28
business case
generally, 8.3
introduction, 8.1
business planning, 8.31
competition law, 8.29–8.30
conflicts of interest, 8.23
Council as shareholder, 8.20–8.21
directors' liability, 8.25
directors' remuneration
governance framework, 8.24
proprietary controls, 8.14
establishment
conclusion, 8.34
introduction, 8.1
prior considerations, 8.2–8.3
type of company, 8.4–8.9
exit strategies, 8.32
features, 7.8
financial controls
generally, 8.13
introduction, 8.12
funding, 8.28
governance framework
additional risks, 8.26
conflicts of interest, 8.23
directors' fees, 8.24
introduction, 8.2
liability of directors, 8.25
role of Board, 8.22
shareholders, 8.20–8.21

Local authority companies—*cont.*
grants, 8.28
guarantee companies, 8.7
Industrial and Provident
  Societies Act, under, 8.8
information, 8.19
introduction
  features, 7.8
  legal requirement, 7.7
  power to establish, 7.11
  regulatory regimes, 7.9
  type of vehicle, 7.10
joint venture company
  commercial issues, 9.11–9.12
  conclusion, 9.15
  generally, 9.1
  introduction, 9.9
  legal issues, 9.13–9.14
  practical issues, 9.11–9.12
  procurement issues, 9.10
  staffing, 9.11
  structure, 9.14
  taxation, 9.12
  vires of establishing, 9.13
legal constraints
  financial controls, 8.12–8.13
  placing contracts with in-house
    companies, 8.11
  proprietary controls, 8.14–8.19
  tendering for own authority
    work, 8.10
legal requirement, 7.7
liability of directors, 8.25
limited by guarantee, 8.7
limited by shares, 8.6
loans, 8.28
not-for-profit community
  enterprise, 8.1
political activity, 8.17
power to establish, 7.11
proprietary controls
  audit, 8.18
  generally, 8.14
  information, 8.19
  introduction, 8.12
  payment to directors, 8.16
  political activity prohibition,
    8.17

Local authority companies—*cont.*
proprietary controls—*cont.*
  stationery and publications,
    8.15
prudential accounting, and, 8.1
regulatory regimes, 7.9
role of Board, 8.22
share issue, 8.28
shareholders, 8.20–8.21
staffing issues, 8.24
state aid, 8.29–8.30
stationery and publications, 8.15
subsidies, and
  introduction, 8.1
  state aid, 8.29–8.30
taxation, 8.33
type of company
  aims of business, 8.4
  generally, 8.5
  Industrial and Provident
    Societies Act, 8.8
  introduction, 7.10
  limited by guarantee, 8.7
  limited by shares, 8.6
  unlimited, 8.9
unlimited companies, 8.9
wholly owned company
  business case, 9.3
  commercial issues, 9.3
  conclusion, 9.8
  directors' duties, 9.7
  establishing the company, 9.4
  funding, 9.3
  generally, 9.1
  introduction, 9.2
  legal advice, 9.5–9.6
  legal issues, 9.4
  memorandum and articles, 9.6
  practical issues, 9.3
  taxation, 9.3
**Local Authority (Goods and
  Services) Act 1970**
existing powers, and
  abuse of power, 4.8
  drafting of the power, 4.4
  introduction, 4.3
  limitations, 4.7–4.8

Local Authority (Goods and Services) Act 1970—*cont.*
existing powers, and—*cont.*
relevant public bodies, 4.5
services, 4.6
surplus capacity agreement, 4.7–4.8
Northern Ireland, and, 14.3
statutory instruments, 16.4
strategic planning, and, 3.17
Local government
abolition of *ultra vires* doctrine, 13.9
attitude to trading
introduction, 13.10
1980–1995, 13.11
1995–2005, 13.12–13.14
conclusion, 13.15
court's role, 13.7–13.8
framework legislation, 13.6
inspection, 13.5
introduction, 13.1
regulation, 13.5
relationship with central government
control via statutes, 13.6
inspection, 13.5
introduction, 13.4
regulation, 13.5
structure, 13.2–13.3
Local Government Act 1972, s.101
drafting of the power, 4.10–4.11
introduction, 4.9
Local Government Act 1972, s.111
commercial trading, and, 7.13
existing powers, and, 4.24
Local Government Act 1972, s.145
drafting of the power, 4.18
introduction, 4.17
Local Government Act 2000, s.2
drafting of the power, 4.13–4.14
introduction, 4.12
Local Government Act 2003, s.93
and see **Charging for discretionary services**
examples, 6.1–6.8
generally, 5.1–5.12

Local Government Act 2003, s.93—*cont.*
Northern Ireland, and, 14.3
statutory instruments, 16.3
text of provision, 16.2
Wales, and, 14.10
Local Government Act 2003, s.95
and see **Commercial trading**
examples, 9.1–9.16
generally, 7.1–7.14
Northern Ireland, and, 14.3
practical issues, 8.1–8.34
statutory instruments, 16.3
text of provision, 16.2
Wales, and, 14.10
Local Government and Housing Act 1989, s.150
drafting of the power, 4.33
introduction, 4.32
Local legislation
introduction, 4.28
local education authorities, 4.30
London, 4.31
police authorities, 4.29

Management
implementation issues, and, 10.11–10.12
Mandatory language
ultra vires, and, 2.3
Marginal costs
charging for discretionary services, and, 5.9
Market analysis
implementation issues, and, 10.6
Market place
disturbance of functioning market, 3.9
filling gaps in the market, 3.7
introduction, 3.6
regulation of market, 3.8
Maturity of local market
strategic planning, and, 3.9
Members of the public
charging for discretionary services, and, 6.2–6.3
Memorandum and articles
wholly owned company, and, 9.6

Methodology
charging for discretionary
services, and, 5.8
**Miscellaneous Provisions Act 1976,
s.19**
drafting of the power, 4.20
introduction, 4.19
**Miscellaneous Provisions Act 1976,
s.32**
existing powers, and, 4.23
**Miscellaneous Provisions Act 1976,
s.38**
drafting of the power, 4.22
introduction, 4.21
Modification of power
charging for discretionary
services, and, 5.10
Monitoring
transfer of staff, and, 12.26
Municipal trading
existing powers, and, 4.1

New joiners
transfer of staff, and, 12.24
Non-financial resources
availability of asset, 3.11
generally, 3.10
staff resources, 3.12
Northern Ireland
Best Value, 14.5
conclusion, 14.6
generally, 14.1
introduction, 14.2
local government powers, 14.3
reliance on "old" law, 14.4
**Not-for-profit community
enterprise**
trading companies, and, 8.1

ODPM guidance
charging for discretionary
services, and, 5.1
commercial trading, and, 7.5
Organisation
implementation issues, and,
10.11–10.12
Outsourcing
trading powers, and, 3.26

Pensions
'admission body' option,
12.33–12.34
'broadly comparable' scheme,
12.31–12.32
generally, 12.29
introduction, 12.8
LGPS, 12.30
post-transfer working, 12.35
Performance levels
implementation issues, and, 10.8
**Placing contracts with in-house
companies**
trading companies, and, 8.11
Planning of activity
ultra vires, and, 2.25
Police Act 1996, s.25
existing powers, and, 4.29
Policy issues
charging for discretionary
services, and, 5.6
Political activity
trading companies, and, 8.17
Powers of local authority
charging, 2.12–2.16
conflict between powers, 2.11
distinction from duties, 2.3–2.4
introduction, 2.2
overlap with duties, 2.11
types, 2.5–2.8
Pre-contractual statements
generally, 11.2
**Private sector, charging and
trading with**
available powers, 4.8
catering for the public
drafting of the power, 4.16
introduction, 4.15
entertainment provision
drafting of the power, 4.18
introduction, 4.17
introduction, 4.2
leisure
drafting of the power, 4.20
introduction, 4.19
spare computer capacity
drafting of the power, 4.22
introduction, 4.21

Private sector, charging and trading with—*cont.*
working outside your area, 4.23
Procedural impropriety
ultra vires, and, 2.23
Procurement
joint venture company, and, 9.10
Profit motive
ultra vires, and, 2.27
Prudential accounting
trading companies, and, 8.1
Public, charging and trading with
available powers, 4.11
introduction, 4.2
Public sector, charging and trading with
introduction, 4.2
joint arrangements
drafting of the power,
4.10–4.11
introduction, 4.9
trading with other public bodies
abuse of power, 4.8
drafting of the power, 4.4
introduction, 4.3
limitations, 4.7–4.8
relevant public bodies, 4.5
services, 4.6
surplus capacity agreement,
4.7–4.8
wellbeing of the community
drafting of the power,
4.13–4.14
introduction, 4.12
Public to private activities
charging for discretionary
services, and, 6.6–6.7
Public to public activities
charging for discretionary
services, and, 6.4–6.5
Purpose of activity
charging for discretionary
services, and, 5.1

Quantum meruit
contractual terms, and, 11.5

Raising money
charging for discretionary
services, and, 5.9
Reasonableness
ultra vires, and, 2.18
Regulation of market
strategic planning, and, 3.8
Relevant considerations
ultra vires, and, 2.20
Reliance on policy
ultra vires, and, 2.18
Representations
pre-contractual statements, and,
11.2
Risk analysis
implementation issues, and,
10.4–10.5
Risk of challenge
implementation issues, and,
10.15–10.16
s.111 Local Government Act 1972 power
use, 2.13–2.14
Sale of goods
implied terms, and, 11.10
Scale of activity
ultra vires, and, 2.25
Scotland, trading powers in
background, 14.1
conclusion, 14.33
construction activity, 14.23
generally, 14.21–14.22
Guidance, 14.25
introduction, 14.20
operation
competitiveness, 14.28
discharge of functions, 14.28
external trading, 14.29
introduction, 14.26
public trading, 14.27
Regulations, 14.25
significance test, 14.31–14.32
statutory provisions, 14.21–14.25
trading accounts
operation,. 14.30
statutory provision, 14.24
trading operations, 14.31–14.32

Secondment
contractual issues, 12.14
implied conditions, 12.17
health and safety, 12.18
introduction, 12.11
legal issues, 12.12–12.13
practical issues, 12.16–12.18
supervision, 12.16
TUPE, 12.13
value added tax, 12.15
vires, 12.12
working practices, 12.17
Share issue
trading companies, and, 8.28
Shareholders
trading companies, and,
8.20–8.21
Significance test
trading powers in Scotland, and,
14.31–14.32
Social and environmental wellbeing
implementation issues, and, 10.10
Spare capacity
introduction, 4.25
legal basis, 4.27
meaning, 4.26
Spare computer capacity
drafting of the power, 4.22
introduction, 4.21
Specific powers
generally, 4.32–4.33
ultra vires, and, 2.7
Staff resources
joint venture company, and, 9.11
strategic planning, and, 3.12
trading companies, and, 8.24
State aid
trading companies, and,
8.29–8.30
Stationery and publications
trading companies, and, 8.15
Statutory implied terms
introduction, 11.9
sale of goods, 11.10
supply of goods and services,
11.11
unfair terms, 11.12

Strategic planning
business case, 3.15
charging powers
generally, 3.23–3.24
introduction, 3.20
classification of authority, 3.4–3.5
choice of charging or trading
business case, 3.15
factors, 3.3–3.14
introduction, 3.2
commercial trading powers
existing private sector
company, 3.28
incremental planning, 3.21
joint ventures, 3.27
outsourcing, 3.26
strategy, 3.25–3.28
conclusion, 3.29
delivery of efficiency, 3.14
development of strategy, 3.15
discretionary charging
generally, 3.23–3.24
introduction, 3.20
factors in choice of charging or
trading
classification of authority,
3.4–3.5
delivery of efficiency, 3.14
introduction, 3.3
market place, 3.6–3.9
non-financial resources,
3.10–3.12
specialist areas, 3.13
filling gaps in the market, 3.7
Goods and Services Act, 3.17
incidental powers, 3.22
incremental plan
commercial trading powers,
3.21
discretionary charging powers,
3.20
Goods and Services Act, 3.17
incidental powers, 3.22
introduction, 3.16
other specific powers, 3.18
wellbeing powers, 3.19
introduction, 3.1

Strategic planning—*cont.*
market place
  disturbance of functioning
    market, 3.9
  filling gaps in the market, 3.7
  introduction, 3.6
  regulation of market, 3.8
non-financial resources
  availability of asset, 3.11
  generally, 3.10
  staff resources, 3.12
other specific powers, 3.18
regulation of market, 3.8
selection of charging or trading,
  3.2
specialist areas, 3.13
three year plan, 3.16
trading powers
  existing private sector
    company, 3.28
  generally, 3.25
  introduction, 3.21
  joint ventures, 3.27
  outsourcing, 3.26
wellbeing powers, 3.19
Sub-contracting
transfer of staff, and, 12.25
Subsidies to trading companies
introduction, 8.1
state aid, 8.29–8.30
Supervision
secondment, and, 12.16
Supply of goods and services
implied terms, and, 11.11
Surplus capacity agreement
existing powers, and, 4.7–4.8
Surpluses
charging for discretionary
  services and, 5.9

Tactics
implementation issues, and, 10.14
Taking on additional resources
ultra vires, and, 2.26
Taxation
corporation tax, 11.20
introduction, 11.19

Taxation—*cont.*
joint venture company, and, 9.12
trading companies, and, 8.33
value added tax, 11.21
wholly owned company, and, 9.3
Tendering for own authority work
trading companies, and, 8.10
Terms of contract
"battle of the forms", 11.4
implied by law
  consumer contracts, 11.8
  custom or usage, by, 11.7
  introduction, 11.6
  sale of goods, 11.10
  statute, by, 11.9–11.12
  supply of goods and services,
    11.11
  unfair terms, 11.12
introduction, 11.3
quantum meruit, 11.5
Three year plan
strategic planning, and, 3.16
Time period
charging for discretionary
  services and, 5.8
Total costs
charging for discretionary
  services and, 5.9
Trading accounts
Scotland, and
  operation, 14.30
  statutory provision, 14.24
Trading companies
arm's length entity, 8.1
audit, 8.18
borrowing, 8.28
business case
  generally, 8.3
  introduction, 8.1
business planning, 8.31
competition law, 8.29–8.30
conflicts of interest, 8.23
Council as shareholder, 8.20–8.21
directors' liability, 8.25
directors' remuneration
  governance framework, 8.24
  proprietary controls, 8.16

Trading companies—*cont.*
establishment
 conclusion, 8.34
 introduction, 8.1
 prior considerations, 8.2–8.3
 type of company, 8.4–8.9
exit strategies, 8.32
features, 7.8
financial controls
 generally, 8.13
 introduction, 8.12
funding, 8.28
governance framework
 additional risks, 8.26
 conflicts of interest, 8.23
 directors' fees, 8.24
 introduction, 8.2
 liability of directors, 8.25
 role of Board, 8.22
 shareholders, 8.20–8.21
grants, 8.28
guarantee companies, 8.7
Industrial and Provident
 Societies Act, under, 8.8
information, 8.19
introduction
 features, 7.8
 legal requirement, 7.7
 power to establish, 7.11
 regulatory regimes, 7.9
 type of vehicle, 7.10
joint venture company
 commercial issues, 9.11–9.12
 conclusion, 9.15
 generally, 9.1
 introduction, 9.9
 legal issues, 9.13–9.14
 practical issues, 9.11–9.12
 procurement issues, 9.10
 staffing, 9.11
 structure, 9.14
 taxation, 9.12
 vires of establishing, 9.13
legal constraints
 financial controls, 8.12–8.13
 placing contracts with in-house
  companies, 8.11

Trading companies—*cont.*
legal constraints—*cont.*
 proprietary controls, 8.14–8.19
 tendering for own authority
  work, 8.10
legal requirement, 7.7
liability of directors, 8.25
limited by guarantee, 8.7
limited by shares, 8.6
loans, 8.28
not-for-profit community
 enterprise, 8.1
political activity, 8.17
power to establish, 7.11
proprietary controls
 audit, 8.18
 generally, 8.14
 information, 8.19
 introduction, 8.12
 payment to directors, 8.16
 political activity prohibition,
  8.17
 stationery and publications,
  8.15
prudential accounting, and, 8.1
regulatory regimes, 7.9
role of Board, 8.22
share issue, 8.28
shareholders, 8.20–8.21
staffing issues, 8.24
state aid, 8.29–8.30
stationery and publications, 8.15
subsidies, and
 introduction, 8.1
 state aid, 8.29–8.30
taxation, 8.33
type of company
 aims of business, 8.4
 generally, 8.5
 Industrial and Provident
  Societies Act, 8.8
 introduction, 7.10
 limited by guarantee, 8.7
 limited by shares, 8.6
 unlimited, 8.9
unlimited companies, 8.9

Trading companies—*cont.*
wholly owned company
business case, 9.3
commercial issues, 9.3
conclusion, 9.8
directors' duties, 9.7
establishing the company, 9.4
funding, 9.3
generally, 9.1
introduction, 9.2
legal advice, 9.5–9.6
legal issues, 9.4
memorandum and articles, 9.6
practical issues, 9.3
taxation, 9.3
Trading operations
Scotland, and, 14.31–14.32
Trading Order
commercial trading, and, 7.4
Trading powers
commercial and consumer issues
and see **Commercial issues**
advertising controls,
11.13–11.15
competition, 11.16–11.18
conclusion, 11.22
introduction, 11.1
pre-contractual statements,
11.2
taxation, 11.19–11.21
terms of contract, 11.3–11.12
conclusion, 15.1–15.2
context
and see **Local government**
attitude to trading, 13.10–13.14
conclusion, 13.15
court's role, 13.7–13.8
introduction, 13.1
relationship with central
government, 13.4–13.6
employee and member issues
and see **Employment issues**
change management,
12.2–12.10
conclusion, 12.37
fixed term employees, 12.19
indemnities, 12.26

Trading powers—*cont.*
employee and member issues—
cont.
introduction, 12.1
pensions, 12.29–12.35
secondment, 12.11–12.18
transfer of staff, 12.20–12.28
existing powers, under
conclusion, 4.34
incidental powers, 4.24
introduction, 4.1
key provisions, 4.2–4.23
local legislation, 4.28–4.31
spare capacity, 4.25–4.27
specific powers, 4.32–4.34
history of the debate
introduction, 13.10
1980–1995, 13.11
1995–2005, 13.12–13.14
implementation
accountability, 10.13
business plan, 10.2–10.3
conclusion, 10.17
cost/benefit analysis, 10.9
economic, social and
environmental wellbeing,
10.10
introduction, 10.1
management, 10.11–10.12
market analysis, 10.6
organisation, 10.11–10.12
performance levels, 10.8
risk analysis, 10.4–10.5
risk of challenge, 10.15–10.16
tactics, 10.14
user surveys, 10.7
legal basis
and see **Legal basis for
charging and trading**
case law, 2.28–2.31
conclusion, 2.32
introduction, 2.1
ultra vires, 2.2–2.27
Northern Ireland, in
background, 14.1
Best Value, 14.5
conclusion, 14.6

Trading powers—*cont.*
legal basis—*cont.*
  generally, 14.2
  local government powers, 14.3
  reliance on "old" law, 14.4
overview, 1.1–1.3
s.95 LGA 2003, under
  and see **Commercial trading**
  examples, 9.1–9.16
  generally, 7.1–7.14
  practical issues, 8.1–8.34
Scotland, in
  background, 14.1
  conclusion, 14.33
  introduction, 14.20
  operation of provisions,
    14.26–14.32
  statutory provisions,
    14.21–14.25
strategic planning
  and see **Strategic planning**
  existing private sector
    company, 3.28
  generally, 3.25
  introduction, 3.21
  joint ventures, 3.27
  outsourcing, 3.26
ultra vires, and
  and see **Ultra vires**
  Code, as, 2.15
  express, 2.12
  incidental, 2.13–2.16
Wales, in
  background, 14.1
  conclusion, 14.19
  generally, 14.13–14.17
  introduction, 14.7
  local government powers, 14.8
  modification of enactments,
    14.18
  "old" law position, 14.4
  statutory provision, 14.10
  Wales Improvement
    Programme, 14.9
Trading with other public bodies
abuse of power, 4.8
drafting of the power, 4.4

Trading with other public bodies—
  cont.
introduction, 4.3
limitations, 4.7–4.8
relevant public bodies, 4.5
services, 4.6
surplus capacity agreement,
  4.7–4.8
Transfer of staff
Code of Practice, 12.23
enforcement via service contract,
  12.22
failure to comply with Code,
  12.27
introduction, 12.20
monitoring, 12.26
new joiners, 12.24
rights under TUPE, 12.28
secondment, and, 12.13
statutory provision, 12.21
sub-contracting, 12.25

***Ultra vires* doctrine**
abolition, 13.9
acting in bad faith, 2.22
blind reliance on policy, 2.19
capacity of local authority
  introduction, 2.2
  overlap between powers and
    duties, 2.11
  powers and duties, 2.3–2.10
charging powers
  Code, as, 2.15
  express, 2.12
  incidental, 2.13–2.16
conflict between powers, 2.11
consequential powers, 2.8
court's role, 13.7–13.8
discretionary language, 2.3
duties of local authority
  distinction from powers,
    2.3–2.4
  introduction, 2.2
  overlap with powers, 2.11
exercise of powers
  acting in bad faith, 2.22

Ultra vires—cont.
exercise of powers—*cont.*
blind reliance on policy, 2.19
examples of limitations,
2.19–2.23
improper motives, 2.21
introduction, 2.17
irrelevant considerations, 2.20
procedural impropriety, 2.23
reasonableness, 2.18
relevant considerations, 2.20
express prohibitions, 2.4
functions of local authority, 2.9
general powers, 2.6
impact, 2.24–2.27
implied powers, 2.8
improper motives, 2.21
incidental powers
charging powers, 2.13–2.16
generally, 2.8
interest rate swap cases, 2.9
introduction, 2.1
irrelevant considerations, 2.20
joint venture company, and, 9.13
mandatory language, 2.3
planning of activity, 2.25
powers of local authority
charging, 2.12–2.16
conflict between powers, 2.11
distinction from duties, 2.3–2.4
introduction, 2.2
overlap with duties, 2.11
types, 2.5–2.8
procedural impropriety, 2.23
profit motive, 2.27
reasonableness, 2.18
relevant considerations, 2.20
reliance on policy, 2.19
scale of activity, 2.25
secondment, and, 12.12
specific powers 2.7
taking on additional resources,
2.26
Unfair terms
implied terms, and, 11.12
Unlimited companies
trading companies, and, 8.9

Usage and custom
implied terms, and, 11.7
User surveys
implementation issues, and, 10.7

Value added tax
generally, 11.21
secondment, and, 12.15
Vires
and see Ultra vires
joint venture company, and, 9.13
secondment, and, 12.12

Wales
charging for discretionary
services, 14.12
commercial trading, 14.13–14.17
conclusion, 14.19
generally, 14.1
Guidance, 17.65–17.80
introduction, 14.7
local government powers, 14.8
modification of enactments, 14.18
"old" law position, 14.4
statutory provision, 14.10
Wales Improvement Programme,
14.9
Wellbeing powers
existing powers, and
drafting of the power,
4.13–4.14
introduction, 4.12
general powers, and, 2.6
implementation issues, and, 10.10
Northern Ireland, and, 14.3
strategic planning, and, 3.19
White Papers
commercial trading, and, 7.1
Wholly owned company
business case, 9.3
commercial issues, 9.3
conclusion, 9.8
directors' duties, 9.7
establishing the company, 9.4
funding, 9.3
generally, 9.1
introduction, 9.2
legal advice, 9.5–9.6

Wholly owned company—*cont.*
  legal issues, 9.4
  memorandum and articles, 9.6
  practical issues, 9.3

Wholly owned company—*cont.*
  taxation, 9.3
Working outside you area
  existing powers, and, 4.23